If it's APRIL 2004
and you are still using this Directory,
it's time to order the NEW Edition.

Please visit our website

www.cabells.com

or contact us at

Cabell Publishing Company
Box 5428, Beaumont, Texas 77726-5428
(409) 898-0575
Fax (409) 866-9554

Cabell's Directory
of Publishing Opportunities in

Educational
Psychology and Administration

VOLUME II   J of C thru Y, INDEX
SIXTH EDITION 2002-2003

David W. E. Cabell, Editor
McNeese State University
Lake Charles, Louisiana

Deborah L. English, Editor
Nancy A. Guarnieri, Assistant Editor

To order additional copies
visit our web site
www.cabells.com

or contact us at

Box 5428 Beaumont, Texas 77726-5428
(409) 898-0575 Fax (409) 866-9554

$89.95 U.S. for addresses in United States
Price includes shipping and handling for U.S.
Add $50 for surface mail to countries outside U.S.
Add $100 for airmail to countries outside U.S.

ISBN # 0-911753-19-2

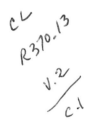

Journal of Career Development

ADDRESS FOR SUBMISSION:

Norman C. Gysbers, Editor
Journal of Career Development
University of Missouri-Columbia
Room 305, Noyes Building
Columbia, MO 65211
USA
Phone: 573-882-6386
Fax: 573-882-5440
E-Mail: 573-882-5440
Web: gysbersn@missouri.edu
Address May Change:

PUBLICATION GUIDELINES:

Manuscript Length: 16-20
Copies Required: Three
Computer Submission: No
Format: N/A
Fees to Review: 0.00 US$

Manuscript Style:
    American Psychological Association

CIRCULATION DATA:

Reader: Academics
Frequency of Issue: Quarterly
Copies per Issue: 1,001 - 2,000
Sponsor/Publisher:
Subscribe Price: 46.00 US$ Individual
    225.00 US$ Institution
    265.00 US$ Foreign

REVIEW INFORMATION:

Type of Review: Blind Review
No. of External Reviewers: 2
No. of In House Reviewers: 0
Acceptance Rate: 11-20%
Time to Review: 2 - 3 Months
Reviewers Comments: Yes
Invited Articles: 21-30%
Fees to Publish: 0.00 US$

MANUSCRIPT TOPICS:
Adult Career & Vocational; Counseling & Personnel Services

MANUSCRIPT GUIDELINES/COMMENTS:

The *Journal of Career Development* is a professional journal dedicated to the study of Career Development. The *journal* publishes manuscripts dealing with career development research, theory, and practice. Research reports and discussion of theory are welcome, but practical applications must be presented.

Manuscript Submission
Authors must use the *Publication Manual of the American Psychological Association* (5th ed., 2001) as a guide for preparing manuscripts for submission. Manuscripts should be submitted in triplicate, typed on one side of the page only, and double-spaced throughout. A margin of at least one inch should be left on all four edges. Manuscripts should not exceed 16-20, 8-1/2" x 11" white pages. Send manuscripts to: Norman C. Gysbers, 305 Noyes Building, University of Missouri-Columbia, Columbia, MO 65211.

Title Page should contain the names of the authors, as well as their academic degrees, affiliations, and phone number of senior author. A name and address for reprint requests should be included. A footnote may contain simple statements of affiliation, credit, and research support. Except for an introductory footnote, footnotes are discouraged.

References should be listed on a separate page and referred to in the text by author(s) and year of publication in accordance with the style described in the *Publication Manual of the American Psychological Association* (5th ed., 2001). Only items cited in manuscripts should be listed as references. Page numbers must be provided for direct quotations.

Illustrations should be self-explanatory and used sparingly. Tables and figures must be in camera-ready condition and include captions.

Manuscript Review
All manuscripts are peer reviewed by Editorial Board members using a blind review system. Two or three months may elapse between acknowledgment of receipt of a manuscript and notification of its disposition.

Personal-Computer Disks
After a manuscript has been accepted for publication and after all revisions have been incorporated, manuscripts may be submitted to the Editor's Office on **personal-computer disks**. Label the disk with identifying information-kind of computer used, kind of software and version number, disk format and file name of article, as well as abbreviated journal name, authors' last names, and (if room) paper title. Package the disk in a disk mailer or protective cardboard. **The disk must be the one from which the accompanying manuscript (finalized version) was printed out.** The Editor's office cannot accept a disk without its accompanying, matching hard-copy manuscript. Disks will be used on a case-by-case basis--where efficient and feasible.

Journal of Cases in Educational Leadership

ADDRESS FOR SUBMISSION:

Gary M. Crow, Editor
Journal of Cases in Educational Leadership
University of Utah
Dept. of Educational Leadership & Policy
1705 E. Campus Center Dr., Rm 339
Salt Lake City, UT 84112-9254
USA
Phone: 801-581-3377
Fax: 801-585-6756
E-Mail: gcrow@ed.utah.edu
Web: www.ucea.org
Address May Change:

PUBLICATION GUIDELINES:

Manuscript Length: 11-15
Copies Required: Four
Computer Submission: Yes
Format: MSWord or WordPerfect
Fees to Review: 0.00 US$

Manuscript Style:
    See Manuscript Guidelines

CIRCULATION DATA:

Reader: Academics
Frequency of Issue: Quarterly
Copies per Issue: Online
Sponsor/Publisher: University Council for
    Educational Administration
Subscribe Price: 0.00 US$ Online

REVIEW INFORMATION:

Type of Review: Blind Review
No. of External Reviewers: 3
No. of In House Reviewers: 2
Acceptance Rate: 44%
Time to Review: 2 - 3 Months
Reviewers Comments: Yes
Invited Articles: 0-5%
Fees to Publish: 0.00 US$

MANUSCRIPT TOPICS:
Education Management/Administration

MANUSCRIPT GUIDELINES/COMMENTS:

Statement of Purpose
The *Journal of Cases in Educational Leadership* (JCEL) publishes in electronic format peer-reviewed cases appropriate for use in programs that prepare educational leaders. Building on a long tradition, the University Council for Education Administration sponsors this journal in an ongoing effort to improve administrative preparation. The journal's editorial staff seeks a wide range of cases that embody relevant and timely presentations of issues germane to the preparation of educational leaders.

Cases published in JCEL may be downloaded and duplicated for non-profit use by any individual or education/public agency. Such reproduction must bear the citation of the article, including author's name, title of case, journal name, issue and page numbers. Commercial use of this journal in whole or in part is strictly prohibited

Submission Guidelines
All cases will be subject to blind, peer review by the Editorial Board of JCEL. As is customary in most scholarly publications, authors should be prepared to work with the editorial staff in revising manuscripts in accordance with editorial policy.

Cases are reviewed with the following criteria in mind:
- Focuses on pertinent and timely issues of educational leadership.
- Relevant to graduate students preparing for educational leadership roles and for educational professionals currently in these roles.
- Useful in graduate teaching environments.
- Presents a practical and realistic problem that requires the integration of knowledge within and/or across disciplines.
- Stimulates self-directed learning by encouraging students to generate questions and access new knowledge.
- Provides the description of a problem that can sustain student discussion of alternative solutions.
- Describes the context in a rich fashion, including the individuals in the case.
- Encourages the clarification of personal and professional values and beliefs.
- Authenticates the connection of theory to practice.
- Includes teaching notes that facilitate the use of the case for leadership development.
- Is clearly written with specific objectives.

Manuscript Submissions
Authors should submit manuscripts electronically in Microsoft Word or WordPerfect formats by email or diskette.
All figures must be submitted as GIF or JPEG images in final form. Manuscripts should include a cover sheet with the title, author's name, address and email address. Ordinarily manuscripts should be between 1200-2000 words, exclusive of teaching notes.

Manuscripts to be considered for publication should be sent to:

Gary M. Crow, Editor
UCEA Journal of Cases in Educational Leadership
University of Utah
Department of Educational Leadership and Policy
1705 E. Campus Center Drive - Room 339
Salt Lake City, UT 84112-9254
gcrow@gse.utah.edu

Preparation of Manuscripts
All cases should include the following:
- *Title*
- *Author Information* Author's name and institutional affiliation
- *Abstract* A short 100 word abstract describing the topic(s) of the case and a brief synopsis of the case.

- **Text** Sections should be typed in Times Roman font (12 pt) with page numbers centered at the bottom of the page.
- **Teaching Notes** All cases should include a one (1) page "Teaching Notes" that outlines how the material might be used in professional preparation programs for educational leaders. Within the "Teaching Note," authors should repeat the abstract describing the topic(s) of the case and a brief synopsis of the case.
- **References** References should follow the style in the fourth edition of the *Publication Manual of the American Psychological Association.*
- **Biographical Statement** Authors should provide a brief (2-3 sentence) biographical statement.
- **ERIC Descriptors** Three (3) ERIC descriptors suitable for searching should be identified.

Figures
Use and submission of figures should be as follows:
- *Tables*Tables should be used only when they can present information more effectively than in running text. Care should be taken to insure that tables can be effectively presented in html, since articles will be in both html and adobe acrobat (pdf).
- *Illustrations* Figures should be numbered in series. Symbols (open or closed circles, triangles, squares) and lettering must be clear when rendered in GIF or JPEG format. Please review all figures after converting to GIF or JPEG format to insure that they are readable.
- *Line drawings and graphs* Original line drawings and graphs should be submitted as GIF or JPEG files.
- *Photographs* Photographs should be submitted as GIF or JPEG files.

Author's Warranty
Authors must assign UCEA copyright of their cases to be published in JCEL and acknowledge that the case is an original work that has not been published elsewhere. UCEA grants its authors the right to republish their own cases wherever they wish, in any format, provided that they cite JCEL as the original source.

Page Layout
The page layout should follow the example below.
**Note Because excessive formatting can significantly delay conversion of a manuscript to the html and pdf formats in which the cases are electronically published, use of additional enhancements (headers, footers, automatic outlines, underlines, etc.) is discouraged unless these features are necessary to the content of the document . Authors with questions about formatting requirements may contact Charles Chiu at UCEA (email: kcc46@mizzou.edu; phone: 573-884-8305).

Page Layout Example

TITLE

Author
Affiliation

380

Abstract

This case was developed for use in a course on learning-centered leadership with a focus on supervision. Varied data are presented about the school, the district, the students, and the community. Students must analyze the data, identify inconsistencies...

Case Narrative

At a district meeting for principals and assistant principals this week, the Superintendent shared the current testing report. Highlights for RRMS are summarized below.

Writing test results - grades 6 and 8
State writing tests are scored on a scale of 1 to 4, with 1 indicating no proficiency, and 4 indicating strong proficiency. A score of 2.5 indicates acceptable performance. At RRMS, 41.8% of sixth graders and 59.0% of eighth graders scored equal to or better than...

Teaching Notes

This case was developed for use in a course on learning-centered leadership with a focus on supervision. Varied data are presented about the school, the district, the students, and the community. Students must analyze the data, identify inconsistencies, formulate additional questions and strategies for gaining additional information, and begin to develop a plan for working in a new leadership role to improve instruction and student performance. In their responses to the case, students are able to demonstrate their ability to:

References

DuFour, R., & Eaker, R. (1998). *Professional learning communities at work: Best practices for enhancing student achievement*. Bloomington, IN: National Education Service.

Glatthorn, A. A. (1997). *Differentiated supervision*(2nd Ed). Alexandria, VA: Association for Supervision and Curriculum Development.

Biographical Statement

Lynn Bradshaw is Associate Professor in the Department of Educational Leadership at East Carolina University. She brings to that role experience as a teacher, principal, state agency consultant, central office administrator and assistant superintendent in the areas of personnel, supervision, and human resource development. Dr. Bradshaw can be reached at edbradsh@eastnet.educ.ecu.edu

ERIC Descriptors

instructional leadership
instructional improvement
instructional effectiveness

Journal of Child Sexual Abuse

ADDRESS FOR SUBMISSION:

Robert Geffner, Editor
Journal of Child Sexual Abuse
Alliant International University
Calif. School of Professional Psychology
6160 Cornerstone Court East
San Diego, CA 92121
USA
Phone: 858-623-2777 ext. 445
Fax: 858-646-0761
E-Mail: bgeffner@alliant.edu
Web:
Address May Change:

PUBLICATION GUIDELINES:

Manuscript Length: 25-35
Copies Required: Five
Computer Submission: Yes Email
Format: MSWord
Fees to Review: 0.00 US$

Manuscript Style:
    American Psychological Association

CIRCULATION DATA:

Reader: , Multidisciplinary
Frequency of Issue: Quarterly
Copies per Issue: 1,001 - 2,000
Sponsor/Publisher: Haworth Press, Inc.
Subscribe Price: 45.00 US$ Individual
    85.00 US$ Institutional
    175.00 US$ Library

REVIEW INFORMATION:

Type of Review: Blind Review
No. of External Reviewers: 3
No. of In House Reviewers: 1
Acceptance Rate: 21-30%
Time to Review: 4 - 6 Months
Reviewers Comments: Yes
Invited Articles. 0-5%
Fees to Publish: 0.00 US$

MANUSCRIPT TOPICS:

Brief Reporrts, Commentary; Counseling & Personnel Services; Sexual Abuse, Intervention; Social Studies/Social Science; Tests, Measurement & Evaluation

MANUSCRIPT GUIDELINES/COMMENTS:

About The Journal

This best-selling, interdisciplinary journal interfaces among researchers, academicians, attorneys, clinicians, and practitioners. Divided into sections to provide clear information, the journal covers research issues, clinical issues, legal issues, case studies, and brief reports, focusing on three subject groups-child and adolescent victims of sexual abuse or incest, adult survivors of childhood sexual abuse or incest, and sexual abuse or incest offenders.

Research, treatment approaches and techniques, prevention, intervention, and other programs concerning any of these groups are emphasized. An international editorial board has been assembled, consisting of about 50 psychologists, sociologists, social workers, clinicians, physicians, nurses, attorneys, and practitioners who have expertise in the diagnosis, treat, prosecution, research, and/or prevention of sexual abuse.

Instructions For Authors

1.Original articles only. Submission of a manuscript to this Journal represents a certification on the Part of the author(s) that it is an original work, and that neither this manuscript nor a version of it has been published elsewhere nor is being considered for publication elsewhere,

2. **Manuscript Length** Your manuscript May be approximately 20-30 typed pages double-spaced (including references and abstract). Lengthier manuscripts may be considered, but only at the discretion of the Editor. Sometimes, lengthier manuscripts may be considered if they can be divided up into sections for publication in successive *Journal* issues. Brief reports, case studies, and commentary concerning important issues in medicine (ie: Grand Rounds), in law (ie: On Trial), or mental health/social service (ie: Case Conference), are encouraged; these should be 5-20 pages double-spaced.

3. **Manuscript Style.** References, citations, and general style of manuscripts for this Journal should follow the APA style (as outlined in the latest edition of the *Publication Manual Of The American Psychological Association).* References should be double-spaced and placed in alphabetical order. Legal manuscripts should follow the style and format of the *Harvard Law Review.*

If an author wishes to submit a paper that has been already prepared in another style, he or she may do so. However, if the paper is accepted (with or without reviewer's alterations), the author is fully responsible for retyping the manuscript in the correct style as indicated above. Neither the Editor nor the Publisher is responsible for repreparing manuscript copy to adhere to the *Journal's* style.

4. **Manuscript preparation.** *Margins*: leave at least a one-inch margin on all four sides. *Paper*: use clean white 8-1/2" x 111 bond paper. *Number of copies*: 5 (the original plus four photocopies). *Cover Page*: Important--staple a cover page to the manuscript, indicating, only the article title (this is used for anonymous refereeing). *Second Title Page*: enclose a regular title page but do not staple it to the manuscript. Include the title again, plus:

- Full authorship.
- An ABSTRACT of about 100 words. (Below the abstract provide 3-10 key words for index purposes).
- An introductory footnote with authors' academic degrees, professional titles, position, a 1 sentence bibliographical background, affiliations, mailing addresses, and any desired acknowledgment of research support or other credit.
- Authors telephone numbers, telefax numbers, and e-mail address if available.
- Address and contact person for reprint requests.
- If an article has been revised based upon Editorial Board reviewer comments, then it is appropriate to acknowledge the "helpful comments of the anonymous reviewers of the JCSA Editorial Board,"

5. **Return Envelopes**. When you submit your five manuscript copies, also include:
- A 9" x 12" envelope, self-addressed and stamped (with sufficient postage to ensure return of your manuscript);

- A regular envelope, stamped and self-addressed. This is for the Editor to send you an "acknowledgement of receipt" letter.

6. **Spelling, Grammar, And Punctuation**. You are responsible for preparing manuscript copy which is clearly written in acceptable scholarly English, and which contains no errors of spelling, grammar, or punctuation. Neither the Editor nor the Publisher is responsible for correcting errors of spelling and grammar; the manuscript, after acceptance by the Editor, must be immediately ready for typesetting as it is finally submitted by the author(s). Check your paper for the following common errors:
- Dangling modifiers,
- Misplaced modifiers,
- Unclear antecedents,
- Incorrect or inconsistent abbreviations

Also, check the accuracy of all arithmetic calculations, statistics, numerical data, text citations, and references.

7. **Inconsistencies Must Be Avoided**. Be sure you are consistent in your use of abbreviations, terminology, and in citing references, from one part of your paper to another.

8. **Preparation Of Tables, Figures, And Illustrations**. All tables, figures, illustrations, etc, must be "camera-ready." That is, they must be cleanly typed or artistically prepared so that they can be used either exactly as they are or also used after a photographic reduction in size. Figures, tables, and Illustrations must be prepared on separate sheets of paper. Always use black ink and professional drawing instruments. On the back of these items, write your, article title and the journal title Lightly in pencil, so they do not get misplaced in text, skip extra Lines and indicate where these figures and tables are to be placed (please do not write on face of art). Photographs are considered part of the acceptable manuscript and remain with the Publisher for use in additional printings.

9. **Alterations Required By Referees And Reviewers**. Many times a paper is accepted by the Editor contingent upon changes that are mandated by anonymous specialist referees and members of the Editorial Board. If the Editor returns your manuscript for revisions, you are responsible for retyping any sections of the paper to incorporate these revisions (if applicable, revisions should also be put on disk).

10. **Typesetting**. You will not be receiving galley proofs of your article. Editorial revisions, if any, must therefore be made while your article is still in manuscript. The final version of the manuscript will be the version you see published. Typesetter's errors will be corrected by the production staff of The Haworth Press. Authors are expected to submit manuscripts, disks, and art that are free from error.

11. **Electronic Media**. Haworth's in-house type-setting unit is able to utilize your final manuscript material as prepared on most personal computers and word processors. This will minimize typographical errors and decrease overall production timelag.

A. Please continue to send your first draft and final draft copies of your manuscript to the journal Editor in print format for his/her final review and approval.

B. Only after the journal editor has approved your final manuscript, you may submit the final approved version both on

- Printed format ("hard copy")
- Floppy diskette.

C. Please make sure that the disk version and the hard copy (printed copy) are exactly the same.

Wrap your floppy diskettes in a strong diskette wrapper or holder and write on the outside of the diskette package:

- The brand name of your computer or word processor
- The word-processing program that you used
- The title of your article, and * file name

Note. Disk and hard copy must agree. In case of discrepancies, it is The Haworth Press's policy to follow hard copy. Authors are advised that no revisions of the manuscript can be made after acceptance by the Editor for publication. The benefits of this procedure are many with speed and accuracy being the most obvious. We look forward to working with you on this, knowing we will be able to serve you more efficiently in the future.

12. **Reprints.** The senior author will receive two copies of the journal issue and 25 complimentary reprints of his or her article. The junior author will receive two copies of the journal issue. These are sent several weeks after the journal issue is published and in circulation. An order form for the purchase of additional reprints will also be sent to all authors at this time. (Approximately 4-6 weeks are necessary for the preparation of reprints.) Please do not query the Journal's Editor about reprints. ALL such questions should be sent directly to The Haworth Press. Inc., Production Department, 21 Broad Street, West Hazleton, PA 18201. To order additional (minimum: 50 copies), please contact The Haworth Document Delivery Center, 10 Alice Street, Binghamton, NY 13904-1580. 1-800-3429678 or Fax (607) 722-6362,

13. **Copyright.** Copyright ownership of your manuscript must be transferred officially to The Haworth Press, Inc. before we can begin the peer-review process. The Editor's letter acknowledging receipt of the manuscript will be accompanied by a form fully explaining this. All authors must sign the form and return the original to the Editor as soon as possible. Failure to return the copyright form in a timely fashion will result in delay in review and subsequent publication.

Manuscript Submission Form

This copyright transmittal form-signed by all authors must be included with any journal article submission to the editor. Original signatures, not photocopies, must be received with submission.

Publication Agreement

1. **Copyright**: In consideration for publication of our Work, if accepted and published by the journal noted on the reverse side of the page, the Author(s) agree to transfer copyright of the Work to The Haworth Press, Inc., including full and exclusive rights to publication in all media now known or later developed, including but not limited to electronic databases and microfilm, and in anthologies of any kind. **(Note to U.S. Government employees: see your Exemption, paragraph 5 below.)**

2. **Author Re-Use Of Work**: As a professional courtesy, the authors retain the right to reprint their article submitted again, after publication in the journal, in any work for which they are sole Author, or in any edited work for which the author is Senior Editor. No further permission is necessary in writing from The Haworth Press, Inc., nor will the Press require fees of any kind for the reprinting. This statement is intended to provide full copyright release for the purposes listed above and a photocopy of this page (front and back) may be used when another Publisher requires a written release.

3. **Author Warranties**: The author(s) represent(s) and warrant(s): a) that the manuscript submitted is his/her (their) own work; b) that the work has been submitted only to this journal and that it has not been submitted or published elsewhere; c) that the article contains no libelous or unlawful statements and does not infringe upon the civil rights of others; d) that the author(s) is (are) not infringing upon anyone else's copyright.

The authors agree that if there is a breach of any of the above representations and warranties that (s)he (they) will indemnify the Publisher, Editor, or Guest Editor and hold them harmless.

4.   a) **Rights Retained By The Author.** This transmittal form conveys copyright to the Publisher, but patent rights are retained by the Author;

      b) **Materials Retained By The Publisher.** Photographs and illustrative material are considered part of the manuscript, and must be retained by the Publisher for use in additional printings in case the journal issue or reprint edition needs to be reprinted.

5. **Note for U.S. Government Employees.** If the article is single-authored by a U.S. government employee as part of his/her official duties, it is understood that the article is not copyrightable. It is called a "Work of the U.S. Government." However, if the article was not part of the employee's official duties, it may be copyrighted. If the article was jointly written, the authors understand that they are delegating the right of copyright to the nongovernmental employee, who must sign this agreement.

6. **"Work For Hire" Authors.** If the article was written by an author who was hired by another person or company to do so, the article is called a "Work for Hire" manuscript. This agreement must then be signed by the "employer" who hired the author, as well as the author.

7. **No Amendments.** No amendments or modifications of the terms of this Agreement are permissible unless same shall be in writing and signed by a duly authorized officer of The Haworth Press, Inc. No Journal Editor, Guest Editor or Special Issue Editor is authorized to waive, amend or modify any of the procedures or other provisions of this Agreement. This

386

form is not valid if the Author(s) add any additional constraints and/or amendments. Please submit the article elsewhere for publication if the Author(s) do not sign this agreement without alteration.

8. Integration. This Agreement embodies the entire agreement and understanding between the Authors and The Haworth Press, Inc. and supersedes all other agreements and understandings, whether oral or written, relating to the subject matter hereof.

Copyright Transfer Form

Name of journal:

_____

_____

Name and EXACT Mailing Address of Contributor:

Special Note: **This Will Be Used For Mailing Reprints**. You must include exact street address, name of your department if at a university, and **Zip Code**. The Haworth Press cannot be responsible for lost reprints if you do not provide us with your exact mailing address.

_____

In reference to your journal article:

☐ If this box is checked...

Thank you for your article submission! Please allow 10-15 weeks for the review process. Before sending out your article for review, however, the Publisher requires us to obtain your signature(s) confirming that you have read the **Publication Agreement** on the reverse side of this page.

All co-authors must sign and return the **Original** signed copy.

It Is Confirmed that I/we have read the **Publication Agreement** on the reverse side of the page, and agree and accept all conditions:

_____
   authors signature date

_____
   authors signature date

☐ If this box is checked ...

Your article has been favorably reviewed. Our reviewers, however, require certain revisions which are indicated on the attached sheets. Please review and incorporate their suggestions, and return your manuscript/disk retyped within 14 days. A decision about publication will be made at that time. Thank you for your help and cooperation.

Please reply to

_____
( )Journal Editor:

_____
( ) Guest Editor/ Special Issue Editor:

☐ If this box is checked ...

We are pleased to inform you that your article has been accepted for publication in the journal noted above. In addition to the standard journal edition, at the editor's discretion, this issue may be also be co-published in a hardcover monographic co-edition.

Please note the following:

1. **Publication.** Your article is currently scheduled to appear in

Volume:_____ Issue:_____

2. **Typesetting**. Your article will be sent to the Production Department of The Haworth Press, Inc., 21 East Broad Street, West Hazleton, PA 18201-3809. They will typeset your article (preferably from your computer disk) exactly as submitted. Please note that you will not be receiving galley proofs. The production staff will proofread the galleys for typesetting errors against the final version of the manuscript as submitted. No revisions are allowed.

3. **Reprints.** Shortly after publication you will receive an order form for purchasing quantities of reprints. (About three weeks after publication, the senior author will receive two complimentary copies of the issue and ten copies of the article, and the junior author(s) will receive two complimentary copies of the issue.) Please note that preparation of reprints takes about eight weeks additional time after the actual issue is printed and in circulation.

☐ If this box is checked...

We are sorry, but the reviewers for this journal did not agree that your article was appropriate for publication in this periodical. If the reviewers consented in having their comments forwarded to you, their critiques are attached. Your submission is appreciated, and we hope that you will contribute again in the future.

Journal of Chinese Language Teachers Association

ADDRESS FOR SUBMISSION:

Cynthia Ning, Editor
Journal of Chinese Language Teachers
    Association
University of Hawaii
c/o Center for Chinese Studies
Moore Hall 416
1890 East-West Road
Honolulu, HI 96822
USA
Phone: 808-956-2692
Fax: 808-956-2682
E-Mail: cyndy@hawaii.edu
Web:
Address May Change:

PUBLICATION GUIDELINES:

Manuscript Length: 11-20 or More
Copies Required: Two
Computer Submission: Yes
Format: MAC, IBM, State Program
Fees to Review: 0.00 US$

Manuscript Style:
    See Manuscript Guidelines

CIRCULATION DATA:

Reader: Academics
Frequency of Issue: 3 Times/Year
Copies per Issue: Less than 1,000
Sponsor/Publisher: University & CLTA
Subscribe Price: US$ Varied
    100.00 US$ Institution
    25.00 US$ Student

REVIEW INFORMATION:

Type of Review: Editorial Review
No. of External Reviewers: 1
No. of In House Reviewers: 1
Acceptance Rate: 21-30%
Time to Review: 2 - 3 Months
Reviewers Comments: Yes
Invited Articles: 6-10%
Fees to Publish: 0.00 US$

MANUSCRIPT TOPICS:
Chinese Language Pedagogy; Chinese Literature; Languages & Linguistics; Reading; Teacher Education; Tests, Measurement & Evaluation

MANUSCRIPT GUIDELINES/COMMENTS:

JCLTA **Style Sheet** (Supplemental to LSA and JAS Style Sheets)
1. **Contributions** to *JCLTA* on linguistic and pedagogical subjects must follow the Linguistic Society of America s style sheet, while those on literary, historical, and other subjects must conform to the Journal of Asian Studies style sheet. Note that the style of punctuation for articles submitted to *JCLTA* must conform to the following: single quotes are used instead of double quotes, and punctuation such as commas, periods, etc. should be enclosed within the final quote.

2. **Manuscripts**. An original and two copies must be submitted to the editor. Upon acceptance, any editorial changes or reviewer's comments will be noted on one copy, which will be returned to the contributor for comment.

Text, notes, and quotations must be neatly typewritten and double spaced with ample margins on paper of standard size (8 1/2 x 11) and weight (16lbs.).

Notes should be numbered consecutively and typed together at the end of the article. Each page, including endnote pages, should be numbered consecutively in the upper right-hand corner.

Brief corrections made after typing the manuscript should be indicated where they occur. Deletions are shown by a single line through the phrase to be omitted; insertions or substitutions are written in the space above the line and indicated with a caret. A change to lower case is indicated by a diagonal line drawn through a capital letter; a change to a capital is shown by three lines under a letter. Authors corrections on galley proofs should be kept to a minimum. Revisions made in proofs may be charged to the author.

3. **Characters**. Characters may be used to accompany a romanization on its first occurrence in a manuscript, and only where they facilitate identification. They should not be inserted for words or names which are well known and can be readily identified. Both simplified and full characters are acceptable, but authors must be consistent.

Language and linguistic examples should be given in romanization, preferably Pinyin, word for-word translation, and an idiomatic English translation; characters need not be inserted.

When characters follow romanization, no intervening punctuation is needed.

4. **Romanization**. Whenever possible, use the Pinyin system and insert tone marks for all words except in titles of books and names of persons.

For place names, use the Zhonghua Renmin Gongheguo Fensheng Dituji (Beijing, 1977), which spells in Pinyin, but without tone marks.

For names of well-known individuals, follow the accepted variant romanization (Sun Yatsen); for other names we prefer Pinyin.

English translations may follow romanized Chinese in the text and should be enclosed in single quotes. The English translation should be used to accompany the Chinese on its first occurrence in a manuscript and only where it facilitates identification. The translation need not be repeated thereafter.

CLTA Headquarters. Chinese Language Association, c/o Center for Chinese Studies, Moore 417, 1890 E-W Road, University of Hawaii, Honolulu, HI 96822, Phone: 808-956-2692, Fax: 808-956-2682, E-mail: cyndy@hawaii.edu

Executive Director. Cynthia Ning, University of Hawaii, e-mail: cyndy@hawaii.edu

Editor. Shou-hsin Teng National Taiwan Normal University Institute of Chinese as a Second Language Taipai, Taiwan 106-10 Email: steng@cc.ntnu.edu.tw

Review Editor. Dana Scott Bourgerie Asian and Near Eastern Languages Brigham Young University, Provo, UT Phone: 801-378-4952, ext.3396, Fax: 801-378-5866 Email: bourgerie@byu.edu

Journal of Chiropractic Education

ADDRESS FOR SUBMISSION:

Robert Ward, Editor
Journal of Chiropractic Education
PO Box 1166
Whittier, CA 90609-1166
USA
Phone: 562-902-3383
Fax: 562-902-3383
E-Mail: robertward@scuhs.edu
Web: N/A
Address May Change:

PUBLICATION GUIDELINES:

Manuscript Length: N/A
Copies Required: Four
Computer Submission: Yes Disk, Email
Format: Any program; English
Fees to Review: 0.00 US$

Manuscript Style:
  See Manuscript Guidelines

CIRCULATION DATA:

Reader: Practicing Teachers,
  Administrators
Frequency of Issue: 2 Times/Year
Copies per Issue: 1,001 - 2,000
Sponsor/Publisher: Association of
  Chiropractic Colleges
Subscribe Price: 25.00 US$ Individual
  30.00 US$ Libraries

REVIEW INFORMATION:

Type of Review: Blind Review
No. of External Reviewers: 3
No. of In House Reviewers: 1
Acceptance Rate: 21-30%
Time to Review: 4 - 6 Months
Reviewers Comments: Yes
Invited Articles: 6-10%
Fees to Publish: 0.00 US$

MANUSCRIPT TOPICS:

Clinical Education; Curriculum Studies; Education Management/Administration; Higher Education; Tests, Measurement & Evaluation

MANUSCRIPT GUIDELINES/COMMENTS:

Instructions For Authors

The mission of the Journal of Chiropractic Education (J Chiropractic Educ) is to promote excellence in chiropractic education through the publication of research and scholarly articles concerned with educational theory, methods and content relevant to the practice of chiropractic. Continuing call for papers includes:

Investigations - reports of new research findings concerning chiropractic students, the efficacy of teaching strategies, and the outcomes of chiropractic education,

Literature Reviews - critical assessments of current knowledge of a particular subject of interest,

Editorials - the presentations of points-of-view or opinion relating to the purpose of the journal, tire discussion of related controversial issues, or the emphasis of evidential support,

Model Lessons - descriptions of lesson plaits and discussions of implementation showing the adaptation of traditional material to meet the needs of chiropractic student through use of instructional strategies, selection of emphasis in content, attitude development, and development of skills unique to chiropractic.

Letters to the Editor - communications which are directed specifically to the editor which critically assess some aspect of the Journal, particularly as such assessment may add to, clarify, or point-up a deficiency in some recently published paper: authors arc afforded the privilege of a counter response,

Conference Reports - documentation of educational conferences, particularly abstracts of presentations prior to their publication in proceeding volume or elsewhere.

Manuscripts are accepted for consideration for publication with the understanding that they represent original, unpublished work which is submitted exclusively to the Journal of *Chiropractic Education:* that is, has not been, and will not be, submitted elsewhere until a final decision has been made by the editor. All manuscripts (meaning any material submitted for consideration to publish) must be accompanied by a properly completed *Transfer of Copyright* form, signed by all authors, and employer if submission represents a "work for hire." Upon such submission, it is to be accepted by all authors that no further dissemination of any part of the material contained in the manuscript is permitted in any planner without prior written approval of the editor. Non-compliance with this copyright holder stipulation may result in withdrawal from consideration for publication.

The following editorial policies will apply:

Authorship - all authors of papers must have an intellectual stake in the material presented for publication. All must be willing to answer for the content of the work, Authors should be willing to certify participation in the work, vouch for its validity, acknowledge reviewing and approving the final version of the paper, acknowledge that the work has not been previously published elsewhere, and be able to produce raw data if requested.

Manuscript Preparation and Submission - manuscripts must be prepared in accordance with the *Declaration of Vancouver* "Uniform Requirements for Manuscripts Submitted to Biomedical Journals." The original and two copies axe to be submitted accompanied by an assignment of copyright. The author should retain a copy in case of loss of submission copies in transit. Manuscripts riot prepared to these standards will be returned for further work before consideration for publication.

Review Process - all manuscripts are subject to *blind* (without author *or* institutional identification) critical review by two *or* more experts in the field or in chiropractic education. The purpose of the review *is to* assist *the* editor *in* determining appropriateness to the Journal objectives, originality, validity, importance of content, substantiation of conclusions, publishability, and possible need for improvement. Reviewers' comments will be returned with manuscript if rejected, or if strong recommendations for improvement were made. All reviewers remain anonymous.

Acceptance for Publication - acceptance of a manuscript for "consideration for publication" and initiation of the review process does not necessarily imply acceptance for publication. After review a manuscript may be accepted for publication as is, accepted after revision, or rejected. Aside for rejection for uncorrectable faults, a manuscript may also be rejected because it adds little new to what has been previously published in the Journal, or addresses a new topic, which it is felt deserves a more in-depth reporting. When there is a decision to require revision or to reject, the editor will usually provide the author with recommendations.

Author Responsibility - manuscripts accepted for publication are subject to such editorial modification and revision as may be necessary to ensure clarity- conciseness- correct usage and conformance to approved style. However, in so far as authors are responsible for all information contained in their published work, they will be consulted if substantive changes are needed and will have further opportunity to make any necessary corrections on the galley proofs.

Reprints and Copies - one complimentary copy of the issue in which the author's work appears will be provided at no charge. Additional copies may be ordered from the office. Reprints may be ordered.

Reproductions - The entire contents of the Journal are protected by copyright and no part may- be reproduced (outside of *the fair use* stipulation of Public Law 94-553) by any means without prior written permission from the editor, In particular this applies to the reprinting of the original article in another publication and the use of any illustrations or text to create a new work.

Manuscript Preparation

Manuscripts submitted for consideration for publication in the *Journal* must be compiled in accordance with the *Declaration of Vancouver* "Uniform Requirements for Manuscripts Submitted to Biomedical Journals." The following instructions are essentially in accordance with those requirements. Those manuscripts not so prepared are subject to return to the author for revision before review.

The entire manuscript must be typed double spaced and on one side only of white bond paper (8 _ x 11" or 130 A4 212 x 297 mm.) with margins of at least 25mm (1 in.)

Each of the following sections must start on a stew page and each paragraph must be indented. Measurements may be reported using the units in which the calculations were originally made. Only standard abbreviations should be used. The list from the Uniform, Standards appears in JMPT. September 1982.

Title Page

The first page is the title page. The title page should carry
a. The concise and informative title of the article.
b. A short running footer based on the title, which will be found on every sheet.
c. First name, middle initial, last name and highest academic degree of each author.
d. Names of the department(s) and institutions) to which the work should be attributed.
e. Disclaimers (if any).

394

f   Name, address, phone and FAX number of author responsible for correspondence and proofreading of galleys (usually the principal author).

g. The sources of support for the work (grants, equipment, etc.).

Abstract and Key Words

The abstract The second page should carry an abstract of no more than 150 words. An abstract should indicate the objectives of the authors; the methods used and summarize the results and conclusions. Structured abstracts are required. (In February 1992 JMPT published information on structured abstracts for original data reports and reviews of the literature. In February/March 1993 JMPT published an editorial on the use of structures abstracts for case studies.)

Key words Below the abstract list 3 to 10 key indexing terms from Index Medicus. ERIC, or CHIROLARS, which best describe what your article is about. These words or short phrases are to help indexers cross-referencing your work. The college librarians axe helpful in the selection of keywords.

Text Pages

The text of the article begins on the third page. Until after *blind review the text should not include the* name of *any institution.* To indicate where you might wish to include a specific name or abbreviation of a name, use "(institution)". This can then be replaced during revisions after review.

(Note: Avoid the use of footnotes. Include any necessary explanatory information within the text in parentheses.) The text should be long enough to clearly present the material and be subdivided with at least the headings; Introduction, Discussion and Conclusion. Articles with original date normally will also have sections entitled: Materials & Methods, arid Results. Other types of articles such as reviews, model lessons, editorials- etc. may need other formats. Long articles may need further sub-dividing with sub-subheadings.

Introduction The introduction serves to introduce the reader to what was done *and* why it was done. It should clearly state the purpose of the article and summarize the rationale that led to the work. Only strictly pertinent references should be given because this is not an extensive review of the subject. (See also Discussion)

Materials and Methods This is the how of the article. Identify your methods and procedures in sufficient detail so that others may reproduce your work for comparison of results. If you used an established method, give a reference to a published description of the method. If the method has been published but is not well known, add a brief description. Describe in detail any new methods that you developed or any- modifications that you have made to the methods of others. When relevant, describe your selection of subjects and indicate whether the work was done *in* accordance with the ethical standards of with the *Helsinki Declaration of 1975* and with the approval of the institution's Committee on Human Rights.

Results Present your results in a logical sequence in the text, tables, and illustrations. The text should highlight and summarize the material in the tables and illustrations rather than repeat all data shown.

Discussion The discussion should emphasize the new and important aspects of the study and the conclusions that follow. Include the implications of the findings, how they relate to the work of others to be found *in* the literature (Don't forget to give the references), and the limitations of the findings and/or the work.

Conclusions The principle conclusions should be directly linked to the goals of the study. Unqualified statements not supported by the evidence presented should be avoided, as should alluding possible evidence from work that has not been completed. Recommendations for further study may be included when appropriate.

Acknowledgements

This section should start on a separate page of paper. Acknowledge only persons who have made substantive contributions. Ordinarily this would include support personnel such as statisticians or consultants, but not subjects or clerical staff. Authors arc responsible for obtaining written permission from persons being acknowledged by name because someone may infer their endorsement of the data or conclusions. Names are not published without written permission of the individuals.

References

References are to be numbered consecutively as they are first used in the text, and listed in that order (not alphabetically) beginning on a separate sheet following the text pages, When a previously used reference is used again, it is designated (in the text) by the by the number originally assigned to it by its first use; do not assign another number by again listing it as "op cit.".

Only those references that provide support for a particular statement in the text, tables or figures should be used. References are published material or material accepted for publication (in press), Abstracts, "unpublished observations" and "personal communications" may no longer be used as references, although reference to written (not verbal) communications may be inserted (in parentheses) in the text. Excessive use of references should be avoided. References must be verified by the authors) against the original document. That is, do not copy a quotation from someone who used the reference without going back to the original article and verifying that is what the reference said.

For the most part sources of information and reference support for a paper should be limited to recent journals (rather than books) since that knowledge is generally more up to date, and (in the case of refereed journals with active sections of letters to the editors) more accurate. Consequently the approved form for an approved reference style is established by journal listings; others (books) are modified from journal listings as required. The journal reference style is as follows:

a. Last name(s) of the author(s) and their initials in capitals separated by a space: a comma is used to separate each author aid a period to conclude the list. (List all authors when six or less: when seven or more list the first three and add et al.

b. Title of the article with the first word capitalized and all other words in lower case, except names of persons or places-

c. The name of the journal abbreviated in accordance with that specified by the National Library of Medicine, a space and the year of publication; Volume number (issue number in parentheses if needed) followed by a colon, and inclusive pages of the article (with redundant numbers dropped, for example 1(14-12), See the January 1994 issue of Index Medicus for a complete listing of their indexed journals.

Specific Examples of References
Journal Article:
1. Kleynhans AM. Implications of distance education for chiropractic. J Chiropractic Educ 1992; 6(2):55-56.

Books:
2. McKeachie WJ. Teaching tips, a guidebook for the beginning teacher. 5th ed. IC Lexington, Massachusetts.Heath Bc Co,, 1986;143-157. 189-93.

3. Jacobs LC. Chase CI. Developing and using tests effectively, a guide for faculty. San Francisco, Jossey-Bass Pub.,1992:123-140.

4. Glasberg M. Selection of patients in therapeutic trials. In: Rose FC, ed. Amyotrophic lateral sclerosis. New York, Demos Pub., 199o;33-38.

Table pages- Type each table on a separate sheet remembering to double-space all data. Using arable numerals, number each table in the order in which they are listed (in parentheses in the text). Supply a brief title to appear above the table. Any necessary explanatory matter should be provided under the bottom of the table and identified with a sequence of alphabetical symbols.

Too many tables may make it impossible to format the material for publication. In such cases the editor may suggest that the authors make available packets of tables for those interested.

Illustration legend pages- Number the illustrations on the back in the same sequence in which they are mentioned in the text (for example, Figure 1). On a separate sheet type the legends for the illustrations using double-spacing and numbering the legends to match the illustrations.

Manuscript Submission
Submit a complete manuscript package. This consists of;
a   The manuscript with all its pacts (original and three blinded copies),
b.   Four sets of illustrations (if applicable) - one for each manuscript.
c.   Transfer of copyright form signed by all authors, and by employer if study was a work for hire.
d.   Letter(s) of permission to use previously published material (if applicable)
e.   Consent forms to publish photographs in which subjects may be identifiable, to publish names in acknowledgements.
f.   Cover letter from principal author (or author specified as correspondent) providing any special information regarding the submission, which may be helpful in its consideration for publication.

The material should be packaged securely in a heavyweight envelope with illustrations placed between cardboard to prevent bending. The manuscript should be mailed first class or express, insured (return receipt requested, if desired) to the *Journal of Chiropractic Education,* Los Angeles College of Chiropractic, 16200 E. Amber Valley Drive, Whittier, CA 90609 –1166.

Letters To The Editor

In keeping with the standard practice of providing an open forum for readers to participate in the improvement of related knowledge, the *Journal* welcomes *Letters to the editors,* which seek to add to or clarify the information contained in a recent article.

Letters should be double-spaced with wide margins on standard bond paper. The title of the article being referred to should be at the top of the first page and the nacre and address of the writer at the end. The original and one vicar photocopy should be submitted to the editor, along with a cover letter (on the writer's letterhead and signed by the writer), which specifies that the accompanying letter is being submitted for consideration for publication. No unsigned letters arc accepted for publication.

If a letter is accepted for publication, a copy will be sent to the author of the article in question, who will have the opportunity to provide a rebuttal and new information that will be considered for publication along with the letter. This indirect communication provides all readers with information and can reduce irritations and biases.

Submission Of Revised Manuscript

When a manuscript has been provisionally accepted for publication, reviewers' comments will be returned to the author for consideration in the revision process. The authors should revise the manuscript in accordance with the reviewers' suggestions. Before submission for publication the final draft should be checked for spelling and other such problems. It should be submitted before the designated deadline, This draft should be sent as a hard copy and as either an attachment to au e-mail or a copy on. a 3.5" disk formatted IBM compatible. The file name should indicate the author and the disk should be labeled to indicate the word processing format used. The draft is subject to editorial revision for clarity and consistency of style, to fit the format of the Journal, or other reasons. The author will receive a galley to proof and should be sure to inform the editor if the editing has caused any changes in the meaning of the material. Galley proofs should be returned within 48 hours.

Journal of Clinical Psychology

ADDRESS FOR SUBMISSION:

Larry E. Beutler, Editor
Journal of Clinical Psychology
University of California Santa Barbara
Graduate School of Education
Santa Barbara, CA 93106
USA
Phone: 805-893-2923
Fax: 805-893-7264
E-Mail: beutler@education.ucsb.edu
Web:
Address May Change:

PUBLICATION GUIDELINES:

Manuscript Length: 5-25
Copies Required: Three
Computer Submission: No
Format: N/A
Fees to Review: 0.00 US$

Manuscript Style:
       American Psychological Association

CIRCULATION DATA:

Reader: Academics, Clinicians
Frequency of Issue: Bi-Monthly
Copies per Issue: 2,001 - 3,000
Sponsor/Publisher: John Wiley & Sons
Subscribe Price: 45.00 US$

REVIEW INFORMATION:

Type of Review: Blind Review
No. of External Reviewers: 2
No. of In House Reviewers: 1
Acceptance Rate: 21-30%
Time to Review: 1 - 2 Months
Reviewers Comments: Yes
Invited Articles: 6-10%
Fees to Publish: 0.00 US$

MANUSCRIPT TOPICS:
Higher Education; School Law; Special Education; Tests, Measurement & Evaluation

MANUSCRIPT GUIDELINES/COMMENTS:

Aims and Scope
Founded in 1945, the *Journal of Clinical Psychology* is a peer-reviewed forum devoted to research, assessment, and practice. Published eight times a year, the *Journal* includes research studies; articles on contemporary professional issues, single case research; dissertations in brief; notes from the field; and news and notes. In addition to papers on psychopathology, psychodiagnostics, and the psychotherapeutic process, the journal welcomes articles focusing on psychotherapy effectiveness research, psychological assessment and treatment matching, and clinical outcomes. From time to time, the *Journal* publishes Special Sections, featuring a selection of articles related to a single particularly timely or important theme; individuals interested in Guest Editing a Special Section are encouraged to contact the Editors.

IN SESSION: Psychotherapy in Practice
The twin challenges for mental health practitioners are to stay abreast of emerging therapeutic innovations and to identify the treatment methods and relationship stances that will prove

most effective for each client. *In Session*, a branch of the *Journal of Clinical Psychology*, focuses on the clinical challenges confronting psychotheapists, in the form of either a distinct patient population or a therapeutic dilemma. Each issue of *In Session* features original articles illustrated through case reports by seasoned clinicians and informed by research reviews translated into clinical practice. Each issue examines a variety of theoretical orientations and treatment formats in jargon-free language. Case examples, clinical recommendations, and relevant research findings are combined to facilitate the selection and integration of effective methods.

Editorial Policy. The opinions expressed here are those of the authors, and do not necessarily reflect those of the editors or the publisher. Names and identifying information have been changed to ensure the confidentiality of all individuals mentioned in case material.

Manuscript Submission
Please submit **four** originals (including all illustrations and tables) of manuscripts for consideration to the editor, Larry E. Beutler, Ph.D. at the following address:
> Journal of Clinical Psychology
> Department of Education
> Counseling/Clinical/School Psychology Program
> University of California
> Santa Barbara, CA 93106

All *In Session* articles are published by invitation only. Individuals interested in nominating, organizing, or guest editing an issue are encouraged to contact the editor-in-chief:
> John C. Norcross, Ph.D.
> Department of Psychology
> University of Scranton
> Scranton, PA 18510-4596
> E-mail: norcross@uofs.edu

Manuscript Preparation
Format. Final manuscripts should be typed (or laser-printed) double-spaced with a 1" margin on all sides. Please use good quality white bond 8½ × 11 paper. Number all pages of the manuscript sequentially. Manuscripts should contain each of the following elements in sequence: 1) Title page 2) Abstract 3) Text 4) Acknowledgments 5) References 6) Tables 7) Figures 8) Figure Legends 9) Permissions. Start each element on a new page. Because the *Journal of Clinical Psychology* utilizes an anonymous peer-review process, authors' names and affiliations should appear ONLY on the title page of the manuscript.

Style. Please follow the stylistic guidelines detailed in the *Publication Manual of the American Psychological Association, Fourth Edition*, available from the American Psychological Association, Washington, D.C. *Webster's New World Dictionary of American English, 3rd College Edition*, is the accepted source for spelling. Define unusual abbreviations at the first mention in the text. The text should be written in a uniform style, and its contents as submitted for consideration should be deemed by the author to be final and suitable for publication.

400

Title Page. The title page should contain the complete title of the manuscript, names and affiliations of all authors, institution(s) at which the work was performed, and name, address, telephone and telefax numbers of the author responsible for correspondence. Authors should also provide a short title of not more than 45 characters (including spaces), and five to ten key words, that will highlight the subject matter of the article.

Abstract. Abstracts are required for research articles; dissertations in brief; and notes from the field. Abstracts must be 150 words or less, and should be intelligible without reference to the text.

Permissions. Reproduction of an unaltered figure, table, or block of text from any non-federal government publication requires permission from the copyright holder. All direct quotations should have a source and page citation. Acknowledgment of source material cannot substitute for written permission. It is the author's responsibility to obtain such written permission from the owner of the rights to this material.

Final Revised Manuscript. A final version of your accepted manuscript should be submitted on diskette as well as hard copy, using the Diskette Submission Instructions form included in most issues of the journal.

Article Types

Research Reports. Research reports may include quantitative or qualitative investigations, or single-case research. They should contain Introduction, Methods, Results, Discussion, and Conclusion sections conforming to standard scientific reporting style (where appropriate, Results and Discussion may be combined).

Review Articles. Review articles should focus on the clinical implications of theoretical perspectives, diagnostic approaches, or innovative strategies for assessment or treatment. Articles should provide a critical review and interpretation of the literature. Although subdivisions (e.g. introduction, methods, results) are not required, the text should flow smoothly, and be divided logically by topical headings.

Dissertations in Brief. The journal encourages the submission of important work by young investigators and researcher/practitioners. This section of the journal spotlights innovative research conducted during the student's graduate studies. Dissertations in Brief should contain an abstract, and provide a concise synopsis (10 manuscript pages or less) of the major findings presented in the student's final dissertation. The format of manuscripts submitted for this section may adhere to the Research Report or Review Article format as appropriate.

Notes from the Field. Notes from the Field offers a forum for brief descriptions of advances in clinical training; innovative treatment methods or community based initiatives; developments in service delivery; or the presentation of data from research projects which have progressed to a point where preliminary observations should be disseminated (e.g., pilot studies; significant findings in need of replication). Articles submitted for this section should be limited to a maximum of 10 manuscript pages, and contain logical topical subheadings.

News and Notes. This section offers a vehicle for readers to stay abreast of major awards, grants, training initiatives; research projects; and conferences in clinical psychology. Items for this section should be summarized in 200 words or less. The Editors reserve the right to determine which News and Notes submissions are appropriate for inclusion in the journal.

Editorial Policy

Manuscripts for consideration by the *Journal of Clinical Psychology* must be submitted solely to this journal, and may not have been published in another publication of any type, professional or lay. This policy covers both duplicate and fragmented (piecemeal) publication. Although, on occasion it may be appropriate to publish several reports referring to the same data base, authors should inform the editors at the time of submission about all previously published or submitted reports stemming from the data set, so that the editors can judge if the article represents a new contribution. If the article is accepted for publication in the *Journal*, the article must include a citation to all reports using the same data and methods or the same sample. Upon acceptance of a manuscript for publication, the corresponding author will be required to sign an agreement transferring copyright to the Publisher; copies of the Copyright Transfer form are available from the editorial office. All accepted manuscripts become the property of the Publisher. No material published in the *Journal* may be reproduced or published elsewhere without written permission from the Publisher, who reserves copyright.

Any possible conflict of interest, financial or otherwise, related to the submitted work must be clearly indicated in the manuscript and in a cover letter accompanying the submission. Research performed on human participants must be accompanied by a statement of compliance with the Code of Ethics of the World Medical Association (Declaration of Helsinki) and the standards established by the author's Institutional Review Board and granting agency. Informed consent statements, if applicable, should be included with the manuscript stating that informed consent was obtained from the research participants after the nature of the experimental procedures was explained.

The *Journal of Clinical Psychology requires* that all identifying details regarding the client(s)/ patient(s), including, but not limited to name, age, race, occupation, and place of residence be altered to prevent recognition. By signing the *Copyright Transfer Agreement*, you acknowledge that you have altered all identifying details, or obtained all necessary written releases.

All statements in, or omissions from, published manuscripts are the responsibility of authors, who will be asked to review proofs prior to publication. Reprint order forms will be sent with the page proofs. No page charges will be levied against authors or their institutions for publication in the journal. Authors should retain copies of their manuscripts; the journal will not be responsible for loss of manuscripts at any time.

Disk Submission Instructions

Please return your final, revised manuscript on disk as well as hard copy. The hard copy must match the disk. The Journal strongly encourages authors to deliver the final, revised version of their accepted manuscripts (text, tables, and, if possible, illustrations) on disk. Given the near-universal use of computer word-processing for manuscript preparation, we anticipate that providing a disk will be convenient for you, and it carries the added advantages of maintaining the integrity of your keystrokes and expediting typesetting. Please return the disk submission slip below with your manuscript and labeled disk(s).

Guidelines for Electronic Submission

Text

Storage medium. 3-1/2" high-density disk in IBM MS-DOS, Windows, or Macintosh format. **Software and format**. Microsoft Word 6.0 is preferred, although manuscripts prepared with any other microcomputer word processor are acceptable. Refrain from complex formatting; the Publisher will style your manuscript according to the Journal design specifications. Do not use desktop publishing software such as Aldus PageMaker or Quark XPress. If you prepared your manuscript with one of these programs, export the text to a word processing format. Please make sure your word processing program's "fast save" feature is turned off. Please do not deliver files that contain hidden text: for example, do not use your word processor's automated features to create footnotes or reference lists.

File names. Submit the text and tables of each manuscript as a single file. Name each file with your last name (up to eight letters). Text files should be given the three-letter extension that identifies the file format. Macintosh users should maintain the MS-DOS "eight dot three" file-naming convention.

Labels. Label all disks with your name, the file name, and the word processing program and version used.

Illustration

All print reproduction requires files for full color images to be in a CMYK color space. If possible, ICC or ColorSync profiles of your output device should accompany all digital image submissions.

Storage medium. Submit as separate files from text files, on separate disks or cartridges. If feasible, full color files should be submitted on separate disks from other image files. 3-1/2" high-density disks, CD, Iomega Zip, and 5 1/4" 44- or 88-MB SyQuest cartridges can be submitted. At author's request, cartridges and disks will be returned after publication.

Software and format. All illustration files should be in TIFF or EPS (with preview) formats. Do not submit native application formats.

Resolution. Journal quality reproduction will require grayscale and color files at resolutions yielding approximately 300 ppi. Bitmapped line art should be submitted at resolutions yielding 600-1200 ppi. These resolutions refer to the output size of the file; if you anticipate that your images will be enlarged or reduced, resolutions should be adjusted accordingly.

File names. Illustration files should be given the 2- or 3-letter extension that identifies the file format used (i.e., .tif, .eps).

Labels. Label all disks and cartridges with your name, the file names, formats, and compression schemes (if any) used. Hard copy output must accompany all files.

Journal of Cognition and Development

ADDRESS FOR SUBMISSION:

Phillip David Zelazo, Editor
Journal of Cognition and Development
University of Toronto
Department of Psychology
100 St. George Street
Toronto, Ontario, M5S 3G3
Canada
Phone: 416-978-3904
Fax: 416-978-4811
E-Mail: jcd@psych.utoronto.ca
Web: www.cogdevsoc.org
Address May Change:

PUBLICATION GUIDELINES:

Manuscript Length: 30+
Copies Required: Four
Computer Submission: No
Format: N/A
Fees to Review: 0.00 US$

Manuscript Style:
    American Psychological Association

CIRCULATION DATA:

Reader: Academics
Frequency of Issue: Quarterly
Copies per Issue: No Reply
Sponsor/Publisher: Lawrence Erlbaum
    Associates
Subscribe Price: 60.00 US$ Individual
    180.00 US$ Institution

REVIEW INFORMATION:

Type of Review: Blind Review
No. of External Reviewers: 2
No. of In House Reviewers: 0
Acceptance Rate: No Reply
Time to Review: 4 - 6 Months
Reviewers Comments: Yes
Invited Articles: No Reply
Fees to Publish: 0.00 US$

MANUSCRIPT TOPICS:
Elementary/Early Childhood

MANUSCRIPT GUIDELINES/COMMENTS:

Editorial Scope
The *Journal of Cognition and Development* will publish the very best articles on all aspects of cognitive development. In addition to empirical reports, it will feature theoretical essays (occasionally accompanied by peer commentaries), and essay reviews of new and significant books. Criteria for acceptance of submitted manuscripts will include:

- relevance of the work to issues of broad interest;

- substance of the argument (including methodological rigor and support for conclusions drawn);

- ingenuity of the ideas or approach; and quality of expression.

Instructions to Contributors
Four copies of the manuscript should be sent to:

Dr. Philip David Zelazo, Editor
Journal of Cognition and Development
Dept. of Psychology
University of Toronto
100 St. George St.
Toronto, Canada M5S 3G3
phone: 416-978-3904

Manuscripts must conform to the conventions specified in the *Publication Manual of the American Psychological Association, 4th Edition* (see www.apa.org), with the exceptions and considerations listed below. Copies of the manual may be ordered from 750 First St. NE, Washington, D.C. 20002-4242

1. Figures and Tables: A note should be inserted in the text to indicate the approximate placement of each figure and table.

2. Title Page: Acknowledgements and a complete mailing address (including a fax number and an e-mail address) should appear on the title page of the manuscript. Authors will receive reviews and most editorial correspondence by e-mail.

3. Electronic Copy: Once a manuscript has been accepted, authors will be required to submit an electronic copy of the manuscript on diskette. The diskette should be IBM compatible; the text should be saved in WordPerfect or MS Word; any tables and/or figures should be saved in a separate file. Manuscripts that are currently under consideration by another journal, or that have been published previously, in whole or in part, may not be submitted. For further information, please direct enquiries to the Editorial Assistant, via e-mail: jcd@psych.utoronto.ca.

Journal of Collective Negotiations in the Public Sector

ADDRESS FOR SUBMISSION:

Harry Kershen, Editor
Journal of Collective Negotiations in the
    Public Sector
25 E Shore Drive
Massapequa, NY 11758
USA
Phone: 516-798-2688
Fax: 516-797-7146
E-Mail:
Web:
Address May Change:

PUBLICATION GUIDELINES:

Manuscript Length: 16-20
Copies Required: Three
Computer Submission: No
Format: N/A
Fees to Review: 0.00 US$

Manuscript Style:
    See Manuscript Guidelines

CIRCULATION DATA:

Reader: Academics, Administrators,
    Practicing Teachers
Frequency of Issue: Quarterly
Copies per Issue: 1,001 - 2,000
Sponsor/Publisher:
Subscribe Price: 36.00 US$ Individual
    96.00 US$ Institution

REVIEW INFORMATION:

Type of Review: Blind Review
No. of External Reviewers: 1
No. of In House Reviewers: 2
Acceptance Rate: 40%
Time to Review: 1 - 2 Months
Reviewers Comments: No
Invited Articles: 11-20%
Fees to Publish: 0.00 US$

MANUSCRIPT TOPICS:

Bilingual/E.S.L.; Education Management/Administration; Everything Related to Applied Gerontology; Labor Relations; Collective Bargaining

MANUSCRIPT GUIDELINES/COMMENTS:

The increase in the number of public employees during the past three decades, the spread of collective bargaining throughout the public sector, and the recent financial woes of many governmental entities have all dramatically influenced public employee-employer labor relations. *The Journal of Collective Negotiations In The Public Sector* as well as the volumes in the *Public Sector Contemporary Issues Series* present clear discussions of the problems involved in negotiating contracts, resolving impasses, strikes and grievances, and administering contracts in the various areas of public employment.

Each volume in the book series is based on material originally published in the *Journal of Collective Negotiations In The Public Sector*. Articles have been selected for their long range relevance, varied perspectives and depth of analysis. Containing papers ranging from time-tested practical tips, to theoretical analyses, to detailed discussions of legislation,

406

administrative rulings and court decisions, each offering in the series provides a wealth of useful, timely information.

Contributors to the *Public Sector Contemporary Issues Series* include experienced negotiators, public officials, and academic analysts of public sector labor issues. The differing viewpoints and expertise of the authors expose readers to diverse, comprehensive, stimulating presentations on a broad range of topics. Throughout the series, however, those characteristics unique to public sector bargaining - and the political context in which it occurs--are emphasized.

Public sector bargaining demands a comprehensive grasp of laws as well as a broad familiarity with the background information pertinent to each type of negotiation. Aspirations of employees, attitudes of law-makers and of the community-at-large, decisions of regulatory agencies, goals of management, and the feelings of those who sit at the bargaining table are just some of the factual-intangible components of all collective bargaining situations.

Manuscript Preparation
Manuscripts are to be submitted in triplicate (1 original, and 2 copies) to the Executive Editor. Retain one copy, as manuscript will not be returned. Manuscript must be typewritten on 8 1/2" x 11', white paper, one side only, double-spaced, with wide margins. Paginate consecutively starting with the title page. An abstract of 100 to 125 words is required. The organization of the paper should be clearly indicated by appropriate headings and subheadings (note the use of such headings throughout this manual).

The receipt of all manuscript will be acknowledged by return mail. Authors should note that only original articles are accepted for publication. Submission of a manuscript represents certification on the part of the author(s) that neither the article submitted nor a version of it has been published or is being considered for publication elsewhere.

Copyright Agreement
The author's Warranty and Transfer of Copyright Agreement must be signed and received before an article is refereed and composition begins. Current laws state that publishers must receive signed agreements for all manuscripts, in order to protect the copyright.

The publisher grants permission to the author/s to use their articles in whole, or part, without further consent of the publisher. In reuse state journal name, volume, issue and date of original appearance. The use of this copywritten material, by other than the author, is prohibited without expressed written permission of the publisher.

Title Page And Affiliation
The title page should include the complete title of the article, the author's name(s), the academic or professional affiliation(s), and complete address(es). If the title contains fifty or more characters submit a shortened version to be used in the running head. When a source footnote is used for the article, indicate it by an asterisk placed after the title and type the footnote at the bottom of the title page. The complete name and address, including zip code, of the person to whom proofs and reprint requests are to be sent should be shown on the title page.

References

In text - A reference is a direction to or a consultation of books, periodicals, etc., for information that is cited within text. References are, indicated numerically. Each new reference is listed in numerical order. Where previously cited reference material is used again, it bears its original reference number. Reference number(s) are to be enclosed in brackets with a dash separating consecutive numbers (1--57 and a comma separating individual. numbers C 1, 3, 57 Where it is necessary to show the pages cited in text t following sample is used 11, p. 57.

In Listing - A compiled list of reference citings, in numerical sequence appears at the end of text. Ibid., op. cit., etc., are not to be used, as ea new referenced work receives its new numerical listing, and previously cited, referenced material retains its numerical listing. The following is a model a reference listing.

Journal/Periodical

1. Author's name, first and middle initials, surname, i.e. J. J. Jones
2. Title of referenced work, i.e. Instructions to Authors
*3. Editor's name; first and middle initials, surname (abbreviate word editor and place in parentheses after surname), i.e. T. A. Smith (ed.4.Title of journal/periodical, underlined, i.e. 4. Journal of Publishing Specifications
5. Volume number, underlined, i.e. 3
6. Issue number, i.e. 2
7. Pages, i.e. p. or pp. 1-4
8. Year of publication, i.e. 1976

Sample:

1. J. J. Jones, Instructions to Authors, Journal of Publishing Specifications, 3:2,pp. 1-4, 1976.

*Where applicable use this sample for editor inclusion
1. J. J. Jones, Instructions to Authors, T. A. Smith (ed.), Journal of Publishing Specifications, 3:2, pp. 1-4, 1976.

Book Model

1. Author's name; first and middle initials, surname, i.e. J. J. Jones
2. Title of book, underlined, i.e. Publishing Specifications and Styles
3. Editor's name; first and middle initials, surname, i.e. J. E. Grenbourg (ed.)
4. Publisher, i.e. Baywood Publishing Company, Inc.
5. Location, i.e. Farmingdale, New York
6. Page, i.e. p. 10
7. Year of publications, i.e. 1976

Sample:

1. J. J. Jones, Publishing Specifications and Styles, J. E. Grenbourg (ed.), Baywood Publishing Company, Inc., Farmingdale, New York, p. 10, 1976.

Bibliography

A bibliography is an unnumbered, alphabetical list of writings relating to a given subject or author, and not necessarily cited within text. Publisher's format requires an alphabetized list of author's last name followed by his first and middle initials. The balance of entry utilizes the same style as references.

Footnotes

Footnotes are notes placed at the foot of the page where cited. They give information or commentary which, though related to the subject discussed, would interrupt the flow of the narrative or argument; or give additional evidence or illustration in support. Footnotes should be numbered with superior Arabic numbers without parentheses or brackets. Table footnotes are indicated by lower case letters. Footnotes should be brief with an average Length of three lines.

Figures

All line figures submitted must be original drawings in black ink on a good quality paper done to professional standards. Two color work will not be accepted. Photographs should be glossy prints with high contrast. Plan all figures to be proportionate to the 4 1/2 " x 7 1/2" final size image area. Figures Larger than final size must remain easily readable with points and lines clearly distinguishable after reduction; 8 point is the standard callouts (labeling) size. All figures must be referenced in text and positioned as close to citation as possible. Identify all figures on front, outside image area, with author's name, article title, figure number, figure title, and figure top. If additional space is needed attach a paper to the bottom of the illustration. Please be accurate as the position of this material will identify the correct reading position of the illustration. All figures appear in strict numerical sequence starting with Figure 1. Clearly indicate on manuscript page margin where each figure is to appear.

Tables

Tables must be cited in text in numerical sequence. Use arabic numbers starting with Table 1. Place each table as close to citation as possible and indicate placement in margin on the manuscript. Keep in mind the 4 1/2" X 7 1/2" final size when planning tabular material. Tables larger than this size will have to be reduced and type must remain large enough to be easily read. Each table must have a descriptive title. Footnotes to tables are indicated by superior lower case letters. Each table will have one opening rule, a rule under column heads, and a closing rule. Avoid vertical ruling.

Scheduling

After editor's acceptance the manuscript is sent to the publisher for production editing and composition. On completion of these phases, proofs are sent to the editor and author for careful proofreading and checking. After author and editor review the proofs, corrections will be made as required, and the article is considered final.

It is mandatory that the author review proofs and mail them within 48 hours of receipt in order that the publisher may fulfill the rigorous scheduling requirements. Authors may order reprints of their articles by completing the reprint order form enclosed with the proofs. All reprint orders must be prepaid.

Journal of College & University Student Housing

ADDRESS FOR SUBMISSION:

Sharon Blansett, Editor
Journal of College & University Student
    Housing
University of Florida
University Housing Office
PO Box 112100
Gainesville, FL 32611-2100
USA
Phone: 352-392-2161
Fax: 352-392-6819
E-Mail: sharonb@housing.ufl.edu
Web: www.acuho.ohio-state.edu
Address May Change:

PUBLICATION GUIDELINES:

Manuscript Length: 11-15
Copies Required: Three
Computer Submission: Yes Email
Format: Word Attachment
Fees to Review: 0.00 US$

Manuscript Style:
    American Psychological Association

CIRCULATION DATA:

Reader: Administrators, Faculty
Frequency of Issue: 2 Times/Year
Copies per Issue: 3,001 - 4,000
Sponsor/Publisher: Association of College
    and University Officers-International
Subscribe Price: 30.00 US$ Individual
    20.00 US$ Members

REVIEW INFORMATION:

Type of Review: Masked
No. of External Reviewers: 0
No. of In House Reviewers: 3
Acceptance Rate: 40%
Time to Review: 2 - 3 Months
Reviewers Comments: Yes
Invited Articles: 6-10%
Fees to Publish: 0.00 US$

MANUSCRIPT TOPICS:
College and University Housing; Higher Education; Student Affairs Administration

MANUSCRIPT GUIDELINES/COMMENTS:

The Editorial Board will consider articles on current research, literature reviews, and other scholarly material for housing officers with particular interest in housing-related research.

Electronic submission of manuscripts is encouraged. To submit a manuscript, send or e-mail attachment of the manuscript typed, double-spaced with generous margins on 8 ½ x 11 inch page set-up in Word format or send an original (typed double-spaced with generous margins on 8 ½ x 11 inch white paper) and three clear copies.

Text and reference style should conform to that in the *Publication Manual of the American Psychological Association*, (4th ed.). Manuscripts should generally not exceed 3,000 words (approximate 12 pages, including references, tables, and figures) or be less than 1,000 words. Place each figure (camera-ready if possible) and table on pages separate from text. Include only essential data in tables; combine tables if feasible. No more than four tables and/or figures will be published per article. Do not use general masculine or sexist terms. Avoid footnotes. Authors are responsible for the accuracy of all material and should recognize individuals who contributed as co-authors, joint researchers, consultants, or student supervisees.

Do not submit material that has been published or is being considered for publication by another medium. Manuscript receipt is acknowledged promptly, but editorial decisions may require several months. Upon article publication, each author receives two copies of the issue. Published material becomes the property of ACUHO-I. The Editor reserves the right to edit as necessary.

Journal of College and University Law

ADDRESS FOR SUBMISSION:

William P. Hoye, Editor
Journal of College and University Law
Notre Dame Law School
Notre Dame, IN 46556
USA
Phone: 219-631-6749 or 6411
Fax: 219-631-6731 or 8233
E-Mail: jcul@nd.edu
Web: www.nd.edu/~jcul
Address May Change:

PUBLICATION GUIDELINES:

Manuscript Length: More than 20
Copies Required: Three
Computer Submission: Yes , Online
Format: Word or Wordperfect
Fees to Review: 0.00 US$

Manuscript Style:
    Uniform System of Citation (Harvard
    Blue Book)

CIRCULATION DATA:

Reader: Academics, Administrators
Frequency of Issue: 3 Times/Year
Copies per Issue: 3,001 - 4,000
Sponsor/Publisher: Notre Dame Law
    School
Subscribe Price: 61.00 US$

REVIEW INFORMATION:

Type of Review: Editorial Review
No. of External Reviewers: 1
No. of In House Reviewers: 3
Acceptance Rate: 40%
Time to Review: 1 - 2 Months
Reviewers Comments: Yes
Invited Articles: 50% +
Fees to Publish: 0.00 US$

MANUSCRIPT TOPICS:
Education Management/Administration; Gifted Children; Higher Education; School Law; Special Education; Teacher Education

MANUSCRIPT GUIDELINES/COMMENTS:

The *Journal of College and University Law* is a quarterly publication of the Association of College and University Attorneys (NACUA) and the Notre D School. It is a refereed, professional journal specializing in contemporary I issues and developments important to postsecondary education.

The Journal publishes articles, commentaries (scholarly editorials), book r student notes and student case comments. Experts in the law of higher ed review all manuscripts.

Manuscripts should be typewritten on 8 1/2"x 11" paper and should be double-spaced. Set-off quotations should be double-spaced. Footnotes should re format specified in the sixteenth edition of A Uniform System of Citation (the "Bluebook"). A paragraph on the title page should provide the position, ed background, address and telephone number of the author. Each author is to disclose in a footnote any affiliation or position, past present or prospective, that could be perceived to influence the author's views on ma discussed in the manuscript.

Decisions on publication usually are made within four weeks of a manuscript receipt. A student editor, an outside reviewer, and the Faculty Editor edit a accepted for publication. The Journal submits editorial changes to the auth approval before publication. The Faculty Editor reserves the right of final d concerning all manuscript changes.

When an article is approved for publication, the Journal retains the exclusive right to publish it, and the copyright is owned by NACUA.

Manuscripts may be submitted electronically by completing the form on the journal's website www.nd.edu/~jcul/authors.htm or by submitting by mail to: Professor William P. Hoye, Faculty Editor, Office of the General Counsel, 203 Main Building, Notre Dame, IN 46556. To submit a work electronically, please email the work as a Word or WordPerfect document.

Deadlines for Manuscript Receipt:
August 25   Winter distribution
October 1   Spring distribution
January 1   Summer distribution
March 1   Fall distribution

Journal of College Orientation and Transition

ADDRESS FOR SUBMISSION:

Michael Miller, Editor
Journal of College Orientation and
   Transition
San Jose State University
College of Education
One Washington Square
San Jose, CA 95192-0071
USA
Phone: 408-924-3600
Fax: 408-924-3713
E-Mail: mmiller5@email.sjsu.edu
Web: noda.tamu.edu
Address May Change:

PUBLICATION GUIDELINES:

Manuscript Length: 11-15
Copies Required: Five
Computer Submission: Yes Disk
Format: MSWord, pdf
Fees to Review: 0.00 US$

Manuscript Style:
   American Psychological Association

CIRCULATION DATA:

Reader: Administrators
Frequency of Issue: 2 Times/Year
Copies per Issue: 1,800
Sponsor/Publisher: National Orientation
   Directors Assn.
Subscribe Price: 20.00 US$
   25.00 US$ International

REVIEW INFORMATION:

Type of Review: Blind Review
No. of External Reviewers: 3
No. of In House Reviewers: 1
Acceptance Rate: 50%
Time to Review: 2 - 3 Months
Reviewers Comments: Yes
Invited Articles: 0-5%
Fees to Publish: 0.00 US$

MANUSCRIPT TOPICS:
Higher Education; Student Affairs

MANUSCRIPT GUIDELINES/COMMENTS:

The Journal of College Orientation and Transition focuses on the trends, practices, research, and development of programs, policies, and activities related to the matriculation, orientation, transition, and retention of college students. Also encouraged are literature reviews, "how-to" articles, innovative initiatives, successful practices, and new ideas.

Publication Schedule. Spring and fall editions.

Style Guide. *Publication Manual of the American Psychological Association,* Fourth Edition.

Recommended Length
Should not exceed 3,000 words (approximately 12 pages of double-spaced, type-written copy with one inch margins and including abstract, tables and figures, and references).

"Campus Notes" Submission
Manuscripts briefs on campus programs, "how-to" articles, successful innovations and pragmatic issues relevant to the orientation and transition of students are encouraged. They should not exceed 1,000 words and should be submitted directly to the "Campus Notes" Associate Editor.

Book Reviews
Book reviews of current appropriate professional publications are encouraged. Submissions should not exceed 1,500 words and should be submitted directly to the "Book Reviews" Associate Editor.

Perspectives
Points-of-view and reflections written in editorial or speech writing style.

Abstract
Include an abstract on a separate page following the title page (except for "Campus Notes" and "Perspectives" manuscripts). The abstract should be 50 words.

Accepted Manuscripts
Once the manuscript has been accepted for publication, a revised copy should be submitted on a 3 1/2 " disk (Macintosh™ preferred; MS-DOS acceptable) with word processing software specified

Figures and Graphs. Supply camera-ready art.

Special Format Guideline
Place the name(s) of the author(s), position(s), and institutional affiliation(s) on a separate title page. The article's text page should include the manuscript title, but not the author name(s). Subsequent pages are to be identified by the running head and page number.

Review Process
The journal is refereed using a blind review system. The manuscript will be judged based on relevance of the topic, usefulness to the orientation, transition, and/or student affairs profession; writing skill; and quality of methodology and/or information. Notification of acceptance or rejection of all manuscripts will be made by the editor. All manuscripts received and approved for publication become the property of the association. All others will be returned upon request. The editor reserves the right to edit or rewrite accepted articles to meet the journal standards.

Concurrent Submissions to Other Publications
Never submit an article which has been previously published or one which has been submitted to another publication.

Appropriate Language
Avoid the use of the term "subject;" instead, use specific references such as "student" or "participant." Avoid sexist terminology and the perpetuation of stereotypes.

Manuscript Submission
Submit five copies on 8.5" x 11" paper with a running head (see APA Manual) to the Editor.

Manuscripts and Perspectives
Dr. Michael T. Miller, Editor
Journal of College Orientation and Transition
Associate Dean
San Jose State University
One Washington Square
San Jose, CA 95192-0071
(408) 924-3600 fax: (408) 924-3713
mmiller5 @email.sjsu.edu

Campus Notes
Dr. Denise L. Rode, Associate Editor
Journal of College Orientation and Transition
Director of Orientation Northern Illinois University 120 Campus Life Building
DeKalb, IL 60115
(815)7536781 fax: (815)753-7480
drode@niu.edu

Book Reviews
Dr. Daniel P. Nadler
Associate Dean of Students
Tulane University
Suite 204, University Center
New Orleans, LA 70118-5698
(504)865-5141 fax: (504)862-8730
nadler@mailhost.tcs.tulane.edu

The members of the editorial board are dedicated to a quality publication and are always willing to discuss manuscript ideas and publication policies with potential authors. Authors are not required to be NODA members to publish in its journal

Journal of College Science Teaching

ADDRESS FOR SUBMISSION:

Lester G. Paldy, Editor
Journal of College Science Teaching
State University of New York
  at Stony Brook
Science Outreach Program
Stony Brook, NY 11794-3733
USA
Phone: 631-632-7026
Fax: 631-632-7220
E-Mail: lpaldy@notes.cc.sunysb.edu
Web: www.nsta.org
Address May Change:

PUBLICATION GUIDELINES:

Manuscript Length: 3,500 words or less
Copies Required: Three
Computer Submission: Yes
Format: any, prefer MSWord
Fees to Review: 0.00 US$

Manuscript Style:
    Chicago Manual of Style

CIRCULATION DATA:

Reader: Academics
Frequency of Issue: 7 Times/Year
Copies per Issue: 5,001 - 10,000
Sponsor/Publisher: National Science
  Teachers Association
Subscribe Price: 65.00 US$ Membership
    12.00 US$ Single Copy

REVIEW INFORMATION:

Type of Review: Blind Review
No. of External Reviewers: 2
No. of In House Reviewers: 1
Acceptance Rate: 40%
Time to Review: 2 - 3 Months
Reviewers Comments: Yes
Invited Articles: 0-5%
Fees to Publish: 0.00 US$

MANUSCRIPT TOPICS:
Curriculum Studies; Higher Education; Library Science/Information Resources; Science Math & Environment; Teacher Education

MANUSCRIPT GUIDELINES/COMMENTS:

Editorial Objectives

- To explore ways of teaching about the nature of science and the scientific disciplines; the relationships between science and society; the science/technology overlap; and the responsibilities of scientists and science faculty for the undergraduate science curriculum

- To provide a forum for the exchange of ideas and experiences with undergraduate science courses, particularly those for the nonscience major

- To report and discuss innovative media and other teaching materials, methods, and evaluative criteria

- To serve as a sounding board for controversial ideas relating to undergraduate science teaching

- To disseminate contributions toward improving college science instruction

- To describe work in disciplinary science courses that is broad enough in its approach to appeal to teachers in other disciplines

- To publish articles of general interest to teachers of undergraduate science courses

- To provide information on numbers and characteristics of undergraduate science students, teachers, and curricula

Manuscript Preparation

JCST prefers to publish articles that stress interdisciplinary aspects of science teaching, so please keep topics general; other fine journals exist (e.g., *Journal of Chemical Education, American Journal* of Physics, etc.) for more specialized articles. **Please write articles in the active voice.** For specific style criteria and questions involving grammar and punctuation consult *The Chicago Manual of Style, 1993, 14th* edition. Consult the first listing in *Webster's Collegiate Dictio*nary for correct spelling.

In general, articles should not exceed *3,000* words. On the title page include the title, name of author(s), present position or title of author(s), and home, work, and e-mail addresses. Number each page following the title page. Each submission should include a 50-word abstract at the opening of the manuscript.

If you use quotations, give the *complete* source, including page numbers. Copy all quoted material **exactly** as it appears in the original, indicating any omissions by ellipses. The editor will request permission to use copyrighted material. Acknowledge financial support for work reported (including grants under which a study was made) as a note below the title.

Define any words or phrases that cannot be found in *Webster 's Unabridged Dictionary.*

Avoid using specialized jargon and acronyms. Define or explain new or highly technical terminology. Use abbreviations sparingly, and only in standard form.

Present all data and measurements in metric units unless there is a special reason for using other units. Type or print all mathematical material carefully, using a separate line for each equation. Prepare tables on separate sheets at the end of the article and refer to them by number in the text. Avoid complicated column headings.

Unlike the literature of scientific research, too many manuscripts describing teaching innovations and curriculum development efforts make few if any references to related work. We require all manuscripts to reference related *JCST* material. Manuscripts that do not include *JCST* references (when such references exist) will be returned to authors prior to review with a request that references be included. We also expect authors to explain in the text of their submissions how their material builds upon, expands, or otherwise relates to work that has preceded theirs. To conduct a search of *JCST* volumes 21-29 (1991-2000), visit our web site at www.nsta.org/pubs/jcst. Of course, manuscripts may also reference literature from other journals.

References within the text should cite in parenthesis the author's name and year of publication only. The full citation should be included alphabetically by the author's last name in a reference list at the end of the article.

Publication Process

Once your manuscript is in the correct form, send the original and three copies to the *JCST* Arlington office and another copy to the JCST editor at Stony Brook. The three copies will be sent out for blind review, so please do NOT include any data that will identify you (name, address, etc.) on those three copies. Keep a copy for your files. Include a cover letter introducing the manuscript and stating that it has not been published and is not under consideration elsewhere. You may also submit manuscripts via e-mail to lpaldy@notes.cc.sunysb.edu and clink@nsta.org

Manuscripts are acknowledged as they are received. Acknowledgment does not constitute a commitment to publish. Authors are asked to sign a copyright release form at the time of submission.

Each manuscript is reviewed as quickly as possible by members of the science community with expertise pertinent to the manuscript topic. This process normally takes no more than five months. After the review process is complete, the editor will make a decision to accept, reject, or recommend a revision of the manuscript, based on reviewer comments and editorial policies. The author will be notified of this decision.

Accepted manuscripts are published more or less in order of acceptance, although theme issues, general balance of subject matter, and space requirements are considered in scheduling.

All manuscripts are edited for publication. Authors receive copies of the edited version at least one month before the projected publication date. Read this proof carefully; it is the last time you will see the article before publication.

All contributors are invited to consider NSTA membership as a way to participate fully in the programs. Each author will receive complimentary copies of JCST and tear sheets of his/her article.

Photographs

Photographs are preferable and should be black and white glossy prints with the subject in sharp focus. Photos must comply with generally accepted laboratory safety requirements. (For example, people in laboratories must be wearing goggles.) Never use paper clips or hard points on photographs. Never draw crop marks on the face of a photo. Type the captions on a separate sheet of paper, identifying them with the picture numbers. Send the original photos to the NSTA office, with a photocopy to Stony Brook. Authors should retain negatives, duplicate irreplaceable photos, and send valuable artwork by certified mail.

JCST covers are made from color slides. To be considered for the cover, a slide must be an original (not a duplicate), in clear focus, and free from scratches or nicks. Be sure to use a vertical format that will fit the shape of the cover. We look for unusual or eye-catching images and color combinations, as well as a clear connection to one or more articles inside the issue.

Addresses

Submit one copy of your manuscript to the *JCST* Editor:
Professor Lester G. Paldy, Science Outreach Program, State University of New York at Stony Brook, Stony Brook, NY 11794.

Submit the original manuscript and photos, with three review copies, to:
Editorial Office, JCST, National Science Teachers Association, 1840 Wilson Blvd., Arlington, VA 22201-3000.

Journal of College Student Development

ADDRESS FOR SUBMISSION:

Gregory Blimling, Editor
Journal of College Student Development
Applachian State University
Vice Chancelor for Student Development
105 Administration Bldg.
Boone, NC 28608
USA
Phone: 828-262-2060
Fax: 828-262-2615
E-Mail: blimlinggs@appstate.edu
Web: www.jcsd.appstate.edu
Address May Change:

PUBLICATION GUIDELINES:

Manuscript Length: 20
Copies Required: Three
Computer Submission: Yes
Format: After Acceptance Only
Fees to Review: 0.00 US$

Manuscript Style:
American Psychological Association

CIRCULATION DATA:

Reader: Academics, Student Development
Educators
Frequency of Issue: Bi-Monthly
Copies per Issue: 5,001 - 10,000
Sponsor/Publisher: American College
Personnel Association
Subscribe Price: 45.00 US$

REVIEW INFORMATION:

Type of Review: Blind Review
No. of External Reviewers: 2
No. of In House Reviewers: 1
Acceptance Rate: 11-20%
Time to Review: 2 - 3 Months
Reviewers Comments: Yes
Invited Articles: 0-5%
Fees to Publish: 0.00 US$

MANUSCRIPT TOPICS:
Counseling & Personnel Services; Higher Education; Student Development

MANUSCRIPT GUIDELINES/COMMENTS:

The *Journal of College Student Development* is interested in manuscripts concerning student development, professional development, professional issues, administrative concerns, and creative programs to improve student services. Authors may focus on recent original research, replication of research, reviews of research, or essays on theoretical, organizational, and professional issues. Manuscripts should address one of the following:

- Support for the extension of knowledge in the area of developmental theory;
- Support for increasing sophistication in the assessment of developmental change and the factors contributing thereto;
- Support for practitioner efforts to apply theoretical developmental constructs to programs in the field; or

- Support for increasing our knowledge of organizational behaviors so that effective tactics and strategies might be applied to the implementation of developmentally focused programs on the campus.

Style Guidelines

Manuscripts must be clear, concise, and interesting with a well-organized development of ideas. The *Publication Manual of the American Psychological Association,* Fifth Edition should be followed for reference style and general guidelines. When preparing a manuscript for publication, the author(s) must carefully follow the instructions Listed below:

1. Avoid use of the term "subject," Use more specific references such as "student," or "participant."

2. Use titles that are short and descriptive. Place the title on a separate page with the names of the authors, their professional titles, and their institutional affiliations.

3. Include an abstract on the second page beneath the title and before the first paragraph of the article (except for manuscripts submitted for "On the Campus" or "'Research in Brief "). The abstract or capsule statement should clearly describe the main intent or outcome of the manuscript in 50 words or fewer.

4. Place each table and figure on separate pages following the reference section of the manuscript. Supply figures as camera-ready art. Include only essential data in tables and combine tables whenever possible. Indicate in the narrative of the manuscript, on a separate tine and in square brackets, where to place the table or figure. Final placement is at the discretion of the layout editor.

5. Only citations referred to in the manuscript should be listed in the references. Check all references before mailing the manuscript to ensure that all sources cited in the text appear in the references and vice versa, and that all references are accurate and complete. Use the reference style in the *APA Publication Manual,* Fourth Edition.

6. Lengthy quotations (a total of 300 or more words from one source) require written permission from the copyright holder for reproduction. Adaptation of tables and figures also requires such approval. The author is responsible for securing such permission. A copy of the publisher's written permission must be provided to the Journal editor immediately upon acceptance of the article for publication.

7. Use a common type style, such as Courier or Times Roman, and set all text (including references, quotations, tables, and figures) in 12pitch type, double-spaced, or 12-point type with 30 points of leading. Set the title in upper and lower case. Set the first-level subheading in ALL CAPS: set the second-level subheading in upper and Lower case; set the third-Level heading in upper and lower case, underlined, and run-in with the paragraph. Underlining is preferred for elements that are to be set in italics, because underlining is easily seen on the hard copy. Allow generous margins (at Least one inch) around each page.

8. Because manuscripts are processed through a masked review system, they should contain no clues to the author's identity or institutional affiliation (with the exception of the title page

previously mentioned). Where appropriate, institutional identification will be inserted after acceptance of the manuscript.

9. Avoid footnotes. The Journal will not publish acknowledgments except on rare occasions for recognition of external funding.

10. Authors are responsible for the accuracy of references, quotations, tables, and figures. Authors should make sure these are complete and correct.

11. Submission of a manuscript indicates the author's agreement to furnish information beyond the actual manuscript. The editor may request such information in order to assist with the review process.

12. Specific instructions for submission of accepted manuscripts on computer disk will be sent to the author(s) at the time of acceptance. Authors are responsible, for making the changes recommended by the copy editor and for proofreading their manuscript, prior to submitting the final correct copy on disk.

Submission Instructions
Never submit manuscripts under consideration by another publication. Authors must sign a statement affirming non-duplication of submission prior to review of their manuscripts.

Full-length articles generally should not exceed 5,000 words (approximately 19 pages of double-spaced, typewritten copy including references. tables. and figures).

Articles submitted for "On the Campus" should describe new practices, programs, and techniques. Practices reviewed should be related to theory and research. Manuscripts generally should not exceed 750 words. Authors should be able to provide additional background or supplemental information at the request of interested readers.

Articles submitted for "Research in Brief" should report meaningful research that does not require a full-length manuscript. Manuscripts generally should not exceed 1,500 words. Articles should present research about instruments, methods, or analytical tools which may be helpful to researchers or consumers of research in conducting and understanding student services, student development, and the student affairs profession.

Send an original (printed on 8 1/2 x 11 paper) and two clear copies of all material to:
Gregory S. Blimling, Editor, *Journal of College Student Development,* 109 Admin. Bldg., Appalachian State University, Boone, NC 28608. 704-262-2060 - bliminggs@appstate.edu

Associate Editor John Schuh accepts submission of manuscripts for "On the Campus" and "Research in Brief" and distributes information about the book review process. Unsolicited book reviews are not accepted by the *Journal.*
John Schuh, Associate Editor, *Journal of College Student Development,* Iowa State University N247E Lagomarcino Hall, Ames, IA 50014. 515-294-6393 - jschuh@iastate.edu

Journal of College Student Psychotherapy

ADDRESS FOR SUBMISSION:

Leighton Whitaker, Editor
Journal of College Student Psychotherapy
220 Turner Road
Wallingford, PA 19086
USA
Phone: 610-565-7643
Fax:
E-Mail: leighwhit@home.com
Web: haworthpressinc.com
Address May Change:

PUBLICATION GUIDELINES:

Manuscript Length: Any length
Copies Required: Three
Computer Submission: No
Format: N/A
Fees to Review: 0.00 US$

Manuscript Style:
    American Psychological Association

CIRCULATION DATA:

Reader: Academics, Administrators,
    Counselors
Frequency of Issue: Quarterly
Copies per Issue: Less than 1,000
Sponsor/Publisher: Haworth Press, Inc.
Subscribe Price: 60.00 US$ Individual
    95.00 US$ Institution
    375.00 US$ Library

REVIEW INFORMATION:

Type of Review: Blind Review
No. of External Reviewers: 0-2
No. of In House Reviewers: 0-2
Acceptance Rate: 50%
Time to Review: 2 - 3 Months
Reviewers Comments: Yes
Invited Articles: 50% +
Fees to Publish: 0.00 US$

MANUSCRIPT TOPICS:
Educational Psychology; Mental Health of College and University Students; Psychotherapy

MANUSCRIPT GUIDELINES/COMMENTS:

The *Journal of College Student Psychotherapy* is dedicated to enhancing the lives of college and university students by featuring high-quality articles about practice, theory, and research in mental health and personal development. It strives to promote greater caring for and knowledge of students. Contributions to the journal come from professionals in the field of mental health and counseling and from college staff, faculty, and students.

The journal is written specifically for college and university administrative staff and faculty as well as counselors and mental health professionals. Regular quarterly issues of the journal feature articles of central interest to psychotherapists and counselors while also expressing broader implications for everyone who wishes to understand students. Issues focus on important developments in individual and group psychotherapy with students, the knowledge that is generated by these approaches, and the significance that this knowledge may have for institutions of higher learning.

The journal covers such topics as emergency and brief interventions, short-term counseling and psychotherapy, ethics and confidentiality, referral, research on personal development during the college years, and psychotherapeutic approaches to eating, sleeping, sexual, and academic problems.

Special thematic issues of the journal have covered such topics as prevention of college student suicide, psychosomatic disorders in the college age group, psychological and social concerns of the minority student, male and female identity and support, and information for parents about college students' problems.

Instructions For Authors

1. **Original Articles Only**. Submission of a manuscript to this journal represents a certification on the part of the author(s) that it is an original work, and that neither this manuscript nor a version of it has been published elsewhere nor is being considered for publication elsewhere.

2. **Manuscript Length**. Your manuscript may be approximately 5-50 typed pages double-spaced (including references and abstract). Lengthier manuscripts may be considered, but only at the discretion of the Editor. Sometimes, lengthier manuscripts may be considered if they can be divided up into sections for publication in successive Journal issues.

3. **Manuscript Style**. References, citations, and general style of manuscripts for this Journal should follow the Chicago style (as outlined in the latest edition of the *Manual of Style* of the University of Chicago Press). References should be double-spaced and placed in alphabetical order.

If an author wishes to submit a paper that has been already prepared in another style, he or she may do so. However, if the paper is accepted (with or without reviewer's alterations), the author is fully responsible for retyping the manuscript in the correct style as indicated above. Neither the Editor nor the Publisher is responsible for re-preparing manuscript copy to adhere to the Journal's style.

4. **Manuscript Preparation**.
Margins: leave at least a one-inch margin on all four sides.
Paper: use clean white, 8 1/2 " x 11" bond paper.
Number of Copies: 4 (the original plus three photocopies).
Cover Page: Important--staple a cover page to the manuscript, indicating only the article title (this is used for anonymous refereeing).
Second "Title Page": enclose a regular title page but do not staple it to the manuscript. Include the title again, plus:
• full authorship
• an ABSTRACT of about 100 words. (Below the abstract provide 3-10 key words for index purposes)
• an introductory footnote with authors' academic degrees, professional titles, affiliations, mailing addresses, and any desired acknowledgment of research support or other credit.
Manuscripts may be submitted to the editor via e-mail provided the editor approves this method in advance.

5. **Return Envelopes**. When you submit your four manuscript copies, also include:
- a 9" x 12" envelope, self-addressed and stamped (with sufficient postage to ensure return of your manuscript);
- a regular envelope, stamped and self-addressed. This is for the Editor to send you an "acknowledgement of receipt" letter.

6. **Spelling, Grammar, and Punctuation**. You are responsible for preparing manuscript copy which is clearly written in acceptable scholarly English, and which contains no errors of spelling, grammar, or punctuation. Neither the Editor nor the Publisher is responsible for correcting errors of spelling and grammar: the manuscript, after acceptance by the Editor, must be immediately ready for typesetting as it is finally submitted by the author(s). Also, check the accuracy of all arithmetic calculations, statistics, numerical data, text citations, and references.

7. **Inconsistencies Must Be Avoided**. Be sure you are consistent in your use of abbreviations, terminology, and in citing references, from one part of your paper to another.

8. **Preparation of Tables, Figures, and Illustrations**. All tables and figures, illustrations, etc. must be "camera-ready". That is, they must be cleanly typed or artistically prepared so that they can be used either exactly as they are or else used after a photographic reduction in size. Figures, tables, and illustrations must be prepared on separate sheets of paper. Always use black ink and professional drawing instruments. On the back of these items, write your article title and the journal title lightly in pencil, so they do not get misplaced. In text, skip extra lines and indicate where these figures and tables are to be placed (please do not write on the face of art). Photographs are considered part of the acceptable manuscript and remain with the publisher for use in additional printings. If submitted art cannot be used, the Publisher reserves the right to redo the art and to charge the author a fee of $35.00 per hour for this service.

9. **Alterations Required By Referees And Reviewers**. Many times a paper is accepted by the Editor contingent upon changes that are mandated by anonymous specialist referees and members of the Editorial Board. If the Editor returns your manuscript for revisions, you are responsible for retyping any sections of the paper to incorporate these revisions (if applicable, revisions should also be put on disk).

10. **Typesetting**. You will not be receiving galley proofs o your article. Editorial revisions, if any, must therefore be made while your article is still in manuscript. The final version of the manuscript will be the version you see published. Typesetter's errors will be corrected by the production staff of The Haworth Press. Authors are expected to submit manuscripts, disks, and art that are free from error.

11. **Electronic Media**. Haworth's in-house typesetting unit is able to utilize your final manuscript material as prepared on most personal computers and word processors. This will minimize typographical errors and decrease overall production timelag. Please send the first draft and final draft copies of you manuscript to the journal Editor in print format for his/her final review and approval.

426

After approval of your final manuscript, please submit the final approved version both on printed format ("hard copy") and floppy diskette. On the outside of the diskette package write:
A. The brand name of your computer or word processor
B. The word-processing program that you used
C. The title of your article, and
D. File name

Note: Disk and hard copy must agree. In case of discrepancies, it is The Haworth Press' policy to follow hard copy. Authors are advised that **No Revisions** of the manuscript can be made after acceptance by the Editor for publication. The benefits of this procedure are many with speed and accuracy being the most obvious. We look forward to working with you on this, knowing we will be able to serve you more efficiently in the future.

12. **Reprints**. The senior author will receive two copies of the journal issue and 25 complimentary reprints of his or her article. The junior author will receive two copies of the journal issue. These are sent several weeks after the journal issue is published and in circulation. An order form for the purchase of additional reprints will also be sent to all authors at this time. (Approximately 4-6 weeks is necessary for the preparation of reprints.) Please do not query the Journal's Editor about reprints. All such questions should be sent directly to The Haworth Press, Inc. Production Department, 21 East Broad Street, West Hazleton, PA 18201 USA. To order additional reprints (minimum: 50 copies), please contact The Haworth Document Delivery Center, 10 Alice Street, Binghamton, NY 13904-1580 USA; 1-800-342-9678 or Fax (607) 722-6362.

13. **Copyright**. Copyright ownership of your manuscript must be transferred officially to The Haworth Press, Inc. before we can begin the peer-review process. The Editor's letter acknowledging receipt of the manuscript will be accompanied by a form fully explaining this. All authors must sign the form and return the original to the Editor as soon as possible. Failure to return the copyright form in a timely fashion will result in delay in review and subsequent publication.

COPYRIGHT TRANSFER FORM

Name of journal:
Journal of College Student Psychotherapy

Name and **Exact** Mailing Address of Contributor:

Special note: This will be used for mailing reprints. You must include exact street address, name of your department if at a university, and ZIP CODE. The Haworth Press cannot be responsible for lost reprints if you do not provide us with your exact mailing address.

In Reference To Your Journal Article:

☐ **If this box is checked...**

Thank you for your article submission! Please allow 10-15 weeks for the review process. Before sending out your article for review, however, the Publisher requires us to obtain your signature(s) confirming that you have read the PUBLICATION AGREEMENT on the reverse side of this page.

All co-authors must sign and return the ORIGINAL signed copy.

IT IS CONFIRMED that I/we have read the PUBLICATION AGREEMENT on the reverse side of the page, and agree and accept all conditions:

author's signature	date
author's signature	date
author's signature	date

☐ It this box is checked...

Your article has been favorably reviewed. Our reviewers, however, require certain revisions which are indicated on the attached sheets. Please review and incorporate their suggestions, and return your manuscript/disk retyped within 14 days. A decision about publication will he made at that time. Thank you for your help and cooperation.

Please reply to

( ) Journal Editor:
Leighton Whitaker, Ph.D., ABPP
220 Turner Road
Wallingford, PA   19086-6037

☐If this box is checked...

We are pleased to inform you that your article has been accepted for publication in the journal noted above. In addition to the standard journal edition, at the editor's discretion, this issue may also be co-published in a hardcover monographic co-edition.

Please note the following:

1. Publication: Your article is currently scheduled to appear in

Volume: _____ Number: _____

428

2. **Typesetting**: Your article will be sent to the Production Department of The Haworth Press, Inc., 21 East Broad Street, West Hazleton, PA 18201. They will typeset your article (preferably from your computer disk) exactly as submitted. Please note that you will not be receiving galley proofs. The production staff will proofread the galleys for typesetting errors against the final version of the manuscript as submitted. No revisions are allowed.

3. **Reprints**: Shortly after publication you will receive an order form for purchasing quantities of reprints. (About three weeks after publication, the senior author will receive two complimentary copies of the issue and ten copies of the article, and the junior author(s) will receive two complimentary copies of the issue.) Please note that preparation of reprints takes about eight weeks additional time after the actual issue is printed and in circulation.

□ **If this box is checked...**

We are sorry, but the reviewers for this journal did not agree that your article was appropriate for publication in this periodical. If the reviewers consented in having their comments forwarded to you, their critiques are attached. Your submission is appreciated, and we hope that you will contribute again in the future.

Journal of College Student Retention: Research, Theory, & Practice

ADDRESS FOR SUBMISSION:

Alan Seidman, Editor
Journal of College Student Retention:
  Research, Theory, & Practice
30 Windsong Circle
Bedford, NH 03110
USA
Phone: 603-471-1490
Fax:
E-Mail: aseidman@aol.com
Web: www.collegeways.com
Address May Change:

PUBLICATION GUIDELINES:

Manuscript Length: 6-30+
Copies Required: Three
Computer Submission: Yes Disk, Email
Format: MSWord; English
Fees to Review: 0.00 US$

Manuscript Style:
  American Psychological Association

CIRCULATION DATA:

Reader: Academics, Administrators
Frequency of Issue: Quarterly
Copies per Issue: Less than 1,000
Sponsor/Publisher: Baywood Publishing
  Company, Inc.
Subscribe Price: 47.00 US$ Individual
  132.00 US$ Institution

REVIEW INFORMATION:

Type of Review: Blind Review
No. of External Reviewers: 2
No. of In House Reviewers: 0
Acceptance Rate: 45%
Time to Review: 1 - 2 Months
Reviewers Comments: Yes
Invited Articles: 0-5%
Fees to Publish: 0.00 US$

MANUSCRIPT TOPICS:
College Retention; Education Management/Administration

MANUSCRIPT GUIDELINES/COMMENTS:

Aim & Scope
The aim and scope of the Journal are to provide the educational community, federal and state government officials and the public with the latest research findings regarding the retention of students in higher education. Although access to higher education is virtually universally available, many students who start in a higher education program drop out prior to completing a degree or achieving their individual academic and/or social goals. Over the years colleges have spent vast amounts of money setting up programs and services for a variety of groups who will attend their college and may be in need of extra services to develop the necessary skills to graduate. In spite of all of the programs and services to help retain students, according to the U.S. Department of Education, Center for Educational Statistics, only 50% of those who enter higher education actually earn a bachelors degree. Retaining students remains a top priority of colleges and universities.

The Journal of College Student Retention: Research, Theory & Practice is intended to provide the educational community, federal and state governmental officials and the general public a medium to exhibit and explore the complex issue of student retention and attrition. The Journal will feature articles pertaining to current and new theoretical constructs and current research on student retention and attrition in higher education. In addition, the Journal will provide practitioners an avenue to highlight and disseminate current practices, programs and services, which help students persist.

Features & Departments
Refereed Articles, Occasional Commentary, & Guest Editorials

Need for This Journal
Current U.S. retention figures have not improved over time, even with large amounts of money expended by colleges and universities on programs and services to retain students. In spite of these programs and services, retention figures have not improved. In fact, only about 66% of high school graduates attend college and about 50% of those who attend college earn a bachelor degree. Put in real numbers, about 2,800,000 students will graduate from high school this year, 1,850,000 will attend college and only 925,000 of these students will earn a bachelor degree. Colleges are looking for ways to keep the students that they recruit. The Journal will provide the educational community with current theoretical foundations, research and practice results, which will help educators and institutions to retain students.

Submission of Manuscripts
The editor will accept manuscripts in a number of formats including paper copy (in triplicate), 3 ½ diskette, or as email attachment in MS Word format. Manuscripts should be submitted using the *Publication Manual of the American Psychological Association* and include a title page, affiliation, and an abstract of 100-125 words. Submit manuscripts to: Dr. Alan Seidman, Journal of College Student Retention, 30 Windsong Circle, Bedford, NH 13110, Email: aseidman@aol.com, www.collegeways.com.

Originality. Only original articles are accepted for publication. Submission of a manuscript represents certification on the part of the author(s) that neither the article submitted, nor a version of it has been published, or is being considered for publication elsewhere

Manuscripts. Submit four copies. Retain one copy, as manuscript will not be returned. Manuscript must be word processed or typewritten on 8-1/2" x 11" white paper, one side only, double-spaced, with wide margins. Paginate consecutively starting with the title page. The organization of the paper should be indicated by appropriate headings and subheadings. Manuscripts will also be accepted on 3½ diskette in Microsoft Word, and as an E-mail attachment in Microsoft Word.

Abstracts. Abstracts of 100 to 150 words are required to introduce each article.

Format. Prepare manuscripts according to the Publication Manual of the American Psychological Association (4th ed.) A synopsis of this manual is available from the American Psychological Association.

Style. Technical terms specific to a particular discipline should be defined. Write for clear comprehension by readers from a broad spectrum of scholarly and professional backgrounds. Avoid acronyms and footnoting, except for acknowledgments

Permissions. Authors are responsible for all statements made in their manuscript and for obtaining from copyright owners to reprint or adapt a table or figures, or to reprint a quotation of 500 words or more. Authors should write to original author(s) and publisher to request nonexclusive world rights in all languages to use the material in the article and in future editions. Provide copies of all permission and credit lines obtained at the time of manuscript submission.

Reprints. Authors will receive twenty complimentary reprints of their published article and a copy of the Journal issue. Additional reprints may be ordered, using the form provided when proofs are sent for correction.

Journal of Communication

ADDRESS FOR SUBMISSION:

William Benoit, Editor
Journal of Communication
University of Missouri
Department of Communication
115 Switzler
Columbia, MO 65211-2310
USA
Phone: 573-882-0545
Fax:
E-Mail: joc@missouri.edu
Web:
Address May Change: 12/31/05

PUBLICATION GUIDELINES:

Manuscript Length: 26-30
Copies Required: Four
Computer Submission: No
Format: N/A
Fees to Review: 0.00 US$

Manuscript Style:
    American Psychological Association

CIRCULATION DATA:

Reader: Academics
Frequency of Issue: Quarterly
Copies per Issue: 5,001 - 10,000
Sponsor/Publisher: International
    Communication Association
Subscribe Price: 50.00 US$

REVIEW INFORMATION:

Type of Review: Blind Review
No. of External Reviewers: 2
No. of In House Reviewers: 0
Acceptance Rate: 11-20%
Time to Review: 2 - 3 Months
Reviewers Comments: Yes
Invited Articles: 0-5%
Fees to Publish: 0.00 US$

MANUSCRIPT TOPICS:
Communication Theory and Research; Languages & Linguistics

MANUSCRIPT GUIDELINES/COMMENTS:

The *Journal of Communication* is a general forum for communication scholarship and publishes articles and book reviews examining a broad range of issues in communication theory and research. *JoC* publishes the best available scholarship on all aspects of communication. All methods of scholarly inquiry into communication are welcome. Manuscripts should be conceptually meaningful, methodologically sound, interesting, clearly written, and thoughtfully argued.

Manuscripts must not have been published elsewhere or be currently under consideration for any other publication. Manuscripts are processed by blind review so author identification must be removed from all pages except the title page, which is retained by the editor.

Ordinarily (unless a compelling argument is made), data- or text-based manuscripts must follow specific guidelines depending upon method. Quantitative manuscripts should report reliability estimates for dependent variables, the amount of variance accounted for in significance tests, and power when a result is not significant. When measures of central tendency are reported, appropriate measures of variability should be included. Quantitative content analyses should report inter-coder reliability, preferably using a statistic that controls for agreement by chance. Survey research should describe the population, sampling procedures, and response rate. Qualitative research should articulate the standards employed to assure the quality and verification of the interpretation presented (e.g., member checking, negative case analysis).

Prepare manuscripts in strict accordance with the 5th edition of the *Publication Manual of the American Psychological Association*. Submissions are *rarely* longer than 30 pages, including references, appendixes, endnotes, tables, and figures (keep endnotes to a minimum). The editor may return manuscripts (without review) that do not follow these requirements or that are otherwise unsuitable for review. Include a cover letter with author(s) address, telephone, email address, and title of the manuscript. Submit four (4) copies of article manuscripts; attach abstract to each copy of the manuscript; do not identify author(s) except on the detachable title page. Send to:

William L. Benoit, Editor
Journal of Communication
Department of Communication-115 Switzler
University of Missouri
Columbia, MO 65211-2310.

Submissions are **not** accepted by email attachment or fax (authors from outside of North America may request exceptions to this rule prior to submission).

Manuscripts meriting review will be read anonymously by two or three referees. In most instances, authors can expect decisions on their work within 90 days. Because manuscripts receive expert review, and because the Editorial Board of *JoC* is international in scope, this time may vary. No manuscripts will be returned to authors. The *Journal* retains the right to make changes in accepted manuscripts that (in the opinion of the editor) do not substantially alter meaning as well as for grammatical, stylistic and space considerations.

Authors should submit book review manuscripts to:

Mary Beth Oliver, Book Review Editor
Journal of Communication
College of Communication
210 Carnegie Building
Pennsylvania State University
University Park, PA 16801
mbo @psu.edu

Manuscripts that are accepted for publication must be submitted both as a hard (printed) copy and as a WordPerfect or Microsoft Word file.

Questions can be addressed to the editor at: joc@missouri.edu or (573) 882-0545.

Journal of Communications & Minority Issues

ADDRESS FOR SUBMISSION:

Delindus Brown, Editor
Journal of Communications & Minority
    Issues
St. Augustine's College
Department of Communication
1315 Oakwood Avenue, Boyer 300 E
Raleigh, NC 27610
USA
Phone: 919-516-4078
Fax:
E-Mail: drbrown@st-aug.edu
Web: www.st-aug.edu
Address May Change:

PUBLICATION GUIDELINES:

Manuscript Length: 21-25
Copies Required: Two
Computer Submission: Yes
Format: MSWord
Fees to Review: 0.00 US$

Manuscript Style:
    American Psychological Association

CIRCULATION DATA:

Reader: Academics, Administrators;
    Minorities
Frequency of Issue: 1 Time/Year
Copies per Issue: Less than 1,000
Sponsor/Publisher: St. Augustine's College;
    WAUG TV; Outside Sources
Subscribe Price: 15.00 US$ Individual
    75.00 US$ Institution

REVIEW INFORMATION:

Type of Review: Blind Review
No. of External Reviewers: 2
No. of In House Reviewers: 1
Acceptance Rate: 40%
Time to Review: 2 Months
Reviewers Comments: Yes
Invited Articles: 0-5%
Fees to Publish: 0.00 US$

MANUSCRIPT TOPICS:
Minority Issues/Communication; Urban Education, Cultural/Non-Traditional

MANUSCRIPT GUIDELINES/COMMENTS:

Journal of Community Development Society

ADDRESS FOR SUBMISSION:

A.E. Luloff, Editor
Journal of Community Development
    Society
Pennsylvania State University
111 Armsby Agrs
University Park, PA 16802
USA
Phone: 814-863-8646
Fax: 814-865-3746
E-Mail: ael3@psu.edu
Web: www.comm-dev.org/journal
Address May Change:

PUBLICATION GUIDELINES:

Manuscript Length: 16-20
Copies Required: Six
Computer Submission: Yes
Format: WordPerfect/Word
Fees to Review: 0.00 US$

Manuscript Style:
    See Manuscript Guidelines

CIRCULATION DATA:

Reader: Academics, Practitioners;
    Development Specialists
Frequency of Issue: 2 Times/Year
Copies per Issue: 1,200
Sponsor/Publisher: Pennsylvania State
    University
Subscribe Price: 85.00 US$

REVIEW INFORMATION:

Type of Review: Blind Review
No. of External Reviewers: 3+
No. of In House Reviewers: No Reply
Acceptance Rate: 45%
Time to Review: 4 Months
Reviewers Comments: Yes
Invited Articles: 0-5%
Fees to Publish: 35.00 US$ per page

MANUSCRIPT TOPICS:
Community Development & Studies; Economic Development; Human Development; Rural Education & Small Schools; Tests, Measurement & Evaluation; Urban Education, Cultural/Non-Traditional

MANUSCRIPT GUIDELINES/COMMENTS:

The *Journal of Community Development Society* is devoted to improving knowledge and practice in the field of purposive community change. The purpose of the *Journal* is to disseminate information on theory, research, and practice. The Editor welcomes manuscripts that report research; evaluate theory, techniques, and methods; examine community problems; or analyze, critically, the profession itself.

Instructions to Authors: Address submissions to the Editor (Address for Submission above.)

Submission Requirements
Submit six printed copies of the manuscript on 8 1/2" by 11 inch bond in near-letter quality type. Double space **all** material, including indented passages, footnotes, and references, with

ragged right margins and no hyphenation. Up to five copies of each paper without author identification will be submitted to referees for review.

Printed Manuscript

Cover Page. Show article title, institutional affiliation(s) and professional position(s) of author(s). Omit author name(s) and affiliation(s) from the manuscript itself

Abstract. Include on a separate page the article title and a summary of 100 to 150 words.

Keywords. Authors must supply from three(3) to five(5) alphabetized key words, or phrases that identify the most important subjects covered by the paper. Place key words on the bottom of the **Abstract** page.

Footnotes. Use footnotes in the text for **substantive comments only**, not for bibliographic references. Footnotes should be numbered consecutively on a separate page following the text. Include Location notes at appropriate places in the text.

Tables and Figures. Append tables and figures on separate pages at the end of the manuscript. Include location notes, e.g., "Table 1 about here," "Fig. 1 near here," at appropriate places in the text. Art for figures must be camera-ready ropy and sized to fit within the Journal's 4 ½" by 7" page format.

References in the Text. References in the body of the text should include the name of the author(s) cited and date of reference in parentheses within the manuscript, e.g., (Carrey, 1972). Do not use ibid., op. sit., loc. sit., etc. If reference is a direct quote, include page number also, e.g., (Carrey, 1972, p. 241). For repeat citations, continue to use name of author(s) and date. In case of multiple works with the same authors? and publication year, use 111991a," "1991b," etc.

References at the End of Text. Complete data on all references should be listed alphabetically at the end of the article. Include page numbers, volume and issue numbers of journals, and all authors' names. Double-space the listing of references. Forms for articles, books, and articles in books are as follows:

William, Fern K. & Donald M. Crider. 1993. Pennsylvania's view economic development: A ten year perspective. Journal of the Community Development Society 24(1):30-45.

Babbie, Earl. 1993. The Practice of Social Research. Belmont: Wadsworth Publishing.

Fear, Frank, Larry Gamm & Fredrick Fisher. 1989. The technical assistance approach. In James A. Christenson & Jerry W. Robinson, Jr. (eds.), Community Development in Perspective. Ames, IA: Iowa State University Press.

Diskette Text File [Only after Acceptance and Final Editing]. Cover page, abstract, manuscript text (excluding footnotes, tables and 1 figures) and references at the end of the text should be in WordPerfect or Word. Footnotes should be in a separate file; and each table an each figure should be in a separate file.

Footnotes. Put contents of all footnotes in one file. Mark Location of notes at the appropriate places in the main text file. Do not use the footnote function of word processing software.

Tables. Put contents of each table in a separate file. Include Location notes at the appropriate places in the main text file.

Figures. In addition to camera-ready copy mentioned above, figures may be submitted in Harvard Graphics or Powerpoint or in EPS or TIFF files. Include location notes at the appropriate places in the main text file.

The *Journal of Community Development Society* regards submission of a manuscript as a commitment by the author(s) that is not to be breached by submission to another journal while the manuscript is under review. There is an institutional charge of $35per printed page, which is payable by the granting agency or employer who supports the work. If no support exists, an exemption may be granted.

Journal of Community Psychology

ADDRESS FOR SUBMISSION:

Raymond Lorion, Editor
Journal of Community Psychology
University of Pennsylvania
Graduate School of Education
3700 Walnut Street
Philadelphia, PA 19104
USA
Phone: 215-898-7367
Fax: 215-573-2115
E-Mail: lorian@gse.upenn.edu
Web: www.interscience.wiley.com
Address May Change:

PUBLICATION GUIDELINES:

Manuscript Length: 26-30
Copies Required: Three
Computer Submission: No
Format: N/A
Fees to Review: 0.00 US$

Manuscript Style:
    American Psychological Association

CIRCULATION DATA:

Reader: Academics
Frequency of Issue: Quarterly
Copies per Issue: 3,001 - 4,000
Sponsor/Publisher: John Wiley & Sons
Subscribe Price: 40.00 US$

REVIEW INFORMATION:

Type of Review: Blind Review
No. of External Reviewers: 2
No. of In House Reviewers: 1
Acceptance Rate: 11-20%
Time to Review: 1 - 2 Months
Reviewers Comments: Yes
Invited Articles: 6-10%
Fees to Publish: 0.00 US$

MANUSCRIPT TOPICS:
Emotional/Behavioral/Academic Disorders; Prevention of Child/Adolescent Disorders; Tests, Measurement & Evaluation; Urban Education, Cultural/Non-Traditional

MANUSCRIPT GUIDELINES/COMMENTS:

The *Journal of Community Psychology* is devoted to research, evaluation, assessment, intervention, and review articles that deal with human behavior in community settings. This includes an emphasis on the community as meeting needs and supporting growth and development of its residents. Applied psychology in community settings will need to have clear implications drawn to the community. Descriptive reports on particular groups or persons are considered as appropriate to the journal when the community relevance is made clear. Reviews and articles dealing with theory will be considered.

Manuscripts should be submitted in triplicate to the Editor. Authors are requested to adopt the style requirements suggested in the *APA Publication Manual*, 5th Edition, 2001, with the following exceptions: (1) Either metric or non metric measurements are acceptable, and (2) Authors are requested **not** to rule tabular material. In order to allow blind review, authors are requested to avoid identifying information in the body of a manuscript. Full identifying information, including address for correspondence, should be placed on a cover page. Reprint purchase information will accompany the printer's galleys. Authors are requested to retain a copy of the manuscript since the edited ms. does not accompany the galleys.

Submission is a representation that the manuscript. has not been published elsewhere and is not currently under consideration elsewhere. A statement transferring copyright from the authors (or their employers, if they hold the copyright) to Clinical Psychology Publishing Company will be required before the manuscript can be accepted for publication. The Editor will supply the necessary forms for this transfer. Such a written transfer of copyright, which previously was assumed to be implicit in the act of submitting a manuscript, is necessary under the new U.S Copyright Law in order for the publisher to carry through the dissemination of research results and reviews as widely and effectively as possible. Authors are required to state in their initial submission letter or to provide a signed statement that they have complied with APA ethical standards in the treatment of their subjects (human or animal). (A copy of the *APA Ethical Principles* may be obtained from the APA Ethics office, 1200 17th Street NW, Washington, D.C. 20036.) Particular emphasis should be given to the matter of informed consent and to whether the persons serving as data sources could be seen to be participants in the research process. Authors should describe the research setting, indicating how entry and consent were obtained, how and what feedback was given, and how the findings were used.

Manuscripts will not be returned unless the author includes a self-addressed, postage-paid envelope. A 100-200 word abstract should be provided, as well as a footnote indicating where reprint requests should be sent and, where appropriate, acknowledgements for funding and assistance. Microform editions of the journal are available, after a three-year publication tag, from MIMC, Fairview Parks, Elmsford, NY 10523.

Journal of Computing in Higher Education

ADDRESS FOR SUBMISSION:

Carol B. MacKnight, Editor
Journal of Computing in Higher Education
PO Box 2593
Amherst, MA 01004-2593
USA
Phone: 413-549-5150
Fax: 413-253-9525
E-Mail: cmacknight@oit.umas.edu
Web: See Guidelines
Address May Change:

PUBLICATION GUIDELINES:

Manuscript Length: 16-20
Copies Required: Four
Computer Submission: Yes
Format: English
Fees to Review: 0.00 US$

Manuscript Style:
    American Psychological Association

CIRCULATION DATA:

Reader: Academics
Frequency of Issue: 2 Times/Year
Copies per Issue: Less than 1,000
Sponsor/Publisher:
Subscribe Price: 35.00 US$ Individual
    75.00 US$ Institution

REVIEW INFORMATION:

Type of Review: Blind Review
No. of External Reviewers: 2
No. of In House Reviewers: 1
Acceptance Rate: 21-30%
Time to Review: 1 - 2 Months
Reviewers Comments: Yes
Invited Articles: 0-5%
Fees to Publish: 0.00 US$

MANUSCRIPT TOPICS:
Educational Psychology; Higher Education; Information Technologies; Teacher Education

MANUSCRIPT GUIDELINES/COMMENTS:

Instructions to Authors
Please prepare manuscripts in accordance with the *Publication Manual of the American Psychological Association* (APA), fifth edition, and with these guidelines below. Address all Editorial Correspondence to the Editor, Carol B. MacKnight, at PO Box 2593 Amherst, MA 01004-2593, or through e-mail: cmacknight@oit.umass.edu. A complete submission consists of four hard-copies and one diskette containing the document and all graphics. Manuscripts should be accompanied by a stamped return-mail envelope. Authors should recommend two reviewers in their field who can pass judgment on their work.

Format
List of authors with their affiliations, present addresses, telephone number, electronic mail address, and fax telephone numbers on a separate title page.

Biography of 100 to 150 words, on a separate sheet.

The full manuscript (5,000 words maximum) in quadruplicate and in **Times** font.
Order of Presentation: Title page, Abstract, Keywords, Body of Article, Acknowledgements, Footnotes, References, Tables, Figure captions, and Figures.

Typewritten, double-spaced throughout. **One space** between words.

Referencing

All sources (25 maximum) are listed alphabetically at the end of the manuscript under the heading References using APA style:

Journals - Brown, J.D. & Harding, W. (1993). Technology in the next century. *Journal of Computing in Higher Education*, 10(2), 23-55.

Books - Lauer, T.W., Peacock, E. & Graesser, A.C. (Eds.). (1992). *Questions and information system*. Hillsdale, N.J.: Lawrence Erlbaum Associates, Inc.

Proceedings - Carroll, J. & Rosson, M.B. (1990). Human computer interaction scenarios as a design representation. *Proceedings of HICSS-23: Hawaii International Conference on System Sciences* (pp. 555-561). Los Alamitos, CA: IEEE Computer Society Press.

Web – Gilbert, S. (2000). campus portal decisions. AAHESGIT #51, [Online] Available: http://wwwlcren.net:8080/guest/archieves/aahesgit/log0009/mgs0003.html

Reference list must be **left justified** and original source in italics.

References in the text should be cited as follows: Smith (1993) reported that…

Direct quotes of 40 words or less in double quotation marks are incorporated into the text; those longer than 40 words should be in indented block format. All quotes must be in this style: Smith, 1999, pp. 23-26.

Graphics

Each table and figure on a separate page at the end of the manuscript. All table, figures, charts and diagrams must be provided in camera-ready format. All titles must be on a separate sheet.

Number tables in Arabic numerals and center Table 1 over each heading.
Number figures in Arabic numerals before the caption at the foot of each graph, i.e., Figure 1. Trusted Products Status Summary.

Style

JCHE's editorial style conforms closely to the recommendations of the Publication Manual of the APA

Hard Copy and Diskettes

Four copies. Please submit text in MS Word or WordPerfect formats and graphics in TIFF or JPEG formats at 300 dpi.(limits are width 5" and length 6"). Submissions may be on a PC or a Macintosh formatted disks

Types of Articles

The *Journal of Computing in Higher Education* publishes scholarly essays, reviews, reports, and research articles that contribute to our understanding of the issues, problems, and research associated with instructional technology and educational management systems. Our focus is to improve teaching and learning. Articles representing all aspect of academic computing are encouraged. Types of contributions solicited: General interest articles, Applications, Case Studies, Research, Reports, Professional Reports, and Book Reviews and Software Reviews. Fields of interest include: Development of Novel Applications, Hypermedia Design Strategies, Authoring Tools, Assessment, Intelligent Interfaces, Expert Systems, Use of Knowledge Bases, User Interface Methodology, Impact of Cognitive Psychology on instructional Technology, Pedagogy, Learner Centered Technologies, User models, Information Management, Publishing, Libraries, Business.

Audience

Our audience includes faculty, administrators, designers, developers, programmers, researchers, academic computer people, and book publishers.

Journal of Continuing Education in the Health Professions

ADDRESS FOR SUBMISSION:

Paul Mazmanian, Editor
Journal of Continuing Education in the
   Health Professions
Virginia Commonwealth University
School of Medicine
Office of Continuing Medical Education
Box 980048
Richmond, VA 23298-0048
USA
Phone: 804-828-7438
Fax: 804-828-0492
E-Mail: paul.mazmanian@ucu.edu
Web: jcehp.com
Address May Change: 12/31/02

PUBLICATION GUIDELINES:

Manuscript Length: 6-10
Copies Required: No Paper Copy
Computer Submission: Yes Electronic Only
Format: MSWord
Fees to Review: 0.00 US$

Manuscript Style:
   , Uniform Requirements for Manuscripts
   Submitted to Biomedical Journals

CIRCULATION DATA:

Reader: Administrators
Frequency of Issue: Quarterly
Copies per Issue: 4,001 - 5,000
Sponsor/Publisher: Alliance for Continuing
   Medical Eduction Assn. (more sponsors
   in Guidelines)
Subscribe Price: 70.00 US$ Individual
   109.00 US$ Institution

REVIEW INFORMATION:

Type of Review: Blind Review
No. of External Reviewers: 2
No. of In House Reviewers: 0
Acceptance Rate: 21-30%
Time to Review: 2 - 3 Months
Reviewers Comments: Yes
Invited Articles: 6-10%
Fees to Publish: 0.00 US$

MANUSCRIPT TOPICS:
Education Management/Administration; Educational Technology Systems; Health & Physical Education; Higher Education; Tests, Measurement & Evaluation

MANUSCRIPT GUIDELINES/COMMENTS:

Sponsors: Alliance foe Continuing Medical Education, Society of Academic Continuing Medical Education, Council on CME, Association for Hospital Medical Education

New Instructions to Authors will be released with Vol 21 #4, appearing in early January 2002. Uniform requirements for manuscripts submitted to Biomedical Journals should be followed.

The *Journal of Continuing Education in the Health Professions* invites the submission of manuscripts relevant to theory and practice in continuing education in the health sciences. The intent is to provide information that is practical for use by those who plan, implement, or evaluate continuing education activities. Topics of special interest include cognition, motivation, and behavior; health policy and professional performance; lifelong learning skills development; and the measurement of educational and patient outcomes.

Manuscripts. Manuscripts should be submitted either as hard copy in triplicate to: Evelyn R. Hebberd, Office of Continuing Medical Education, School of Medicine, Virginia Commonwealth University, Medical College of Virginia Campus, Box 980048, Richmond, VA 23298-0048. Tel: 804-828-1537; fax: 804-828-7438; or as an attached file of an e-mail message to evelyn.hebberd@vcu.edu.

A diskette with the files) in Word should accompany the hard copy of the manuscript. Hard copy of manuscripts will not be returned unless accompanied by a SASE. Manuscripts will be accepted with the understanding that their content is unpublished and not being submitted for publication elsewhere. A manuscript's suitability for publication will be judged on the basis of style as well as content. All parts of the manuscript, including the title page, abstract, tables, and legends should be typewritten in English, double-spaced on one side of white bond. Allow margins of at least one inch (3 cm) on all sides of the typed pages. Number manuscript pages consecutively throughout the paper. Ordinarily articles should not exceed 3,000 words (15 text pages); under exceptional consideration articles longer than 4,000 words will be published. Translations of papers previously published in languages other than English can be considered, but this information must be provided by the author at the time of submission.

Title. All titles must be as brief as possible, 6 to 12 words. Authors should also supply a shortened version of the title suitable for the running head, not exceeding 50 character spaces.

Affiliation. On the title page include full names of authors, academic and/or other professional affiliations, as well as academic or professional titles, and the complete mailing address, telephone and fax numbers, and email address (if available) of the author to whom proofs and correspondence should be sent.

Abstract. Each paper should be summarized in a structured abstract of not more than 250 words. Avoid abbreviations, diagrams, and references to the text. The abstract should include four components: (1) the background including a literature review and problem statement, 2) a statement of methods describing how data were collected and managed, 3) a synopsis of results, and 4) a short account of the findings, including implications for practice.

Key Words. Authors must supply from three to ten key words or phrases that identify the most important subjects covered by the paper.

Lessons for Practice. Two to four key points intended for reader focus should be included.

References. All references are to be numbered consecutively in the order of first mention and listed at the end of every paper. In the text, references should be cited consecutively by the corresponding superscript number. All papers that are published, in press, personal communications, and unpublished observations must be included. Abbreviations for journal titles should conform to those used in *Index Medicus*. For further information consult the "Uniform Requirements for Manuscripts Submitted to Biomedical Journals," in the *New*

England Journal of Medicine 1997; 336:309-315. All (up to eight) author names with initials should be provided in the reference listing.

Journal articles
1. Caplan R.M. A fresh look at some bad ideas in continuing medical education. Mobius 1983; 3(1):55-61.

Books
2. Campbell DT, Stanley JC. Experimental and quasi experimental designs for research. Chicago: Rand McNally and Company, 1963.

Figures. All figures must be submitted in camera-ready form, either as black & white glossy photographs or photostats. Xerox copies are not acceptable. Maximum image size is 5" x 7.75". Label each figure with article title, author's name, and figure number, by attaching a separate sheet of white paper to the back of each figure. Do not write on the camera-ready art. Each figure should be provided with a brief, descriptive legend. All legends should be typed on a separate page at the end of the manuscript.

Tables. All tables must be discussed or mentioned in the text and numbered in order of mention. Each table should have a brief descriptive tide. Do not include explanatory material in the title: use footnotes, keyed to the table with superior lower-case letters. Place all footnotes to a table at the end of tile table. Define all data in the column heads. Every table should be fully understandable even without references to the text. Type all tables on separate sheets; do not include them within the text.

Permissions. If any figure, table, or more than a few lines of text from previously published material are included in a manuscript, the author must obtain written permission for republication from the copyright holder and forward a copy to the publisher.

Copyright. Under the copyright law, the transfer of copyright from author to publisher must be explicitly stated. A copyright form will be sent to the author and must be completed and returned before an accepted manuscript can be scheduled for publication.

Proofs. All proofs must be corrected and returned to the publisher within 48 hours of receipt. If the manuscript is not returned within the allotted time, the editor will proofread the article, and it will be printed per his instruction. Only correction of typographical errors is permitted. The author will be charged for additional alterations to text at the proof stage.

Journal of Continuing Higher Education

ADDRESS FOR SUBMISSION:

Barbara E. Hanniford, Editor
Journal of Continuing Higher Education
Kent State University
PO Box 5190
Kent, OH 44242
USA
Phone: 330-672-8672
Fax: 330-672-2079
E-Mail: bhannifo@kent.edu
Web: www.ACHEinc.org
Address May Change:

PUBLICATION GUIDELINES:

Manuscript Length: 21-25
Copies Required: Four
Computer Submission: Yes
Format: MSWord compatible
Fees to Review: 0.00 US$

Manuscript Style:
    American Psychological Association

CIRCULATION DATA:

Reader: Administrators
Frequency of Issue: 3 Times/Year
Copies per Issue: 2,001 - 3,000
Sponsor/Publisher: Association for
    Continuing Higher Education
Subscribe Price: 40.00 US$

REVIEW INFORMATION:

Type of Review: Blind Review
No. of External Reviewers: 3
No. of In House Reviewers: 1
Acceptance Rate: 21-30%
Time to Review: 1 - 2 Months
Reviewers Comments: Yes
Invited Articles: 11-20%
Fees to Publish: 0.00 US$

MANUSCRIPT TOPICS:
Adult Career & Vocational; Higher Education

MANUSCRIPT GUIDELINES/COMMENTS:

The Journal of Continuing Higher Education strives to support continuing higher education by serving as a forum for the reporting and exchange of information based on research, observations, and the experience relevant to the field. It is published in January, May, and September.

Author's Guidelines
Manuscripts submitted should have theoretical, as well as practical, implications. We encourage the following types of submissions:
* Articles of up to 7,000 words on:
    * Organization and administration of continuing higher education
    * Development and application of new continuing education program thrusts
    * Adult and nontraditional students
    * Continuing education student programs and services
    * Research within continuing higher education and related fields

- Book reviews of current publications in the field--prospective authors are advised to consult with the editor prior to preparing book reviews.

- Opinion pieces addressing issues directly relevant to continuing professional education.

All manuscripts should be typewritten and double spaced. Please submit **four** copies with the author's name, title, address, and telephone number on a separate sheet of paper. The author's name should not appear on the manuscript itself. *The Publication Manual of the American Psychological Association, Fourth Edition* should be used to provide stylistic guidance, including reference formatting.

We acknowledge receipt of each manuscript. The *Journal* uses a blind review process for evaluation of all manuscripts submitted, with each manuscript read by three reviewers. We make every effort to notify authors of the disposition of their manuscripts within 60 days of receipt.

If a manuscript is accepted for publication, we ask the author will be asked to provide the final version on a 3.5-inch computer disk in Microsoft Word, WordPerfect or an ASCII file, compatible with Windows software. Authors may also transmit files electronically. We reserve the right to edit the manuscript without notice to the author so that it conforms to style, usage, and space requirements.

Please note: Manuscript submission indicates that the piece is not under consideration for publication elsewhere, and has not been published previously.

Address correspondence to:
Barbara Haniford, Editor, *The Journal of Continuing Higher Education,* College of Continuing Studies, Kent State University, P.O. Box 5190, Kent, OH 44242-0001.
Telephone: (330) 672-8672 Fax (330) 672-2079 E-Mail: barb@ccs.kent.edu.

Journal of Counseling and Development

ADDRESS FOR SUBMISSION:

Scott McGowan, Editor
Journal of Counseling and Development
Long Island University
2 Kingman Terrace
Yonkers, NY 10701
USA
Phone: 516-299-2815
Fax: 516-299-4167
E-Mail: amcgowan@liu.edu
Web: www.counseling.org/journals
Address May Change:

PUBLICATION GUIDELINES:

Manuscript Length: 20-35
Copies Required: Three
Computer Submission: No
Format: N/A
Fees to Review: 0.00 US$

Manuscript Style:
    American Psychological Association

CIRCULATION DATA:

Reader: , Practicing Counselors
Frequency of Issue: Quarterly
Copies per Issue: 60,500
Sponsor/Publisher: American Counseling
    Association
Subscribe Price: 138.00 US$

REVIEW INFORMATION:

Type of Review: Blind Review
No. of External Reviewers: 2
No. of In House Reviewers: 0
Acceptance Rate: 20%
Time to Review: 3-4 Months
Reviewers Comments: Yes
Invited Articles: No Reply
Fees to Publish: 0.00 US$

MANUSCRIPT TOPICS:
Counseling & Personnel Services; Topics pertinent to the practice of counseling

MANUSCRIPT GUIDELINES/COMMENTS:

The *Journal of Counseling & Development (JCD)* publishes articles that inform counseling practice with diverse client populations in a variety of settings and that address issues related to counselor education and supervision, as represented by the membership of the American Counseling Association (ACA). Articles should be scholarly, be based on existing literature, and include implications for practice. Manuscripts typically fall into one of the following categories, although other kinds of submissions may be appropriate for *JCD* readers:

Practice. These manuscripts focus on innovative approaches, counseling programs, ethical issues, and training and supervision practices. They are grounded in counseling or educational theory and empirical knowledge. Some evidence of effectiveness in practice is provided.

Theoretical. These manuscripts provide a new theoretical perspective on a particular issue or integrate existing bodies of knowledge in an innovative way. A review of the literature, one type of conceptual piece, provides a critical overview of existing conceptual and empirical knowledge in a particular area. All theoretical pieces include implications for counseling practice.

Research. Both qualitative and quantitative studies are published in *JCD*. In these manuscripts, the review of the literature provides the context and need for the study, logically leading to the purpose and research questions. The methodology includes a full description of the participants, variables and instruments used to measure them, data analyses, and results. Authors are expected to discuss the clinical significance of the results (one means to accomplish this is to report effect size). The discussion section includes conclusions and implications for future research and counseling practice.

Assessment and Diagnosis. These manuscripts are focused on broad assessment and diagnosis issues that have direct relevance for the practitioner. In general, *JCD* does not publish developmental work on individual scales or tests.

Profiles. These manuscripts are focused on one or more persons who have made significant contributions to the profession through scholarship, leadership, and/or innovative practices. This section is also devoted to profiling organizational aspects of ACA. One example is a historical review of one of ACA's Divisions in relation to significant achievements that have positively affected the counseling field.

Trends. These manuscripts are designed to provide readers with information about significant counseling-related literature (i.e., journal articles or special issues) not published and distributed by ACA. The manuscript should not exceed 3,000 words with half of its length devoted to a review of the material selected and half devoted to implication for counselors and/or the counseling profession.

Additional Information Concerning Topic Areas. For information related to multi-culturalism, research, profiles, assessment and diagnosis, and trends potential authors should contact the associate editor affiliated with a topic area. Areas of affiliations are listed on the front, inside cover of JCD. E-mail addresses:

Thomas H. Hohenshil (thohen@vt.edu),
Pamela O. Paislcy (ppaisley@arches.uga.edu),
Tracy L. Robinson (robinson@poe.coe.ncsu.cdu),
Floyd F. Robison (flip@iupui.edu).

All manuscripts should be prepared according to the *Publication Manual of the American Psychological Association* (5th ed.). Authors should consult the APA *Publication Manual Manual* for guidelines regarding the format of the manuscript, abstract, citations and references, tables and figures, and other matters of editorial style. Tables and figures should be used only when essential. Authors should not submit more than three tables or two figures with each manuscript. Figures (graphs, illustrations, line drawings) should be supplied as camera-ready art (glossies prepared by commercial artists) whenever possible. Figure captions should be on an attached page, as required by APA style. JCD does not publish footnotes. Instead, incorporate any footnotes into text or include an endnote. Manuscript titles should be limited to 80 characters.

Authors should also carefully follow *APA Publication Manual* guidelines for nondiscriminatory language regarding gender, sexual orientation, racial and ethnic identity, disabilities, and age. In addition, the terms *counseling, counselor,* and *client* are preferred, rather than their many synonyms.

Lengthy quotations (generally 500 cumulative words or more from one source) require written permission from the copyright holder for reproduction, as do adaptations of tables and figures. It is the author's responsibility to secure such permission, and a copy of the publisher's written permission must be provided to the Editor immediately upon acceptance for publication.

JCD uses an anonymous review system. Thus, authors should make every effort to submit a manuscript that contains no clues to the authors' identity. Citations that may reveal the authors' identity (e.g., "in an extension of our previous work [citation of work with authors' names]") should be masked (e.g., ["Authors, 1995"]). The authors' names, positions or titles, places of employment, and mailing addresses should appear on one cover title page only, not in authors' footnotes. Other title pages should include the title only.

JCD expects authors to follow the *Code of Ethics and Standards of Practice (1995)* of the American Counseling Association (ACA) related to publication, including authorship, concurrent submission to only one publication, informed consent for research participants, and piecemeal publication of research data. In a cover letter, authors should include statements indicating that they have complied with specified ACA ethical standards relevant to their manuscript.

Submit an original and three copies of the manuscript to Scott McGowan, Editor, Counseling and Human Development Services, 2 Kingman Terrace, Long Island University, Yonkers, NY 10701. Do not send manuscripts to the Virginia office of ACA; this will delay handling. Submissions that do not adhere to the above guidelines will be returned to the author without review. Manuscripts are reviewed by at least two editorial board members. Manuscripts typically undergo revision before final acceptance. Final decisions regarding publication are made by the Editor. Authors whose manuscripts are accepted for publication will be required to provide a 3.5 diskette copy of the final version in either MS Word 98 or generic (ASCII) format for IBM compatible computers or in text file format for Macintosh computers. The submitting author's name and the hardware and software used in preparing the diskette must be clearly labeled on the diskette.

A copy of guidelines for submitting proposals for a special issue or feature section in *JCD* may be obtained from the Editor.

Note: Authors bear full responsibility for the accuracy of references, quotations, tables, figures, and the overall content of the article. The ACA Publications Department will send authors a computer printout of the edited article for their final review.

Journal of Creative Behavior

ADDRESS FOR SUBMISSION:

Thomas Ward
Journal of Creative Behavior
Texas A&M University
College of Liberal Arts
Department of Psychology
College Station, TX 77843
USA
Phone: 979-845-2506
Fax: 979-845-4727
E-Mail: jcb@psyc.tamu.edu
Web: www.cef-dpsi.org
Address May Change:

PUBLICATION GUIDELINES:

Manuscript Length: 16-20
Copies Required: Four
Computer Submission: Yes Disk, Email
Format: MSWord - IBM
Fees to Review: 0.00 US$

Manuscript Style:
    American Psychological Association

CIRCULATION DATA:

Reader: Academics
Frequency of Issue: Quarterly
Copies per Issue: 2,001 - 3,000
Sponsor/Publisher: Creative Education
    Foundation
Subscribe Price: 75.00 US$ Individual
    95.00 US$ Institution
    85.00 US$ & $110 Foreign

REVIEW INFORMATION:

Type of Review: Blind Review
No. of External Reviewers: 2
No. of In House Reviewers: 1
Acceptance Rate: 11-20%
Time to Review: 4 - 6 Months
Reviewers Comments: Yes
Invited Articles: 0-5%
Fees to Publish: 0.00 US$

MANUSCRIPT TOPICS:
Art/Music; Curriculum Studies; Education Management/Administration; Educational Psychology; Educational Technology Systems; Elementary/Early Childhood; English Literature; Gifted Children; Higher Education; Languages & Linguistics; Science Math & Environment; Secondary/Adolescent Studies; Social Studies/Social Science; Teacher Education; Tests, Measurement & Evaluation

MANUSCRIPT GUIDELINES/COMMENTS:

The *Journal of Creative Behavior* is published quarterly and is interdisciplinary in nature. Contributions relating to creativity and problem solving are invited. articles should be of interest to individuals who have either a vocational or avocational interest in these areas.

Papers should be as concise as possible with illustrations and tables kept to a minimum. They should not exceed 8,000 words in length; however, consideration will be given to longer articles of special interest.

JCB Format

Author's name in full caps.

Title in upper/lower case; if asterisk after title, description follows at bottom of first page (reference to grant, author, etc.)

Paragraphing: First paragraph flush with side heads
Main heading – full caps – paragraph flush
Subheadings – upper/lower case – paragraph indented
All other paragraphs indented.

Quotations: One or two short sentences – include in main paragraph -- example
"One of the main reasons..." (author, date).

More than two or lengthy sentences – indented without marks with author and date cited in sentence before quotation or at end of quotation -- examples

Getzels and Jackson (1962) summarized Freud's position as follows:
Creativity has its genesis in conflict, and the unconscious forces motivated...
or
This person is characterized by his or her creativity: With his sensitive openness to his world, his trust of his own ability...(Rogers, 1961).

Number
Indentations: To be indented completely -- example:
1. That creativity is a process which when communicated and
described, etc....

Figures: Citation below figures -- example:
FIGURE 1. Targeting on type III.

Tables: Citation above table -- example:
TABLE 1. A comparison of a facilitative model.

Bibliographic Any reference that appears in the text of the manuscript must be cited
References: in the Reference Section.

In the text -- author and year of publication, e.g.,
(Parnes, 1981)

When author's name is part of a sentence, e.g.,
(Guilford, 1979; MacKinnon, 1980; Parnes, 1981)

In reference section, alphabetized in APA style (*American Psychological Association Manual*)

Footnotes: Numerical order, citation at bottom of same page (should be kept to a minimum).

Articles should be submitted in quadruplicate (even if submitting on a diskette). Acknowledgement of receipt is sent. If accepted, articles will undergo editorial revision and be sent to authors for final approval before typesetting. No proofs are sent to authors.

Authors will receive two copies of the *Journal* in which their article appears.

Journal of Developmental Education

ADDRESS FOR SUBMISSION:

Barbara Calderwood, Managing Editor
Journal of Developmental Education
Appalachian State University
National Center for Developmental Edu.
Boone, NC 28608
USA
Phone: 828-262-6101
Fax: 828-262-2128
E-Mail: calderwoodbj@appstate.edu
Web: www.ncde.appstate.edu
Address May Change:

PUBLICATION GUIDELINES:

Manuscript Length: 16-20
Copies Required: Four
Computer Submission: No
Format: N/A
Fees to Review: 0.00 US$

Manuscript Style:
    American Psychological Association

CIRCULATION DATA:

Reader: Academics
Frequency of Issue: 3 Times/Year
Copies per Issue: 4,001 - 5,000
Sponsor/Publisher: Appalachian State
    University/National Center for
    Developmental Education
Subscribe Price: 23.00 US$ Individual
    28.00 US$ Institution

REVIEW INFORMATION:

Type of Review: Blind Review
No. of External Reviewers: 3
No. of In House Reviewers: 2
Acceptance Rate: 11-20%
Time to Review: 4 - 6 Months
Reviewers Comments: Some
Invited Articles: 0-5%
Fees to Publish: 0.00 US$

MANUSCRIPT TOPICS:
Developmental Education/Learning Assistance; Higher Education; Remediation

MANUSCRIPT GUIDELINES/COMMENTS:

The *Journal of Developmental Education* is published as a forum for educators concerned with the practice, theory, research, and news of the post secondary developmental and remedial education community. The *Journal's* content focuses on basic skills education in post secondary education but also treats adjacent fields of knowledge. Editorial emphasis is placed on manuscripts that relate education theory to practical and successful teaching and Learning. The Journal also publishes manuscripts that expand current knowledge or have a clearly demonstrated impact on the field.

The Review Process
Articles submitted to the *Journal* are reviewed by editorial staff. Those considered appropriate are acknowledged and submitted to a blind review by three or more members of the Board of Editors. The process is completed by the Editor and Managing Editor who rely heavily on the judgment of reviewers but are not bound by it. The review process takes three to five months.

Only articles that have not been published previously and are not scheduled for publication, wholly or in part, in any other publication will be considered. Not accepted are book reviews, reviews of educational materials, essays, interviews or dialogues, surveys of literature, or articles which promote a commercial service or product. Low priority is placed on articles which deal broadly with a subject, are based on unique situations, or are extremely technical in topic or presentation.

Writing the Article

When preparing an article for the *Journal*, write simply and clearly. Document your assertions and give proper credit to other authors, for the burden of plagiarism belongs to you, not to the *Journal*. Use the *Publication Manual of the American Psychological Association* to answer questions of style and form, paying particular attention to citations in text and reference formats. Articles which fail to conform will be returned.

Because the *Journal* places editorial emphasis on the implications of education theory for practice, the majority of manuscripts require a statement of an appropriate theoretical base and supporting literature search. Whenever possible, include descriptive examples of procedures, processes, interaction, and outcomes in the manuscript. Include an evaluation component as appropriate. Use headings and subheadings to divide your paper into manageable sections, using one heading for about every two pages of copy. Tables, charts, and figures must be camera ready; poorly prepared documents will discourage acceptance of the manuscript. An abstract of about 100 words is required.

The optimum length of a *Journal* manuscript is 15 to 20 pages, although shorter articles are accepted. The manuscript should have a short, informative title which aids indexing; the initial word of the title should refer to the subject of the paper. For example, use "Cognitive Skills in the Reading Classroom," not "Classroom Cognition: Developmental Reading in College."

Presentation Format

Type the abstract, body, and references of the article, entirely double spaced , using a b-inch line on non-erasable paper. Do not justify the right-hand margin, for this impedes editing and copy fitting. Headings should be centered; subheadings should be flush left. Pages should be numbered. **Your name should not appear on any of these pages**.

Prepare a single cover sheet that bears the title of the article, your name, title, address, institutional affiliation, and telephone number.

* Make four copies of the abstract, body and references only: three for reviewers, and one for yourself.

* If you want your original manuscript returned, prepare a large, self-addressed stamped envelope to include with the manuscript.

Journal of Distance Learning Administration

ADDRESS FOR SUBMISSION:

Janet Gubbins, Managing Editor
Journal of Distance Learning
    Administration
State University of West Georgia
Honors House
1803 Maple Street
Carrollton, GA 30118
USA
Phone: 770-838-3017
Fax: 770-836-4666
E-Mail: distance@westga.edu
Web: www.westga.edu/distance/
Address May Change:

PUBLICATION GUIDELINES:

Manuscript Length: No Reply
Copies Required: One
Computer Submission: Yes Disk, Email
Format: MSWord or WordPerfect
Fees to Review: 0.00 US$

Manuscript Style:
    American Psychological Association

CIRCULATION DATA:

Reader: Administrators
Frequency of Issue: Quarterly
Copies per Issue: 5,001 - 10,000
Sponsor/Publisher: State University of West
    Georgia's Distance & Distributed
    Education Center
Subscribe Price: 0.00 US$ Online

REVIEW INFORMATION:

Type of Review: Blind Review
No. of External Reviewers: 2
No. of In House Reviewers: 1
Acceptance Rate: 70%
Time to Review: 4 - 6 Months
Reviewers Comments: Yes
Invited Articles: 0-5%
Fees to Publish: 0.00 US$

MANUSCRIPT TOPICS:

Distance Education Administration; Education Management/Administration; Educational Technology Systems; Higher Education; Tests, Measurement & Evaluation

MANUSCRIPT GUIDELINES/COMMENTS:

Mission

The Journal of Distance Learning Administration is a peer-reviewed electronic journal offered free each quarter over the World Wide Web. The Journal welcomes manuscripts based on original work of practitioners and researchers with specific focus or implications for the management of distance education programs.

Submission is of Articles

Original articles up to 6500 (normally between 2000 and 6000) words required. We welcome practical distance education management ideas as well as more theoretical works. Articles should be submitted electronically, as HTML documents, or as Microsoft Word files. Graphics should be either in Gif or JPEG format.

Articles will be reviewed by two or three persons with expertise in the area. Authors will be notified of acceptance within one month.

Manuscripts can be submitted in WordPerfect or Microsoft Word. All submissions should be preceded by a header containing the title of the manuscript, the name(s) of the author, any affiliations, mail, and e-mail addresses, and telephone numbers. As much as possible typescript should conform to the style set forth in the *Publications Manual of the American Psychological Association.*

Articles may be submitted to *jgubbins@westga.edu*

If the author/s do not have access to an email account, articles may also be submitted on a disk to:

The Journal of Distance Learning Administration
Janet Gubbins, Managing Editor
Honors House
State University of West Georgia
Carrollton, Georgia 30118

It is the standard policy to include the email address of all contributors so they can be directly contacted by interested readers. Any contributor who does not want their email address provided should inform the editor.

Journal of Education Finance

ADDRESS FOR SUBMISSION:

Mary F. Hughes, Executive Editor
Journal of Education Finance
University of Arkansas
College of Education
238 Graduate Education Bldg.
Fayetteville, AR 72701
USA
Phone: 501-575-7019
Fax: 501-575-2492
E-Mail: mhughe@comp.uark.edu
Web: www.uark.edu/misc/elfc/jef/
Address May Change:

PUBLICATION GUIDELINES:

Manuscript Length: 30 double-spaced
Copies Required: Five
Computer Submission: Upon Acceptance
Format: MSWord 6.0 or higher
Fees to Review: 0.00 US$

Manuscript Style:
    Chicago Manual of Style

CIRCULATION DATA:

Reader: Academics, Technical Personnel
Frequency of Issue: Quarterly
Copies per Issue: 1,001 - 2,000
Sponsor/Publisher: Association of School
    Business Officials Internation (ASBO)
Subscribe Price: 40.00 US$ Individual
    60.00 US$ Group/Library
    8.00 US$ Add for Foreign

REVIEW INFORMATION:

Type of Review: Blind Review
No. of External Reviewers: 3
No. of In House Reviewers: 0
Acceptance Rate: 21-30%
Time to Review: 2 - 3 Months
Reviewers Comments: Yes
Invited Articles: 0-5%
Fees to Publish: 0.00 US$

MANUSCRIPT TOPICS:
Education Management/Administration; Higher Education; Public School/Higher Education
Finance; School Law; Special Education

MANUSCRIPT GUIDELINES/COMMENTS:

Editorial Policy
The Editorial Staff welcomes articles concerned with the problems and issues of education
finance. The *Journal of Education Finance* exists to disseminate knowledge in the field of
education finance. There are three sets of criteria applied to the review and selection of
articles for publication. First, articles must advance knowledge, theory, and practice. Second,
the content of articles must be accurate and technically competent. Third, articles must be well
written; they must be clear, well organized, and stylistically correct.

A manuscript which is published in the *Journal* should not have appeared in other
publications. When the manuscript is published by the *Journal*, it becomes the property of the
Journal with the *Journal* possessing exclusive right to publication. All rights in copyright will
belong to the *Journal of Education Finance*.

General Information for Contributors
The Journal's website: http://www.uark.edu/misc/elfc/jef/home.html
Publication Schedule: Quarterly; summer, fall, winter, and spring.
Scope: The *Journal of Education Finance* is a blind reviewed scholarly journal committed to the dissemination of knowledge in the field of education finance.
Editorial Style: *Manual of Style*, University of Chicago Press
Copies to be Submitted: Five. An original and four copies
Author Responsibilities: If the article is accepted for publication, all graphs and illustrative materials must be provided in camera-ready form by the author. Specifications will be sent on request.

Editorial Procedures
Articles submitted to the *Journal of Education Finance* are processed as follows. Upon receipt, the article is initially reviewed by the staff. If the article fails to fall within the scope of the Journal, it is returned to the author.

If an article is in accord with the guidelines, a letter of acknowledgment is sent to the author. All references to the author's name and affiliation are removed and the paper is submitted for review to two or more members of the Editorial Advisory Board. With the advice of the reviewers, the editors make one of four decisions: accept, accept contingent on revision, revise and resubmit, or reject. In the case of conditional acceptance, the editor will specify necessary revisions in writing to the author. In the case of a request for revision and resubmission, the editor will suggest or specify revisions in writing to the author; upon resubmission, the manuscript will be treated to the same blind review as the initial process. Copies of manuscripts which have been rejected will not be returned to the author unless the author provides a stamped, self-addressed envelope.

Manuscripts submitted to the *Journal of Education Finance* should not be under consideration for publication by other journals. If a paper has been presented at a meeting or conference, the author should state where and when such a paper was presented. After acceptance, a paper or any portion of a paper may not be published elsewhere without written approval from the editor of the *Journal of Education Finance*.

If an article is accepted, the author will be notified and given an indication of the volume and issue in which the article will be published. At this time, the author must submit a copy of the article on diskette in MSWord 6.0 or higher, or ASCII. The diskette label should indicate the file(s) name(s) and the software used. Any graphs or other illustrative materials contained in the article must be provided in camera-ready form by the author. Footnotes should not be, embedded in the text, but on a separate page at the end of the manuscript. The staff on the *Journal of Education Finance* agrees to process manuscripts promptly. In most cases, an editorial decision may be expected between eight to ten weeks after submission.

Technical and Stylistic Requirement
Articles submitted to the *Journal of Education Finance* must be grammatically correct and stylistically consistent. The University of Chicago's *Manual of Style* is the editorial style required.

The copy should be double-spaced with margins of 1 1/2" at top, bottom, and both sides. Dot matrix type is not acceptable. Manuscript on both sides of typing sheet is not acceptable. There should be no hyphenated words on line endings; not printed borders; and no numbered line indicators on the left margin. Footnotes should be typed on separate pages and not at the bottom of the manuscript page. Five copies must be submitted; an original and four copies. Each copy should be stapled together. Any other form of binding is not acceptable. Tables and graphs should be kept to maximum of five.

The title page should contain the following: title of the paper; full name of the author(s); institutional affiliation and position held by the author(s); telephone number of the author(s); statement of place and date of previous oral presentation of the paper, if any; and a disclaimer statement, if applicable. All correspondence and contact during the review and production processes will be addressed to the first author listed. The *Journal of Education Finance* does not publish statements of acknowledgment to colleagues who assisted in the preparation of the manuscript.

The title of the article should appear at the top of the first page. The name of the author(s) should not appear on the first page of the manuscript nor on any subsequent pages.

The Editorial Staff and Board welcome any inquiries concerning the policies, review, and production processes of the *Journal of Education Finance*.

Sample
TABLE 2
Trends in Public Elementary and Secondary School Finance

| School Year | Total Expenditures | | Total Revenues | | |
| | Gross National Product | Personal Income | Federal | State | Local |
	%	%	%	%	%
1959-60	3.1	4.0	4.4	35.2	60.4
1969-70	4.2	5.1	8.3	38.5	53.2
1974-75	4.3	5.2	9.2	41.8	48.8
1979-80	3.7	4.5	9.9	46.8	43.3
1981-82	3.7	4.4	8.6	47.7	43.7

Source: Computed by author from data from United States Department of Education National Center for Education Statistics and United States Department of Commerce, Bureau of Economic Analysis.

Journal of Education for Business

ADDRESS FOR SUBMISSION:

Isabella Owen Perelman, Editor
Journal of Education for Business
c/o Heldref Publications
1319 Eighteenth Street NW
Washington, DC 20036
USA
Phone: 202-296-6267 ext 258
Fax: 202-296-5149
E-Mail: jeb@heldref.org
Web:
Address May Change:

PUBLICATION GUIDELINES:

Manuscript Length: 11-15
Copies Required: Two
Computer Submission: Yes
Format: MSWord
Fees to Review: 0.00 US$

Manuscript Style:
    American Psychological Association

CIRCULATION DATA:

Reader: Practicing Teachers, Academics,
    Administrators
Frequency of Issue: 6 Times/Year
Copies per Issue: 4,001 - 5,000
Sponsor/Publisher: Heldref Publications,
    Inc.
Subscribe Price: 28.00 US$ Individual
    46.00 US$ Institution

REVIEW INFORMATION:

Type of Review: Blind Review
No. of External Reviewers: 2
No. of In House Reviewers: 0
Acceptance Rate: 33%
Time to Review: 3-4 Months
Reviewers Comments: Yes
Invited Articles: 0-5%
Fees to Publish: 0.00 US$

MANUSCRIPT TOPICS:

Business Education Trends & Issues; Communications; Curricular Issues- Accounting, Econ.
& Finance; Curriculum Studies; Education Management/Administration; Mgt, Marketing &
Business Disciplines

MANUSCRIPT GUIDELINES/COMMENTS:

Scope of JEB

The *Journal of Education for Business* is designed to appeal to individuals whose primary
focus is education and training for business. Articles are basic and applied research based and
are selected through a blind peer-review process.

The *Journal* entertains articles that deal with:

* Significant trends and issues affecting education for business
* Curriculum development and evaluation of educational programs in traditional and
  nontraditional settings
* The process of instruction in accounting and finance, business fundamentals (math, law,
  economics, communications, organization), consumer economics, management,

marketing, microcomputers, and office systems (office support staff training, information processing)

Instructions To Contributors

The *Journal of Education for Business* is designed to appeal to persons interested in education and particularly teachers, supervisors and administrators at the post secondary levels, and to educators in colleges and universities.

Manuscripts should normally not exceed 2,500 words, should be submitted exclusively to this journal, and should not have been previously published elsewhere.

1. Contributors should submit two copies of each manuscript to be considered for publication. In addition, the author should keep an extra copy so the editors can refer to specific pages and lines if a question arises. The manuscript should be double-spaced but right lines should not be justified.

2. *Publication Manual* (4th edition), American Psychological Association, Washington, DC, should be used as a style reference in preparation of manuscripts.

3. Reproduction of figures (graphs and charts) may be submitted for review purposes, but the originals must be supplied if the manuscript is accepted for publication. Tables and figures should be prepared in accord with the instructions given in the APA's *Publication Manual* (see pp. 120-162).

4. Avoid explanatory notes whenever possible by incorporating their content in the text. For essential notes, identify them with consecutive superscripts and list them in a section entitled "Notes" at the end of the text.

5. References should be listed alphabetically according to the author's last name at the end of the manuscript in APA style.

6. An abstract of 75-100 words should be provided on the first page.

7. Authors receive two complimentary copies of the issue in which their article appears and permission to reproduce additional copies of that article.

The manuscript should contain the author's mailing address and telephone number. Once received, the manuscript is reviewed by a consulting editor, and then by one of the executive editors. This process takes approximately six weeks.

Journal of Education Policy

ADDRESS FOR SUBMISSION:

M.M. Maguire, Deputy Editor
Journal of Education Policy
King's College London
Educational and Professional Studies
Franklin-Wilkins Bldg., (WBW)
Waterloo Road
London, 8E1 9NN
UK
Phone: +44 0 2076 126973
Fax: +44 0 2076 126818
E-Mail: s.ball@ioe.ac.uk
Web: www.tandf.co.uk/journals
Address May Change:

PUBLICATION GUIDELINES:

Manuscript Length: 26-30
Copies Required: Three
Computer Submission: No
Format: N/A
Fees to Review: 0.00 US$

Manuscript Style:
    See Manuscript Guidelines

CIRCULATION DATA:

Reader: Practicing Teachers, Academics,
    Administrators, Policy Makers
Frequency of Issue: 6 Times/Year
Copies per Issue: Less than 1,000
Sponsor/Publisher: Taylor & Francis
Subscribe Price: No Reply

REVIEW INFORMATION:

Type of Review: Blind Review
No. of External Reviewers: 2
No. of In House Reviewers: 1
Acceptance Rate: 21-30%
Time to Review: 2 - 3 Months
Reviewers Comments: Yes
Invited Articles: 0-5%
Fees to Publish: 0.00 US$

MANUSCRIPT TOPICS:
Education Management/Administration; Education Policy

MANUSCRIPT GUIDELINES/COMMENTS:

The *Journal of Education Policy* aims to discuss, analyze and debate policymaking, policy-implementation and policy impact at all levels of an in all facets of education. It offers a forum for theoretical debate, and historical and comparative studies, as well as policy analysis and evaluation reports. The journal also analyses key policy documents and reviews, relevant texts and monographs.

Contacting the Editors:
Managing Editors:
Stephen Ball, Karl Mannheim Professor of Sociology of Education, Institute of Education, University of London, 59 Gordon Square, London WC1H ONT, UK email: s.ball@ioe.ac.uk

464

Ivor Goodson (Founding Editor), Centre for Applied Research in Education, School of Education and Professional Development, University of East Anglia, Norwich NR4 7TJ, UK
email: igoodson@uea.ac.uk

Deputy Editor:
Meg Maguire (address as for Stephen Ball, above)

Submitting a Paper
In writing your paper, you are encouraged to review articles in the area you are addressing which have been previously published in the journal, and where you feel appropriate, to reference them. This will enhance context, coherence, and continuity for our readers.

Please read these Guidelines with care and attention: failure to follow them may result in your paper being delayed. Note especially the referencing conventions used *by Journal of Education Policy* and for all manuscripts, non-discriminatory language is mandatory. Sexist or racist terms should not be used.

Journal of Education Policy considers all manuscripts on condition they are the property (copyright) of the submitting author(s) and that copyright will be transferred to *Journal of Education Policy* and Taylor & Francis Ltd if the paper is accepted. *Journal of Education Policy* considers all manuscripts on the strict condition that they have been submitted only to *Journal of Education Policy*, that they have not been published already, nor are they under consideration for publication, nor in press elsewhere. Authors who fail to adhere to this condition will be charged all costs, which *Journal of Education Policy* incurs, and their papers will not be published.

Please write clearly and concisely, stating your objectives clearly and defining your terms. Your arguments should be substantiated with well-reasoned supporting evidence. For all manuscripts, non-discriminatory language is mandatory. Sexist or racist terms should not be used. Abstracts of around 100 - 200 words are required for all papers submitted and should precede the text of a paper. Manuscripts should be typed on one single side of A4 or 8 x 11 inch white good quality paper, double-spaced throughout, including the reference section. Accepted manuscripts in their final, revised versions, may also be submitted as electronic word processing files on disk - see 'Electronic Processing'.

Three copies of your manuscript must be submitted. Authors should include telephone and fax numbers as well as e-mail addresses on the cover page of manuscripts. Bionotes should be contained on a separate sheet and be located at the beginning of a paper. In writing your paper, you are encouraged to review articles in the area you are addressing which have been previously published in the journal, and where you feel appropriate, to reference them. This will enhance context, coherence, and continuity for our readers.

Articles for consideration should be sent to the managing editors: Ivor Goodson (General Section—North America); Stephen Ball (General Section—UK, Europe, Australasia; Reviews); and Robert Burgess (Documents and Debates Section) Penn State University, University Park, PA 16802, but may be also be submitted through any member of the executive editorial board.

Electronic Processing

We strongly encourage you to send us the final, revised version of your article in both hard (paper) and electronic (disk) forms. This Guide sets out the procedures, which will assure we can process your article efficiently. It is divided into three sections:

- a guide for authors using standard word-processing software packages
- a guide for authors using LaTeX mathematical software packages
- a guide for authors using graphics software packages

There are some general rules, which apply to all three options.

- These guides do not apply to authors who are submitting an article for consideration and peer review; they apply only to authors whose articles have been reviewed, revised, and accepted for publication
- Print out your hard (paper) copy from the disk you are sending; it is essential that the hard-copy printout is identical to the material on the disk; where versions differ, the hard copy will take precedence. We advise that you maintain back-ups of your files
- Save and send your files on a standard 3.5 inch high density disk (Mac or PC); please do not attempt to send the article via file transfer protocol or email
- When saving your article onto a disk, please make sure that the files do not exceed a manageable size. Please ensure that figures are saved on a separate disk
- Ensure that the files are **not** saved as read only
- Virus-check your disk before sending it to the Editor
- Label your disk
- Package disks in such a way as to avoid damage in the post
- Disks are not returnable after publication

If you are not sure about the usability of your disk, contact the Editorial Manager Journals, Taylor & Francis, 11 New Fetter Lane, London EC4P 4EE, UK

1. A guide for authors using standard word-processing software packages

For the main text of your article, most standard PC or Mac word-processing software packages are acceptable, although we prefer Microsoft Word in a PC format. Word-processed files should be prepared according to the journal style. Avoid the use of embedded footnotes. For numbered tables, use the table function provided with the word-processing package. All text should be saved in one file with the complete text (including the title page, abstract, all sections of the body of the paper, references), followed by numbered tables and the figure captions.

You should send the following to the Editor:

- A 3.5-inch disk containing the final, accepted version of the paper
- Include an ASCII/text only version on the disk as well as the word processed version if possible
- Two hard copy printouts

Disks should be clearly labeled with the following information:

Journal title, Name of author, File names contained on disk, Hardware used (PC or Mac), Software used (name and version)

2. A guide for authors using LaTeX mathematical software packages

Authors who wish to prepare their articles using the LaTeX document preparation system are advised to use article.sty (for LaTex 2.09) or article.cls (for LaTex2e). The use of macros should be kept to an absolute minimum but if any are used they should be gathered together in the file, just before the \begin{document} command.

You should send the following to the Editor:
- A 3.5-inch disk containing the final, accepted version of the paper
- The files you send must be text-only (often called an ASCII file), with no system-dependent control codes
- Two hard copy printouts

Disks should be clearly labeled with the information as previously listed

3. A guide for authors using graphics software packages

We welcome figures on disk, but care and attention to these guidelines is essential, as importing graphics packages can often be problematic. Figures must be saved on a separate disk from the text. Avoid the use of color and tints for aesthetic reasons. Figures should be produced as near to the finished size as possible. High quality reproducible hard copy for all line figures (printed out from your electronic files at a minimum of 600 dpi) must be supplied in case the disks are unusable; photographs and transparencies can be accepted as hard copy only. Photocopies will not be accepted.

All figures must be numbered in the order in which they occur (e.g. figure 1, figure 2 etc.). In multi-part figures, each part should be labeled (e.g. figure 1 (a), figure 1 (b) etc.) The figure captions must be saved as a separate file with the text and numbered correspondingly. The filename for the graphic should be descriptive of the graphic e.g. Figure1, Figure2a. Files should be saved as TIFF (tagged image file format), PostScript or EPS (encapsulated PostScript), containing all the necessary font information and the source file of the application (e.g., CorelDraw/Mac, CorelDraw/PC).

Disks should be clearly labeled with the following information:
Journal title, Name of author, Figures contained on disk, Hardware used (PC or Mac)
Software used (name and version)

Abstracts

Structured abstracts are required for all papers, and should be submitted as detailed below, following the title and author's name and address, preceding the main text. For papers reporting original research, state the **primary objective** and any hypothesis tested; describe the **research design** and your reasons for adopting that methodology; state the **methods and procedures** employed, including where appropriate tools, hardware, software, the selection and number of study areas/subjects, and the central **experimental interventions**; state the **main outcomes and results**, including relevant data; and state the **conclusions** that might be drawn from these data and results, including their implications for further research or application/practice. For review essays, state the **primary objective** of the review; the reasoning behind your literature selection; and the way you critically analyse the literature; state the **main outcomes and results** of your review; and state the **conclusions** that might be drawn, including their implications for further research or application/practice. Abstracts should not exceed 200 words.

Copyright permission

Contributors are required to secure permission for the reproduction of any figure, table, or extensive (more than fifty word) extract from the text, from a source which is copyrighted - or owned - by a party other than Taylor & Francis or the contributor.

This applies both to direct reproduction or 'derivative reproduction' - when the contributor has created a new figure or table which derives substantially from a copyrighted source.

The following form of words can be used in seeking permission:

Code Of Experimental Ethics And Practice

Contributors are required to follow the procedures in force in their countries, which govern the ethics of work done with human or animal subjects. The Code of Ethics of the World Medical Association (Declaration of Helsinki) represents a minimal requirement.

When experimental animals are used, state the species, strain, number used, and other pertinent descriptive characteristics.

For human subjects or patients, describe their characteristics. For human participants in a research survey, secure the consent for data and other material - verbatim quotations from interviews, etc. - to be used.

When describing surgical procedures on animals, identify the pre anaesthetic and anaesthetic agents used and state the amount of concentration and the route and frequency of administration for each. The use of paralytic agents, such as curare or succinylcholine, is not an acceptable substitute for anaesthetics. For other invasive procedures on animals, report the analgesic or tranquilizing drugs used; if none were used, provide justification for such exclusion.

When reporting studies on unanaesthetized animals or on humans, indicate that the procedures followed were in accordance with institutional guidelines. Specific permission for facial photographs of patients is required. A letter of consent must accompany the photographs of patients in which a possibility of identification exists. It is not sufficient to cover the eyes to mask identity.

Mathematics

Special care should be taken with mathematical scripts, especially subscripts and superscripts and differentiation between the letter 'ell' and the figure one, and the letter 'oh 'and the figure zero. If your keyboard does not have the characters you need, it is preferable to use longhand, in which case it is important to differentiate between capital and small letters, K, k and x and other similar groups of letters. Special symbols should be highlighted in the text and explained in the margin. In some cases it is helpful to supply annotated lists of symbols for the guidance of the sub-editor and the typesetter, and/or a 'Nomenclature' section preceding the 'Introduction'.

For simple fractions in the text, the solidus / should be used instead of a horizontal line, care being taken to insert parentheses where necessary to avoid ambiguity, for example, $1/(n-1)$.

Exceptions are the proper fractions available as single type on a keyboard. Full formulae or equations should be displayed, that is, written on a separate line. Horizontal lines are preferable to solidi, for example:

$$\underline{6l + 5h + q}$$

$$3n + 3yz^2$$

But: $\underline{a/b + c/d + a/d}$

$$P = (a^2 + b^2)(c^2 + d^2)$$

The solidus is not generally used for units: ms^{-1} not m/s, but note electrons/s, counts/channel, etc. Displayed equations referred to in the text should be numbered serially (1, 2, etc.) on the right hand side of the page. Short expressions not referred to by any number will usually be incorporated in the text. Symbols should not be underlined to indicate fonts except for tensors, vectors and matrices, which are indicated with a wavy line in the manuscript (not with a straight arrow or arrow above) and rendered in heavy type in print: upright sans serif **r** (tensor), sloping serif **r** (vector) upright serif **r** (matrix).

Typographical requirements must be clearly indicated at their first occurrence, e.g. Greek, Roman, script, sans serif, bold, italic. Authors will be charged for corrections at proof stage resulting from a failure to do so. Braces, brackets and parentheses are used in the order {[( )]}, except where mathematical convention dictates otherwise (i.e. square brackets for commutators and anticommutators).

Notes On Style

All authors are asked to take account of the diverse audience of *Journal of Education Policy*. Clearly explain or avoid the use of terms that might be meaningful only to a local or national audience. However, note also that the *Journal of Education Policy* does not aspire to be international in the ways that McDonald's restaurants or Hilton Hotels are 'international'; we much prefer papers that, where appropriate, reflect the particularities of each higher education system

Some specific points of style for the text of articles, research reports, case studies, reports, essay reviews, and reviews follow:

1. *Journal of Education Policy* prefers US to 'American', USA to 'United States', and UK to 'United Kingdom'.

2. *Journal of Education Policy* uses conservative British, not US, spelling, i.e. colour not color; behaviour (behavioural) not behavior; [school] programme not program; [he] practises not practices; centre not center; organization not organisation; analyse not analyze, etc.

3. Single 'quotes' are used for quotations rather than double "quotes", unless the 'quote is "within" another quote'.

4. Punctuation should follow the British style, e.g. 'quotes precede punctuation'.

5. Punctuation of common abbreviations should follow the following conventions: e.g. i.e. cf. Note that such abbreviations are not followed by a comma or a (double) point/period.

6. Dashes (M-dash) should be clearly indicated in manuscripts by way of either a clear dash (-) or a double hyphen (- -).

7. *Journal of Education Policy* is sparing in its use of the upper case in headings and references, e.g. only the first word in paper titles and all subheads is in upper case; titles of papers from journals in the references and other places are not in upper case.

8. Apostrophes should be used sparingly. Thus, decades should be referred to as follows: 'The 1980s [not the 1980's] saw...'. Possessives associated with acronyms (e.g. APU), should be written as follows: 'The APU's findings that...', but, NB, the plural is APUs.

9. All acronyms for national agencies, examinations, etc., should be spelled out the first time they are introduced in text or references. Thereafter the acronym can be used if appropriate, e.g. 'The work of the Assessment of Performance Unit (APU) in the early 1980s...'. Subsequently, 'The APU studies of achievement...', in a reference ... (Department of Education and Science [DES] 1989a).

10. Brief biographical details of significant national figures should be outlined in the text unless it is quite clear that the person concerned would be known internationally. Some suggested editorial emendations to a typical text are indicated in the following with square brackets: 'From the time of H. E. Armstrong [in the 19th century] to the curriculum development work associated with the Nuffield Foundation [in the 1960s], there has been a shift from heurism to constructivism in the design of [British] science courses'.

11. The preferred local (national) usage for ethnic and other minorities should be used in all papers. For the USA, African-American, Hispanic, and Native American are used, e.g. 'The African American presidential candidate, Jesse Jackson...' For the UK, African-Caribbean (not 'West Indian'), etc.

12. Material to be emphasized (italicized in the printed version) should be underlined in the typescript rather than italicized. Please use such emphasis sparingly.

13. n (not N), % (not per cent) should be used in typescripts.

14. Numbers in text should take the following forms: 300, 3000, 30 000. Spell out numbers under 10 unless used with a unit of measure, e.g. nine pupils but 9 mm (do not introduce periods with measure). For decimals, use the form 0.05 (not .05).

15. When using a word which is or is asserted to be a proprietary term or trade mark authors' must use the symbol ® or TM or alternatively a footnote can be inserted using the wording below:

This article includes a word, which is or is asserted to be a proprietary term or trade mark. Its inclusion does not imply it has acquired for legal purposes a non-proprietary or general significance, nor is any other judgment implied concerning its legal status.

Notes On Tables And Figures

Artwork submitted for publication will not be returned and will be destroyed after publication, unless you request otherwise. Whilst every care is taken of artwork, neither the Editor nor Taylor & Francis shall bear any responsibility or liability for non-return, loss, or damage of artwork, nor for any associated costs or compensation. You are strongly advised to insure appropriately. Illustrations are as important as the text, and should be as simple, relevant and clear as possible. A potential reader, after reading the title, often glances next at the figures, and their main purpose should be evident from the legend beneath the figure and the words used in labeling the parts of diagrams and the axes of graphs without reference to the text.

Black-and-white photographs should have adequate contrast. Colour illustrations can be printed if they are necessary to convey the scientific content of the illustration.

Labeling of axes of graphs should be in words, whenever possible, and the dimensionless numbers on the axes should be those obtained by dividing the quantities measured by the units employed. For example, the numbers relating to density should be labeled Density/(kg M-3) , and numbers relating to temperature in degrees celsius should be labeled temperaturePC.

Please use different line thicknesses for emphasis; for example, thinner lines for axes of graphs and thicker lines for curves. Use different data points and lines, dashed or dotted, when more than one curve appears in a graph, and identify their meaning in the legend or by labeling, legends should explain any abbreviations used in the figures.

1. Tables and figures should be valuable, relevant, and visually attractive. Tables and figures must be referred to in the text and numbered in order of their appearance. Each table and figure should have a complete, descriptive title; and each table column an appropriate heading. Tables and figures should be referred to in text as follows: figure 1, table 1, i.e. lower case. 'As seen in table [or figure] 1 ...' (not Tab., fig. or Fig).

2. The place at which a table or figure is to be inserted in the printed text should be indicated clearly on a manuscript:
[Insert table 2 about here]

3. Each table and/or figure must have a title that explains its purpose without reference to the text.

4. All figures and tables must be on separate sheets and not embedded in the text. Original copies of figures should be supplied. All figures should allow for reduction to column width (130 mm) or page width (160mm). Please avoid figures that would require landscape reproduction, i.e., reading from bottom to top of the page. Photographs may be sent as glossy prints or negatives. Please number each figure on the reverse in pencil. Do not type the caption to a figure on that figure; the legends to any illustrations must be typed separately following the main text and should be grouped together.

Acknowledgements
Any acknowledgements authors wish to make should be included in a separate headed section at the end of the manuscript. Please do not incorporate these into the bionote or notes.

Book Reviews
1. The following header material should appear in all reviews in the following order (note also the punctuation):
The Politics of Social Research.

By Martyn Hammersley (Sage, London, 1995), 192 pp., £35.00 (hbk), ISBN 0-8039-7718-2, £11.95 (pbk), ISBN 0-8039-7719.

2. Page references within reviews should be given as follows: (p. 337) or (pp. 36-37).

Citations in Text
References should be cited using the author-date, or Harvard, system.
1. 'Ibid.' (and the like) are not used when repeating citations. Simply repeat the original citation verbatim, e.g. (Orwell 1945).

2. Citations should be included in prefatory material to quotes (wherever possible) rather than placing them at the end. Thus, for example, 'Orwell (1945: 23) reduces the principles of animalism to seven commandments, namely, ...' is preferred to 'Orwell reduced the principles of animalism to seven commandments, namely, ... (Orwell 1945: 23)'.

3. Multiple citations within parentheses should be divided by a comma, not a semi-colon, and there should be no use of '&' within such multiple references. References to works published in the same year should be cited as, e.g. (Smith 1991a, b).

4. Multiple citations within a text should be ordered by date, not alphabetically by authors name, e.g. (Smith 1902, Jones and Bower 1934, Brown 1955, 1958a, b, Green 1995).

5. 'et al.' may be used in references within the text when a paper or book has three or more authors, but note that all names should be given in the reference itself.

6. Page spans in references should be given in full, e.g. 'Sedgewick (1935: 102-103; emphasis added) outlines them as follows:'

References
Journal of Education Policy uses the following conventions for references:
1. Reference to a book:
Lacey, C. (1977) *The Socialization of Teachers* (London: Methuen).

2. Reference to a chapter in a book:
Crozier, M. (1969) The vicious circle of bureaucracy, in T. Burns (ed.), *Industrial Man* (Harmondsworth: Penguin), 250-262

472

3. Reference to an article in a journal:
Buswell, C. (1980) Pedagogic change and social change, *British Journal of Sociology of Education.*

4. Proceedings, reports and unpublished literature:
Smith, R. J. M. (1995) Accountability to the state: an exploration of the educational market and parental choice literature. Paper presented to the Annual Conference of the New Zealand Association for Research in Education, Massey University, Palmerston North, 7–10 December.
Burnham, C. A. and Anderson, T. H., 1991 Learning to sew on a button by reading a procedural text. CSR Technical Report, No. 543, Center for the Study of Reading, University of Illinois at Urbana-Champaign. ERIC ED 332 157.

Cohen, D. K. and Ball, D. L. (1997) Policy, Cognition, and Instruction. Unpublished manuscript.

5. Reference to a newspaper or magazine:
Richards, H., 1996, Republican lite? *The Times Higher Education Supplement,* 1 November, 16.

6. Reference to an Internet source:
Give the universal resource locator in full: http://acsinfo.acs.org/instruct/instruct.html

7. Reference to a personal communication:
Brannen, J., 1996, Personal communication.

8. Reference to a case in law:
In text, italicize names of plaintiffs and defendants: Miranda v. *Arizona* 1974

9. Reference to government legislation:
US Congress, Senate Committee on Foreign Relations, 1956, *The Mutual Security Act of 1956,* 84th Congress, second session, report 2273.

United Kingdom Parliament, Committee on the Working of the Monetary System [Radcliffe Committee] 1960, *Principal Memoranda of Evidence*, vol. 2, Cmd 1958.

Journal of Educational Administration

ADDRESS FOR SUBMISSION:

A. Ross Thomas, Editor
Journal of Educational Administration
PO Box 1201
Armidale
New South Wales, NSW 2350
Australia
Phone: +61 (0)2 6772 7612
Fax: +61 (0)2 6772-7612
E-Mail: athomas@metz.une.edu.au
Web: www.mcb.co.uk/jea.htm
Address May Change:

PUBLICATION GUIDELINES:

Manuscript Length: 21-25
Copies Required: Three
Computer Submission: Yes
Format: see guidelines
Fees to Review: 0.00 US$

Manuscript Style:
   See Manuscript Guidelines

CIRCULATION DATA:

Reader: Academics, Practicing Educational
   Leaders
Frequency of Issue: 6 Times/Year
Copies per Issue: No Reply
Sponsor/Publisher: MCB University
   Press/Emerald
Subscribe Price: 3199.00 US$
   3759.00 AUS$
   1999.00 Pounds

REVIEW INFORMATION:

Type of Review: Blind Review
No. of External Reviewers: 3
No. of In House Reviewers: 0
Acceptance Rate: 21-30%
Time to Review: 1 - 2 Months
Reviewers Comments: Yes
Invited Articles: 11-20%
Fees to Publish: 0.00 US$

MANUSCRIPT TOPICS:

Administrative/Managerial Emphasis; Education Management/Administration; Higher Education; Rural Education & Small Schools; School Law; Special Education

MANUSCRIPT GUIDELINES/COMMENTS:

Articles submitted to the journal should be original contributions and should not be under consideration for any other publication at the same time.

Submissions should be sent to the Editor:
Dr. A. Ross Thomas, PO Box 1201, Armidale, New South Wales 2350, Australia.

Editorial Objectives

The *Journal of Educational Administration* is for all interested in the practice and theory of educational administration worldwide. It is designed to meet the needs of principals, inspectors, superintendents and directors of education, and of university teachers and students of educational administration.

In seeking to advance thinking in the field, the editor believes that there is no aspect of education more deserving of disciplined study and research than the administrative process, on which the efficacy of the teaching-learning process so much depends, and that this will best be achieved through an international approach to the field. The editor is prepared to consider for publication articles of interest to practising administrators and to students of administration in any country. Articles in the theory and practice of educational administration will be welcomed, but preference will be given to reports of research projects in the area.

The Reviewing Process

Each paper submitted to the *Journal of Educational Administration* is subject to the following review procedures:
1.   It is reviewed by the editor for general suitability for this publication.
2.   If it is judged suitable at least three reviewers are selected, each from a different country, to carry out a blind review of the manuscript.
3.   Based on the recommendations of the reviewers, the Editor then decides whether the particular article should be accepted as it is, revised or rejected.

The process described above is the normal procedure followed. The editor, however, may, in some circumstances, vary this process.

Article Features and Formats Required of Authors

Linkage to the literature is essential in papers submitted for publication. To enable authors to carry out a comprehensive literature search, free access, via the Internet, to Anbar Management Intelligence is available for a trial period of 30 days. Anbar Management Intelligence provides on-line access to more than 420 of the world's leading management journals, has an archive going back to 1989 and is updated monthly. Please go to http://www.anbar.co.uk/anbar.htm for access.

There are also a number of specific requirements with regard to article features and formats which authors should note carefully:

1. **Word Length.** Articles should be between 3,000 and 6,000 words in length.

2. **Methodology.** In papers reporting upon surveys and case studies, methodology should be clearly described under a separate heading. Particularly for survey-based articles full details should be given, i.e. type and size of sample, data instruments used including, for mailed surveys, the final percentage response and the treatment of bias.

3. **Title.** A title, ideally, of not more than eight words in length should be provided.

4. **Autobiographical Note.** A brief autobiographical note should be supplied including full name, appointment, name of organization and e-mail address.

5. **Word Processing.** Please submit to the Editor three copies of the manuscript in double line spacing with wide margins.

6. **Headings and Sub-Headings.** These should be short and to-the-point, appearing approximately every 750 words. Headings should be typed in capitals and underlined;

subheadings should be typed in upper and lower case and underlined. Headings should not be numbered.

7. **References**. References to other publications should be in Harvard style. They should contain full bibliographical details and journal titles should not be abbreviated. For multiple citations in the same year use a, b, c immediately following the year of publication. References should be shown as follows:

Within the text - author's last name followed by a comma and year of publication all in round brackets, e.g. (Fox, 1994) at the end of the article a reference list in alphabetical order as follows:
    a.   for books
surname, initials, year of publication, title, publisher, place of publication, e.g. Casson, M. (1979), Alternatives to the Multinational Enterprise, Macmillan, London.
    b.   for chapter in edited book
surname, initials, year, "title", editor's surname, initials, title, publisher, place, pages, e.g. Bessley, M. and Wilson, P. (1984), "Public policy and small firms in Britain", in Levicki, C. (Ed.), Small Business Theory and Policy, Croom Helm, London, pp. 111-26. Please note that the chapter title must be underlined.
    c.   for articles
surname, initials, year "title", journal, volume, number, pages, e.g. Fox, S. (1994) "Empowerment as a catalyst for change: an example from the food industry", Supply Chain Management, Vol 2 No 3, pp. 29-33.

If there is more than one author list surnames followed by initials. All authors should be shown.

Electronic sources should include the URL of the electronic site at which they may be found.

Notes/Endnotes should be used only if absolutely necessary. They should be identified in the text by consecutive numbers enclosed in square brackets and listed at the end of the article.

8. **Figures, Charts, Diagrams.** Use of figures, charts and diagrams should be kept to a minimum and information conveyed in such a manner should instead be described in text form. Essential figures, charts and diagrams should be referred to as figures and numbered consecutively using Arabic numerals. Each figure should have a brief title and labelled axes. Diagrams should be kept as simple as possible and avoid unnecessary capitalization and shading. In the text, the position of the figure should be shown by typing on a separate line the words "take in Figure 1".

9. **Tables.** Use of tables should be kept to a minimum. Where essential, these should be typed on a separate sheet of paper an numbered consecutively and independently of any figures included in the article. Each table should have a number in roman numerals, a brief title, and vertical and horizontal headings. In the text, the position of the table should be shown by typing on a separate Line the words "take in Table I". Tables should not repeat data available elsewhere in the paper.

10. **Photos, Illustrations**. Half-tone illustrations should be restricted in number to the minimum necessary. Good glossy bromide prints should accompany the manuscripts but not be attached to manuscript pages. Illustrations unsuitable for reproduction, e.g. computer screen capture will not be used. Any computer programs should be supplied as clear and sharp print-outs on plain paper. They will be reproduced photographically to avoid errors.

11. **Emphasis.** Words to be emphasized should be limited in number and italicized. Capital letters should be used only at the start of sentences or in the case of proper names.

12. **Abstracts**. Authors must supply an abstract of 100-150 words when submitting an article. It should be an abbreviated, accurate representation of the content of the article. Major results, conclusions and/or recommendations should be given, followed by supporting details of method, scope or purpose. It should contain sufficient information to enable readers to decide whether they should obtain and read the entire article.

13. **Keywords**. Up to six keywords should be included which encapsulate the principal subjects covered by the article. Minor facets of an article should not be key worded. These keywords will be used by readers to select the material they wish to read and should therefore be truly representative of the article's main content.

Preparation For Publication
14. **Final Submission of the Article**. Once accepted by the Editor for publication, the final version of the article should be submitted in manuscript accompanied by a 3.5" disk of the same version of the article marked with: disk format; author names(s); title of article; journal title; file name. This will be considered to be the definitive version of the article and the author should ensure that it is complete, grammatically correct and without spelling or typographical errors. In preparing the disk, please use one of the following formats:
- for text prepared on a PC - AMI Pro, FrameMaker, Office Writer, Professional write, RTF, Word or WordPerfect
- for text prepared on a macintosh system - FrameMaker, MacWrite, MS Works, Nisus 3, RTF, Word, WordPerfect, WriteNow or ASCII
- for graphics, figures, charts and diagrams, please use one of the following formats:

File Type	Programs	File Extension
Windows Metafile	Most Windows	.wmf
WordPerfect Graphic	All WordPerfect	.wpg
Adobe Illustrator	Adobe Illustrator	.ai
	Corel Draw	
	Macromedia Freehand	
Harvard Graphics	Harvard Graphics	.cgm
PIC	Lotus graphics	.pic
Computer/Graphics Metafile	Lotus Freelance	.cgm
DXF	Autocad	.dxf
	Many CAD	
GEM	Ventura Publisher	.gem
Macintosh PICT	Most Macintosh Drawing	

Only "vector" type drawings are acceptable, as bitmap files (extension .bmp, .pcx or .gif) print poorly. If graphical representations are not available on disk, black ink line drawings suitable for photographic reproduction and of dimensions appropriate for reproduction on a journal page should be supplied with the article.

If you require technical assistance in respect of submitting an article please consult the relevant section of MCB's World Wide Web Literati club on http://www.mcb.co.uk/Literati/nethome.htm or contact Mike Massey at MCB, e-mail mmasseyamcb.co.uk.

15. **Journal Article Record Form.** Each article should be accompanied by a completed and signed Journal Article Record Form. This form is available from the Editor or can be downloaded from MCB's World Wide Web Literati Club on http://222.mcb.co.uk/Literati/nethome.htm

Copyright
Authors submitting articles for publication warrant that the work is not an infringement of any existing copyright and will indemnify the publisher against any breach of such warranty. For ease of dissemination and to ensure proper policing of use, papers and contributions become the legal copyright of the publisher unless otherwise agreed.

Journal homepage
Copyright MCB University Press
cperry@mcb.co.uk

Journal of Educational and Behavioral Statistics (JEBS)

ADDRESS FOR SUBMISSION:

Larry Hedges, Editor
Journal of Educational and Behavioral
    Statistics (JEBS)
University of Chicago
Department of Education
5835 S Kimbark Avenue
Chicago, IL 60637
USA
Phone: 773-702-1587
Fax: 773-702-0248
E-Mail: jebs@uchicago.edu
Web:
Address May Change:

PUBLICATION GUIDELINES:

Manuscript Length: Any length <50
Copies Required: Four
Computer Submission: No
Format: N/A
Fees to Review: 0.00 US$

Manuscript Style:
    American Psychological Association

CIRCULATION DATA:

Reader: Academics
Frequency of Issue: Quarterly
Copies per Issue: 2,001 - 3,000
Sponsor/Publisher: Amer. Educational
    Research Assn., Amer. Statistical Assn.
Subscribe Price: 55.00 US$ Individual
    65.00 US$ Institution
    20.00 US$ ASA Member

REVIEW INFORMATION:

Type of Review: Blind Review
No. of External Reviewers: 2
No. of In House Reviewers: 1
Acceptance Rate: 21-30%
Time to Review: 4 - 6 Months
Reviewers Comments: Yes
Invited Articles: 0-5%
Fees to Publish: 0.00 US$

MANUSCRIPT TOPICS:
Educational Statistics; Tests, Measurement & Evaluation

MANUSCRIPT GUIDELINES/COMMENTS:

The *Journal of Educational And Behavioral Statistics* is a quarterly publication sponsored by the American Statistical Association and the American Educational Research Association. Members of these societies may subscribe at special rates.

Journal of Educational And Behavioral Statistics (JEBS) provides an outlet for papers demonstrating, preferably through concrete example, how the educational statistician can contribute to sound, productive, and creative educational decision-making and practice. The goal of authors seeking to publish in *JEBS* should be to communicate to the readers why, when, and how a statistical method should be used. Typically, papers will present new methods of analysis or new applications of better know methods. It is hoped that the journal will thus serve as a source from which educational statisticians can learn of the latest developments in their profession from those who are able to demonstrate the usefulness of these new methods. Additionally, it is the aim of the *Journal* to serve as a link between substantively oriented educators, who have need of new statistical techniques to solve their problems, and mathematical statisticians, who can benefit from having new mathematical problems on which to work with the expectation that this linkage would provide an enrichment of the accomplishments of both groups. The educational statistician is seen as the link between the two groups, defining mathematical problems for the mathematical statistician and obtaining practical solutions for the substantive worker, either through new applications of old methods or through the development of new methods. Thus a journal article is generally expected to contain an application to a nontrivial data set as part of the paper. (Monte Carlo studies are obvious exceptions, but the objects of the study should already have established practicality.) The journal also welcomes papers which demonstrate the need for new or more powerful techniques by showing the shortcomings of currently accepted techniques when dealing with commonly encountered data sets.

Send all manuscripts (four copies) to Jan de Leeuw, Editor, JEBS, Department of Mathematics, Math Sciences Building, Room 8118, UCLA, Los Angeles, CA 90024-1554. Manuscripts must be typed double spaced and should include an abstract of 100 to 150 words.

Instructions for Contributors
Because of the nature of JEBS and how it is being typeset, there are some author guidelines which need to be followed for marking the manuscript before it is sent to the Central Office for copyediting. The final manuscript should follow *APA Style*, except for the variations below. If followed, there will be no confusion on the copy editor or the typesetter's part, and author's alterations should be reduced.

1. Do not mark symbols and variables for italic (i.e., do not underline). The typesetter automatically programs these for italic and does not need them marked.
   Exceptions: (1) when a letter like "a" is used as a variable, but might be mistaken for a word, it should be marked for italic. (2) Every occurrence of italic "O" should be marked. This exception is based on the premise that the compositor is instructed to set all circles, near circles, and "O's" as zero unless marked for italic or a mathematical symbol.
2. All vectors and matrices should be marked with the accepted wavy line underneath, indicating boldface.
3. Greek letters need not be marked if they are typewritten or handwritten legibly.
   Exceptions: The Greek letters epsilon, capital sigma, and capital pi should be underlined every time they occur. If they are not underlined, typesetters will set them as the special symbols: is a member of, summation, and product, respectively.
4. Be consistent.
5. Always supply camera-ready copy for figures; key words; author's bio at the end.

General Information for Contributors to AERA Journals

Specifications for Manuscripts
The preferred style guide for most AERA journals is the *Publication Manual of the American Psychological Association,* 5th ed., 2001 (available from order Department, American Psychological Association, P.O. Box 2710, Hyattsville, MD 20784). The *Chicago Manual of*

Style, 14th ed., 1993, is also acceptable for all AERA journals, and it is the preferred style guide for the Social and Institutional Analysis section of AERJ.

Manuscripts should be typed on 8 ½ X 11-inch white paper, upper and lower case, double spaced in entirety, with 1-inch margins on all sides. The type size should be at least 10 pitch (CPI) or 12 point. Subheads should be at reasonable intervals to break the monotony of lengthy text. Only words to be set in italics (according to the rules of the style manual) should be underlined; sentence structure should be used to create emphasis. Words should not be typed in italic or bold fonts. Abbreviations and acronyms should be spelled out at first mention unless they are found as entries in their abbreviated form in *Webster's Tenth Collegiate Dictionary* (e.g., IQ needs no explanation). Pages should be numbered consecutively, beginning with the page after the title page. Mathematical symbols and Greek letters should be clearly marked to indicate italics, boldface, superscript, and subscript.

Requirements for Computer Disks

Whenever possible, a 3 ½ -inch computer disk should be sent to the editor once and article has been accepted (the disk may accompany the manuscript for book reviews). The computer file must contain all revisions and must agree with the final version of the manuscript. We prefer a file in WordPerfect 3.0 for Macintosh, but can convert from WordPerfect 6.0 as well as RFT, Microsoft Word for Macintosh, and ASCII. We cannot process tables or figures on disk.

It would be most helpful if you would use the following practices in typing your manuscript on disk.

1. Continue to follow the *APA Manual* to differentiate among subhead levels; the managing editor will convert these to the proper codes.
2. Do not use bold or italics anywhere. Use underlining to indicate italics in   either text or references.
3. Begin each paragraph with a tab, not the spacebar.
4. In text, use hard returns only at the ends of paragraphs, heads, and subheads. Do not use hard returns in block quotations.
5. Despite the instructions in the *APA Manual*, do not use indents or margins changes in the References. Just type straight copy and use one hard return at the end of each entry.
6. Type only one space after a period or other punctuation.
7. We prefer to have footnotes typed in as normal text at the end of the text section of the manuscript rather than as part of the footnote or endnote feature of a computer program.

Author Identification

The complete title of the article and the author(s) should be typed only on the first sheet to ensure anonymity in the review process. Subsequent pages should have no author names, but may carry a short title at the top. Information in text or references that would identify the author should be deleted from the manuscript (e.g., text citations of "my previous work," especially when accompanied by a self-citation; a preponderance of the author's own work in the reference list). These may be reinserted in the final draft. The first named author or the co-author who will be handling correspondence with the editor, clearing valley ?roofs, and working with the Association's Publications Department should submit a complete address and contact telephone number.

Footnotes and References
Footnotes are explanations or amplifications of textual material. Because footnotes are distracting to readers and expensive to set, the information should be incorporated into the text whenever possible. When they must occur, they should be typed on a separate sheet (to be inserted at the end of the manuscript before tables and figures). Footnotes must be numbered consecutively throughout the article.

The accuracy and completeness of all references are the responsibility of the author(s). A reference list should contain only those references that are cited in the text. Examples of references to a book, a chapter in a book, and a journal article follow.

Garner, R. (1987). *Metacognition and Reading Comprehension*. New York: Ablex.

Tatsuoka, M., & Silver, P. (1988). quantitative research methods in educational administration. In N. J. Boyan (Ed.), *Handbook of Research on Educational Administration* (pp. 677-701). New York: Longman.

Tyack. D. B., & Hansot, (1988). Silence and policy talk: Historical puzzles about gender and education. *Educational Researcher*, 17(3), 33-41.

Reference notes referring to material that is not readily available to the public (e.g., reports of limited circulation, unpublished works, personal communications, papers presented at meetings, some technical reports, and works in progress) should include as much information as possible to make them retrievable.

Tables, Figures and Illustrations
The purpose of tables and figures is to present data to the reader in a clear and unambiguous manner. The author should not describe the data in the text in such detail that either illustrations or the text is redundant.

Figures and tables should be keyed to the text. They should be typed on a separate sheet and attached at the end of the manuscript (after the refcrences). Tables will be typeset.

Figure captions should also be typed on a scparate sheet (and should not appear in full on the original figures). One high-quality, camera-ready version of each figure must be submitted with the manuscript that is to be typeset, and photocopies may be submitted with the additional copies of the manuscript.

Review Process
Manuscripts will be acknowledged by the editor upon receipt. After preliminary editorial review, articles will be sent to reviewers whose area of expertise conforms to the subject of the article.

The review process takes anywhere from 6 weeks to 3 months, depending on the individual journal. Authors should expect to hear from editors within that time regarding the status of their manuscript.

AERA publications have traditionally used the blind review system. The names of referees are published in the journals periodically.

Originality of Manuscript

Manuscripts are accepted for consideration with the understanding that they are original material and are not under consideration for publication elsewhere.

Copyright

To protect the words of authors and the Association, AERA copyrights all of its publications. Rights and permissions regarding the uses of AERA-copyrighted materials are handled by the AERA Publications Department. Authors who wish to use material, such as figures or tables, for which they do not own the copyright must obtain written permission from the copyright holder (usually the publisher) and submit it to AERA with their manuscripts.

Grievances

Authors who believe that their manuscripts were not reviewed in a careful or timely manner and in accordance with the American Educational Research Association's procedures should call the matter to the attention of the Association's President or Executive Officer.

Comments

The Publications committee welcomes comments and suggestions from authors. Please send these to the Publications Committee in care of the AERA central office.

Right of Reply

The right of reply policy encourages comments on articles recently published in an AERA Publication. Such comments are subject to editorial review and decision. If the comment is accepted for publication, the editor shall inform the author of the original article. If the author submits a reply to the comment, the reply is also subject to editorial review and decision. The editor may allot a specific amount of journal space for the comment (ordinarily about 1,500 words) and for the reply (ordinarily about 750 words). The reply may appear in the same issue as the comment or in a later one.

Journal of Educational and Psychological Consultation

ADDRESS FOR SUBMISSION:

Emilia C. Lopez, Editor
Journal of Educational and Psychological
    Consultation
Queens College - CUNY
Educational & Community Programs
65-30 Kissena Blvd.
Flushing, NY 11367
USA
Phone: 718-997-5234
Fax: 718-997-5248
E-Mail: lopez@cedx.com
Web: www.erlbaum.com
Address May Change:

PUBLICATION GUIDELINES:

Manuscript Length: 26-30+
Copies Required: Five
Computer Submission: No
Format: N/A
Fees to Review: 0.00 US$

Manuscript Style:
    American Psychological Association

CIRCULATION DATA:

Reader: Practicing Teachers, Academics,
    Counselors, Educational Psychologists
Frequency of Issue: 4 Times/Year
Copies per Issue: Less than 1,000
Sponsor/Publisher: Lawrence Erlbaum
    Associates
Subscribe Price: 45.00 US$ Individual
    380.00 US$ Institution
    40.50 US$ Electronic

REVIEW INFORMATION:

Type of Review: Blind Review
No. of External Reviewers: 3
No. of In House Reviewers: 3
Acceptance Rate: 21-30%
Time to Review: 2 - 3 Months
Reviewers Comments: Yes
Invited Articles: 0-5%
Fees to Publish: 0.00 US$

MANUSCRIPT TOPICS:
Consultation Training; Counseling & Personnel Services; Individual, Group, and
Organizational Consultation

MANUSCRIPT GUIDELINES/COMMENTS:

Editorial Scope
The *Journal of Educational and Psychological Consultation (JEPC)* provides a forum for
improving the scientific understanding of consultation and for describing practical strategies
to increase the effectiveness and efficiency of consultation services. Consultation is broadly
defined as a process that facilitates problem solving for individuals, groups, and organizations.
JEPC publishes articles and special thematic issues that describe formal research, evaluate
practice, examine the program implementation process, review relevant literature, investigate
systems change, discuss salient issues, and carefully document the translation of theory into
practice. Examples of topics of interest include individual, group, and organizational
consultation; collaboration; community-school-family partnerships; consultation training;
educational reform; ethics and professional issues; health promotion; personnel preparation;

preferral interventions; prevention; program planning, implementation, and evaluation; school to work transitions; services coordination; systems change; and teaming. Of interest are manuscripts that address consultation issues relevant to clients of all age groups, from infancy to adulthood. Manuscripts that investigate and examine how culture, language, gender, race, ethnicity, religion, and exceptionality influence the process, content, and outcome of consultation are encouraged. *JEPC* publishes empirical investigations as well as qualitative studies that use methodologies such as case studies and ethnography. In addition to publishing research and theoretical articles, *JEPC* publishes three special columns. The Book and Material Reviews Column features reviews of books and other professional materials (e-g., software programs, training modules) relevant to the process of consultation. The Consultant's Corner column provides a forum for papers that explore new ideas or discuss content areas that arc of interest to consultants. The Diversity Column features articles that examine the process of consultation within the context of human diversity. Prospective authors are encouraged to contact the Editor by phone at 718-997-5234 or via email at. lopez@cedx.com to discuss suggestions for manuscript and special issues, as well as questions regarding the appropriateness of papers for *JECP* .

Guidelines for Authors

Manuscripts should be prepared according to the *Publication Manual of the American Psychological Association* (5th edition). Type all components of the manuscript double-spaced, including title page, abstract, text quotes, acknowledgments, references, appendices, tables, figure captions, and footnotes. The abstract should be 100-150 words in length. A dot matrix or unusual typeface is acceptable only if it is clear and legible. To enable authors to address their topics comprehensively, manuscript of up to 35 pages of text (excluding references, tables, and figures) will be considered. Articles for the Book and Material Reviews, Consultant's Corner, and Diversity Columns should be a maximum of 15 double-spaced pages. Authors of empirical treatment studies are asked to include information regarding the quality of the implementation process and about intervention fidelity. Papers describing qualitative investigations should carefully document procedures for data collection and data analyses. Authors are expected to discuss the practical significance of their findings using effect size indicators and/or narrative analyses. Manuscripts must address implications for the practice of consultation by a broad, interdisciplinary audience. The content should be original and should not have been published (in whole or part) in any other journal or source.

Guidelines. For Special Issues Proposals

JEPC will publish one: or two guest-edited special issues each year. At least two-thirds of the journal space in a special issue will he devoted to articles that have been solicited to be part of a thematic discussion on topics of importance to practitioners, researchers, and/or trainers in the field of educational and psychological consultation. Because the procedure for submitting a special issue proposal is different than unsolicited manuscripts, the following information is provided as a guideline to assist individuals who are interested in developing a special issue.

Purpose of Special Issues. A special issue is designed to provide cohesive and comprehensive coverage of a given topic. The special issue should reflect a conceptual framework that underlies the various articles and attempts to address important questions related to the topic under discussion. One of the primary purposes of a special issue is to offer readers of *JEPC* a means of accessing and thinking about issues that may be occurring in areas important to educational and psychological consultation but in related disciplines such as school psychology and special education. The special issue can also serve as a forum for timely discussion of issues that have direct impact on the field of educational and psychological consultation. By using a thematic approach to presenting information, *JEPC* can offer a source for readers for synthesizing large bodies of research and practice.

Guest Editors. Given that the selection of topics for a special issue rests primarily with the *JEPC* Editor and Associate Editor for Special Issues, prospective guest editors should consult with the Associate Editor for Special Issues early in the process of developing a special issue. The Guest Editor will be responsible for the following: submitting the special issue proposal to the *JEPC* Associate Editor for Special Issues, communicating with the Associate Editor for Special Issues, coordinating the. work of contributing authors, supervising the reviews of submitted papers, summarizing reviewer comments and sharing those with contributing authors and the Associate Editor for Special Issues, submitting the reviewed/revised papers to the Associate Editor for Special Issues, communicating information from the Associate Editor for Special Issues and the Editor to contributing authors, and submitting the final product to the Associate Editor for Special Issues.

Submission of Proposal. The.- proposal should begin with an introductory statement that develops a rationale, need, and objectives for the special issue. Within this information, the proposal should provide a link to current literature and/or policy, providing a clear statement on the conceptual framework within which the special issue will be written. The introduction should also indicate the importance and potential impact of the special issue to the practice of educational and psychological consultation. After the introduction, each specific article should be identified by title and authors), along with a brief biography of the author(s) and a Summary of the content. Incorporated within the articles for the special issue, there should be one introductory article that provides a description for the theme and the content of the special issue as well as a summary and/or reaction article. Guest editors should limit their contributions to one article beyond the introductory and reaction articles. The description of the articles in the special issue should be brief but contain enough detail to allow reviewers to clearly understand the contents of each article. The guest editor will be responsible for identifying multiple reviewers for the papers in the special issue. 'The names and brief biographies of each reviewer should be included in the proposal. After the article summaries and biographies, there should be a proposed timeline for completion of the special issue. The following steps should be considered in the development of the timeline: date for submission of special issue proposal, one month for review of proposal by *JEPC* editors, author submission of articles to guest editor, review of articles by guest editor and blind reviewers, author revisions based on review, two months for *JEPC*(-review, revisions based on *JEPC* review, final draft of entire special issue. As an addendum to the proposal, brief vita(e) of guest editor(s) should be attached.

Submission of Proposals for Special Issues. A total of-5 copies of the proposal and vitae should be sent to: Kathleen C. Harris, Ph.D., *JEPC* Associate Editor for Special Issues, College of Education, Arizona State University West, 4701 W. Thunderbird Road, P.0. Box 37100, Phoenix, A7. 85069-7100 (602-543-6339) (Kathlecn.Harris@asu.cdu).

Review Process for Special Issues Proposals. The Editor, the Associate Editor for Special Issues, and additional Associate Editors, when necessary, review special issue proposals. Proposals arc examined in terms of interest to the journal readership, organization and coverage o f the topic, qualifications of the guest editor(s), qualifications of the potential contributors, and qualifications of blind reviewers. Once the special issue proposal is accepted, the *JEPC* Editor and Associate Editor for Special Issues will negotiate the anticipated publication date with the guest editor.

Manuscript Submission

1n a cover letter, authors should state that they have complied with APA ethical standards in the treatment of their subjects, and that the manuscript has not been previously published and is not simultaneously being submitted to another journal. 1'o facilitate anonymous review by members of the Editorial Board, each copy of the manuscript should include a separate title page with authors' names, affiliations, and an introductory footnote with the mailing address of the corresponding author. This information should not appear anywhere else in the manuscript. It is the authors' responsibility to make every effort to see that the manuscript itself contains no clue as to their identities. Authors should supply their addresses; phone and fax numbers; and electronic mail addresses for potential use by the editorial and production offices.

Submission Of Research And Theoretical Articles. Five copies of each manuscript should be submitted on good duality paper to Emilia C.. Lopez; Fditor; Queens College, CUNY; Educational arid Community Programs; 65-:30 Kissena Blvd., Flushing, NY 11367; 718-997-5234; lopez@cedx,com; Fax: 718-997-5248.

Submission Of Special Issues. The total page limit of the special issue should be 120 manuscript pages, following *APA* style. The guest editor is responsible for working closely with the *JEPC* Associate Editor for Special Issues toward completion of the issue. Adhering to negotiated timelines is critical for successful completion of the special issue. Five copies of each article in the special issue and 5 copies of a brief biography for each author should be submitted to Kathleen C. Harris, Ph.D., *JEPC* Associate Editor for Special Issues, College of Education, Arizona State University West, 4701 W. Thunderbird Road, P.O. Box 37100, Phoenix, AZ 85069-7100; 602-543-6339; Kathleen.Harris@asu.cdu; Fax: 602-543-6350.

Submission Of Manuscripts To The Book And Material Reviews Column. Three copies of each review should be submitted on good quality paper to Clyde Crego, Ph.D.; *JEPC*; Associate Editor for the Book and Material Reviews Column; 2.26 Brotman Hall; California State University-Long Beach; Long Beach, CA 90840; 562-985-4001; ccrego@csulb.edu; Fax: 562-985-8817.

Submission Of Manuscripts To The Consultant's Corner Column. Three copies of each manuscript should be submitted on good quality paper to Margaret R. Rogers, Ph.D.; Associate Editor for the Consultant's Corner Column; Psychology Department; University of Rhode Island; Woodward 16; Kingston, RI 02881; 401-874-7999; mrogres@uri.edu; Fax: 401-874-2157.

Submission Of Manuscripts To The Diversity Column. Three copies of each manuscript should be submitted on good quality paper to Mary Henning-Stout, Ph.D.; Associate Editor for the Diversity Column; MSG 86, Counseling Psychology; Lewis & Clark College; Portland, OR 97219; 503-768-6069; henning@lclark.edu; Fax: 503-768-6065.

Review Policy
All manuscripts submitted for consideration as regular articles are mask reviewed. Reviews typically arc completed within 3 months of submission, with the revision process (as needed) taking additional time.

Permissions
Authors are responsible for all statements made in their work and for obtaining permission from copyright owners to reprint or adapt a table or figure or to reprint a quotation of 500 words or more. Authors should write to original author(s) and publisher(s) to request nonexclusive world rights in all languages to use the material in the article arid in future editions. Copies of all permissions and credit lines obtained must be provided prior to publication.

Publication Policy
Authors of research reports are expected to have available their data throughout the editorial review process and for 5 years following publication.

Production Notes
After a manuscript is accepted for publication, its author .is asked to provide a computer disk containing the manuscript file. Files are copyedited and typeset into page proofs. Authors read proofs to correct errors and answer editors' queries. Authors receive a complementary copy of the issue in which their article appears, and they may order reprints of their articles only when they receive page proofs.

Journal of Educational Measurement

ADDRESS FOR SUBMISSION:

Barbara G. Dodd, Editor
Journal of Educational Measurement
University of Texas at Austin
Department of Educational Psychology
SZB 504
Austin, TX 78712-1296
USA
Phone: 512-471-4155
Fax: 512-471-1288
E-Mail: bg.dodd@mail.utexas.edu
Web:
Address May Change:

PUBLICATION GUIDELINES:

Manuscript Length: 11-25
Copies Required: Three
Computer Submission: No
Format: N/A
Fees to Review: 0.00 US$

Manuscript Style:
    American Psychological Association

CIRCULATION DATA:

Reader: Academics
Frequency of Issue: Quarterly
Copies per Issue: 3,001 - 4,000
Sponsor/Publisher: National Council on
    Measurement in Education
Subscribe Price: 45.00 US$ Individual
    50.00 US$ Institution

REVIEW INFORMATION:

Type of Review: N/A
No. of External Reviewers: 2
No. of In House Reviewers: 0
Acceptance Rate: 11-20%
Time to Review: 2 - 3 Months
Reviewers Comments: Yes
Invited Articles: 0-5%
Fees to Publish: 0.00 US$

MANUSCRIPT TOPICS:
Tests, Measurement & Evaluation

MANUSCRIPT GUIDELINES/COMMENTS:

The *Journal of Educational Measurement* seeks manuscripts containing generalizable contributions to educational measurement. In keeping with the purposes of NCME, preferred topics are those likely to be of interest to persons concerned with the practice of measurement in field settings as well as measurement theorists. In addition to presenting new contributions to measurement theory, *JEM* is a vehicle for the improvement of measurement application in a variety of educational settings, especially the public and nonpublic schools. When considering prospective audiences for manuscripts submitted to *JEM*, authors should keep these objectives in mind.

The types of manuscripts sought for *JEM* include reports of research on measurement processes, techniques, tools, and procedures; generalizable procedures for reporting and interpreting measurement results; scholarly expositions on measurement practice or the philosophy of measurement; and reports on novel and generalizable use of educational measurement in education or related disciplines

Submitted manuscripts within the broad domain of educational measurement will be reviewed for the accuracy of their designs, analyses and interpretations; their appropriateness for an audience of educational measurement practitioners and theorists; the significance and generalizability of their contributions; and the novelty of their content.

Certain types of manuscripts are unlikely to be published in JEM. These include: 1. Manuscripts with a focus outside the domain of educational measurement (e.g., manuscripts that describe the development or routine evaluation of new curricula); 2. Manuscripts that deal principally with new statistical methods, except as these clearly pertain to educational measurement theory and practice; 3. Manuscripts more suitable for a journal addressed to an exclusive audience of measurement theorists; 4. Manuscripts that report routine investigations of the psychometric adequacy of specific measurement instruments; 5. Manuscripts concerned with psychological rather than educational measurement; and 6. Manuscripts that describe computer programs.

Manuscript Submission And Procedure

All material submitted for publication should conform to the style of the *Publication Manual of the American Psychological Association* (5th ed., 2000), obtainable from the American Psychological Association, 1200 17th Street, NW, Washington, DC 20036. Note that in this style the year of publication directly follows the author's name in the reference list.

Three copies of each manuscript must be submitted, two of which are prepared for the "blind" review procedure by the removal of references to the author and the author's institution. Each manuscript must be accompanied by an abstract of 100-150 words and a suggested running head. The first text page of the article should have the complete title, but no list of the authors. Subsequent pages should carry only a running head.

Manuscripts should be typed, double spaced, with ample margins. Subheadings should be used at reasonable intervals to aid the reader's comprehension and break the monotony of lengthy texts. Only words to be italicized should be underlined. Abbreviations and acronyms not easily recognized by the average reader should be explained. All pages should be numbered consecutively.

Manuscripts are accepted for consideration with the understanding that they are original material and are not currently being considered for publication elsewhere. The latest issue of JEM contains the name and address of the person to whom manuscripts should be submitted.

Review Procedures

Each manuscript submitted to *JEM* will be screened for consistency with the editorial policies of the journal. If found to be appropriate for *JEM*, manuscripts will be sent, with author identification removed, to at least two qualified reviewers. Upon receiving the recommendations of reviewers, the editor will report a decision to the author, including reasons for the decision and the comments of reviewers. The review process typically takes two to three months, but exceptional cases may require more or less time.

Final Manuscripts
The tables and figures to be published aye reproduced photographically from camera-ready copy provided by the author. Final versions of accepted manuscripts must include originals or glossy prints of all figures and tables prepared in *APA style*. All figures should be drawn in black ink, one to

New Instruments Section
This section of *JEM* contains reports on the development and psychometric properties of measurement instruments that are new and unavailable commercially. Articles usually will be limited to three journal pages (about six double-spaced typed pages). They should contain a description of the intended use of the instrument, a brief review of the development process, information on the psychometric quality of the instrument, and supporting technical material. Articles for this section will be reviewed for the completeness with which they describe the instrument and its purposes, the quality of the instrument and its availability, the quality and completeness of the evidence presented in support of the psychometric quality of the instrument, and its potential usefulness to practitioners and researchers.

For purposes of the review process, unsolicited manuscripts submitted for the "New Instruments" section should be accompanied by three copies of the instrument and three copies of a longer, more detailed description of development and analysis procedures and results. Additional materials submitted for review purposes should be concise and of publication quality, but may be of any length and in any internally consistent style.

Review Section
Reviews are included in *JEM* to provide up-to-date information about the content and quality of new publications in the field of educational measurement. Reviews of all publications and materials, including software, are expected to be both descriptive and evaluative in character. They are intended primarily, although not exclusively, for readers who make practical use of measurement in various kinds of educational settings.

The policy of *JEM* is to publish only solicited reviews. Two reviews of the same publication will occasionally be included. Insofar as feasible, authors will be invited to respond to reviews that are critical of their works.

The Review Editor will welcome suggestions regarding particular publications or types of publications for which reviews would be most helpful.

Comments
Comments on technical or substantive issues addressed in articles or reviews previously published in *JEM* are encouraged. Comments will be reviewed and the author of the original article will be invited to respond.

Journal of Educational Psychology

ADDRESS FOR SUBMISSION:

Karen R. Harris, Editor
Journal of Educational Psychology
University of Maryland
Department of Special Education
Benjamin Building
College Park, MD 20742
USA
Phone: 301-405-6515
Fax:
E-Mail: kh9@umail.umd.edu
Web: www.apa.org/journals/edu.html
Address May Change:

PUBLICATION GUIDELINES:

Manuscript Length: 10-40 Typically
Copies Required: Five
Computer Submission: No
Format: N/A
Fees to Review: 0.00 US$

Manuscript Style:
American Psychological Association

CIRCULATION DATA:

Reader: Academics
Frequency of Issue: Quarterly
Copies per Issue: 5,001 - 10,000
Sponsor/Publisher: American Psychological
    Association
Subscribe Price: 102.00 US$ Individual
    194.00 US$ Institution
    51.00 US$ APA Member

REVIEW INFORMATION:

Type of Review: Blind Review
No. of External Reviewers: 2
No. of In House Reviewers: 1
Acceptance Rate: 11-20%
Time to Review: 2 - 3 Months
Reviewers Comments: Yes
Invited Articles: 0-5%
Fees to Publish: 0.00 US$

MANUSCRIPT TOPICS:

Curriculum Studies; Educational Psychology; Elementary/Early Childhood; Foreign Language; Gifted Children; Reading; Science Math & Environment; Secondary/Adolescent Studies; Special Education; Tests, Measurement & Evaluation

MANUSCRIPT GUIDELINES/COMMENTS:

Editorial. What can one rightfully expect from a journal called the *Journal of Educational Psychology?* The *Journal* is receptive to educational-psychological research stemming from a wide variety of methodological and statistical approaches, assuming that such approaches are applied with care and precision. Yes we have much quantitative research; we have some qualitative analyses as well. In short, we welcome methodological approaches and data analyses of all kinds, as long as supportable conclusions logically follow from the application of the procedure. Substantively, we are soliciting interesting, informative, and innovative primary research studies that focus on psychological processes associated with the process of education. In seeking such pieces, we regard the overall quality of the research as one of the most important criteria for inclusion.

Because the *Journal* no longer has a separate category of Brief Reports, manuscript length per se is not a consideration for acceptance. Rather, length should be related to the manuscript's "information value". For example, the development of a theoretical position, with accompanying data in a series of experiments, might easily exceed 40 manuscript pages, whereas a single, tightly conducted, and concisely reported study might require fewer than 10 manuscript pages. The author should be the initial manuscript-length judge; our reviewers may ultimately help the author decide.

Instructions to Authors. Authors should prepare manuscripts according to the *Publication Manual of the American Psychological Association* (5th ed.). All manuscripts must include an abstract containing a maximum of 960 characters and spaces (which is approximately 120 words) typed on a separate sheet of paper. Typing instructions (all copy must be double-spaced) and instructions on preparing tables, figures, references, metrics, and abstracts appear in the Publication Manual. All manuscripts are subject to editing for sexist language. Manuscript length per se is not an issue, although length should be related to the manuscript's "information value."

APA policy prohibits an author from submitting the same manuscript for concurrent consideration by two or more journals. *APA* policy also prohibits duplicate publication, that is, publication of a manuscript that has already been published in whole or in substantial part elsewhere. Prior and duplicate publication constitutes unethical behavior, and authors have an obligation to consult journal editors if there is any chance or question that the paper might not be suitable for publication in an APA journal. Authors of manuscripts submitted to *APA* journals are expected to have available their raw data throughout the editorial review process and for at least 5 years after the date of publication. Authors will be required to state in writing that they have complied with APA ethical standards in the treatment of their sample, human or animal, or to describe the details of treatment. (A copy of the APA Ethical Principles may be obtained from the APA Ethics Office, 750 First Street. NE, Washington, DC 20002-4242.)

Because the *Journal* has an anonymous review policy, authors submitting manuscripts are requested to include with each copy of the manuscript a cover sheet that shows the title of the manuscript, the authors' names and institutional affiliations, the date the manuscript is submitted, and footnotes identifying the authors or their affiliations. The first page of the manuscript should omit the authors' names and affiliations but should include the title of the manuscript and the date it is submitted. Every effort should be made by the authors to see that the manuscript itself contains no clues to their identities.

Authors should submit five (5) copies of the manuscript. All copies should be clear, readable, and on paper of good quality. A dot matrix or unusual typeface is acceptable only if it is clear and legible. Manuscripts not meeting readability and *APA Publication Manual* specifications will be returned for repair before being reviewed. Authors should keep a copy of the manuscript to guard against loss. To facilitate correspondence, authors (and especially those overseas) with an electronic mail address are encouraged to submit that address and FAX number with their manuscript. Mail manuscripts to the Editor.

Journal of Employment Counseling

ADDRESS FOR SUBMISSION:

Norman Amundson, Editor
Journal of Employment Counseling
University of British Columbia
Faculty of Education
Van Couver, BC V6T 1Z4
Canada
Phone: 604-822-6757
Fax: 604-822-2328
E-Mail: amundson@unixg.ubc.ca
Web:
Address May Change:

PUBLICATION GUIDELINES:

Manuscript Length: 11-15
Copies Required: Three
Computer Submission: No
Format: N/A
Fees to Review: 0.00 US$

Manuscript Style:
    American Psychological Association

CIRCULATION DATA:

Reader: , Employment Counselors
Frequency of Issue: Quarterly
Copies per Issue: 3,001 - 4,000
Sponsor/Publisher:
Subscribe Price: 11.00 US$ Individual
    5.00 US$ Member

REVIEW INFORMATION:

Type of Review: Blind Review
No. of External Reviewers: 2
No. of In House Reviewers: 2
Acceptance Rate: 50%
Time to Review: 2 - 3 Months
Reviewers Comments: Yes
Invited Articles: 0-5%
Fees to Publish: 0.00 US$

MANUSCRIPT TOPICS:
Adult Career & Vocational; Counseling & Personnel Services; Curriculum Studies

MANUSCRIPT GUIDELINES/COMMENTS:

The *Journal of Employment Counseling* invites articles of interest to readers. If you wish to contribute to the *Journal*, follow these guidelines.

Edited copy is sent to the senior author of each article in the journal. Changes at this stage must be Limited to correcting inaccuracies and typographical errors. Authors must bear responsibility for the accuracy of references, tables, and figures.

Upon publication of an article, one complimentary copy is sent to all authors.

Send an original and two clean copies of all material. The original should be on good quality white bond: do not use colored, airmail, onionskin, erasable, or other nonstandard papers.

Double-space everything, including references and quotations. Allow wide margins.

Manuscripts should be well organized so the development of ideas is logical: try to write clearly, concisely, and interestingly. The reader should have no difficulty in following the writer's development of ideas. A good reference is "Getting into Print in P & G: How It's Done," by Judy Wall, *The Personnel And Guidance Journal*, Vol. 52, No. 9, May 1974, pp. 594-602.

The title of the article should appear on a separate page accompanying the manuscript. Include on this page the names of authors followed by a paragraph that repeats the names of authors and gives the institutional affiliation of each.

Include an abstract as a separate page. The abstract should clearly summarize the main idea of the manuscript (100 120 words). If it is a research article, reference should be made to method, results, and conclusions.

Also include a 25-word abstract with your manuscript.

Note that we do not use the generic masculine pronoun or other sexist terminology.

Article titles and headings within the article should be as short as possible.

Avoid footnotes wherever possible. Use the *APA style* of referencing instead.

Check all references for completeness: adequate information should be given to allow the reader to retrieve the referenced material from the most available source.

Tables should be kept to a minimum. Include only essential data, and combine tables wherever possible. Each table should be on a separate sheet of paper following the reference section of the article. Final placement of tables is at the discretion of the production editor: in all cases tables will be placed after the first reference to the table in the text.

Lengthy quotations (generally 300-500 cumulative words or more from one source) require written permission from the copyright holder for reproduction. Adaptation of tables and figure also requires reproduction approval from the copyrighted source. It is the author' responsibility to secure such permission, and a copy of the publisher's written permission must be provided the journal editor immediately upon acceptance of the article for publication by AACD.

Figures (graphs, illustrations, line drawings) should be checked for possible duplication of information in text or tabular presentation. Figures should be submitted as clean, camera-ready art.

References, tables, and figures should follow the style of the last Issue of the Journal or the *Publication Manual of the American Psychological Association*, Third Edition, 1983, which is available from APA Order Department, 1400 North Uhle St., Arlington, VA 22201.

Never submit material for concurrent consideration by another periodical.

Authors are required to provide an additional copy of submitted manuscripts (final version) on a computer diskette for final editing. This facilitates manuscript editing and production processing. This diskette should be labeled with the first author's name, and the manuscript should be in WordPerfect or an ASCII file on the diskette. The manuscript should be formatted to be read by an IBM PC. Diskettes will be returned to authors after processing.

Journal of English for Academic Purposes

ADDRESS FOR SUBMISSION:

Liz Hamp-Lyons, Editor
Journal of English for Academic Purposes
The Hong Kong Polytechnic University
Hung Hom
Kowloon,
Hong Kong
Phone: 852 2766 7544
Fax: 852 2333 6569
E-Mail: eglhl@polyu.edu.hk
Web: www.eslevier.com
Address May Change:

PUBLICATION GUIDELINES:

Manuscript Length: 21-25
Copies Required: Three
Computer Submission: No Disk
Format: MSWord
Fees to Review: 0.00 US$

Manuscript Style:
American Psychological Association

CIRCULATION DATA:

Reader: Academics
Frequency of Issue: 3 Times/Year
Copies per Issue: Less than 1,000
Sponsor/Publisher: Elsevier Science
Publishing Co.
Subscribe Price: 211.00 US$ Institution
189.00 US$ European Countries

REVIEW INFORMATION:

Type of Review: Blind Review
No. of External Reviewers: 2-3
No. of In House Reviewers: 0
Acceptance Rate: No Reply
Time to Review: 2 - 3 Months
Reviewers Comments: Yes
Invited Articles: 6-10%
Fees to Publish: 0.00 US$

MANUSCRIPT TOPICS:
Languages & Linguistics; Writing

MANUSCRIPT GUIDELINES/COMMENTS:

Description
The *Journal of English for Academic Purposes* provides a forum for dissemination of information and views which enables practitioners of and researchers in EAP to keep current with developments in their field and to contribute to its continued updating. *JEAP* publishes articles, book reviews, conference reports, and academic exchanges in the linguistic, sociolinguistic and psycholinguistic description of English as it occurs in the contexts of academic study and scholarly exchange itself. A wide range of linguistic, applied linguistic and educational topics may be treated from the perspective of English for academic purposes; these include: classroom language, teaching methodology, teacher education, assessment of language, needs analysis; materials development and evaluation, discourse analysis, acquisition studies in EAP contexts, research writing and speaking at all academic levels, the sociopolitics of English in academic uses and language planning.

Also of interest are review essays and reviews of research on topics important to EAP researchers. No worthy topic relevant to EAP is beyond the scope of the journal. The journal also carries reviews of scholarly books on topics of general interest to the profession.

Submission Requirements

Submission of a paper requires the assurance that the manuscript is an original work which has not been published previously and is not currently being considered for publication elsewhere. Article submissions should not normally exceed 20 pages excluding tables. Articles must be written in English and should be related to the teaching of English. Manuscript pages should be consecutively numbered in the upper right hand corner. All artwork must be suitable for publication and need no further work. Submit three copies of the manuscript, including all artwork, to one of the editors: Professor Liz Hamp-Lyons, Chair Professor of English, Director, Asian Centre for Language Assessment Research, The Hong Kong Polytechnic University, Hung Hom, Kowloon, Hong Kong or Dr. Ken Hyland, Department of English and Communication, City University of Hong Kong, Tat Chee Avenue Kowloon Tong, Hong Kong. On a separate sheet, please supply the senior author's telephone number, fax number, and e-mail address (if available), along with a brief biographical sketch (see below).

Receipt of manuscripts will be acknowledged, but they cannot be returned; therefore, authors should retain a copy of the paper exactly as it was submitted. Since page proofs cannot be sent to authors for last minute corrections, authors must proofread manuscripts carefully, giving special attention to the accuracy of quotations and references. Authors will receive 25 offprints of their own contributions. Writers of reviews will receive 10 offprints. If extra prints are desired, authors must request them with the offprint order form that the editorial office sends before publication of the journal.

All authors must sign the 'Transfer of Copyright' agreement before the article can be published. This transfer agreement enables Elsevier Science Ltd to protect the copyrighted material for the authors, but does not relinquish the author's proprietary rights. The copyright transfer covers the exclusive rights to reproduce and distribute the article, including reprints, photographic reproductions, microform or any other reproductions of similar nature and translations, and includes the right to adapt the article for use in conjunction with computer systems and programs, including reproduction or publication in machine-readable form and incorporation in retrieval systems. Authors are responsible for obtaining from the copyright holder permission to reproduce any figures for which copyright exists.

Style

Articles must be written in English and should be related to the teaching of English, Grammatical, lexical, and orthographic features may conform to either British or American norms. Citations may be given of lexical material from languages other than English; however, citations from languages not employing a Roman alphabet must be given in a Romanized transliteration or in a transcription which uses standard symbols available in the International Phonetic Alphabet.

References And Footnotes
In the text, references are cited using author's last name publication date (Wilkins 1976). If quotations are cited, these should additionally have page numbers (Wilkins 1976: 21-22). The reference list should be arranged in alphabetical order following the style sheet of the American Psychological Association and should appear on a separate page at the end of the article. The reference list should include only those items specifically cited in the body of the text. Generally speaking, comments and references should be incorporated into the text; but when necessary, footnotes should be typed at the bottom of the page on which the reference appears and should be set off from text with a horizontal line.

Abstracts
All articles should have abstracts which summarize the scope and purpose of the article and, if applicable, the results of the study. The abstracts should be between 100 and 200 words in length.

Keywords
Authors should provide up to six keywords, to appear just underneath the abstract. These keywords will be used to help provide efficient indexing, search and retrieval mechanisms as articles become available through electronic systems. As far as possible, keywords should conform to those used in LLBA (*Linguistics and Language Behaviour Abstracts*).

Tables And Figures
Certain numerical tables can be typeset. Other types of material (figures, graphs, illustrations, tables involving non horizontal matter or special symbols) cannot and must be submitted as camera-ready. Prepare each table, figure, graph or illustration on its own page and number all such material clearly. Make sure that the text refers to the figures and tables in consecutive order. Artwork that is not suitable for publication will be returned to the author with a request for better art. Footnotes to tables should be typed below the table and should be referred to by superscript lowercase letters. No vertical rules should be used. Tables should not duplicate results presented elsewhere in the manuscript, (e.g. in graphs).

Guidelines For Preparation of Manuscripts
1. Articles should be typed with double- spacing throughout and, in general, be no longer than 25 pages, including bibliographical references. Research Notes and Discussions should be no longer than 10 such pages.

2. Type on standard white bond paper (81/2 x 11 in.) or the closest possible equivalent. Type on only one side of the paper.

3. On a separate page, type the name, mailing address, e-mail address, home and work telephone and fax numbers of the senior author, and a brief biographical sketch of each author. Do not put the name(s) of the author(s) on any other pages. Skip two lines and type the title of the paper. Skip four lines and type the word "Abstract." Skip four lines from the end of the abstract and begin typing the text of the article.

4. On the author information sheet, provide a brief biographical sketch of the authors (maximum of 50 words per author). Include the professional affiliation, highlights of professional experience, and important publications.

Electronic Submission

Authors should submit an electronic copy of their paper with the final version of the manuscript. The electronic copy should match the hardcopy exactly. Always keep a backup copy of the electronic file for reference and safety. Full details of electronic submission and formats can be obtained from http://www.elsevier.com/locate/disksub and http://www.elsevier.com/locate/authorartwork and from Author Support at Elsevier Science.

Proofs

Proofs will be sent to the author (first named author if no corresponding author is identified of multi-authored papers) and should be returned within 48 hours of receipt. Corrections should be restricted to typesetting errors; any others may be charged to the author. Any queries should be answered in full. Please note that authors are urged to check their proofs carefully before return, since the inclusion of late corrections cannot be guaranteed. Proofs are to be returned to the Log-in Department, Elsevier Science Ltd, Stover Court, Bampfylde Street, Exeter EX1 2AH, UK.

Offprints

Additional offprints and copies of the issue can be ordered at a specially reduced rate using the order form sent to the corresponding author after the manuscript has been accepted. Orders for reprints (produced after publication of an article) will incur a 50% surcharge.

Copyright

All authors must sign the "Transfer of Copyright" agreement before the article can be published. This transfer agreement enables Elsevier Science Ltd to protect the copyrighted material for the authors, without the author relinquishing his/her proprietary rights. The copyright transfer covers the exclusive rights to reproduce and distribute the article, including reprints, photographic reproductions, microfilm or any other reproductions of a similar nature, and translations. It also includes the right to adapt the article for use in conjunction with computer systems and programs, including reproduction or publication in machine-readable form and incorporation in retrieval systems. Authors are responsible for obtaining from the copyright holder permission to reproduce any material for which copyright already exists.

Author Support

For queries relating to the general submission of manuscripts (including electronic text and artwork) and the status of accepted manuscripts, please contact Author Support at authorsupport@elsevier.ie. Authors can also keep track of the progress of their accepted article through our OASIS system on the Internet. For information on an article go to this Internet Page and key in the corresponding author's name and the Elsevier reference number.

Journal of Entrepreneurship Education

ADDRESS FOR SUBMISSION:

Editor's Name/Check Web Page
Journal of Entrepreneurship Education
Submission Address/Check Web Page
Address All Other Questions To:
Jim or Joann Carland,
USA
Phone: 828-293-9151
Fax: 828-293-9407
E-Mail: carland@wcu.edu
Web: www.alliedacademies.org
Address May Change:

PUBLICATION GUIDELINES:

Manuscript Length: 26-30
Copies Required: Four
Computer Submission: Yes
Format: MSWord or Wordperfect
Fees to Review: 0.00 US$

Manuscript Style:
American Psychological Association

CIRCULATION DATA:

Reader: Academics, Business People
Frequency of Issue: 2 Times/Year
Copies per Issue: 1,001 - 2,000
Sponsor/Publisher: Allied Academies
Subscribe Price: 50.00 US$

REVIEW INFORMATION:

Type of Review: Blind Review
No. of External Reviewers: 3
No. of In House Reviewers: 1
Acceptance Rate: 21-30%
Time to Review: 2 - 3 Months
Reviewers Comments: Yes
Invited Articles: 0-5%
Fees to Publish: 0.00 US$

MANUSCRIPT TOPICS:

Business Education Entrepreneurship; Curriculum Studies; Education
Management/Administration; Educational Psychology

MANUSCRIPT GUIDELINES/COMMENTS:

Editorial Policy Guidelines for Educational and Pedagogic Manuscripts

The Allied Academies affiliates which handle educational and pedagogic manuscripts include the Academy of Entrepreneurship, the Academy of Accounting and Financial Studies, the Academy of Marketing Studies, the Academy of Strategic and Organizational Leadership, the Academy of Managerial Communications, the Academy of Educational Leadership, the Academy of Information and Management Sciences, and, the Academy for Studies in Business Law. These editorial guidelines reflect the Academies' policy with regard to reviewing education and pedagogic manuscripts for publication and presentation in each of these affiliates.

The primary criterion upon which manuscripts are judged is whether the research advances the teaching profession. The specific guidelines followed by referees show the areas of evaluation to which each manuscript is subjected. Key points include currency, interest, relevancy and usefulness to educators. In order for educational or pedagogic manuscripts to be useful to educators, they must address appropriate Literature to support conclusions, teaching methodologies or pedagogies. Consequently, referees pay particular attention to completeness of literature review and appropriateness of conclusions drawn from that review.

Pedagogies or teaching methodologies must be well described with sound foundations in order to be useful to educators. Referees will pay particular attention to such issues in judging manuscripts, documented ideas in order to be useful to educators. Referees will pay close attention to the ideas presented in the manuscript and how well they are presented and supported.

We ask referees to be as specific as possible in indicating what must be done to make a manuscript acceptable for journal publication. This embodies a primary objective of the Academy: to assist authors in the research process. Our editorial policy is one which is supportive, rather than critical. We encourage all authors who are not successful in a first attempt to rewrite the manuscript in accordance with the suggestions of the referees. We will be pleased to referee future versions and rewrites of manuscripts and work with authors in achieving their research goals.

Journal of Gerontology: Biological Sciences

ADDRESS FOR SUBMISSION:

John A. Falukner, Editor
Journal of Gerontology: Biological Sciences
University of Michigan
Institute of Gerontology
300 N. Ingalls, Room 964
Ann Arbor, MI 48109-2007
USA
Phone: 734-764-4378
Fax: 734-936-2116
E-Mail: jheibel@umich.edu
Web:
Address May Change: 12/31/01

PUBLICATION GUIDELINES:

Manuscript Length: No Reply
Copies Required: Two
Computer Submission: Yes
Format: MSWord, WordPerfect, pdf files
Fees to Review: 0.00 US$

Manuscript Style:
, AMA Style

CIRCULATION DATA:

Reader: Academics
Frequency of Issue: Monthly
Copies per Issue: 4,001 - 5,000
Sponsor/Publisher: Gerontology Society of
America
Subscribe Price: 195.00 US$ Individual
425.00 US$ Institution

REVIEW INFORMATION:

Type of Review: Editorial Review
No. of External Reviewers: 2-3
No. of In House Reviewers: 0-1
Acceptance Rate: 45%
Time to Review: 1-6 Months
Reviewers Comments: Yes
Invited Articles: 0-5%
Fees to Publish: 0.00 US$

MANUSCRIPT TOPICS:
Adult Career & Vocational; All Areas of Biogerontology

MANUSCRIPT GUIDELINES/COMMENTS:

The Journal Of Gerontology: Biological Sciences publishes articles on the biological aspects of aging in areas such as biochemistry, biodemography, cellular and molecular biology, comparative and evolutionary biology, endocrinology, exercise sciences, genetics, immunology, morphology, neuroscience, nutrition, pathology, pharmacology, physiology, vertebrate and invertebrate genetics, and biological underpinnings of late life diseases. All submissions are peer reviewed. Manuscripts should be directed to John A. Faulkner, Ph.D., Editor, Journal of Gerontology: Biological Sciences, Institute of Gerontology, University of Michigan, 300 N. Ingalls, Room 964, Ann Arbor, MI 48109-2007.

1. Submission and Acceptance of Manuscripts
Submission of a manuscript to the Journal implies that it has not been published or is not under consideration elsewhere. If accepted for this Journal, it is not to be published elsewhere without permission. As a further condition of publication, the corresponding author will be

responsible, where appropriate, for certifying that permission has been received to use copyrighted instruments or software employed in the research and that human or animal subjects approval has been obtained. In the case of co-authored manuscripts, the corresponding author will also be responsible for submitting a letter, signed by all authors, indicating that they actively participated in the collaborative work leading to the publication an agree to a listed as an author on the paper. These assurances will be requested at the time a paper has been formally accepted for publication.

2. Manuscript Preparation for Articles Describing Original Research

a. *Preparing the manuscript.* Print out paper double spaced, including references and tables, on 8-1/2" x 11" white paper using 1" margins. Number pages consecutively, beginning with the title page and including all pages of the submission. A total of four copies must be submitted. Conciseness of expression is imperative. The *Journal* follows the abbreviations and other conventions *American Medical Association (AMA) Manual of Style,* 8th ed. (1989), which is available at many academic and technical bookstores. A summary of some style aspects is presented below. Use of IBM-compatible software is encouraged to facilitate electronic typesetting, and a disk including the text, tables, and preferable all figures, must accompany the submission of the manuscript. An updated disk is required upon acceptance. Failure to comply with these aspects of submission will delay handling of the manuscript.

b. *Title page. A* title page should include the title of the manuscript and the author's full names) and affiliations. A short running page headline not to exceed 40 letters and spaces should be placed at the foot of the title page.

c. *Abstract.* An abstract of not more than 150 words should be typed, *double spaced,* on a separate page. It should state the purpose of the study, basic procedures (study participants or experimental animals and observational and analytical methods), main findings, and conclusions.

d. *Text.* The text of observational and experimental articles is usually (but not necessarily) divided into sections with the headings: Introduction, Method, Results, and Discussion. Articles may need subheadings within some sections to clarify their content. The Discussion should not merely restate the results but should interpret the results.

e. *Text references.* Number references in the text in the order in which they appear. Use arabic numbers in parentheses, *not superscripts. .*

f. *Reference list.* Type double-spaced. List references by number in the order in which they were first cited in the text. The reference style should conform to that given in the *AMA Manual of Style.* For periodicals, utilize the title observation as given in *Index Medicus* and list all authors when six or fewer; when seven or more, list only the first three and add et al. Examples are shown below.

Journal article
1. Milunsky A. Prenatal detection of neural tube defects, VI: experience with 20,000 pregnancies. JAMA. 1980; 244:2731-2735.

Books and other monographs
2. Stryer L. *Biochemistry.* 2nd ed. San Francisco, Calif: WH Freeman Co; 1981; 559-596.

Part of a book
3. Kavet J. Trends in the utilization of influenza vaccine: an examination of the implementation of public policy in the United States. In: Selby P, ed. *Influenza: Virus, Vaccines, and Strategy.* Orlando, Fla: Academic Press; 1976:297-308. Notations of "unpublished work" or "personal communications" will not be accepted without documentation.

g. *Acknowledgments.* Sources of research support, acknowledgments, preliminary reports or abstract presentation, and current location of authors, if different from the title page, may be indicated. Give name and mailing/E-mail addresses of author to whom correspondence should be addressed.

h. *Tables.* Each table should be typed, double-spaced, on a separate sheet. Number tables consecutively using Arabic numbers and supply a brief title at the top for each. Legends and footnotes for the table are typed immediately below the table and should follow the sequence cited in the AMA *Manual of Style:* *, †, ‡, §, ∥, ¶, ** ††, etc.

i. *Illustrations.* For a graph or drawing, one glossy or laser print and four photocopies must be included. If *photomicrographs* are submitted, five *glossy* prints should be supplied for review purposes. Color photos are published at the expense of the author. Sharp, glossy *prints are required for high-quality reproduction.* Figures must be professionally lettered in a sans-serif type (e.g., Univers or Helvetica) or from a laser printer. Typewritten/dot matrix lettering will not be acceptable. Letters should be of sufficient size that, when reduced for publication, they will be legible.

j. *Captions for tables and illustrations.* Type captions *double spaced* on a separate page with numbers corresponding to the illustrations. Explain symbols, arrows, numbers, or letters used in illustrations. Explain internal scale and identify staining method in photomicrographs. Captions for Tables and Illustrations should be adequate to interpret the content of the table or figure without reference to the text.

3. High-Priority Manuscripts
High-priority manuscripts are identified by the Editor or Deputy Editor and the appropriate Associate Editor as: (a) well written and requiring no/minimal revisions; (b) describing a well-designed experiment; and (c) pertaining to an important or topical subject. Such manuscripts will be processed within weeks and published within 3 months of acceptance. Manuscripts should be prepared as in Section 2.

4. Perspectives
Perspectives are usually invited by the Editor, although unsolicited Perspectives may be submitted for consideration. Perspectives are not comprehensive reviews; rather they are focused treatments of controversial or insightful issues of immediate concern. Manuscripts should be prepared as in Section 2.

5. Letters to the Editor

Letters must be typewritten, *double spaced,* approximately 500 to 750 words. Submit four copies. If appropriate, a copy will be sent to the author of the original article to provide an opportunity for rebuttal. Letters and rebuttals will be reviewed and are subject to editing. Usually both letter and rebuttal will be published in the same issue.

6. Guest Editorials

Guest editorials may be invited but unsolicited editorials may also be submitted. These should not exceed one printed page. Manuscript preparation should follow the guidelines of Section 2. The decision to publish will be exclusively the Editor's.

Journal of Gerontology: Psychological Sciences

ADDRESS FOR SUBMISSION:

Margie Lachman, Editor
Journal of Gerontology: Psychological
   Sciences
Brandeis University
Department of Psychology, MS 062
415 South Street
Waltham, MA 02454-9110
USA
Phone: 781-736-3295
Fax: 781-736-3296
E-Mail: jgerops@brandeis.edu
Web:
Address May Change:

PUBLICATION GUIDELINES:

Manuscript Length: 35
Copies Required: Four
Computer Submission: No
Format: N/A
Fees to Review: 0.00 US$

Manuscript Style:
   American Psychological Association

CIRCULATION DATA:

Reader: Practicing Teachers, Academics,
   Administrators
Frequency of Issue: Bi-Monthly
Copies per Issue: 5,001 - 10,000
Sponsor/Publisher: Gerontological Society
   of America
Subscribe Price: 62.00 US$ Individual
   95.00 US$ Institution

REVIEW INFORMATION:

Type of Review: Peer Review
No. of External Reviewers: 2
No. of In House Reviewers: 0
Acceptance Rate: 15%
Time to Review: 3-6 Months
Reviewers Comments: Yes
Invited Articles: Yes
Fees to Publish: 0.00 US$

MANUSCRIPT TOPICS:

Audiology/Speech Pathology; Curriculum Studies; Educational Psychology; Social
Psychology in Aging; Tests, Measurement & Evaluation

MANUSCRIPT GUIDELINES/COMMENTS:

The *Journal of Gerontology: Psychological Sciences* publishes articles on applied, clinical
and counseling, developmental, experimental, and social psychology of aging. Appropriate
topics include, but are not limited to, attitudes, cognition, educational gerontology, emotion,
health psychology, industrial gerontology, interpersonal relations, neuropsychology,
perception, personality, physiological psychology, psychometric tests, and sensation.
Manuscripts reporting work that relates behavioral aging to neighboring disciplines are also
appropriate. The Journal publishes four types of articles: 1) articles reporting original
research; 2) brief reports; 3) invited reviews and position papers; and 4) theoretical or
methodological contributions. All submissions are peer reviewed, with final decisions made
by the Editor. Manuscripts should be addressed to the Editor,

1. Submission and Acceptance of Manuscripts

Submission of a manuscript to the Journal implies that it has not been published or is not under consideration elsewhere. If accepted for this *Journal,* it is not to be published elsewhere without permission. As a further condition of publication, the corresponding author will be responsible, where appropriate, for certifying that permission has been received to use copyrighted instruments or software employed in the research and that human or animal subjects approval has been obtained. In the case of co-authored manuscripts, the corresponding author will also be responsible for submitting a letter, signed by all authors, indicating that they actively participated in the collaborative work leading to the publication and agree to be listed as an author on the paper. These assurances will be requested at the time a paper has been formally accepted for publication.

2. Manuscript Preparation

a. *Preparing the manuscript.* Print out paper double spaced, including references and tables on 8 1/2" x 11" white paper using at least 1" margins. Number pages consecutively, beginning with the title page. A total of four (4) complete copies including tables and figures must be submitted. Use of IBM-compatible software is encouraged to facilitate electronic typesetting, and a disk wilt be requested upon acceptance.

b. *Title Page.* A title page should include the title of the manuscript, the author's full name, and the author's institution. A short running head not to exceed 40 Letters and spaces should be placed at the foot of the title page.

c. *Abstract.* A one-paragraph abstract not exceeding 150 words should be typed, double spaced, on a separate page. The abstract should state the purpose of the study, basic procedures used (study participants or experimental animals and observational or analytical methods), principal findings, and conclusions.

d. *Text.* The text of observational and experimental articles is usually (but not necessarily) divided into major sections with headings such as Introduction, Methods, Results, and Discussion. Articles may require subheadings within sections to clarify their content. The discussion section may include conclusions derived from the study and supported by the data. White full exposition of a study is desirable, conciseness of expression is imperative. Sexist or ageist use of language should be avoided.

e. *Text References.* References in text are shown by citing in parentheses the author's surname and the year of publication. Example:". . . a recent study (Jones, 1987) has shown . . ." If a reference has two authors the citation includes the surnames of both authors each time the citation appears in the text. When a reference has more than two authors and fewer than six authors, cite all authors the first time the reference occurs; in subsequent citations, and for all citations having more than six authors, include only the surname of the first author followed by "et al." If more than one publication in the same year by a given author or multiple authors is cited, distinguish citations by adding, a, b, etc. to the year of publication. Example: ". . . a recent study (Jones, 19876) has shown . . ." Multiple references cited at the same point in the text are separated by semicolons and enclosed in one pair of parentheses. The order within one pair of parentheses is alphabetical by first author's surname or, if all by the same author, in sequence by year of publication. Examples: "Recent studies (Brown, 1986: Jones, 1982) have shown . . ." "Recent studies (Jones, 1985a, 19856). . ."

f. *Reference List*. Type double-spaced and arrange alphabetically by author's surname; do not number. The reference list includes only references cited in the text and in most cases should not exceed 25 entries. Do not include references to private communications. Consult the *Publication Manual of the American Psychological Association* for correct form.

g. *Footnotes*. A footnote related to the title, each author's affiliation and address, source of research support, and other acknowledgments should be placed on a separate page after the references. Please indicate where correspondence should be addressed. Reference footnotes should not be used.

h. *Tables*. Each table should be typed double spaced on a separate sheet. Tables should be numbered consecutively and have a brief title. Footnotes to a table are typed Immediately below the table. Table footnotes are referenced by superscript letters (a, b,c...) with footnotes arranged alphabetically by their superscripts. Asterisks are used only to indicate the probability levels of tests of significance.

i. *Illustrations*. Each figure must be arranged by the author. One glossy or laser print and three copies should be provided for each graph and drawing. Color photos are at the expense of the author. Sharp, laser printed or glossy prints are required for high-quality reproduction. Figures must be professionally lettered in a sans-serif type (e.g., Univers or Helvetica) or from a laser printer. Typewritten/dot matrix lettering is not acceptable. Letters should be of sufficient size that, when reduced for publication, they will be Legible.

j. *Captions for illustrations*. Type captions double spaced on a separate page with numbers corresponding to the illustrations. Captions should explain the scale used in the figure.

k. *Author Anonymity*. Anonymous review is available on request. Manuscripts, in this case, should be prepared to conceal the identity of the author(s). The cover page and footnotes that identify author(s) should be omitted from two copies of the manuscript. Manuscripts not prepared in this manner will receive open review.

l. Other than as specified above, manuscripts should be prepared according to the *Publications Manual of the American Psychological Association* (5th ed.), obtainable from APA, 750 First St. N.E., Washington, DC 20002-4242.

3. Brief Reports
Manuscripts (including references) must be no Longer than six (b) double spaced typewritten pages, including no more than one (1) table, graph, or illustration. Four (4) copies of the manuscript must be submitted.

4. Review Articles and Position Papers
These articles are solicited only by the editor.

5. Theoretical or Methodological Articles

Theoretical papers must include an integration and critical analysis of existing views in a specific area as well as proposed resolutions) of controversial positions. Methodological contributions should be supported with examples based upon empirical data if possible.

Journal of Gerontology: Social Sciences

ADDRESS FOR SUBMISSION:

Fredric D. Wolinsky, Editor
Journal of Gerontology: Social Sciences
Saint Louis University
School of Public Health
3663 Lindell Blvd., Room 408
St. Louis, MO 63108-3342
USA
Phone: 314-977-8101
Fax: 314-977-1658
E-Mail: wolinsky@slu.edu
Web: www.geron.org
Address May Change:

PUBLICATION GUIDELINES:

Manuscript Length: Up to 5,000 words
Copies Required: Five
Computer Submission: No
Format: N/A
Fees to Review: 0.00 US$

Manuscript Style:
    See Manuscript Guidelines

CIRCULATION DATA:

Reader: Academics
Frequency of Issue: Bi-Monthly
Copies per Issue: 5,001 - 10,000
Sponsor/Publisher: Gerontological Society
    of America
Subscribe Price: 62.00 US$ Individual
    95.00 US$ Institution

REVIEW INFORMATION:

Type of Review: Editorial Review
No. of External Reviewers: 3
No. of In House Reviewers: 1
Acceptance Rate: 28%
Time to Review: 2 Months
Reviewers Comments: Yes
Invited Articles: 0-5%
Fees to Publish: 0.00 US$

MANUSCRIPT TOPICS:
Gerontology; Social Studies/Social Science; Tests, Measurement & Evaluation

MANUSCRIPT GUIDELINES/COMMENTS:

The *Journal of Gerontology: Social Sciences* is a bimonthly journal of the Gerontological Society of America that publishes articles dealing with aging issues from the fields of anthropology, demography, economics, epidemiology, geography, health services research, political science, public health, social history, social work, and sociology. The Journal publishes five types of contributions: 1) articles reporting original research; 2) brief reports; 3) letters to the editor; 4) reviews; and 5) theoretical and methodological articles. All submissions are peer-reviewed, with the Editor making the final decision. All manuscripts should be addressed to the Editor.

1. Submission and Acceptance of Manuscripts
Manuscripts submitted to the *Journal* must be accompanied by a fully executed certifications page. The certifications page can be obtained from the GSA's website or from the editorial

office. Each author must read and sign the exclusive review, 'authorship, financial disclosure, copyright transfer, and data availability statements prior to manuscript submission.

Submission of a manuscript to the Journal implies that it has not been published or is not under consideration elsewhere. All authors must have participated sufficiently in the conception and design of the work, the analysis of the data, as well as the writing of the manuscript to take public responsibility for it. They must also have approved the manuscript for submission. Any affiliations with or involvement in any organization or entity with a financial interest in the subject matter or materials presented in the manuscript must be declared. All authors must agree to produce the data on which the manuscript is based for examination by the Editor or his assignees should they request it in order to document procedures, clarify controversies, or verify results. Upon acceptance of the manuscript for publication, copyright will be transferred to The Gerontological Society of America. If accepted for this Journal, the manuscript is no to be published elsewhere without permission. As a further condition of publication, the corresponding author will be responsible, where appropriate, for certifying that permission has been received to use copyrighted instruments or software employed in the research and that human or animal subjects approval has been obtained.

2. Manuscript Preparation for Articles Reporting Original Research

a. *Preparing The Manuscript*. The text of articles can normally range up to 5,000 words, if concisely expressed, with shorter texts welcome. Print out paper double spaced, including references and tables, on 8 1/2" x 111' white paper using 1" margins. Number pages consecutively, beginning with the title page and including all pages of the submission. A total of five (5) copies must be submitted. Use of IBM-compatible software is encouraged to facilitate electronic typesetting, and a disk will be requested upon acceptance.

b. *Title Page*. A title page should include the title of the manuscript and the full name and (with footnotes) affiliation of each author. A short running page headline not to exceed 40 letters and spaces should be placed at the foot of the title page.

c. *Author Anonymity*. Anonymous review is available upon request. Manuscripts should be prepared to conceal the identity of the author(s). The title page that identifies author(s) should be omitted from four copies of the manuscript. Manuscripts not prepared in this manner will not receive this type of review.

d. *Abstract*. A structured abstract of not more than 200 words should be typed, double spaced, on a separate page. It should have four sections: Objectives, Methods, Results, and Discussion.

e. *Text*. The text of articles is usually divided into sections with the headings: Introduction, Methods, Results, and Discussion. Articles may need subheadings within some sections to clarify their content. Do not use appendices.

f. *Text References*. References in the text are shown by citing in parentheses the authors surname and the year of publication. Example: 1'...a recent study (Jones, 1987) has shown..." If a reference has two authors the citation includes the surnames of both authors each time the

512

citation appears in the text. Example: "...c recent study (Jones R Brown,. 1988) has shown... " When a reference has more than two authors and fewer than six authors, cite all authors the first time the reference occurs; in subsequent citations, and for all citations having more than six authors, include only the surname of the first author followed by "et al." If more than one publication in the same year by a given author or multiple authors is cited, distinguish citations by adding, a, b, etc. to the year of publication. Example: "...A recent study (Jones, 1987b) has shown..." Multiple references cited at the same point in the text are separated by semicolons and enclosed in one pair of parentheses. The within one pair of parentheses is alphabetical by first author's surname or, if all are by the same author, in sequence by year of publication. Examples: "Recent studies (Brown, 1986; Jones, 1982) have shown..." "Recent studies (Jones, 1985a, 1985b)."

g. *Reference List*. Type double spaced and arrange alphabetically by author's surname; do not number. The reference list includes only references cited in the text. Do not include private communications. Consult the *Publication Manual of the American Psychological Association* for correct form.

h. *Footnotes and Acknowledgments*. Reference and content footnotes should not be used. Acknowledgments, including source of research support, should be placed on a separate page before the references. Please indicate where correspondence should be addressed; list E-mail address after the zip code.

i. *Tables*. Each table should be typed double-spaced on a separate sheet. Numbers tables consecutively and supply a brief title at the top for each. Footnotes to a table are typed immediately below the table. The reference marks are superscript small letters (a, b, c...) with the footnotes arranged alphabetically by their superscripts. Asterisks are used only for indicating the probability level of tests of significance. Indicate in the text the preferred placement for each table by noting [Table 1 about here].

j. *Illustrations*. Figures must be professionally lettered in a sans-serif type (e.g., Univers or Helvetica) or from a laser printer. Typewritten/dot matrix lettering will not be acceptable. Do not send original copy with a manuscript submitted for review. Include 5 photocopies of original or roughly drawn, legible draft. Upon acceptance of article, 2 original prints must be submitted. Type captions double spaced on a separate page.

k. Other than as specified above, manuscripts should be prepared according to the *Publication Manual Of The American Psychological Association* (5th ed.), obtainable from APA, 750 First Street, N.E., Washington, DC 20002-4242.

3. **Brief Reports**
Manuscripts (excluding references) must be no longer than 2,500 words, including no more than a total of two (2) tables, graphs, or illustrations. Five (5) copies of the manuscript must be submitted.

4. **Review Articles**
These articles are mainly solicited by the Editor.

5. Theoretical or Methodological Articles

Theoretical papers must include an integration and critical analysis of existing views in a specific area as well as proposed resolutions) of controversial positions. Methodological contributions should be supported wit examples based upon empirical data if possible.

Journal of Higher Education

ADDRESS FOR SUBMISSION:

Lee Mobley, Editor
Journal of Higher Education
Ohio State University Press
180 Pressey Hall
1070 Carmack Road
Columbus, OH 43210-1002
USA
Phone: 614-292-7700
Fax: 614-292-2065
E-Mail: baird.62@osu.edu
Web: www.ohiostatepress.org
Address May Change:

PUBLICATION GUIDELINES:

Manuscript Length: 25-30
Copies Required: Three
Computer Submission: Yes
Format: MSWord or WordPerfect
Fees to Review: 0.00 US$

Manuscript Style:
American Psychological Association

CIRCULATION DATA:

Reader: Administrators
Frequency of Issue: Bi-Monthly
Copies per Issue: 4,001 - 5,000
Sponsor/Publisher: The Ohio State
    University Press
Subscribe Price: 42.00 US$ Individual
    90.00 US$ Institution
    28.00 US$ Student

REVIEW INFORMATION:

Type of Review: Blind Review
No. of External Reviewers: 2
No. of In House Reviewers: 0
Acceptance Rate: 6-10%
Time to Review: 2 - 3 Months
Reviewers Comments: Yes
Invited Articles: 0-5%
Fees to Publish: 0.00 US$

MANUSCRIPT TOPICS:

Adult Career & Vocational; Counseling & Personnel Services; Curriculum Studies; Education Management/Administration; Educational Psychology; Higher Education

MANUSCRIPT GUIDELINES/COMMENTS:

Manuscript Submission

Manuscripts, which should meet the criteria outlined in the Editorial Policy, should be mailed - in triplicate - to: Leonard L. Baird, Editor, The Journal of Higher Education, The Ohio State University Press, 1070 Carmack Road, Columbus, OH 43210-1002, USA.

Style

The *Journal of Higher Education* has adopted as its official guide, *Publication Manual of the American Psychological Association*, Fifth Edition, and all manuscripts should be, brought into conformity with this guide before they are submitted, Papers should be typed, double-spaced, on white 8 1/2 x 11 inch paper, with wide margins. An abstract of fifty words or less, summarizing the main points of the article, should accompany the manuscript. Since the Journals readers represent a variety of professional interests, it is recommended that any statistical material be presented as briefly and simply as possible. Although each paper submitted should deal with the methodology employed in addressing the subject in sufficient detail to place the data within the proper methodological setting, the editors of the journal are not primarily interested in papers setting forth practices of research methods (an acquaintance with fundamental procedures of scholarly analysis being assumed on the part of the reader) except for those papers that develop innovative methodological approaches. Illustrations should be of professional quality and ready for production. They should be executed on white Paper or vellum in black ink, and should be capable of legible reduction to a size no larger than 4 1/2 x 7 inches (full page) and preferably no larger than 4 1/2 x 3 1/2 inches (half page). All illustrations should be accompanied by typed captions. Authors should employ a Reference List format to list bibliographic data. Endnotes should be reserved for supplementary comment and typed on a separate page at the end of the manuscript.

Manuscript Length
Manuscripts approximately 25-30 pages of double-spaced typescript are strongly preferred, The editors will consider somewhat longer papers on occasion.

Review Process
Those unsolicited manuscripts that are refereed are reviewed "blind." Authors are thus requested to submit their name, professional position, and institution on a removable cover sheet. They should also mask any items of self-reference where they appear. Authors must not submit the manuscript of any article that is still under consideration by another publisher.

Editorial Reaction
Papers will be returned to authors soon after submission if they fail to meet by a wide margin the basic criteria for selection. Otherwise, authors may expect to receive some notification within two months. If an article is accepted, it will usually appear in print within twelve months after acceptance. If an article which has been subjected to a full review is rejected, the opinions of the referees will be transmitted to the author.

Criteria For Selection
Papers are evaluated on the following points: Form: writing style and readability: logical development; appropriate length; appropriateness of author's stated objectives to treatment as defined below. Content: significance to *JHE* readers. Additional criteria are based upon the following manuscript orientations: as a research paper, as a technical paper, as a professional practice paper, as a literature review, and as a policy paper. It should be emphasized that the editors respond most favorably to manuscripts that evidence both a freshness of vision and a vitality that may be informed by, but certainly go beyond, methodological qualities, and that are in congruence with our publishing goals and directions. The most effective approach in learning about our interests is to read previous issues of the journal. We expect that authors, the journal, and the field will develop through the publication process.

Journal of Higher Education Policy & Management

ADDRESS FOR SUBMISSION:

Ian Dobson & Angel Calderon, Editors
Journal of Higher Education Policy &
   Management
Monash University
PO Box 8001
Victoria, 3168
Australia
Phone: +61 3 9905 5860; +61 4 1951 4232
Fax: +61 3 9905 1010
E-Mail: ian.dobson@adm.monash.edu.au
Web: www.tandf.co.uk/journals
Address May Change:

PUBLICATION GUIDELINES:

Manuscript Length: 5,000 words
Copies Required: One
Computer Submission: Yes , Preferred
Format: MSWord
Fees to Review: 0.00 US$

Manuscript Style:
   Chicago Manual of Style

CIRCULATION DATA:

Reader: Administrators
Frequency of Issue: 2 Times/Year
Copies per Issue: 3,001 - 4,000
Sponsor/Publisher: Carfax Publishing
   (Taylor & Francis)
Subscribe Price: 81.00 US$ Individual
   243.00 US$ Institution
   48.00 Pounds Indv., 147 Pounds Inst.

REVIEW INFORMATION:

Type of Review: Editorial Review
No. of External Reviewers: 3
No. of In House Reviewers: 2
Acceptance Rate: No Reply
Time to Review: 1 - 2 Months
Reviewers Comments: Yes
Invited Articles: 10%
Fees to Publish: 0.00 US$

MANUSCRIPT TOPICS:
Education Management/Administration; Higher Education

MANUSCRIPT GUIDELINES/COMMENTS:

Ian R. Dobson, Editor, Monash University, Australia. Email: (see below).
Angel J. Calderon, Editor RMIT, Australia. Email: angel.calderon@rmit.edu.au

Aims and Scope
The Journal of Higher Education Policy and Management is an international, peer-reviewed journal of professional experience and ideas in post-secondary education. It supports higher education managers by disseminating ideas, analyses and reports of professional experience relevant to colleagues internationally.

The journal caters for practising managers and administrators of universities, colleges and vocational education and training institutes. It attracts the interest of, and contributions from, vice chancellors, presidents, vice presidents, directors, registrars, business managers and deans. It is also read by, and frequently publishes papers by, middle level managers and academic staff who seek to place their work and interests in a broad context.

Journal of Higher Education Policy and Management is the journal of Association for Tertiary Education (http:// www.atem.org.au) Management and is the leading journal in its field in Australasia.

Instructions for Authors

The *Journal of Higher Education Policy and Management* welcomes contributions. *JHE* prefers papers to be no longer than 5000 words. *JHE* also invites short comments, reports and book reviews. The editors are happy to discuss with authors initial ideas and to review preliminary outlines and drafts of possible contributions.

Contributors should bear in mind that they are addressing an international audience.

Submission of papers and books for review.

Contributions are preferred by email (ian.dobson@adm.monash.edu.au) or on disk. Editorial correspondence should be addressed to:

The Editors
Journal of Higher Education Policy and Management
PO Box 8001
Monash University
Victoria 3168
Australia

References and style. *JHE* uses British spelling conventions.

References should be indicated in the text in this form:

A distinctive feature of higher education in the first world in the later part of the twentieth century is that is has become mass if not universal (Trow, 1974) but Karmel (1993, p. 2) has shown that in Australia at least increased participation has not necessarily resulted in increased access, particularly for disadvantaged groups.

If more than one paper by the same author in the same year are cited, a, b, c, etc., should be put after the year of publication. The references should be listed in full at the end of the paper in this standard form:

For books: MARTIN, L. M. (1994) *Equity and General Performance Indicators in Higher Education*. Canberra: Australian Government Publishing Service.

For articles: BAKER, E. L. & O'NEIL, H. F. Jr. (1994) Performance assessment and equity: a view from the USA, *Assessment in Education*, 1, pp. 11-26.

For chapters: STIMPSON, C. R. (1990) Knowing women, in: D. R. JONES & S. L. DAVIES (Eds) *Women in Higher Education: an agenda for the decade*. Armidale: University of New England.

Titles of journals should not be abbreviated. Footnotes to the text should be avoided where this is reasonably possible.

Figures will not normally be re-drawn by the publisher. Please supply one set of artwork in finished form suitable for reproduction.

Proofs will not normally be sent to authors.

Copyright. Papers accepted become the copyright of the *Journal* unless otherwise specifically agreed.

Offprints. Fifty offprints of each paper, together with a complete copy of the relevant issue, are supplied free. Additional copies may be purchased from the publisher.

Journal of Instructional Psychology

ADDRESS FOR SUBMISSION:

George E. Uhlig, Editor
Journal of Instructional Psychology
PO Box 8826, Spring Hill Station
Mobile, AL 36608
USA
Phone: 334-343-1878
Fax: 334-343-1878
E-Mail: guhlig007@yahoo.com
Web: journals825.home.mindspring.com
Address May Change:

PUBLICATION GUIDELINES:

Manuscript Length: 11-15
Copies Required: Two
Computer Submission: Yes Disk + 1
    Hardcopy
Format: Mac
Fees to Review: 0.00 US$

Manuscript Style:
    American Psychological Association

CIRCULATION DATA:

Reader: Academics
Frequency of Issue: Quarterly
Copies per Issue: Less than 1,000
Sponsor/Publisher:
Subscribe Price: 40.00 US$ Institution
    60.00 US$ Foreign

REVIEW INFORMATION:

Type of Review: Editorial Review
No. of External Reviewers: 1
No. of In House Reviewers: 1
Acceptance Rate: 50%
Time to Review: 1 - 2 Months
Reviewers Comments: Yes
Invited Articles: 0-5%
Fees to Publish: 30.00 US$

MANUSCRIPT TOPICS:
Counseling & Personnel Services; Education Management/Administration; Educational Psychology; Educational Technology Systems; Elementary/Early Childhood; Gifted Children; Higher Education; Science Math & Environment; Secondary/Adolescent Studies; Social Studies/Social Science; Teacher Education; Tests, Measurement & Evaluation; Urban Education, Cultural/Non-Traditional

MANUSCRIPT GUIDELINES/COMMENTS:

Journal of Instructional Psychology publishes original articles dealing with issues related to instruction and educational management and gives preferences to manuscripts focusing on bilingual and multicultural issues, at risk youth, and educational technology.

Manuscript Submission
Manuscripts must be submitted in duplicate and should be prepared to conform to the style and procedures described in the *Publication Manual of the American Psychological Association.* Manuscripts must be accompanied by an abstract of 100 to 200 words typed on a separate sheet of paper. The abstract should contain statements of the (a) problem, (b) method, (c) results, and (d) conclusions when appropriate. The abstract should provide the reader with an idea of the theme and scope of the article.

At least one copy of the manuscript and the abstract must be original with clear, clean typing or printing. We prefer disk-based manuscripts in either Macintosh or MS-DOS format. However, at least one printed copy of the manuscript must be included with the disk.

Review Process

Manuscripts are reviewed by at least two reviewers knowledgeable in the field of study. An attempt is made to review manuscripts within two weeks of receipt when possible.

Fees To Publish

This journal is not supported by either membership or association dues, or advertising. Authors or their institutions share the cost of publication. Except for invited articles, authors will be invoiced for their share of publication costs at the time the manuscript is accepted for publication. The article will be scheduled for publication after payment or an institutional purchase order is received.

Reprints

Information concerning reprints and reprint policy is disseminated with page proofs/galleys.

Journal of Interactive Learning Research

ADDRESS FOR SUBMISSION:

Gary Marks, Editor
Journal of Interactive Learning Research
c/o Joe McDonald
ONLINE SUBMISSIONS ONLY
AACE
PO Box 3728
Norfolk, VA 23514-3728
USA
Phone: 757-623-7588 ext 232
Fax: 703-997-8760
E-Mail: pubs@aace.org
Web: www.aace.org/pubs/submit.org
Address May Change:

PUBLICATION GUIDELINES:

Manuscript Length: Max/30 pages
Copies Required: No paper copy
Computer Submission: Yes Online
   Submission
Format: MS Word, html or rtf
Fees to Review: 0.00 US$

Manuscript Style:
   See Manuscript Guidelines

CIRCULATION DATA:

Reader: Academics, Corporate Researchers
Frequency of Issue: Quarterly
Copies per Issue: 1,001 - 2,000
Sponsor/Publisher: AACE - Assn. For the
   Advancement of Computers in Education
Subscribe Price: 85.00 US$ Individual
   120.00 US$ Institution

REVIEW INFORMATION:

Type of Review: Blind Review
No. of External Reviewers: 2-4
No. of In House Reviewers: 2
Acceptance Rate: 11-20%
Time to Review: 1 - 2 Months
Reviewers Comments: Yes
Invited Articles: 31-50%
Fees to Publish: 0.00 US$

MANUSCRIPT TOPICS:
Educational Technology Systems; Higher Education; Secondary/Adolescent Studies

MANUSCRIPT GUIDELINES/COMMENTS:

The *Journal of Interactive Learning Research (JILR)* publishes papers related to the underlying theory, design, implementation, effectiveness, and impact on education and training of the following interactive learning environments:

authoring systems, cognitive tools for learning computer-assisted language learning, computer-based assessment systems, computer-based training, computer-mediated communications, computer-supported collaborative learning, distributed learning environments, electronic performance support systems, interactive learning environments, interactive multimedia systems, interactive simulations and games, intelligent agents on the Internet, intelligent tutoring systems, microworlds, virtual reality based learning systems.

Guidelines

Publishing policy and selection of articles are governed by the editorial objectives of AACE, by each Journal's content, and by the general guidelines that follow.

Please only send all submissions electronically via the **Journal Submissions Form** found on the journal website.

Editorial Objectives

AACE publications have the overall objective to advance the knowledge, theory, and quality of teaching and learning at all levels with computing technologies. The international readership of each Journal is multidisciplinary and includes professors, researchers, classroom teachers, developers, teacher educators, and administrators.

Editorial objectives are to:

- Serve as a forum to report the interdisciplinary research, development, integration, and applications of computing in education.
- Contribute toward the professional development of all who seek in-depth yet practical knowledge about the important research results, latest developments and applications of teaching and learning with computers.
- Present articles of interest on educational computing problems.
- Provide creative ideas, practical strategies, and experiences on instruction with computers.
- Offer information on various aspects of computer literacy for educators.
- Provide information on new computer materials, methods of use, and evaluative criteria.

General Guidelines

Material must be original, scientifically accurate, and in good form editorially. The manuscript should be informative, summarizing the basic facts and conclusions, and maintaining a coherence and unity of thought.

Tutorial or how-to-do-it articles should preferably include a section on evaluation. Controversial topics should be treated in a factually sound and reasonably unbiased manner.

The format of headings, tables, figures, citations, references, and other details should follow the *(APA)* style as described in the *Publication Manual of the American Psychological Association* available from *APA*, 750 1st St., NE, Washington, DC 20002 USA.

Preview

Manuscripts sent to the Editor for review are accepted on a voluntary basis from authors. Before submitting an article, please review the following suggestions. Manuscripts received in correct form serve to expedite the processing and prompt reviewing for early publication.

Spelling, punctuation, sentence structure, and the mechanical elements of arrangements, spacing, length, and consistency of usage in form and descriptions should be studied before submission. Due to the academic focus of AACE publications, the use of personal pronoun (I, we, etc.) and present tense is strongly discouraged.

Pre-publication
No manuscript will be considered which has already been published or is being considered by another journal. Authors should include a statement with their letter that the manuscript has not been published and is not under consideration elsewhere.

Copyright
These journals are copyrighted by the Association for the Advancement of Computing in Education. Material published and so copyrighted may not be published elsewhere without the written permission of the AACE.

Author Note(s)
Financial support for work reported or a grant under which a study was made should be noted just prior to the Acknowledgments. Acknowledgments or appreciation to individuals for assistance with the manuscript or with the material reported should be included as a note to appear at the end of the article prior to the References.

Handling of Manuscripts
All manuscripts are acknowledged upon receipt. Review is carried out as promptly as possible. The manuscript will be reviewed by at least two members of the Editorial Review Board, which takes usually no more than two months. When a decision for publication or rejection is made, the senior author or author designated to receive correspondence is notified. At the time of notification, the author may be asked to make certain revisions in the manuscript, or the Editor may submit suggested revisions to the author for approval.

Presentation
Accepted Submission File Formats - All submissions must be sent in electronic form using the Article Submission Form. **No hard copy submission papers will be accepted.** A format which best preserves the "document look" is preferred. Do NOT submit compressed files. Do not use any word processing options/tools, such as--strike through, hidden text, comments, merges, and so forth.

Submit your manuscript in either of the following formats:
* **WORD** - Microsoft Word (preferred)
* **RTF** - Rich Text Format
* **HTML**

Manuscripts should be double-spaced and a font size of 12 is preferred. All graphics should be embedded in the file in the correct location of the paper. Do not send separate graphic files or compressed files.

Length - In general, articles should not exceed 30 double-spaced pages. Long articles, or articles containing complex material should be broken up by short, meaningful subheads.

Title sheet - Do NOT include a title sheet. Manuscripts are blind reviewed so there should be no indication of the author(s) name on the pages.

524

Abstract - An informative, comprehensive abstract of 75 to 200 words must accompany the manuscript. This abstract should succinctly summarize the major points of the paper, and the author's summary and/or conclusions.

Citations

Citations should strictly follow *American Psychological Association (APA)* style guide. Examples of references cited within the texts of articles are as follows: (Williams, Allen, & Jones, 1978) or (Moore, 1990; Smith, 1991) or Terrell (1977). In citations, et al., can only be used after all authors have been cited or referenced. As per *APA* all citations must match the reference list and vice versa. Over use of references is discouraged.

Quotations

Quoted material of more than two lines should be set in a narrower width than the remainder of the text but continue to double space. At the close of the quotation, give the complete source including page numbers. Copy all quoted material exactly as it appears in the original, indicating any omissions by three spaced periods.

A block quote must be a minimum of 40 words or four lines, single spaced (not 20 and double spaced as is presently noted).

Tables and Figures

All tables and figure graphics must be embedded within the file and of such quality that when printed be in camera-ready form (publication quality). Within the submitted file, number and type captions centered at the top of each table. Figures are labeled at the bottom of the figure, left justified, and numbered in sequence.

Terminology and Abbreviations

Define any words or phrases that cannot be found in Webster's Unabridged Dictionary. Define or explain new or highly technical terminology. Write out the first use of a term that you expect to use subsequently in abbreviated form. Abbreviations (i.e., e.g., etc.) are only acceptable in parenthesis, otherwise they must be spelled out, that is, for example, and so forth, respectively. Please avoid other foreign phrases and words such as via.

Mathematics

Math or other formulas'/codes/programs/text tables, should be submitted as graphics (jpeg, gif, tiff, png), graphics should be embedded in the file where they are to appear. (Do not send separate files.) Graphics, tables, figures, photos, and so forth, must be sized to fit a 6 x 9 publication with margins of: top, 1," inside 1," outside, .75," and bottom, 1," an overall measurement of 4 ½ X 6 ¾ is the absolute limit in size. A table or figure sized on a full size 8 ½ by 11 piece of paper does not always reduce and remain legible. Please adhere to the size stipulation or your manuscript will be returned for graphics/figure's or tables to be re-done.

Program Listings

Program listings will appear with the published article if space permits. Listings should be publication quality. The brand of computer required should be included. Lengthy program listings (more than four 6 x 9 pages) can not be published, but may be made available from the author; a note to that effect should be included in the article.

References
A **maximum** of 40 references is recommended. References should strictly follow the *APA* style guide. References must be checked with great care. All references should be in alphabetical order by author (unnumbered), as shown below. In the references there are no spaces between the author's initials. Use the following style when referencing a book or an article in a periodical:

O'Shea, T., & Self, J. A. (1983). *Learning and teaching with computers.* Englewood Cliffs, NJ: Prentice-Hall Inc.

Porter, R., & Lehman, J. (1984). Projects for teaching physics concepts using a microcomputer. *Journal of Computers in Mathematics and Science Teaching, 3*(4), 14-15.

Post-publication
Upon publication, each author will receive a complimentary copy of the journal issue in which the article appears and an article reprint order form.

Please carefully read and adhere to these guidelines. Manuscripts not submitted according to the guidelines must be returned.

Please only send all submissions electronically via the **Journal Submissions Form**.

All correspondence concerning your submission should be directed to the Publications Coordinator at: pubs@aace.org.

Journal of Latinos and Education

ADDRESS FOR SUBMISSION:

Enrique G. Murillo, Jr., Editor
Journal of Latinos and Education
California State Univ., San Bernardino
College of Education
Center for Equity in Education
5500 University Parkway
San Bernardino, CA 92407-2397
USA
Phone: 909-880-5632
Fax: 909-880-5992
E-Mail: emurillo@csusb.edu
Web: www.erlbaum.com/Journals
Address May Change:

PUBLICATION GUIDELINES:

Manuscript Length: See Guidelines
Copies Required: Four
Computer Submission: No
Format: N/A
Fees to Review: 0.00 US$

Manuscript Style:
    American Psychological Association

CIRCULATION DATA:

Reader: Practicing Teachers, Academics
Frequency of Issue: Quarterly
Copies per Issue: Not Yet Determined
Sponsor/Publisher: Lawrence Erlbaum
    Associates
Subscribe Price: 65.00 US$

REVIEW INFORMATION:

Type of Review: Blind Review
No. of External Reviewers: 2
No. of In House Reviewers: 1
Acceptance Rate: New J
Time to Review: 2 - 3 Months
Reviewers Comments: Yes
Invited Articles: New Journal
Fees to Publish: 0.00 US$

MANUSCRIPT TOPICS:
Latinos and Education; Urban Education, Cultural/Non-Traditional

MANUSCRIPT GUIDELINES/COMMENTS:

Editorial Scope
The *Journal of Latinos and Education (JLE)* provides a cross, multi and interdisciplinary forum for scholars and writers from diverse disciplines who share a common interest in the analysis, discussion, critique, and dissemination of educational issues that impact Latinos. There are four broad arenas which encompass most issues of relevance: (1) Policy, (2) Research, (3) Practice, and (4) Creative & Literary works.

JLE encourages novel ways of thinking about the ongoing and emerging questions around the unifying thread of Latinos and education. The journal supports dialogical exchange for researchers, practitioners, authors, and other stakeholders who are working to advance understanding at all levels and aspects, be it theoretical, conceptual, empirical, clinical, historical, methodological, and/or other in scope.

JLE seeks to identify and stimulate more relevant research, practice, communication, and theory by providing a rich variety of information and fostering an outlet for sharing. The various manifestations of the diverse frameworks and topical areas typically range anywhere from but aren't limited to theoretical and empirical analyses, policy discussions, research reports, program recommendations, evaluation studies, finding and improving practical applications, carefully documenting the transition of theory into real world practice, linking theory and research, new dissertation research, literature reviews, reflective discussions, cultural studies, and literary works.

JLE is open to varying research methodologies and narrative models so as to encourage submissions from varied disciplines, areas, and fields. "Education" is defined in the broad cultural sense and not limited to just formal schooling. Particular attention is given to geographical equity to assure representation of all regions and "Latino" groups in the United States. Policies and practices promoting equity and social justice for linguistically and culturally diverse groups are particularly encouraged and welcomed for consideration. A range of formats for articles is encouraged, including research articles, essay reviews and interviews, practitioner and community perspectives, book and media reviews, and other forms of creative critical writing.

Audience
The broad spectrum of researchers, teaching professionals and educators, academics, scholars, administrators, independent writers and artists, policy and program specialists, students, parents, families, civic leaders, activists and advocates. In short, individuals, grpups, agencies, organizations and institutions sharing a common interest in educational issues which impace Latinos.

Guidelines For Submission
Prepare manuscripts according to the *Publication Manual of the American Psychological Association (APA)*, 4th edition. Any manuscript not in this style will be returned to the authors without review. Special consideration is given for creative and literary works whose work is not appropriately covered by APA. All others: type all components of the manuscript, including title page, abstract, text, quotes, acknowledgments, references, appendices, tables, figure captions, and footnotes. The title page of the manuscript should include the title of the manuscript, authors' names, affiliations if any, complete mailing addresses (including e-mail), and the telephone and fax numbers of the author to whom editorial correspondence is to be addressed. The second page should consist of a brief descriptive abstract or synopsis (maximum of 100 words). The rest of the manuscript, including references, should be double-spaced and in the form determined by the *APA*. Authors should be certain that each citation in the text is listed in the reference section and that each publication listed in the reference section appears in the text. Table and figures should also conform to *APA* guidelines. References to all tables and figures should be explicit in text, and notes as to their approximate placement should be made in the manuscript. All figures must be camera-ready.

Four identical copies of each manuscript should be submitted for publication consideration to the Editor. All copies should be clear, readable, and on 8'/2 X 11-inch nonsmear paper of good quality, with pages numbered, a 12-point font size, and 1-inch margins on all sides. Only original material will be accepted.

Authors are responsible for all statements made in their work and for obtaining permission from copyright owners to reprint or adapt a table or figure or to reprint a quotation of 500 words or more. Authors should write to original author(s) and publisher to request nonexclusive world rights in all languages to use the material in the article and in future editions. Provide copies of all permissions and credit lines at the time of manuscript submission. Contact the editor for sample permission request forms.

In a cover letter, authors should state that the findings reported in the manuscript have not been published previously and that the manuscript is not being simultaneously submitted elsewhere. If pertinent, authors should also state that they have complied with American Psychological Association ethical standards in the treatment of their samples. In this same cover letter, provide 6 key words describing your manuscript. These words will be used for identification and to ensure the proper matching for reviews.

All manuscripts submitted will be acknowledged promptly if an e-mail address is provided. Authors should keep a copy of their manuscript to guard against an unexpected loss.

All manuscripts are reviewed by nationally and internationally renowned scholars, professionals and others with special competence in the area represented by the manuscript. Most commonly, manuscripts are reviewed by two or more members of the Editorial Advisory Board, the Editor and Associates, members of the Executive Council, and other invited reviewers with expertise. Unless otherwise solicited, reviews are anonymous. The names and affiliations of the authors, as well as any other identifying information, should not appear in the body of the manuscript. The process of blind peer review may take up to four months.

JLE welcomes proposals for Thematic Issues. These are special issues having components that link together meaningful conceptual or theoretical questions. The proposer of the Thematic Issue becomes the Guest Editor. Examining topics that bring together inquirers from several disciplines that do not normally engage with each other are particularly welcome. These may be invited or open competitions, but all submissions are peer-reviewed. In the cover letter, the authors should identify the section under which they are making their submission:

Feature Articles: Theory, Research, Policy And Practice - rigorous, innovative and critical scholarship comprised of empirical, methodological, applied, theoretical, programmatic, perspective and policy articles relevant to educational issues which impact Latinos. All modes of inquiry are welcome: observational, experimental, ethnographic, textual, sociological, historical, philosophical, interpretive, survey and others. Suggested length should range from 20 to 30 pages.

Essay Reviews And Interviews - commentary, literature and conceptual review papers that are integrative and timely, evaluating and synthesizing a relevant issue. Included also may be symposia, point-counterpoint debates, task force reports, position papers, brief letters and reactions to policies and actions, and solicited commentaries and interviews with specialists and other figures who have made an impact. Suggested length should range from 7 to 12 pages.

Voices: Community, Parents, Teachers And Students - descriptions, data-driven research reports and case studies, and/or more reflective essays by school "actors" and practitioners who have important knowledge, research or reflection about educational settings which impact Latinos. Issues of practice and philosophy of teaching and learning are addressed from the voices of community, parents, teachers and students. Suggested length should range from 7 to 15 pages.

Book And Media Reviews - summaries and evaluations of books, periodicals, articles, Websites, software, CD-ROMs, teaching material, textbooks, videotapes, film, art, music and other media. Suggested length should range from 3 to 7 pages.

Alternative Formats - personal perspectives and narratives, short tales, confessional or testimonial stories, humor, poetry, drama, artwork, and other creative productions and representations that transgress or transverse "academic" standards. Suggested length should range from 3 to 7 pages.

Production Notes

After a manuscript is accepted for publication, the authors are required to sign a publication agreement transferring the copyright from the author to the publisher. Accepted manuscripts become the permanent property of the journal. Authors must provide a computer disk containing the manuscript file in an electronic version, along with two hard copies. The content of the two should be identical. This file should be formatted for IBM computers (in WordPerfect or Word) and be clean of all irrelevant codes. Files are copyedited and typeset into page proofs. Authors read proofs to correct any errors, update publication information and respond to editors' queries.

For submissions and additional information contact the Editor.

For additional information on the Center for Equity in Education contact:
(909) 880-5634; http://cee.csusb.edu.

Journal of Legal Education

ADDRESS FOR SUBMISSION:

Kent Syverud, Co-Editor
Journal of Legal Education
Vanderbilt University Law School
131 21st Avenue South
Nashville, TN 37203-1181
USA
Phone: 615-322-2717
Fax: 615-322-6631
E-Mail: kent.syverud@law.vanderbilt.edu
Web: law.vanderbilt.edu/publications
Address May Change:

PUBLICATION GUIDELINES:

Manuscript Length: Less than 50
Copies Required: Two
Computer Submission: No
Format: N/A
Fees to Review: 0.00 US$

Manuscript Style:
    Uniform System of Citation (Harvard
    Blue Book)

CIRCULATION DATA:

Reader: Academics
Frequency of Issue: Quarterly
Copies per Issue: 5,001 - 10,000
Sponsor/Publisher: Vanderbilt University
    Law School/ AALS Publications
Subscribe Price: 38.00 US$ U.S.
    42.00 US$ Foreign
    15.00 US$ Single Copy

REVIEW INFORMATION:

Type of Review: Blind Review
No. of External Reviewers: 2
No. of In House Reviewers: 2
Acceptance Rate: 21-30%
Time to Review: 1 - 2 Months
Reviewers Comments: Yes
Invited Articles: 11-20%
Fees to Publish: 0.00 US$

MANUSCRIPT TOPICS:
Curriculum Studies; Educational Psychology; Higher Education; Tests, Measurement &
Evaluation; Topics of Interest to Law Professors

MANUSCRIPT GUIDELINES/COMMENTS:

The *Journal of Legal Education*, (615) 343-7114, does not review multiple submissions. This
quarterly publication addresses issues confronting legal educators, including curriculum
development and legal scholarship. All full-time members of the faculty of member and fee-
paid schools receive a copy.

Kent D. Syverud, Dean , Co-Editor
Vanderbilt University Law School
(615) 322-2617, Fax (615) 322-6631
kent.syverud@law.vanderbilt.edu

D. Don Welch,Jr., Associate Dean, Co-Editor
Vanderbilt University Law School
(615) 322-0164, Fax (615) 322-6631
don.welch@law.vanderbilt.edu

Journal of Legal Studies Education

ADDRESS FOR SUBMISSION:

Janine Hiller, Editor
Journal of Legal Studies Education
Virginia Tech
Pamplin College of Business
Dept. of Finance, Insurance and Bus. Law
1044 Pamplin Hall
Blacksburg, VA 24061
USA
Phone: 540-231-7346
Fax: 540-231-3155
E-Mail: jhiller@vt.edu
Web: www.alsb.org
Address May Change:

PUBLICATION GUIDELINES:

Manuscript Length: 16-20
Copies Required: Four
Computer Submission: Yes Email
   Attachment
Format: MSWord or Comparable
Fees to Review: 0.00 US$

Manuscript Style:
   Uniform System of Citation (Harvard
   Blue Book)

CIRCULATION DATA:

Reader: Academics
Frequency of Issue: 2 Times/Year
Copies per Issue: 1,001 - 2,000
Sponsor/Publisher: ALSB, Western
   Publishing
Subscribe Price: 12.00 US$ Individual
   16.00 US$ Foreign

REVIEW INFORMATION:

Type of Review: Blind Review
No. of External Reviewers: 3
No. of In House Reviewers: 2
Acceptance Rate: 11-20%
Time to Review: 2 - 3 Months
Reviewers Comments: Yes
Invited Articles: 0-5%
Fees to Publish: 0.00 US$

MANUSCRIPT TOPICS:

Business Law, Ethics; Education Management/Administration; Legal Studies Education

MANUSCRIPT GUIDELINES/COMMENTS:

Manuscripts

The *Journal* does not accept previously published manuscripts or those that will be published elsewhere. Manuscripts may be sent simultaneously to other journals on the condition that the Journal is advised, and that the author(s) undertake to inform the editor immediately if the work is to be published elsewhere.

The *Journal* publishes refereed articles, teaching tips, and review of books, and other media. Topics that relate to teaching and research in legal studies and/or related disciplines such as business ethics, business and society, public policy and individual areas of business law-related specialties which are taught in the non-law schools are appropriate areas for publication in the *Journal*. The *Journal* will also consider short, but well-researched works covering "recent developments" in substantive areas taught by legal studies faculty.

The use of the first person in manuscripts is discouraged.

The editorial board selects high quality manuscripts that are of interest to a substantial portion of the Journal's readers. The editors look for: innovative ideas, some element of novelty, good writing, evidence of literature survey where available, and compliance with *A Uniform System of Citation, 17th* edition, for footnote form.

All articles should be sent blinded (all identifying information dedacted) with four copies in double or triple-spaced format to:

Professor Janine Hiller
Editor, JLSE
Virginia Tech
Department of Finance, Insurance, and Business Law
Pamplin School of Business, Mail Code 0221
Blacksburg, Virginai 24061

Electronic submissions are also accepted by sending a blinded (be certain to delete the automatic settings) attachment to jhiller@vt.edu with the subject line indicating "JLSE submission."

Book reviews should be sent to:
Professor Rachel Kowal
Book Review Editor, JLSE
Stern School of Business
New York University
Tisch Hall
40 West 4th Street
New York, New York 10012-1118

Copy
All copy, including footnotes and indented portions, must be at least double-spaced (triple-spaced is preferred) with wide margins, printed on one side of white 8 1/2" by 11" paper. To permit blind refereeing, the manuscripts must not identify the author or the author's institutional affiliation. A removable cover page should contain the title, the name, position, institutional affiliation, address, and telephone number of each author. The first page of the manuscript should also contain the title. Footnotes or references identifying the author(s) should be deleted or placed on the removable cover page. Footnotes must appear at the end of the manuscript. To set large and small capital letters in Word Perfect for Windows (e.g., authors and titles of books), click on Font, then click on Small Caps under Appearance. Proceed by typing normal upper and lower case letters. This will give you large and small capitals. Five clean copies must be submitted. Manuscripts will not be accepted for publication unless all footnotes and citations are in compliance with a *Uniform System of Citation*, 17th edition. The author is responsible for compliance with this system of citation and footnote accuracy.

Table and Figures

Tables should be included in the manuscript with clear, self-explanatory headings and, if appropriate, the source at the bottom. Tables and figures must be submitted camera ready.

Action

Consideration of manuscripts is normally complete within eight weeks after receipt by the *Journal*. Manuscripts must be submitted in electronic format. Authors are obliged to proofread the galley proofs. It is also the responsibility of authors to obtain permission reprint copyrighted material and to pay any necessary fees. Permission forms are available from the editor. In case of coauthored works the editor will correspond with the lead author. Authors must sign a copyright release.

Journal of Marketing for Higher Education

ADDRESS FOR SUBMISSION:

Thomas J. Hayes, Editor
Journal of Marketing for Higher Education
Xavier University
Marketing Department
3800 Victory Parkway
Cincinnati, OH 45207-1096
USA
Phone: 513-745-3059
Fax: 513-745-3692
E-Mail: hayes@xu.edu
Web: www.haworthpress.com/journals
Address May Change:

PUBLICATION GUIDELINES:

Manuscript Length: 11-15
Copies Required: Three
Computer Submission: Yes On Acceptance
Format: Disk & Hardcopy
Fees to Review: 0.00 US$

Manuscript Style:
    Chicago Manual of Style

CIRCULATION DATA:

Reader: Academics, University
    Administrators
Frequency of Issue: 4 Times/Year
Copies per Issue: Less than 1,000
Sponsor/Publisher: Haworth Press, Inc.
Subscribe Price: 60.00 US$ Individual
    81.00 US$ Institution
    87.00 US$ Library

REVIEW INFORMATION:

Type of Review: Blind Review
No. of External Reviewers: 3
No. of In House Reviewers: 1
Acceptance Rate: 21-30%
Time to Review: 3 Months
Reviewers Comments: Yes
Invited Articles: 6-10%
Fees to Publish: 0.00 US$

MANUSCRIPT TOPICS:
Education Management/Administration; Higher Education

MANUSCRIPT GUIDELINES/COMMENTS:

About The Journal
This journal provides guidance for marketing, admissions, public relations, development, and planning professionals who have the responsibility for enrollments and image enhancement at institutions of higher education. A further goal of the journal is to provide a focus through which the many aspects of marketing for higher education can be integrated into a coherent discipline.

The *Journal of Marketing for Higher Education* welcomes the submission of articles dealing with all phases of admissions, institutional research, planning, public relations, development and academic administration that contribute to the marketing of higher education. Of special interest are papers that aim to combine all or some of the appropriate elements from these separate functions into a formal marketing structure. The journal welcomes papers by practitioners as well as academics and particularly welcomes reports which cover both the positive and negative outcomes of projects that have been implemented, with retrospective discussion designed to aid colleagues who are involved in similar projects.

Instructions For Authors

1. **Original Articles Only**. Submission of a manuscript to this Journal represents a certification on the part of the author(s) that it is an original work, and that neither this manuscript nor a version of it has been published elsewhere nor is being considered for publication elsewhere.

2. **Manuscript Length**. Your manuscript may be approximately 20 typed pages double-spaced (including references and abstract). Lengthier manuscripts may be considered, but only at the discretion of the Editor. Sometimes lengthier manuscripts may be considered if they can be divided up into sections for publication in successive Journal issues.

3. **Manuscript Style**. References, citations and general style of manuscripts for this Journal should follow the "Chicago" style (as outlined in the latest edition of the *Manual of Style of The University of Chicago Press*). References should be double-spaced and placed in alphabetical order.

If an author wishes to submit a paper that has been already prepared in another style, he or she may do so. However, if the paper is accepted (with or without reviewer's alterations), the author is fully responsible for retyping the manuscript in the correct style as indicated above. Neither the Editor nor the Publisher is responsible for re-preparing manuscript copy to adhere to the Journal's style.

4. **Manuscript Preparation**.
Margins: leave at least a one-inch margin on all four sides.
Paper: use clean white, 8-1/2" x 11" bond paper.
Number Of Copies: 3 (the original plus two photocopies).
Cover Page: Important - staple a cover page to the manuscript, indicating only the article title (this is used for anonymous refereeing).
Second "Title Page": enclose a regular title page but do not staple it to the manuscript. Include the title again, plus:
- Full authorship.
- An **abstract** of about 100 words.
- An executive summary of one page pinpointing managerial implications of the paper.
- An introductory footnote with authors' academic degrees professional titles, affiliations, mailing addresses and any desired acknowledgement of research support or other credit.

5. **Return Envelopes**. When you submit your three manuscript copies, also include:
- A 9" x 12" envelope, self-addressed and stamped (with sufficient postage to ensure return of your manuscript);
- A regular envelope, stamped and self-addressed. This is for the Editor to send you an "acknowledgement of receipt" letter.

6. **Spelling, Grammar, And Punctuation**. You are responsible for preparing manuscript copy which is clearly written in acceptable scholarly English, and which contains no errors of spelling, grammar, or punctuation. Neither the Editor nor the Publisher is responsible for correcting errors of spelling and grammar: the manuscript, after acceptance by the Editor, must be immediately ready for typesetting as it is finally submitted by the author(s). Check your paper for the following common errors:

- Dangling modifiers
- Misplaced modifiers
- Unclear antecedents
- Incorrect or inconsistent abbreviations

Also, check the accuracy of all arithmetic calculations, statistics, numerical data, text citations, and references.

7. **Inconsistencies Must Be Avoided**. Be sure you are consistent in your use of abbreviations, terminology, and in citing references, from one part of your paper to another.

8. **Preparation of Tables, Figures, And Illustrations**. All tables, figures, illustrations, etc. must be "camera-ready." That is, they must be cleanly typed or artistically prepared so that they can be used either exactly as they are or else used after a photographic reduction in size. Figures, tables, and illustrations must be prepared on separate sheets of paper. Always use black ink and professional drawing instruments on the back of these items, write your article title and the journal title lightly in pencil, so they do not get misplaced. In text, skip extra lines and indicate where these figures and tables are to be placed (please do not write on face of art).

9. **Alterations Required By Referees And Reviewers**. Many times a paper is accepted by the Editor contingent upon changes that are mandated by anonymous specialist referees and members of the Editorial Board. If the Editor returns your manuscript for revisions, you are responsible for retyping any sections of the paper to incorporate these revisions (if applicable, revisions should also be put on disk).

10. **Typesetting**. You will not be receiving galley proofs of your article. Editorial revisions, if any, must therefore be made while your article is still in manuscript. The final version of the manuscript will be the version you see published. Printer's errors will be corrected by the production staff of The Haworth Press. Authors are expected to submit manuscripts, disks, and art that are free from error.

11. **Electronic Media**. Haworth's in-house type-setting unit will now be able to utilize your final manuscript material as prepared on most personal computers and word processors. This will minimize typographical errors and decrease overall production time lag.

A. Please continue to send your first draft and final draft copies of your manuscript to the journal Editor in print format for his/her final review and approval;

B. Only after the journal editor has approved your final manuscript you may submit the final approved version both on:

- Printed format ("hard copy")
- Floppy diskette

C. Wrap your floppy diskettes in a strong diskette wrapper or holder, and write on the outside of the package:
- The brand name of your computer or word processor
- The word-processing program that you used to create your article, book chapter, or book.
- File name

The benefits of this procedure are many with speed and accuracy being the most obvious. We look forward to working with you on this, knowing we will be able to serve you more efficiently in the future.

12. **Reprints**. The senior author will receive one copy of the journal issue and 10 complimentary reprints of his or her article The junior author will receive one copy of the issue. These are sent several weeks after the journal issue is published and in circulation. An order form for the purchase of additional reprints will also be sent to all authors at this time. (Approximately 4-6 weeks is necessary for the preparation of reprints.) Please do not query the Journal's Editor about reprints. All such questions should be sent directly to The Haworth Press, Inc., Production Department, 10 Alice Street Binghamton, NY 13904-1580.

13. **Copyright**. If your manuscript is accepted for publication, copyright ownership must be transferred officially to The Haworth Press, Inc. The Editor's acceptance letter will include a form fully explaining this. The form must be signed by all authors and returned to the Editor at that time.

Preference is given to applied articles and those that apply to multiple departments or the total institution.

Journal of Mental Health Counseling

ADDRESS FOR SUBMISSION:

M. Carole Pistole, Editor
Journal of Mental Health Counseling
Purdue University
School of Education
Liberal Arts and Eduction Bldg.
Room 5176
West Lafayette, IN 47907-1446
USA
Phone: 765-494-9744
Fax: 765-496-1228
E-Mail: pistole@purdue.edu
Web:
Address May Change:

PUBLICATION GUIDELINES:

Manuscript Length: 16-20
Copies Required: Four
Computer Submission: No
Format: N/A
Fees to Review: 0.00 US$

Manuscript Style:
American Psychological Association

CIRCULATION DATA:

Reader: Academics
Frequency of Issue: Quarterly
Copies per Issue: 10,001 - 25,000
Sponsor/Publisher:
Subscribe Price: 30.00 US$ Individual
      72.00 US$ Institution

REVIEW INFORMATION:

Type of Review: Blind Review
No. of External Reviewers: 3
No. of In House Reviewers: No Reply
Acceptance Rate: 21-30%
Time to Review: 2 - 3 Months
Reviewers Comments: Yes
Invited Articles: 6-10%
Fees to Publish: 0.00 US$

MANUSCRIPT TOPICS:
Counseling & Personnel Services

MANUSCRIPT GUIDELINES/COMMENTS:

Manuscripts are being sought for publication in the *Journal of Mental Health Counseling* on all aspects of practice, theory, and research related to mental health counseling.

Manuscripts should be well organized and concise and follow *APA style*. Avoid the use of jargon. Include an abstract sheet of 100-150 words. Articles and headlines should be as short as possible. The title should appear on a separate page. Include on a separate page the names of the authors, their full professional titles, and the institutional affiliations of each. Send an original and two clean copies of all material on 8 ½ x 11 white paper. Double-space all material. Allow wide margins. Never submit material for concurrent consideration by another publication.

Manuscripts submitted for publication in the *Professional Exchange* section should be 750 words or less and follow *APA style*. Each manuscript will be blindly evaluated by two reviewers.

Submit manuscripts to the Editor.

Journal of Multicultural Counseling and Development

ADDRESS FOR SUBMISSION:

Donald B. Pope-Davis, Editor
Journal of Multicultural Counseling and
    Development
University of Notre Dame
Deparment of Psychology
118 Haggar Hall
Notre Dame, IN 46556
USA
Phone: 219-631-8073
Fax: 219-631-8883
E-Mail: jmcdl@ng.edu
Web: www.nd.edu/~jmcd1
Address May Change:

PUBLICATION GUIDELINES:

Manuscript Length: Limit 20 pages
Copies Required: Three
Computer Submission: No
Format: N/A
Fees to Review: 0.00 US$

Manuscript Style:
    American Psychological Association

CIRCULATION DATA:

Reader: Academics, Counseling
    Practitioners
Frequency of Issue: Quarterly
Copies per Issue: 3,500
Sponsor/Publisher: Assn. For Multicultural
    Counseling and Development - AMCD
Subscribe Price: 40.00 US$

REVIEW INFORMATION:

Type of Review: Blind Review
No. of External Reviewers: 2
No. of In House Reviewers: 0
Acceptance Rate: 11-20%
Time to Review: 2 - 3 Months
Reviewers Comments: Yes
Invited Articles: 0-5%
Fees to Publish: 0.00 US$

MANUSCRIPT TOPICS:
Counseling & Personnel Services; Human Development; Multicultural Education; Urban
Education, Cultural/Non-Traditional

MANUSCRIPT GUIDELINES/COMMENTS:

The *Journal of Multicultural Counseling and Development* invites articles concerned with
research, theory, and program applications pertinent to multicultural and ethnic minority
interests or experiences in all areas of counseling and related areas of human development
with an emphasis on multicultural topics in the United States. If you wish to contribute to the
journal, follow these guidelines:

- Manuscripts should be well organized and concise so that the development of ideas is
  logical. Avoid dull, stereotyped writing and aim for the clear and interesting
  communication of ideas. Limit manuscript length to 20 pages including references,
  Include an abstract of not more than 50 words.

- The article title should appear on a separate page accompanying the manuscript. Include on this page the names of the authors and a paragraph that reports the names of the authors and gives the professional title and institutional affiliation of each. This page must include the corresponding author's full name, mailing address, telephone and fax number, and e-mail address.

- Article titles and headings in the articles should be as short as possible.

- If manuscript is accepted for publication, authors must provide the final version of manuscript on a microcomputer high density floppy diskette (3 1/2") in ASCII or WordPerfect format for IBM compatible computers or in Text file format for Macintosh computers. No other formats will be accepted. The diskette should be labeled with the first author's name, the journal title and the language in which the article was written.

- Send an original and two clean copies of all material on 8 1/2" by 11" white bond paper.

- Double-space all material, including references and extensive quotations.

- Do not use footnotes.

- Check all references for completeness, including volume number, issue number, and pages for journal citations. Make sure all references mentioned in the text are listed in the reference section and vice versa.

- Tables should be kept to a maximum of 3 tables. Include only the essential data and combine tables wherever possible. Refer to a recent copy of the *Journal* for style of tabular presentations. Each table should be on a separate sheet of paper following the reference section of the article. Final placement of tables is at the discretion of the production editor; in all cases, tables will be placed near the first reference of *the* table in the text.

- Figures (graphs, illustrations, line drawings) should be supplied as camera-ready art. Titles for the figures may be attached to the art and will be set in appropriate type.

- Lengthy quotations (generally 300-500 cumulative words or more from one source) require written permission from the copyright holder for reproduction. Adaptations of tables and figures also require reproduction approval from the copyrighted sources. It is the author's responsibility to secure such permission and a copy of the publisher's written permission must be provided to the *Journal* editor immediately on acceptance of the article for publication by ACA.

- Manuscript style is that of the *Publication Manual for the American Psychological Association,* fourth edition, which is available from the Order Department, APA 750 First St. NE, Washington, DC 20002-4242. Only manuscripts conforming to this style will be reviewed by the Editorial Board.

- Never submit material that is under consideration by another periodical.

- Submit manuscripts to Donald B. Pope-Davis, PhD, Editor JMCD, Department of Psychology, 118 Haggar Hall, University of Notre Dame, Notre Dame, IN 46556. You must include an e-mail address, since that is the *Journal's* primary mode of communication. Send inquiries regarding your manuscript to jmcd1@nd.edu. When referencing a submitted article, please include the manuscript number.

ACA journal articles are edited within a uniform style for correctness and consistency of grammar, spelling, and punctuation. In some eases, portions of manuscripts have been reworded for conciseness and clarity of expression. Computer printouts of edited manuscripts are sent to the senior authors of each article in the *Journal*. Changes at this stage must be limited to correcting inaccuracies and typographical errors. Authors must bear responsibility for the accuracy of references, tables, and figures. On publication of an article, a complimentary copy is sent to all authors through the corresponding author.

Journal of Pharmacy Teaching

ADDRESS FOR SUBMISSION:

Noel Wilkin, Editor
Journal of Pharmacy Teaching
University of Mississippi
Faser Hall, Room 219
University, MS 38677
USA
Phone: 662-915-1071
Fax: 662-915-5102
E-Mail: jpt@olemiss.edu
Web: www.haworthpressinc.com
Address May Change:

PUBLICATION GUIDELINES:

Manuscript Length: 16-20
Copies Required: Three
Computer Submission: No
Format: N/A
Fees to Review: 0.00 US$

Manuscript Style:
, American Journal of Health - System
Pharmacy

CIRCULATION DATA:

Reader: Practicing Teachers, Academics
Frequency of Issue: Quarterly
Copies per Issue: Less than 1,000
Sponsor/Publisher: Haworth Press, Inc.
   (Pharmaceutical Products Press Division)
Subscribe Price: 60.00 US$ Individual
      95.00 US$ Institution
      105.00 US$ Library

REVIEW INFORMATION:

Type of Review: Blind Review
No. of External Reviewers: 2
No. of In House Reviewers: 0
Acceptance Rate: 21-30%
Time to Review: 1 - 2 Months
Reviewers Comments: Yes
Invited Articles: 0-5%
Fees to Publish: 0.00 US$

MANUSCRIPT TOPICS:

Adult Career & Vocational; Curriculum Studies; Higher Education; Tests, Measurement &
Evaluation

MANUSCRIPT GUIDELINES/COMMENTS:

The *Journal of Pharmacy Teaching* is a specialized medium of communication designed for
educators at all levels within the field of pharmacy. The *Journal* caters to those in the field
who are engaged in the practice or research of education, particularly those who desire to
learn or remain knowledgeable about the advances in educational principles and strategies. It
is a valuable resource for academicians at all levels, pharmacists who educate students and
patients, graduate students considering academia, and those who educate sales personnel who
interact with pharmacists and other health care professionals. With a variety of article types
and feature sections, the *Journal* responds to educators' needs by publishing articles on active
learning strategies, attitudes toward education, laboratory skills and practices, assessment of
educational outcomes, continuing education for professionals, helpful hints from successful
educators, and other topics that will promote the continuation of excellence in educational
research and practice.

The Journal covers topics that are useful to those engaged in the activities of:

- Undergraduate teaching in classroom, laboratory, and clinical settings
- Graduate education
- Postgraduate education including continuing education, residencies, fellowships, and extension and in-service programs
- Education using distance learning strategies and technologies
- Education of sales personnel who deal with health care professionals
- Education of pharmacy support personnel, other professions, and the general public

Articles report the findings of educational research or communicate information that is useful to educational practice. Subject matter includes but is not limited to lecture materials, lab experiments, syllabi, testing procedures, audiovisuals and computers, performance-based exercise and assessments, active learning exercises, assessment instruments and philosophies, software reviews, book reviews, r3eviews of conferences and seminars, reading lists, clinical innovations, teaching philosophies, students' and practitioners' comments, and educational quality and outcomes.

To ensure the quality and relevance of articles selected for the *Journal of Pharmacy Teaching*, a distinguished editorial board gives direction to this peer-reviewed, quarterly journal.

Instructions For Authors
1. **Original Articles Only**. Submission of a manuscript to this journal represents a certification on the part of the author(s) that it is an original work, and that neither this manuscript nor a version of it has published elsewhere nor is being considered for publication elsewhere.

2. **Manuscript Length**. Your manuscript may be approximately 5-50 typed pages double-spaced (including references and abstract). Lengthier manuscripts may be considered, but only at the discretion of the Editor. Sometimes, lengthier manuscripts may be considered if they can be divided up into sections for publication in successive Journal issues.

3. **Manuscript Style**. References, citations, and general style of manuscripts for this Journal should follow the guidelines outlined in the *American Journal of Health-System Pharmacy* which are generally in conformance with the Uniform Requirements of Manuscripts Submitted to Biomedical Journals (N Engl J Med. 1997. 336(4):309-15). The use of footnotes within the text is discouraged. References should be double-spaced and numbered consecutively as they appear in the text.

If an author wishes to submit a paper that has been already prepared in another style, he or she may do so. However, if the paper is accepted (with or without reviewer's alterations), the author is fully responsible for retyping the manuscript in the correct style as indicated above. Neither the Editor nor the Publisher is responsible for re-preparing manuscript copy to adhere to the Journal's style.

4. **Manuscript Preparation**.
Margins: leave at least a one-inch margin on all four sides.

Paper: use clean white, 8 1/2 " x 11" bond paper.

Number of Copies: 4 (the original plus three photocopies).

Cover Page: Important--staple a cover page to the manuscript, indicating only the article title (this is used for anonymous refereeing).

Second "Title Page": enclose a regular title page but do not staple it to the manuscript. Include the title again, plus:

- full authorship
- an ABSTRACT of about 100 words. (Below the abstract provide 3-10 key words for index purposes)
- an introductory footnote with authors' academic degrees, professional titles, affiliations, mailing addresses, and any desired acknowledgment of research support or other credit.

5. **Return Envelopes**. When you submit your four manuscript copies, also include:

- a 9" x 12" envelope, self-addressed and stamped (with sufficient postage to ensure return of your manuscript);
- a regular envelope, stamped and self-addressed. This is for the Editor to send you an "acknowledgement of receipt" letter.

6. **Spelling, Grammar, and Punctuation**. You are responsible for preparing manuscript copy which is clearly written in acceptable scholarly English, and which contains no errors of spelling, grammar, or punctuation. Neither the Editor nor the Publisher is responsible for correcting errors of spelling and grammar: the manuscript, after acceptance by the Editor, must be immediately ready for typesetting as it is finally submitted by the author(s). Check your paper for the following common errors:

- dangling modifiers
- misplaced modifiers
- unclear antecedents
- incorrect or inconsistent abbreviations

Also, check the accuracy of all arithmetic calculations, statistics, numerical data, text citations, and references.

7. **Inconsistencies Must Be Avoided**. Be sure you are consistent in your use of abbreviations, terminology, and in citing references, from one part of your paper to another.

8. **Preparation of Tables, Figures, and Illustrations**. All tables and figures, illustrations, etc. must be "camera-ready". That is, they must be cleanly typed or artistically prepared so that they can be used either exactly as they are or else used after a photographic reduction in size. Figures, tables, and illustrations must be prepared on separate sheets of paper. Always use black ink and professional drawing instruments. On the back of these items, write your article title and the journal title lightly in pencil, so they do not get misplaced. In text, skip extra lines and indicate where these figures and tables are to be placed (please do not write on the face of art). Photographs are considered part of the acceptable manuscript and remain with the publisher for use in additional printings. If submitted art cannot be used, the Publisher reserves the right to redo the art and to charge the author a fee of $35.00 per hour for this service.

9. **Alterations Required By Referees And Reviewers**. Many times a paper is accepted by the Editor contingent upon changes that are mandated by anonymous specialist referees and members of the Editorial Board. If the Editor returns your manuscript for revisions, you are responsible for retyping any sections of the paper to incorporate these revisions (if applicable, revisions should also be put on disk).

10. **Typesetting**. You will not be receiving galley proofs o your article. Editorial revisions, if any, must therefore be made while your article is still in manuscript. The final version of the manuscript will be the version you see published. Typesetter's errors will be corrected by the production staff of The Haworth Press. Authors are expected to submit manuscripts, disks, and art that are free from error.

11. **Electronic Media**. Haworth's in-house typesetting unit is able to utilize your final manuscript material as prepared on most personal computers and word processors. This will minimize typographical errors and decrease overall production timelag. Please send the first draft and final draft copies of you manuscript to the journal Editor in print format for his/her final review and approval. After approval of your final manuscript, please submit the final approved version both on printed format ("hard copy") and floppy diskette. On the outside of the diskette package write:
A. The brand name of your computer or word processor
B. The word-processing program that you used
C. The title of your article, and
D. File name

Note: Disk and hard copy must agree. In case of discrepancies, it is The Haworth Press' policy to follow hard copy. Authors are advised that **No Revisions** of the manuscript can be made after acceptance by the Editor for publication. The benefits of this procedure are many with speed and accuracy being the most obvious. We look forward to working with you on this, knowing we will be able to serve you more efficiently in the future.

12. **Reprints**. The senior author will receive two copies of the journal issue and 25 complimentary reprints of his or her article. The junior author will receive two copies of the journal issue. These are sent several weeks after the journal issue is published and in circulation. An order form for the purchase of additional reprints will also be sent to all authors at this time. (Approximately 4-6 weeks is necessary for the preparation of reprints.) Please do not query the Journal's Editor about reprints. All such questions should be sent directly to The Haworth Press, Inc. Production Department, 21 East Broad Street, West Hazleton, PA 18201 USA. To order additional reprints (minimum: 50 copies), please contact The Haworth Document Delivery Center, 10 Alice Street, Binghamton, NY 13904-1580 USA; 1-800-342-9678 or Fax (607) 722-6362.

13. **Copyright**. Copyright ownership of your manuscript must be transferred officially to The Haworth Press, Inc. before we can begin the peer-review process. The Editor's letter acknowledging receipt of the manuscript will be accompanied by a form fully explaining this. All authors must sign the form and return the original to the Editor as soon as possible. Failure to return the copyright form in a timely fashion will result in delay in review and subsequent publication.

COPYRIGHT TRANSFER FORM

Name of journal:
Journal of Pharmacy Teaching

Name and **Exact** Mailing Address of Contributor:

Special note: This will be used for mailing reprints. You must include exact street address, name of your department if at a university, and ZIP CODE. The Haworth Press cannot be responsible for lost reprints if you do not provide us with your exact mailing address.

In Reference To Your Journal Article:

☐ **If this box is checked...**

Thank you for your article submission! Please allow 10-15 weeks for the review process. Before sending out your article for review, however, the Publisher requires us to obtain your signature(s) confirming that you have read the PUBLICATION AGREEMENT on the reverse side of this page.

All co-authors must sign and return the ORIGINAL signed copy.

IT IS CONFIRMED that I/we have read the PUBLICATION AGREEMENT on the reverse side of the page, and agree and accept all conditions:

author's signature	date
author's signature	date
author's signature	date

☐ **It this box is checked...**

Your article has been favorably reviewed. Our reviewers, however, require certain revisions which are indicated on the attached sheets. Please review and incorporate their suggestions, and return your manuscript/disk retyped within 14 days. A decision about publication will he made at that time. Thank you for your help and cooperation.

Please reply to
( ) Journal Editor:
Noel E. Wilkin, PhD
The University of Mississippi

548

School of Pharmacy
Faser Hall, Room 219
University, MS 38677

___

□ **If this box is checked...**

We are pleased to inform you that your article has been accepted for publication in the journal noted above. In addition to the standard journal edition, at the editor's discretion, this issue may also be co-published in a hardcover monographic co-edition.

Please note the following:

1. Publication: Your article is currently scheduled to appear in

Volume: _____ Number: _____

2. **Typesetting**: Your article will be sent to the Production Department of The Haworth Press, Inc., 21 East Broad Street, West Hazleton, PA 18201. They will typeset your article (preferably from your computer disk) exactly as submitted. Please note that you will not be receiving galley proofs. The production staff will proofread the galleys for typesetting errors against the final version of the manuscript as submitted. No revisions are allowed.

3. **Reprints**: Shortly after publication you will receive an order form for purchasing quantities of reprints. (About three weeks after publication, the senior author will receive two complimentary copies of the issue and ten copies of the article, and the junior author(s) will receive two complimentary copies of the issue.) Please note that preparation of reprints takes about eight weeks additional time after the actual issue is printed and in circulation.

___

□ **If this box is checked...**

We are sorry, but the reviewers for this journal did not agree that your article was appropriate for publication in this periodical. If the reviewers consented in having their comments forwarded to you, their critiques are attached. Your submission is appreciated, and we hope that you will contribute again in the future.

Journal of Professional Studies

ADDRESS FOR SUBMISSION:

Louisa Kozey, Editor
Journal of Professional Studies
University of Regina
Faculty of Education
Regina, Saskatchewan, S4S 0A2
Canada
Phone: 306-585-4678
Fax: 306-585-4880
E-Mail: Louisa.Kozey@uregina.ca
Web:
Address May Change:

PUBLICATION GUIDELINES:

Manuscript Length: 16-20
Copies Required: Five
Computer Submission: No
Format: N/A
Fees to Review: 0.00 US$

Manuscript Style:
    American Psychological Association

CIRCULATION DATA:

Reader: Academics, Administrators
Frequency of Issue: 2 Times/Year
Copies per Issue: Less than 1,000
Sponsor/Publisher: University
Subscribe Price: 20.00 US$ Individual
    25.00 US$ Institution

REVIEW INFORMATION:

Type of Review: Blind Review
No. of External Reviewers: 3
No. of In House Reviewers: 3
Acceptance Rate: 11-20%
Time to Review: 2 - 3 Months
Reviewers Comments: Yes
Invited Articles: 0-5%
Fees to Publish: 0.00 US$

MANUSCRIPT TOPICS:
Adult Career & Vocational; Teacher Education

MANUSCRIPT GUIDELINES/COMMENTS:

Purpose of The Journal
The *Journal of Professional Studies* provides a forum for the exchange of ideas about teacher education practices and their place in the process of becoming a teacher. The discipline of Professional Studies pertains to the study of the practices of school-based and university-based teacher educators and explores how these practices inform teacher identity. Professionals Studies includes the place of program structure and context, teacher education curriculum, its social, cultural and political contexts, instructional practices, and the relational aspects of learning to teach. It is the intent of the *Journal* to promote the voices of those involved in teacher education - students, cooperating teachers, and faculty - by revealing the lived experiences of these participants engaging in their work. The *Journal* is indexed in *Canadian Education Index* and *ERIC*.

550

Editorial Responsibility
Points of view or opinions expressed in the *Journal of Professional Studies* are not necessarily those of the editors. The *Journal* is printed to stimulate conversation, investigation and experimentation among those interested in teacher education practices. Authors who contribute are encouraged to exert their professional judgment.

The *Journal of Professional Studies* is published at least twice yearly.

Acceptance Policy
Authors will be informed when manuscripts and disks are received. Each manuscript is previewed prior to distribution to appropriate reviewers. Once all reviews are returned, a decision will be made and the author will be notified. To expedite matters, it is important for authors to provide a complete postal address, office and home phone numbers and, if possible, a fax number and E-mail address. Manuscripts will be anonymously reviewed. The *Journal* reserves the right to make changes in manuscripts to improve clarity, to conform to style, to correct grammar and spelling, and to fit available space. Manuscripts should not have been published elsewhere.

Length
The manuscript, including all references. tables, charts or figures, should normally be between 15 to 20 pages and must be numbered. Figures should be included, on separate pages, at the end of the text.

Typing
Double-space all text with 1 inch margins all around, left justify only.

Style
For writing and editorial style, follow the *Publication Manual of the American Psychological Association* (2000, 5th ed.). References should also follow *APA style*. Discriminatory language should be avoided.

Abstract
In 50 to 75 words, describe the essence of the manuscript. Double-space on a separate sheet, and place it at the beginning of the manuscript. Do not include your name or any other identifying information with the abstract.

Cover Page
Include the following: title of the manuscript, date of submission, author's name, title, mailing address, business and home phone numbers, fax number, and E-mail address. Please provide a brief biographical sketch and acknowledge if the article was presented as a paper or reports a funded research project.

Form
- Hard copy: five copies of the manuscript, complete with cover page and an abstract; and,
- Computer disk: state if IBM or Macintosh compatible, and list word processing and/or graphics programs used. Macintosh programs are preferred.

Manuscripts, Editorial Correspondence, and Questions should be directed to the Editor at the above address or: Juanita Ingham, Assistant Editor, Journal of Professional Studies, Faculty of Education, University of Regina, Regina, Saskatchewan S4S 0A2, Canada; Tel: 306-585-5142, Fax: 306-585-4880; Email: Juanita.Ingham@uregina.ca.

Journal of Research Administration

ADDRESS FOR SUBMISSION:

Editor
Journal of Research Administration
1901 North Moore Street
Suite 10004
Arlington, VA 22209
USA
Phone: 703-741-0140
Fax: 603-737-5932
E-Mail: info@srainternational.org
Web: www.srainternational.org/NewWeb/
Address May Change:

PUBLICATION GUIDELINES:

Manuscript Length: Less than 10
Copies Required: One
Computer Submission: Yes Email in
    MSWord
Format: MSWord 6.0/WP 5.0 or higher
Fees to Review: 0.00 US$

Manuscript Style:
    American Psychological Association

CIRCULATION DATA:

Reader: , Research Administrators
Frequency of Issue: Quarterly
Copies per Issue: 2,001 - 3,000
Sponsor/Publisher: Society of Research
    Administrators International
Subscribe Price: 45.00 US$
    50.00 US$ Foreign/Not Canada
    35.00 US$ SRA Members

REVIEW INFORMATION:

Type of Review: Editorial Review
No. of External Reviewers: 3+
No. of In House Reviewers: 0
Acceptance Rate: 80%
Time to Review: 1 - 2 Months
Reviewers Comments: Yes
Invited Articles: 31-50%
Fees to Publish: 0.00 US$

MANUSCRIPT TOPICS:
Education Management/Administration; Educational Technology Systems; Higher Education;
Research Administration

MANUSCRIPT GUIDELINES/COMMENTS:

The *SRA Journal* publishes a variety of articles intended to expand the knowledge and tools of research administration. Manuscripts are solicited on topics such as the role of the administrator (e.g., aspects of professional training, responsibilities, and career advancement); methods to improve administrative management; issues of compliance; higher education-industry partnerships; use of new technology; techniques to enhance the management of research; long-range planning strategies; procedures which stimulate faculty interest in research; and other timely subjects that will be of interest to research administrators employed in the public or private sectors. Contributors need not be a member of SRA to submit an article to the *Journal*.

SRA International is now accepting Journal Articles in Microsoft Word (MSWord) format via email. Completed articles should be emailed to journal@srainternational.org

SRA International Author Guidelines
All submitted articles must follow strict style guidelines outlined in the APA Style Manual. We have made these styles available for download in pdf format.

Download The SRA International Author Guidelines (PDF format) from the website.
   http://www.srainternational.org/NewWeb/articles/pdf/SRAAPAGuidelines.pdf

Author Guidelines to APA Editorial Style for the Journal of Research Administration
(Excerpts from chapter 3, Publication Manual of the American Psychological Association, 2001, 77-214. For full details consult the 5th edition.)

STYLES CONTAINED IN THE SRA JOURNAL TEMPLATE (MS WORD DOC)

SRA Level 1(apply to level 1 headings):
   Centered Uppercase and Lowercase Heading (Double space after)

SRA Level 2 (apply to level 2 headings):
   Italicized Centers Uppercase and Lowercase Heading (Double space after)

SRA Level 3 (apply to level 3 headings):
Flush Left Italicized Uppercase and Lowercase heading (Double space after)

SRA Level 4 (apply to level 1 headings):
   Indented; Italicized Lowercase Paragraph heading ending with a period. Type sentence here and continue the paragraph

SRA Series (apply to Series):
Series: Within a paragraph identify series within a sentence using lowercase letters in parentheses, for example (a) first string, (b) second string, and (c) third string. Separate paragraphs in a series such as steps or conclusions are preceded by an arabic number and period, without parentheses, as seen below.

   1. Paragraph one ...

   2. Paragraph two ...

   3. Paragraph three ...

SRA Quotation (apply to Quotations):
Quotations: Reproduce quotes word for word; short quotations of less than 40 words should appear in the text preceded with " and followed by ". Longer quotes should be indented in a block In both cases provide the author, year and page citation in the text with a complete reference in the reference list.
   She stated, " the federal government..." (USDA, 1986, p.18) but did not clarify...

   Marcle, (2001), stated the following:
   The...   end. (p.288)

SRA Reference (apply to References):
Reference List: The journal articles should provide a reference list at the end of the article. Footnotes and endnotes are not used. Accuracy is the responsibility of the author; references will not be checked in editorial review. Chapter 4 of the publication manual provides detail on the correct format. A brief list of common citation types follow. Use Arabic numbers unless a roman numeral is part of the title.

Hewlett, L.S. (1996). *Title of work*. Location: Publisher.

Hewlett, L.S. (1999). Title of chapter in book. In author or editor of book, *Title of book* (pp. xxx-xxx). Location:Publisher.

Hewlett, L.S., Evans, A. E., & Belfar, S. F. (1998). Title of article. *Title of Periodical*, vol. xx, page numbers xxx-xxx.

Justin, A.A. (2001). Title of on-line article. *Title of Periodical* xx, xxx-xxx. Retrieved day month year from http://www.Rest of source url.

Roberts, N.M. (Ed.). (2001). *Title*. Location: Publisher.

Other APA Style Guidelines

Abbreviations: Use abbreviations after introducing the full spelling followed by the abbreviation in parentheses. Remember units of measure and most company names do not use periods in the abbreviation (8 cm, NIH, NM, DG) but United States when used as an adjective (U S. Army), Latin abbreviations (a.m., vs.), and military titles use the period. Plurals of abbreviations and symbols add an s (Eds., 1980s).

Appendix: When the author has useful detailed information that would distract the reader from the main article, it maybe presented in a 1-2 page appendix.

Date: Note our exception to the APA format is the writing of a full date, 25 December 2001

Numbers: In general, use the figure to express numbers 10 and higher. In the same paragraph numbers below 10 that are grouped in comparison to a number above 10 can be represented by the figure (i.e., 7 of 12 records). Numbers representing time, dates, or subjects are used as well as location in a specific series. Start a sentence with the number written out in full.

Punctuation: Use a comma between elements (before and and or) in a series of three or more. Use a semicolon to separate elements in a series that already contain commas. Use a colon between a grammatically complete introductory clause and a final clause. Do not use a colon to introduce an incomplete sentence. Limit the use of double quoted words to the first time an ironic comment is coined. If the use is common, do not " quote it". If you introduce a key or new technical term, italicize it the first time.

Spelling: The reference dictionary is the Merriam Webster Collegiate Dictionary. Use the first spelling listed. Consult hyphenation and plurals. You may check online at www.m-w.com

Symbols: Use the correct symbol (located on toolbar under Insert). The em dash (–) indicates the sudden interruption in the continuity of a sentence. Mark permanent hyphens (-) using the proper symbol. Find single and double quotes at this location.

Tables and Figures: All tables must follow the APA format with clear, simple lines (see publication at 3.69), labeled columns, and a concise title. A table may have notes (general, specific, and statistical). Use a table to supplement the text. Refer to the tables by number in the text (e.g., As shown in Table 8, the findings were...). A table should be formatted in WORD. Figures are drawn, photographed, or graphed and are presented in black and white in an electronic format. Avoid incorporating commercial references and logos in your figures. Figures should fit into one or two columns of the journal page and still be very clear.

Type Font: Use only New Times Roman 12 point for text and headings. Present nothing (in figure or table) less than 8-point type, 10-point preferred.

MS WORD JOURNAL TEMPLATE

For your convenience, we have also set up a MSWord template, which is preset with the correct style settings. The template is a MSWord 5.0 version, which should be easily adapted to later versions (2000, and XP).

This template is created to help you prepare SRA Journal articles. We have changed the automatic WORD style for margins, headings, quotation marks, series, and references that you will apply when using this template.

We hope that this will assist you in applying the SRA International format. You will still need to consult the Author Guidelines on the web page for more exact style hints, as well as the APA Publishing Manual for less applied style matters.

This template uses the four levels of headings in the APA manual and the SRA International Author Guidelines (available for download above).

For instance:
- Level 1 heading is the title of the article, author(s) name, and the author(s)' employer. This will be produced as centered upper and lower case title heading with double-space between it and the next section.
- Level 2 headers will be automatically italicized, centered, and in title format (upper and lower case); use level 2 for major subdivisions of your article.
- Level 3 headers may be used to set off sections of the major subdivisions.
- Level 4 headers may further segment the Level 3 section and are often used to discuss a key point, rule, or other paragraph so the material is clearly related.

Download the MSWord Template from the website.
(To download, right click and choose "Save Target As ")
http://www.srainternational.org/NewWeb/articles/MSWord/SRAJournalStyleGuide2002.doc

To Apply Styles: The template also contains the numbered series format and quotation styles used in the style guide. First highlight the word(s) to which you want to apply a style, then go to the MS Word Toolbar and select 'Format', then select 'Style'. Highlight the style you would like to apply and hit 'Enter'.

Journal of School Health

ADDRESS FOR SUBMISSION:

Tom Reed, Editor
Journal of School Health
American School Health Association
PO Box 708
Kent, OH 44240-0708
USA
Phone: 330-678-1601
Fax: 330-678-4526
E-Mail: treed@ashaweh.org
Web: www.ashaweh.org
Address May Change:

CIRCULATION DATA:

Reader: Practicing Teachers
Frequency of Issue: 10 Times/Year
Copies per Issue: 5,001 - 10,000
Sponsor/Publisher:
Subscribe Price: 80.00 US$
   90.00 US$ Foreign

PUBLICATION GUIDELINES:

Manuscript Length: 11-15
Copies Required: Five
Computer Submission: No
Format: N/A
Fees to Review: 0.00 US$

Manuscript Style:
   See Manuscript Guidelines

REVIEW INFORMATION:

Type of Review: Blind Review
No. of External Reviewers: 3
No. of In House Reviewers: 0
Acceptance Rate: 11-20%
Time to Review: 2 - 3 Months
Reviewers Comments: Yes
Invited Articles: 0-5%
Fees to Publish: 0.00 US$

MANUSCRIPT TOPICS:
Curriculum Studies; Education Management/Administration; Elementary/Early Childhood; Health & Physical Education; Secondary/Adolescent Studies; Tests, Measurement & Evaluation

MANUSCRIPT GUIDELINES/COMMENTS:

A Note to Authors
These guidelines are provided to assist prospective authors in preparing manuscripts for the *Journal of School Health*. Failure to follow the guidelines completely may delay or prevent consideration of the manuscript. Contact the Journal office for assistance: Journal of School Health, P.O. Box 708, Kent, OH 44240-0708, (216) 678-1601.

Features
Manuscripts may be submitted for publication in five categories. Articles address topics of broad interest and appeal to the readership. Research Papers report the findings of original, stringently reviewed, data based research. Commentaries include position papers, documented analyses of current or controversial issues, and creative, insightful, reflective treatments of topics related to or affecting health promotion in schools. Teaching Techniques present

innovative ideas concerning health instruction. Health Service Applications are practical papers of interest in school nursing, medicine, dentistry, and other aspects of school health services. The *Journal* editorial staff determines placement of accepted manuscripts within the five categories. Communications, such as letters to the editor, about subjects relevant to health promotion in schools also are welcomed.

Submission Requirements
Submit a cover letter with the original manuscript and four copies to Managing Editor. Use only letter quality printers. Poor quality copies will not be considered. Manuscripts must be typed on white, 8 ½" x 11" paper and double-spaced throughout, including the abstract and references. Number the manuscript pages consecutively with the first title page as page one followed by the second title page, abstract, text, references, and visuals. The cover letter should include the name, mailing address, and telephone number of the corresponding author. Rejected manuscripts will not be returned unless accompanied by a pre-addressed envelope with adequate return postage. Authors interested in submitting manuscripts on floppy disks may contact the editorial department for details.

Affirmations Copyright.
In accordance with the Copyright Revision Act of 1976, Public Law 94-553, the following statement must be submitted in writing and be signed by all authors and co-authors before a manuscript will be considered:

"In consideration of the *Journal of School Health* taking action in reviewing and editing my submission, the author(s) undersigned hereby transfer, assign, or otherwise convey all copyright ownership to the *Journal of School Health* in the event such work is published in the *Journal*."

Failure to provide the statement will delay consideration of the manuscript. Following publication, an article may not be published elsewhere without written permission from the *Journal* publisher.

Originality
The cover letter must include the following statement for all manuscripts:

"This manuscript or its essence has not been accepted or published previously and is not under simultaneous consideration for publication elsewhere. "

Also, if the same database was used to prepare multiple manuscripts, the manuscript must describe how this report relates to other components of the larger study.

Manuscript Length
Manuscript length requirements are based on standard margins with approximately 250 words per page. Commentaries, Teaching Techniques, and Health Service Applications should not exceed 6-8 typed pages (approximately 2,000 words) not including a maximum of 20 references and two visuals. Articles should not exceed 12-14 typed pages (approximately 3,500 words) not including a maximum of 30 references and five visuals. Research Papers should not exceed 12-14 typed pages (approximately 3,500 words) not including a maximum

of 35 references and six visuals. Communications, such as letters to the editor, should not exceed 500 words, with a maximum of 10 references.

Title Pages
The first title page should include the manuscript title, the category to which the manuscript is being submitted, and the names, academic degrees, current positions, professional affiliation, and mailing address for all authors. For jointly authored works, indicate the corresponding author and include a telephone number. Joint authors should be listed in the order of their contribution to the work. A maximum of six authors for each manuscript will be Listed. Also include on the first title page the total number of words in the text and the total number of tables and figures. The second title page should include the manuscript title and the category to which the manuscript is being submitted.

Abstract
A 150-word abstract must accompany Articles and Research Papers. The abstract should provide sufficient information for the reader to determine the purpose and relevance of the work.

Style
Prepare manuscripts using the *AMA Stylebook* (1989), *American Medical Association Manual of Style.* Manuscript titles should be brief and specific. Manuscripts normally should be written in the third person, avoiding sexist language. Spell numbers one through nine, and use the % symbol to report percentages.

Research manuscripts should include the year and timeframe in which the data were collected. Also include information concerning the psychometric properties of instrumentation (validity, reliability, readability, etc.) where appropriate.

Unfamiliar acronyms should be preceded by their full title following first usage with the acronym or abbreviation in parentheses. Funding sources may be recognized, but personal acknowledgments will not be printed. Footnotes should be eliminated or incorporated into the text where feasible. Outlines and multi-part manuscripts normally are not considered.

Cite references in the text in numerically consecutive order. List the references as they are cited do not list references alphabetically. Abbreviate journal titles according to *Index Medicus.* Journal citations should include author, title, journal abbreviation, year, volume, issue, and pages. Book citations should include author title, city, publisher, year, and pages. Authors are responsible for the accuracy of all references.

1. McClary DG, Bauer JH, Chang CL. Smoking cessation strategies in review. J Sch Health. 1991;61(1):

2. Wilson T, Steiner AR, Lopez JM: Health Promotion in Schools. Chicago: Professional Publications;1991; 120-126.

Visuals
Use visuals only when necessary. Incorporate basic information into the text in narrative form where feasible. Each chart, graph, diagram, table, figure, and photograph should have a brief, self-explanatory title. Submit each visual on a separately numbered page at the end of the manuscript.

Authors may furnish camera-ready art for visuals, or the *Journal* can prepare the visuals and bill the author. Submit original line art, professionally prepared in the required Journal format, using Helios Condensed typeface or the equivalent. Center visual titles in 9 pt Helios Bold Condensed. Depending on the size of the visual, use a width of 19 picas unless the visual contains six or more separate columns, in which case, use a width of 40 picas to accommodate the *Journal* column format mat.

Editing
Manuscripts and Communications are edited for length and clarity. An edited copy of the manuscript or letter is sent to the corresponding author for proofing before publication. If the corresponding author does not respond as requested, the article is printed as it appears on the proof. Costs for changes requested after the proofing period are billed to the author.

Reprints
Authors and co-authors receive two complimentary copies of the Journal in which their article appears. Authors also receive a form for ordering reprints. Additional copies of the issue may be purchased from the *Journal* office.

Peer Review
Contributed manuscripts normally receive a blind peer review from at least three reviewers. Major reasons for rejection include insufficient relevance to health promotion in schools, lack of originality and uniqueness, improper format and style, faulty research design, poor writing, and space limitations. The *Journal* editor makes the final decision concerning acceptance of manuscripts.

Checklist For Authors
- The manuscript topic is appropriate for the Journal.
- Names and mailing addresses are provided for the senior author and all co-authors.
- The corresponding author is designated clearly including name, mailing address, and telephone number.
- A copyright release statement signed by the senior author and all co-authors, and other appropriate affirmation statements are included.
- The *AMA stylebook* (1989) was followed for format, references, and documentation.
- The manuscript is written in the third person, avoiding sexist language.
- Personal acknowledgments are not included, and footnotes are minimized or deleted.
- Two title pages are enclosed.
- Both title pages indicate the category to which the manuscript is being submitted.
- Manuscript length and number of references and visuals conform to requirements for the category.
- The manuscript title is brief and specific.

- The original and four clear copies are enclosed.
- A 150-word abstract is included for Articles and Research Papers.
- All pages are numbered consecutively from the first title page.
- Visuals are prepared on separately numbered pages and placed at the end of the manuscript.
- Adequate return postage is enclosed, if desired.
- The manuscript has been checked thoroughly for style, readability, and quality of writing.

SUMMARY OF MANUSCRIPT REQUIREMENTS

Category of Manuscript	150-Word Abstract Required	Maximum Page Length*	Maximum References Allowed	Maximum Visuals Allowed	Number of Copies Required	Copyright Release Required
Communications	No	1-2	10	0	0/2	No
Commentaries	No	6-8	20	2	0/4	Yes
Teaching Techniques	No	6-8	20	2	0/4	Yes
Health Service Applications	No	6-8	20	2	0/4	Yes
General Articles	Yes	12-14	30	5	0/4	Yes
Research Papers	Yes	12-14	35	6	0/4	Yes

*Based on a standard of approximately 250 words per page.

Journal of School Leadership

ADDRESS FOR SUBMISSION:

Ulrich C. Reitzug, Editor
Journal of School Leadership
University of North Carolina-Greensboro
Curry 239
PO Box 26171
Greensboro, NC 27402-6171
USA
Phone: 336-334-3491
Fax: 336-334-4737
E-Mail: ucreitzu@uncg.edu
Web: www.scarecroweducation.com
Address May Change:

PUBLICATION GUIDELINES:

Manuscript Length: 26-30
Copies Required: Four
Computer Submission: No
Format: N/A
Fees to Review: 0.00 US$

Manuscript Style:
   See Manuscript Guidelines

CIRCULATION DATA:

Reader: Academics, Administrators
Frequency of Issue: Bi-Monthly
Copies per Issue: Less than 1,000
Sponsor/Publisher: Scarecrow Press
Subscribe Price: 85.00 US$ Individual
   155.00 US$ Institution
   27.00 US$ Single Copy

REVIEW INFORMATION:

Type of Review: Blind Review
No. of External Reviewers: 3
No. of In House Reviewers: 1
Acceptance Rate: 6-10%
Time to Review: 2 - 3 Months
Reviewers Comments: Yes
Invited Articles: 0-5%
Fees to Publish: 0.00 US$

MANUSCRIPT TOPICS:

Education Management/Administration; Leadership in Education; School Law; Special Education; Teacher Education; Urban Education, Cultural/Non-Traditional

MANUSCRIPT GUIDELINES/COMMENTS:

Editorial Policy

The primary purpose of the *Journal of School Leadership is* to provide a forum for the creative exchange of new ideas concerning the future educational administration, particularly for translating research and theory into practice. The *Journal of School Leadership* endeavors to examine educational administration in its broadest sense, including: application of theory in educational administration, innovative preparation and staff development programs for current and future educational administrators, research related to the utilization of educational administration concepts, and practical applications of educational administration concepts, theories and research for practicing administrators.

Fulfillment of this purpose depends almost entirely upon the voluntary contribution of articulate, accurate, and authoritative manuscripts. In addition to the multiple reviewing of

562

manuscripts to assure high standards of technical veracity, editorial selectivity also involves consideration of the equitable coverage of the entire field. In further discharging its responsibilities, the journal may choose to endorse the programs of appropriate professional associations but asserts its independent role in both the recording and, if necessary, appraising of their activities.

Instructions for Authors

1. *Manuscript*. Four hard copies of the manuscript should be submitted to Dr. Ulrich Reitzug, Editor, *Journal of School Leadership,* Carry Building, PO. Box 26171, University of North Carolina at Greensboro, Greensboro, NC 27402-6171. Telephone (336-334-3491). All copy should be typed, double-spaced, on standard white paper and should follow the style in the fourth edition of the *Publication Manual of the American Psychological Association.*

2. *Title Page*. The manuscript's title should be brief, and the title page should include name, affiliation, address, country, postal code and telephone number of the author(s). Indicate to whom correspondence and proofs should be sent. Running headline. A short running title of not more than 60 characters (including spaces), suitable for page headings, should be provided if the full title is longer than this.

3. *Abstract*. Include an abstract of up to 100 words.

4. *Figures*. Submit single copies of camera-ready drawings and glossy photographs. High-resolution laser-printed copies are acceptable for non-photographic illustration, e.g., line drawings, charts and diagrams. Drawings should be uniformly sized and, if possible, planned for 50% reduction. Both line drawings and photographs must be referred to in the text. Appropriate captions should all be typed on a separate sheet.

5. *Photographs*. Black and white original photographs **only** should be submitted separate from the text. Please indicate on the back of the photo where in the text it should appear.

6. *References*. Literature references should be listed at the end of the manuscript, following the style in the fourth edition of the *Publication Manual of the American Psychological Association.*

7. *Tables*. Number tables consecutively and list them, numbered, on a separate page. Please use Arabic numerals and supply a heading. Column headings should carry units if necessary.

Table 3. NSF funding for educational technology research and development, 1987-1989 (in millions of dollars)

NSF program	Fiscal Year		
	1987	1988 (eat.)	1989 (est.)
Instructional materials development	4.1	7.4	9.0
Applications for advanced technology	5.2	5.6	6.0
Teacher preparation and enhancement	2.5	3.5	4.1
Total technology	11.8	16.5	19.1
Total precollege	60.0	63.0	97.0

8. *Corrections to Page Proofs*. Authors will receive page proofs, which should be corrected and returned to Scarecrow Press, Inc., Attn: Ginger Strader, within two weeks of receipt. If they are not retuned within three weeks of the date mailed to the authors, the article will appear as edited by the Editors of the *Journal of School Leadership* and copy edited by the Scarecrow Press, Inc., staff:

9. *Headings*. Your article should be structured throughout with headings. Normally no more than two-three subheadings are used, as follows:

Main Subhead: DISCUSSION (all capital letters centered)

Secondary Subhead: PUPIL PERSONNEL SERVICES (all capital, left justified)

Third Order Subhead: Student Guidance and Counseling (capitalize first letter of main words, left justified)

10. *Indexing*. Please help us generate an index by supplying a list of several key words and phrases that will describe the content of your article. A subject index draws attention to your article and makes the journal more useful to the readers and future workers in the field. Please provide a columnar list of key words on a separate page. This indexing is in addition to the customary author and title indexes.

11. *Copyright information*. All journal articles are copyrighted in the name of the publisher, except in the event of prior agreement with an author.

12. *Permissions*. The author is responsible for obtaining releases from other publishers for Scarecrow Press, Inc., to publish material copyrighted by another party. Please contact Ulrich Reitzug for forms to facilitate this process.

General

The *Journal of School Leadership is* not responsible for the views expressed by individual contributors in articles published in the journal.

Journal of School Violence

ADDRESS FOR SUBMISSION:

Edwin R. Gerler, Jr., Editor
Journal of School Violence
North Carolina State University
College of Education
Box 7801
Raleigh, NC 27695-7801
USA
Phone: 919-515-5975
Fax:
E-Mail: edwin_gerler@ncsu.edu
Web: genesislight.com/JSV.html
Address May Change:

PUBLICATION GUIDELINES:

Manuscript Length: 16-20
Copies Required: Four
Computer Submission: Yes Disk, Email
Format: MSWord
Fees to Review: 0.00 US$

Manuscript Style:
American Psychological Association

CIRCULATION DATA:

Reader: Practicing Teachers, Academics,
    Administrators, Counselors
Frequency of Issue: Quarterly
Copies per Issue: Not Yet Determined
Sponsor/Publisher: Haworth Press, Inc.
Subscribe Price: 36.00 US$ Individual
    75.00 US$ Institution
    185.00 US$ Library

REVIEW INFORMATION:

Type of Review: Blind Review
No. of External Reviewers: 2
No. of In House Reviewers: No Reply
Acceptance Rate: New J
Time to Review: 1 - 2 Months
Reviewers Comments: Yes
Invited Articles: Not Yet Determined
Fees to Publish: 0.00 US$

MANUSCRIPT TOPICS:

Counseling & Personnel Services; Education Management/Administration; Educational Psychology; Educational Technology Systems; Rural Education & Small Schools; School Law; School Violence; Urban Education, Cultural/Non-Traditional

MANUSCRIPT GUIDELINES/COMMENTS:

From playground bullying to mass murder, the *Journal of School Violence* brings you the latest information on this difficult issue. This innovative journal tracks the causes, consequences, and costs of aggressive or violent behavior in children from kindergarten through twelfth grade. It presents up-to-date research, practice, and theory with a focus on prevention and intervention.

The *Journal of School Violence* offers tested information on such urgent matters as threat assessment, hostage situations, stalking behavior, and teacher safety. For longer-range strategic planning, it features articles on social policy, staff training, and international and cross-cultural studies. This peer-reviewed journal helps administrators and policymakers plan effectively to ensure school security by considering issues of administration, assessment, and funding.

Drawing on the expertise of eminent researchers and educational leaders worldwide, the *Journal of School Violence* features information derived from a variety of academic disciplines, including psychology, sociology, criminology, theology, education, political science, and the arts (including music and movies). Ongoing columns include Internet resources and web site reviews.

The *Journal of School Violence* encompasses a wide variety of themes related to aggressive behavior, including:

- gender issues, including girl gangs and the role of masculinity in criminal behavior
- preadolescent violence
- successful interventions, including behavioral approaches and peer counseling
- aftermath of violence
- emotional violence, trauma, and abuse
- self-esteem and violence
- sexuality and violence

The *Journal of School Violence* address some of the leading concerns of educators, child psychologists, parents, and children themselves. Every year, violence at school causes untold anguish. The *Journal of School Violence* helps you cope with the looming threat and provides you with the information and tools you need to confront the challenges of this painful issue.

Instructions For Authors

1. **Original Articles Only.** Submission of a manuscript to this journal represents a certification on the part of the author(s) that it is an original work, and that neither this manuscript nor a version of it has been published elsewhere nor is being considered for publication elsewhere.

2. **Manuscript Length.** Your manuscript may be approximately 15-20 typed pages double-spaced (including references and abstract). Lengthier manuscripts may be considered, but only at the discretion of the Editor. Sometimes, lengthier manuscripts may be considered if they can be divided up into sections for publication in successive Journal issues.

3. **Manuscript Style.** References, citations, and general style of manuscripts for this Journal should follow the *APA* style (as outlined in the latest edition of the *Publication Manual of the American Psychological Association*). References should be double-spaced and placed in alphabetical order.

If an author wishes to submit a paper that has been already prepared in another style, he or she may do so. However, if the paper is accepted (with or without reviewer's alterations), the author is fully responsible for retyping the manuscript in the correct style as indicated above. Neither the Editor nor the Publisher is responsible for re-preparing manuscript copy to adhere to the Journal's style.

4. Manuscript Preparation.

Margins: leave at least a one-inch margin on all four sides.

Paper: use clean white, 8 1/2 " x 11" bond paper.

Number of Copies: 4 (the original plus three photocopies).

Cover Page: Important--staple a cover page to the manuscript, indicating only the article title (this is used for anonymous refereeing).

Second "Title Page": enclose a regular title page but do not staple it to the manuscript. Include the title again, plus:

- full authorship
- an ABSTRACT of about 100 words. (Below the abstract provide 3-10 key words for index purposes)
- an introductory footnote with authors' academic degrees, professional titles, affiliations, mailing addresses, and any desired acknowledgment of research support or other credit. Manuscripts may be submitted to the editor via e-mail provided the editor approves this method in advance.
- Email to the editor (Edwin_gerler@ncsu.edu) a Microsoft Word version of the manuscript, preferably saved as a rich text format (rtf) file.

5. Return Envelopes. When you submit your four manuscript copies, also include:

- a 9" x 12" envelope, self-addressed and stamped (with sufficient postage to ensure return of your manuscript);
- a regular envelope, stamped and self-addressed. This is for the Editor to send you an "acknowledgement of receipt" letter.

6. Spelling, Grammar, and Punctuation. You are responsible for preparing manuscript copy which is clearly written in acceptable scholarly English, and which contains no errors of spelling, grammar, or punctuation. Neither the Editor nor the Publisher is responsible for correcting errors of spelling and grammar: the manuscript, after acceptance by the Editor, must be immediately ready for typesetting as it is finally submitted by the author(s). Check your paper for the following common errors:

- dangling modifiers
- misplaced modifiers
- unclear antecedents
- incorrect or inconsistent abbreviations

Also, check the accuracy of all arithmetic calculations, statistics, numerical data, text citations, and references.

7. Inconsistencies Must Be Avoided. Be sure you are consistent in your use of abbreviations, terminology, and in citing references, from one part of your paper to another.

8. Preparation of Tables, Figures, and Illustrations. All tables and figures, illustrations, etc. must be "camera-ready". That is, they must be cleanly typed or artistically prepared so that they can be used either exactly as they are or else used after a photographic reduction in size. Figures, tables, and illustrations must be prepared on separate sheets of paper. Always use black ink and professional drawing instruments. On the back of these items, write your article title and the journal title lightly in pencil, so they do not get misplaced. In text, skip extra lines and indicate where these figures and tables are to be placed (please do not write on the face of art). Photographs are considered part of the acceptable manuscript and remain with the publisher for use in additional printings. If submitted art cannot be used, the Publisher reserves the right to redo the art and to charge the author a fee of $35.00 per hour for this service.

9. **Alterations Required By Referees And Reviewers**. Many times a paper is accepted by the Editor contingent upon changes that are mandated by anonymous specialist referees and members of the Editorial Board. If the Editor returns your manuscript for revisions, you are responsible for retyping any sections of the paper to incorporate these revisions (if applicable, revisions should also be put on disk).

10. **Typesetting**. You will not be receiving galley proofs o your article. Editorial revisions, if any, must therefore be made while your article is still in manuscript. The final version of the manuscript will be the version you see published. Typesetter's errors will be corrected by the production staff of The Haworth Press. Authors are expected to submit manuscripts, disks, and art that are free from error.

11. **Electronic Media**. Haworth's in-house typesetting unit is able to utilize your final manuscript material as prepared on most personal computers and word processors. This will minimize typographical errors and decrease overall production timelag. Please send the first draft and final draft copies of you manuscript to the journal Editor in print format for his/her final review and approval.
After approval of your final manuscript, please submit the final approved version both on printed format ("hard copy") and floppy diskette. On the outside of the diskette package write:
A. The brand name of your computer or word processor
B. The word-processing program that you used
C. The title of your article, and
D. File name

Note: Disk and hard copy must agree. In case of discrepancies, it is The Haworth Press' policy to follow hard copy. Authors are advised that **No Revisions** of the manuscript can be made after acceptance by the Editor for publication. The benefits of this procedure are many with speed and accuracy being the most obvious. We look forward to working with you on this, knowing we will be able to serve you more efficiently in the future.

12. **Reprints**. The senior author will receive two copies of the journal issue and 25 complimentary reprints of his or her article. The junior author will receive two copies of the journal issue. These are sent several weeks after the journal issue is published and in circulation. An order form for the purchase of additional reprints will also be sent to all authors at this time. (Approximately 4-6 weeks is necessary for the preparation of reprints.) Please do not query the Journal's Editor about reprints. All such questions should be sent directly to The Haworth Press, Inc. Production Department, 21 East Broad Street, West Hazleton, PA 18201 USA. To order additional reprints (minimum: 50 copies), please contact The Haworth Document Delivery Center, 10 Alice Street, Binghamton, NY 13904-1580 USA; 1-800-342-9678 or Fax (607) 722-6362.

568

13. **Copyright**. Copyright ownership of your manuscript must be transferred officially to The Haworth Press, Inc. before we can begin the peer-review process. The Editor's letter acknowledging receipt of the manuscript will be accompanied by a form fully explaining this. All authors must sign the form and return the original to the Editor as soon as possible. Failure to return the copyright form in a timely fashion will result in delay in review and subsequent publication.

COPYRIGHT TRANSFER FORM

Name of journal:
Journal of School Violence

Name and **Exact** Mailing Address of Contributor:

Special note: This will be used for mailing reprints. You must include exact street address, name of your department if at a university, and ZIP CODE. The Haworth Press cannot be responsible for lost reprints if you do not provide us with your exact mailing address.

In Reference To Your Journal Article:

☐ **If this box is checked...**

Thank you for your article submission! Please allow 10-15 weeks for the review process. Before sending out your article for review, however, the Publisher requires us to obtain your signature(s) confirming that you have read the PUBLICATION AGREEMENT on the reverse side of this page.

All co-authors must sign and return the ORIGINAL signed copy.

IT IS CONFIRMED that I/we have read the PUBLICATION AGREEMENT on the reverse side of the page, and agree and accept all conditions:

author's signature	date
author's signature	date
author's signature	date

☐ **It this box is checked...**

Your article has been favorably reviewed. Our reviewers, however, require certain revisions which are indicated on the attached sheets. Please review and incorporate their suggestions, and return your manuscript/disk retyped within 14 days. A decision about publication will he made at that time. Thank you for your help and cooperation.

Please reply to

() Journal Editor:
Edwin R. Gerler, Jr.
Department of Educational Research
Leadership & Counselor Education
College of Education
North Carolina State University
Raleigh, NC 27695-7801

☐ **If this box is checked...**

We are pleased to inform you that your article has been accepted for publication in the journal noted above. In addition to the standard journal edition, at the editor's discretion, this issue may also be co-published in a hardcover monographic co-edition.

Please note the following:

1. Publication: Your article is currently scheduled to appear in

Volume: _____ Number: _____

2. **Typesetting**: Your article will be sent to the Production Department of The Haworth Press, Inc., 21 East Broad Street, West Hazleton, PA 18201. They will typeset your article (preferably from your computer disk) exactly as submitted. Please note that you will not be receiving galley proofs. The production staff will proofread the galleys for typesetting errors against the final version of the manuscript as submitted. No revisions are allowed.

3. **Reprints**: Shortly after publication you will receive an order form for purchasing quantities of reprints. (About three weeks after publication, the senior author will receive two complimentary copies of the issue and ten copies of the article, and the junior author(s) will receive two complimentary copies of the issue.) Please note that preparation of reprints takes about eight weeks additional time after the actual issue is printed and in circulation.

☐ **If this box is checked...**

We are sorry, but the reviewers for this journal did not agree that your article was appropriate for publication in this periodical. If the reviewers consented in having their comments forwarded to you, their critiques are attached. Your submission is appreciated, and we hope that you will contribute again in the future.

Journal of Staff Development

ADDRESS FOR SUBMISSION:

Valerie Von Frank, Editor
Journal of Staff Development
1995 Cimarron Drive
Okemos, MI 48864
USA
Phone: 517-347-3066
Fax: 517-349-6975
E-Mail: NSDCValerie@aol.com
Web: nsdc.org
Address May Change:

PUBLICATION GUIDELINES:

Manuscript Length: 12 Pages Max
Copies Required: Three
Computer Submission: No
Format: N/A
Fees to Review: 0.00 US$

Manuscript Style:
    American Psychological Association

CIRCULATION DATA:

Reader: Practicing Teachers,
    Administrators
Frequency of Issue: Quarterly
Copies per Issue: 10,001 - 25,000
Sponsor/Publisher: National Staff
    Development Council
Subscribe Price: 49.00 US$

REVIEW INFORMATION:

Type of Review: Blind Review
No. of External Reviewers: 0
No. of In House Reviewers: 3
Acceptance Rate: 21-30%
Time to Review: 4 - 6 Months
Reviewers Comments: No
Invited Articles: 6-10%
Fees to Publish: 0.00 US$

MANUSCRIPT TOPICS:
Education Management/Administration; Professional Development

MANUSCRIPT GUIDELINES/COMMENTS:

The *Journal of Staff Development* is the flagship publication for the National Staff Development Council. It is published four times a year (Winter, Spring, Summer, and Fall) and is included in all categories of membership in NSDC. The *JSD* is available only through NSDC and is not sold on newsstands.

NSDC is a nonprofit educational association with 10,000 members who are primarily district administrators, principals, and teachers with an interest in professional development. They are committed to high levels of learning and performing for all students and staff members. NSDC members look to the *JSD* for solid, credible articles by leading educators, reports of effective programs and practices, book reviews, and columns. They expect articles that are interesting, thought provoking, timely, practical, informative, concise, and complete.

Issues are organized around themes but each issue also includes several non-thematic articles. In general, articles that are appropriate for an announced theme are more likely to be published. The *JSD* offers no payment for articles by professional educators. The *JSD* editor and the director of publications make decisions regarding publication. NSDC reserves the right to reject poor quality or untimely material, whether solicited or otherwise, at any time during the editing process.

What We Look For

The *JSD* looks for brief (1,500-2,000 words) manuscripts that are helpful to practicing K-12 educators. Our primary audience is directors of staff development, other district administrators who are responsible for staff development, principals, lead teachers, and classroom teachers.

We prefer articles written in an informal, conversational style. We are not looking for conventional research reports or term papers. Writers should emphasize what they have learned from their experiences. At the beginning of each article, they should describe what they have learned and what they are trying to share with readers. Articles should emphasize the implications of their discoveries for staff developers. We will not accept articles about proposed programs. Highest consideration will be given to effective programs that have demonstrated improvements in student learning.

Writers should avoid educational jargon and complicated phrasing. Write in simple, direct sentences. Writers should look for opportunities to break out interesting information into separate "sidebars" to run with the main article. If methodology is essential for readers' understanding, it should be in a sidebar and not in the manuscript's main text. Writers also may include a list of additional resources (books, articles, videos, web sites) that are not referenced directly in the article. Where appropriate, graphs and charts also may be used to illustrate key points. Writers should provide the raw data for such charts and not attempt to produce a publishable graphic on their own.

How To Submit A Manuscript

NSDC acknowledges every manuscript that is received. Writers should expect a confirmation letter within several weeks of the manuscript's receipt.

The *JSD* editor and director of publications re view each submission to determine its appropriateness for the *JSD*. Manuscripts are accepted as submitted, returned for revisions, or rejected.

For an initial submission, send **three** copies of your manuscript. For the initial review, do not send the manuscript on a disk or by e-mail. Each manuscript should be typed, double-spaced with generous margins all around. Please type on only one side of the page. No manuscript should exceed 12 pages, including references and charts. Please number the pages. The cover page should include:

- The proposed title of article.
- The writer's name.
- The theme and date of issue for which the manuscript is being submitted.
- Complete contact information for the writer (phone, address, fax, e-mail).
- Writer's current professional position. You may also identify any major articles or books you have recently published.
- A word count.

An early option for writers: Well in advance of the final deadline, writers may submit a brief synopsis of no more than 100 words regarding a proposed article. Either the *JSD* editor or the director of publications will respond regarding the appropriateness of the idea and offer early guidance about producing such an article.

Authors bear full responsibility for the accuracy of citations, quotations, and information supplied for figures and charts.

What Style Should Be Used

For references only, follow directions in the *Publication Manual of the American Psychological Assn.* (1994, 4th edition). Cite references in text like this (Sparks, 1997) and list them in bibliographic form at the end of the article. See a recent issue of the *JSD* for examples of citations. For questions of spelling, we use *Webster's Collegiate Dictionary*, Tenth Edition.

What About Computer Disks?

When a manuscript has been accepted for publication, writers must submit the final version on disk as well as on paper. We will accept the final version only on IBM-compatible disks. The file must be compatible with one of these three programs:

* Microsoft Word for Windows 6.0;
* Microsoft Word for Mac 5.1; or
* WordPerfect for Windows 6.0 or 6.1.

Please use your last name as the title for the file. If you want the disk returned, please include an appropriate mailer, and mailing address.

How To Survive Editing

If your article is accepted, both the *JSD* editor and the director of publications will edit it for publication. During this process, one of those individuals is likely to contact you to clarify certain points. One of those editors also may want to e-mail you something to review or clarify. Because we strive for high quality writing, your article may undergo substantial editing. Remember that this is a normal part of the editing process for any publication with high standards. You should not be startled or upset that an editor is changing your article. The editor's goal is to produce the most readable and interesting article possible. Your help with this is greatly appreciated.

You will receive an edited version to review, correct, and approve. Typically, you will be asked to return the article in about a week's time. Please do not retype the article! Simply mark any changes on the hard copy that you receive and return it to us as quickly as possible. If you still need to insert material at this point, please type it separately and indicate with a note where that material should be inserted.

At the same time you receive this final edited version, you will receive a copyright form. Signing that form gives NSDC permission to print your article in the *JSD*, to post it on our web site, and to use it for other electronic purposes.

What About Photographs?

The *JSD* encourages writers to submit appropriate photographs to illustrate their articles. We prefer black and white glossy prints. Do not send photos until you have been notified that your article has been accepted for publication.

Please include a note with each photograph that:

- Identifies the individuals pictured;
- Describes what they are doing and where; and
- Names the photographer.

If the photographs need to be returned, please label the back of each with your name and address. Please do not write on the photograph itself. Writers are responsible for obtaining written permission for publication from the subjects of the photographs.

If photographs have been published by a local newspaper or magazine, we will make the necessary contacts to obtain those photos if you will provide us with the appropriate information. The *JSD* also will bear the cost of purchasing such photographs.

When Your Article Is Published

Writers receive two complimentary copies of the issue containing their published articles. Columnists receive one copy each. Those copies will be mailed as soon as they are received in the JSD office.

Mailing Address

Manuscripts, editorial correspondence, and questions about submissions should be sent to:

Valerie Von Frank
1995 Cimarron Drive
Okemos, MI 48864
E-mail: NSDCValerie@aol.com

Journal of Statistics Education

ADDRESS FOR SUBMISSION:

Thomas H. Short, Editor
Journal of Statistics Education
Villanova University
Department of Mathematical Sciences
Villanova, PA 19805-1699
USA
Phone: 610-519-6961
Fax: 610-519-6928
E-Mail: thomas.short@villanova.edu
Web: www.amstat.org/publications/jse
Address May Change: 12/31/03

PUBLICATION GUIDELINES:

Manuscript Length: 6-10
Copies Required: One
Computer Submission: Yes Disk, Email
Format: MSWord, LaTeX, ascii
Fees to Review: 0.00 US$

Manuscript Style:
, ASA Style Guide

CIRCULATION DATA:

Reader: Academics
Frequency of Issue: 3 Times/Year
Copies per Issue: Online
Sponsor/Publisher: American Statistical
Association
Subscribe Price: 0.00 US$ Online

REVIEW INFORMATION:

Type of Review: Blind Review
No. of External Reviewers: 3
No. of In House Reviewers: 0
Acceptance Rate: 21-30%
Time to Review: 4 - 6 Months
Reviewers Comments: Yes
Invited Articles: 0-5%
Fees to Publish: 0.00 US$

MANUSCRIPT TOPICS:
Curriculum Studies; Educational Technology Systems; Science Math & Environment; Teacher Education; Tests, Measurement & Evaluation

MANUSCRIPT GUIDELINES/COMMENTS:

Editorial Policy
The *Journal of Statistics Education* disseminates knowledge for the improvement of statistics education at all levels, including elementary, secondary, post-secondary, post-graduate, continuing, and workplace education. It is distributed electronically and, in accord with its broad focus, publishes articles that enhance the exchange of a diversity of interesting and useful information among educators, practitioners, and researchers around the world. The intended audience includes anyone who teaches statistics, as well as those interested in research on statistical and probabilistic reasoning. All submissions are rigorously refereed using a double-blind peer review process.

Manuscripts submitted to the journal should be relevant to the mission of *JSE*. Possible topics for manuscripts include, but are not restricted to: curricular reform in statistics, the use of cooperative learning and projects, innovative methods of instruction, assessment, and research (including case studies) on students' understanding of probability and statistics, research on the teaching of statistics, attitudes and beliefs about statistics, creative and tested ideas (including experiments and demonstrations) for teaching probability and statistics topics, the use of computers and other media in teaching, statistical literacy, and distance education. Articles that provide a scholarly overview of the literature on a particular topic are also of interest. Reviews of software, books, and other teaching materials will also be considered, provided these reviews describe actual experiences using the materials.

Submissions

Authors submitting papers for publication in *JSE* warrant that their papers are not currently under consideration by any other publication and that the material contained within the work is not subject to any other copyright, unless required consents have been obtained.

The refereeing process is most efficient when papers are submitted electronically in Microsoft Word, LaTeX (using the "article" document style), or ASCII text format. Submissions in html are also welcome.

New submissions and revisions of manuscripts that have been previously reviewed should be submitted via electronic mail to the Editor, Thomas H. Short, at thomas.short@villanova.edu. Alternately, new submissions may be submitted on diskette to the Editor at the following address:

> Thomas H. Short Editor, Journal of Statistics Education Department of Mathematical Sciences Villanova University Villanova, PA 19085-1699 USA

For authors unable to submit articles electronically, we will accept submissions on paper. These manuscripts will require more handling and may experience slower turnaround than articles submitted electronically. Paper manuscripts should be submitted in quadruplicate.

Technical questions may be addressed to the Editor at thomas.short@villanova.edu.

Refereeing Process

Articles submitted to *JSE* are peer-reviewed by referees who are chosen from the *JSE* Editorial Board and a pool of referees. The refereeing process is double blind; authors and referees are anonymous to each other.

Before sending a submission to the referees, we remove the author's name and affiliation from the beginning of the paper and the contact information from the end of the paper. Authors are responsible for removing any references or clues to their identity in the body of the paper or in supplements such as software programs, datasets, and graphics files.

Style Guidelines

Except for the conventions noted in these instructions, manuscripts should be prepared in accordance with the *American Statistical Association Style Guide*, published in the February 1986 issue of *The American Statistician*. Contact the Editor with any style or format questions that are not covered by these instructions.

PREPARATION OF MANUSCRIPTS

Manuscripts should be submitted in English. Insert blank lines between paragraphs, between headings and text, and between references. Do not hyphenate words across lines. Hyphens may be used in words that normally contain them. Type all material flush left, including headings. Please do **not** number the paragraphs of the paper.

Because italics, bold-facing, and other text-formatting features are not available in ASCII text, *JSE* uses the following conventions: _italics_, *boldfacing*

Use underscore characters to identify titles within the text, for example, _Journal of Statistics Education_Authors submitting manuscripts in Microsoft Word or LaTeX may omit the underscore characters.

Title, Author Information, And Key Words

The title of the manuscript should appear at the beginning of the paper. Leave a blank line and then list each author's name and institutional affiliation. Leave one blank line between each author's name and affiliation.

Leave a blank line, type "KEY WORDS:" and list three to six key words or phrases (separated by semicolons) that may be used to index the manuscript. Do not repeat words or strings of words from the title.

Abstracts

Each manuscript should be accompanied by an abstract. The abstract should appear between the key words and the beginning of the manuscript text.

Headings

Major headings within the text should be flush left and numbered using Arabic numerals followed by a period (e.g., 1. Introduction, 2. Example).

Subheadings should be flush with the left margin and numbered in the following style: 1.1 Review of the Literature, 1.2 New Methods, etc.

When three levels of headings are required, use 5-space indented paragraph headings, followed by a period.

(Authors using the LaTeX commands `\section` and `\subsection` need not number sections and subsections; the appropriate numbering will be generated automatically.)

Mathematical Material

JSE has adopted the syntax of LaTeX (Lamport 1986) for mathematical material. These notes are based on Section 3.3, "Mathematical Formulas."

Subscripts and superscripts are indicated by `_` and `^`, respectively: X_n, $y = ax^2 + bx + c$. Sub- or superscripts of more than one character must be enclosed in braces: $a_{i,j} = r^{|i-j|}$.

Fractions may be represented in-line in the usual way: 1/2, x/y. In displayed material, they are written using the `\frac' command, with the numerator preceding the denominator: \frac{a + bx}{c + dx}.

Greek letters are produced by \sigma or \Sigma, for example.

Mathematical symbols on the standard keyboard are typed: ( ) - + = | / . Many others are also available, as commands with reasonable names: \times, \div, \cap, \cup, \leq, \geq, \equiv (like = but with 3 lines), \in (element of), \rightarrow, \forall, \exists, \infty. Summation and integral signs are `\sum' and `\int', and limits are indicated by subscripts and superscripts: \sum_{i=1}^{n}, \int_0^1.

Tables

Tables should appear within the text itself, as close as possible to their first mention in the manuscript. Skip two lines before and after the presentation of the table. Tables should be numbered with Arabic numerals and must have titles.

If possible, use Microsoft Word to generate tables. As an alternative, use the LaTeX conventions for indicating the layout of data in a table. A simple example is the following table of regression parameter estimates:

\begin{tabular}{lcc}
Parameter & Estimate & Standard error \\
Intercept & 7.63 & 1.35 \\ Height & 1.05 & 0.73 \\
Weight & 4.40 & 1.84
\end{tabular}

The argument string `lcc' indicates that there are three columns (with the first left-justified and the remainder centered; `r' for right-justified is the third possibility). Items in the same row are separated by `&', and rows are separated by `\\'. Empty cells are permissible; if a row ends with one or more empty cells, the trailing `&'s may be omitted.

Figures

The preferred format for submitting graphs and figures is Graphic Interchange Format, i.e., GIF file format. Figures may be sent by e-mail as encoded files or by postal mail on diskette. Alternatively, authors may provide a Web address where figures can be found. Figures should be numbered with Arabic numerals and must have titles.

References

All references should appear in a reference list at the end of the manuscript. Follow the *American Statistical Association Style Guide* for the format of reference citations and the reference list. Insert blank lines between items in the reference list.

Contact Information

Include with your submission the following information:
    a.   First author's name
    b.   First author's address

    c.   First author's E-mail address

    d.   First author's phone number and fax number (if available)

    e.   Other authors' names and addresses

    f.   Acknowledgments and relevant information about the history of the manuscript (thesis/dissertation, presented at conferences, etc.)

References

Lamport, L. (1986), *LaTeX: A Document Preparation System*, Reading, MA: Addison-Wesley.

Journal of Student Financial Aid

ADDRESS FOR SUBMISSION:

Joseph A. Russo, Editor
Journal of Student Financial Aid
University of Notre Dame
Office of Financial Aid
Notre Dame, IN 46556
USA
Phone: 219-631-6445
Fax: 219-631-6899
E-Mail: Joseph.A.Russo.4@nd.edu
Web:
Address May Change:

PUBLICATION GUIDELINES:

Manuscript Length: 16-20
Copies Required: Four
Computer Submission: No
Format: N/A
Fees to Review: 0.00 US$

Manuscript Style:
American Psychological Association

CIRCULATION DATA:

Reader: Administrators
Frequency of Issue: 3 Times/Year
Copies per Issue: 3,001 - 4,000
Sponsor/Publisher: National Association of
Student Financial Aid and Administrators
Subscribe Price: 45.00 US$

REVIEW INFORMATION:

Type of Review: Blind Review
No. of External Reviewers: 3+
No. of In House Reviewers: 3+
Acceptance Rate: 21-30%
Time to Review: 4 - 6 Months
Reviewers Comments: Yes
Invited Articles: 21-30%
Fees to Publish: 0.00 US$

MANUSCRIPT TOPICS:
Counseling & Personnel Services; Education Management/Administration; Higher Education;
School Law

MANUSCRIPT GUIDELINES/COMMENTS:

The *Journal of Student Financial Aid* invites the submission of manuscripts that report original research, discuss policy issues, or describe new and innovative programs and procedures in the field. The Editorial Board also welcomes correspondence about financial aid issues or articles and letters appearing in the *Journal*.

Writing and Organizing Manuscripts
Authors should present their material in clear and concise language appropriate for the general reader as well as for financial aid administrators. Attention should be given to the use of proper English avoiding ambiguities and grammatical distractions. The presentation and development of the theme should be orderly, avoiding irrelevancies and wordiness. Generally, articles are structured into segments with headings that suggest the logical progression from introduction to conclusion. Headings reflect the manuscript organization and denote the relative importance of each topic.

Research Articles

A research article should begin with an introductory statement of purpose, which does not have a heading. It should proceed with a discussion of recent and related research, followed by a presentation of the methodology. The analysis of the evidence follows, then conclusions and implications directly related to the evidence presented. Statistical data should be summarized in the text; tables should be clear and only used when they add to the presentation.

Issue Articles

An issue article should address a position or a perspective on a student aid policy or topic. The headings should reflect the organization of the article. The author presents the issue in the introduction, which is not headed. Unlike the components of a research article, the sections of an issue article are arranged by relationship. The sections display the perspectives of others, the evidence and logical argument, and positive and negative implications. The conclusion should suggest next steps or otherwise finalize what has been introduced and argued earlier.

Practice Articles

Practice articles present new or innovative procedures. They may address the experiences or concepts proposed by others or demonstrate the advantages of one type of practice over another. As with issue articles, the sections are usually ordered by relationship and the headings reveal the outline of the manuscript.

The beginning of the article introduces the concept, followed by a definition of the author's professional setting to enable the reader to assess the adaptability of the practice. The author should include implementation costs, and present benefits and liabilities as well as a systematic evaluation of the practice.

Style Manual

Questions of style should be referred to the most recent edition (third) of the *Publication Manual of the American Psychological Association (APA)*. Although the *APA style* has been historically oriented toward research, the APA stresses the adaptability of the style to more theoretical manuscripts.

Authors unfamiliar with the style should read the first chapter of the manual, "Content and Organization of a Manuscript," from which the primary points of these guidelines are derived.

Copies are available in most college and university bookstores or may be ordered from the Order Department, American Psychological Association, 1200 Seventeenth Street, N.W., Washington, D.C. 20036.

Footnotes

Footnotes are generally avoided because they distract the reader. Reference citations are never footnoted, but are included in a reference list. Whenever possible, information germane to an article should be integrated with the text. Necessary supporting documentation may be included as an appendix. Table notes, author identification notes, and copyright permission footnotes are acceptable and are addressed in the *APA Style Manual.*

References

The use of the APA reference is simple and straightforward. All references cited in the text must be listed alphabetically by author in a reference list at the end of the article. Since this list must enable the reader to locate the works cited, the reference data must be correct and contain all of the information necessary for identification and library research. Reference material not readily available to readers (unpublished works, papers presented at meetings, work in progress) should be cited only when it is essential to the article, and must be included in the reference list. As much information as possible should be noted, following the standard *APA Style* including: author, title, date, address from which material may be obtained, and whatever information is necessary to explain the source (for example, "Paper presented at the ..."). Examples of references to an entire book and a journal article are provided below:

Bowen, H.R., (1980). The Costs of Higher Education. San Francisco: JosseyBass.

Jackson, G.A. (1978). Financial Aid and Student Enrollment. Journal of Higher Education, 46(6), 623-652.

Submission of Manuscripts

An original and three paper copies of your article (using typewritten guidelines below) should be submitted. If possible, articles should also be submitted on a 5-1/4 or 3-1/2 inch IBM compatible diskette in WordPerfect, XyWrite, Multimate, Wordstar, ASCII, or DOS formats. Please indicate on the disk which format was used. Diskettes will be returned if so requested.

If typewritten, manuscript should be in upper and lower case. All copy, including indented material and references, should be double-spaced. The title of the article should appear at the top of the first page of the text. Since the Editorial Board has a blind review policy, the author's name should not appear on any page of the text. A cover sheet should include the title of the manuscript, author's name, institutional affiliation, mailing address, and the date the manuscript is submitted.

Authors are also asked to include on the cover page a 2-3 sentence anecdotal description of the manuscript. Each page after the first page should be numbered. The original manuscript and three copies should be submitted to Joseph A. Russo, Office of Financial Aid, University of Notre Dame, Notre Dame, Indiana

Acceptance Policy

Manuscripts will be acknowledged and then referred to members of the Editorial Board of Review. When the decision of the Board is final, authors will be notified that their respective manuscripts have been accepted as submitted, accepted pending revisions, or rejected. Articles will be reviewed for substance and presentation. Please refer to "Writing and Organizing Manuscripts" above. The Editorial Board will consider the relevance of the article to current needs in the field, the significance of the idea or usefulness of the information, appropriate nature of any research method and/or logic of presentation, as well as clarity, syntax, and style, although these are the responsibilities of the author.

It is the general policy of the Editorial Board to accept articles not previously published elsewhere or not currently under consideration for publication elsewhere. Authors submitting a manuscript do so with the understanding that, if it is accepted for publication, copyright of the article will be assigned exclusively to the *Journal*. The Board will not refuse any reasonable request by the author for permission to reproduce any part of it. The author alone is responsible for quotations from copyrighted materials.

Journal of the Association for Communication Administrators (JACA)

ADDRESS FOR SUBMISSION:

Ronald L. Applbaum, Editor
Journal of the Association for
   Communication Administrators (JACA)
Kean University
President's Office
Assn. for Communication Administration
Union, NJ 07083
USA
Phone: 908-527-2222
Fax: 908-558-4681
E-Mail: rapplbau@kean.edu
Web:
Address May Change:

PUBLICATION GUIDELINES:

Manuscript Length: 1-25
Copies Required: Three
Computer Submission: No
Format: N/A
Fees to Review: 0.00 US$

Manuscript Style:
   American Psychological Association

CIRCULATION DATA:

Reader: Administrators, Faculty
Frequency of Issue: 3 Times/Year
Copies per Issue: Less than 1,000
Sponsor/Publisher: Assn. for
   Communication Administration
Subscribe Price: 75.00 US$ Individual
   100.00 US$ Library
   Free with Membership

REVIEW INFORMATION:

Type of Review: Blind Review
No. of External Reviewers: 2
No. of In House Reviewers: 2
Acceptance Rate: 35%
Time to Review: 1 - 2 Months
Reviewers Comments: Yes
Invited Articles: 21-30%
Fees to Publish: 0.00 US$

MANUSCRIPT TOPICS:
Communication Education; Education Management/Administration; Higher Education

MANUSCRIPT GUIDELINES/COMMENTS:

When the *JACA* was founded, one of its proclaimed goals was to facilitate the collection and dissemination of information important to administrators. The *JACA* was established to assist in attaining that goal. The *JACA* is published in January, May, and October. The Editors and Editorial Board consider for publication papers that deal with topics useful to administrators in their work or with problems over which administrators might exercise some control or influence.

An original manuscript and two copies should be submitted; they should be double-spaced throughout, including extended quotations and endnotes, which should be indented and setoff. Papers should be prepared according to the *Publication Manual Of The American Psychological Association,* 5th edition.

The Editor conceals the identity of the authors when sending papers for evaluation and review. Authors can assist in this policy by preparing a separate title page which includes:

- Title of paper
- Author's name
- Identification (i.e. Head and Associate Professor, Department of Communication Arts, University of Rockies, Jackson, Wyoming)

Authors will be notified of receipt of the paper and will be informed of the disposition of the paper within six weeks. The ACA does not make reprints available.

Persons participating in ACA Convention Programs or annual seminars are required to submit a paper or a report for publication in the *JACA*.

The Editor reserves the right to edit without consulting with the author.

Journal of the Learning Sciences (The)

ADDRESS FOR SUBMISSION:

Janet L. Kolodner, Editor
Journal of the Learning Sciences (The)
Georgia Institute of Technology
College of Computing
801 Atlantic Drive
Atlanta, GA 30332-0280
USA
Phone: 404-894-3285
Fax: 404-894-5041
E-Mail: jls@cc.gatech.edu
Web: www.cc.gatech.edu/lst/jls
Address May Change:

PUBLICATION GUIDELINES:

Manuscript Length: 30+
Copies Required: Four
Computer Submission: Yes
Format: MSWord or pdf
Fees to Review: 0.00 US$

Manuscript Style:
    American Psychological Association

CIRCULATION DATA:

Reader: Academics
Frequency of Issue: Quarterly
Copies per Issue: Less than 1,000
Sponsor/Publisher: Lawrence Erlbaum
    Associates
Subscribe Price: 50.00 US$ Individual
    390.00 US$ Institution
        See Website for Addit'l

REVIEW INFORMATION:

Type of Review: Editorial Review
No. of External Reviewers: 3
No. of In House Reviewers: 0
Acceptance Rate: 21-30%
Time to Review: 4 - 6 Months
Reviewers Comments: Yes
Invited Articles: 0-5%
Fees to Publish: 0.00 US$

MANUSCRIPT TOPICS:

Cognitive Science; Educational Psychology; Educational Technology Systems; Learning Sciences; Science Math & Environment

MANUSCRIPT GUIDELINES/COMMENTS:

Content. The *Journal of the Learning Sciences* is a cognitive science journal that provides a multidisciplinary forum for the presentation and discussion of research on teaching and learning. Emphasis is placed on important ideas that can change our understanding of learning as well as the practice of education. Articles will evolve from disciplines such as artificial intelligence, cognitive science, cognitive and educational psychology, cognitive anthropology, education, and educational technology.

Manuscript Submission. Submit four manuscript copies to Janet L. Kolodner, *The Journal of the Learning Sciences,* College of Computing, Georgia Institute of Technology, 801 Atlantic Drive, Atlanta, GA 30332-0280. Manuscripts may be submitted in MS Word format electronically to jls@cc.gatech.edu (please send one printed copy with electronic method). All copies should be clear, readable, and on paper of good quality. A dot matrix or unusual typeface is acceptable only if it is clear and legible. Authors should keep a copy of their manuscript to guard against loss. Prepare manuscripts according the *Publication Manual of the American Psychological Association* (4th ed.). A synopsis of the conventions in this manual is available by writing to the American Psychological Society Observer. Any manuscript not in this style will automatically be returned to the author. Type all components of the manuscript double-spaced, including title page, abstract, text, quotes, acknowledgements, references, appendixes, tables, figure captions, and footnotes. The title page of the manuscript should include the title of the manuscript, authors' names, affiliations, and complete addresses, including the telephone number of the author to whom editorial correspondence is to be addressed. The second page should consist of a 100- to 200-word abstract. References, like the rest of the manuscript, should be double-spaced and in the form determined by the *APA*. Tables and figures should also conform to *APA* guidelines. References to all tables and figures should be explicit in text, and notes as to their approximate placement should be made in the manuscript. All figures must be camera-ready. Send correspondence and ideas for the Books & Ideas section to Timothy Koschmann, Southern Illinois University, P.O. Box 19622, Springfield, IL 62794-9622.

Style. Avoid or define technical words specific to a particular discipline. Avoid acronyms and terminology not consistent with style guidelines of *Publication Manual of the American Psychological Association* (4th ed).

Review. Manuscripts are reviewed by peers with special competence in the area represented by the manuscript. Articles and reviews must be judged to be of substantial importance to the broad, multidisciplinary readership of *The Journal of the Learning Sciences* as well as meet a high level of scientific acceptability.

Permissions. Authors are responsible for all statements made in their work and for obtaining permission from copyright owners to reprint or adapt a table or figure or to reprint a quotation of 500 words or more. Authors should write to original author(s) and publisher to request nonexclusive world rights in all languages to use the material in the article and in future editions. Provide copies of all permissions and credit lines obtained at the time of manuscript submission.

Regulations. Only original manuscripts written in English are considered. In a cover letter, authors should state that the findings reported in the manuscript have not been published previously and that the manuscript is not being simultaneously submitted elsewhere. Authors should also state that they have complied with American Psychology Association ethical standards in the treatment of their samples. Upon acceptance, the authors are required to sign a publication agreement transferring the copyright from the author to the publisher. Accepted manuscripts become the permanent property of the journal. A statement of Editorial Policy will appear in Volume 1, Number 1.

Production Notes. After a manuscript is accepted for publication, the author is asked to provide a computer disk containing the manuscript file. Files are copyedited and typeset into page proofs. Authors read proofs to correct errors and answer editor's queries.

Journal of Thought

ADDRESS FOR SUBMISSION:

Douglas J. Simpson, Editor
Journal of Thought
University of Louisville
College of Education & Human
    Development
Dean's Office
Louisville, KY 40292
USA
Phone: 502-852-6411
Fax: 502-852-1464
E-Mail: akbari01@athena.louisville.edu
Web: See Guidelines
Address May Change: 6/1/05

PUBLICATION GUIDELINES:

Manuscript Length: 16-20
Copies Required: Three
Computer Submission: Yes Disk, Email
Format: MSWord
Fees to Review: 0.00 US$

Manuscript Style:
    Chicago Manual of Style

CIRCULATION DATA:

Reader: Academics
Frequency of Issue: Quarterly
Copies per Issue: Less than 1,000
Sponsor/Publisher: College of Education,
    University of Louisville/Caddo Gap Press
Subscribe Price: 50.00 US$ Individual
    80.00 US$ Library/Institution
    100.00 US$ Outside of USA

REVIEW INFORMATION:

Type of Review: Blind Review
No. of External Reviewers: 2
No. of In House Reviewers: 1
Acceptance Rate: 21-30%
Time to Review: 2 - 3 Months
Reviewers Comments: Yes
Invited Articles: 0-5%
Fees to Publish: 0.00 US$

MANUSCRIPT TOPICS:

Cultural Foundations; Curriculum Studies; Education Management/Administration; Higher Education; Multicultural Education; Religious Education; Social Studies/Social Science; Teacher Education; Urban Education, Cultural/Non-Traditional

MANUSCRIPT GUIDELINES/COMMENTS:

The *Journal of Thought* is a quarterly publication devoted to the reflective examination of educational issues and problems from the perspective of diverse disciplines. The *Journal* welcomes scholars whose work represents varied viewpoints, methodologies, disciplines, cultures, and nationalities as it seeks to treat the most comprehensive issues and problems confronting education throughout the world. The editors solicit essays that develop a reasoned and supported argument, that offer insightful analysis and critiques of other's arguments, or that report on significant research of interest to the field. The editorial goal is to stimulate synthesis of diverse points of view and encourage interdisciplinary dialogue. To this end, pieces that respond to previously published work in the *Journal of Thought* are especially welcome.

588

Editorial offices for the *Journal of Thought* are at the College of Education and Human Development, University of Louisville. The website for the *Journal of Thought* is http://www.louisville.edu/journal/thought; the *Journal* is published by Caddo Gap Press, San Francisco, California. Editorial correspondence and submissions should be addressed to Douglas J. Simpson, Editor, *Journal of Thought*, College of Education and Human Development, University of Louisville, Louisville, Kentucky, 40292-0001 U.S.A.

Submission Guidelines
Manuscripts should be submitted in triplicate. Submissions will not be returned unless requested and accompanied by a postage-paid return envelope. The proposed article and notes or references should not exceed 20 doubled-spaced pages; slightly shorter articles are preferred. Articles must be original and not have appeared in print previously. The *Journal of Thought* is a refereed journal and articles are submitted for blind review; therefore, a title page without the author's name should be provided. Complete, formatted references, text citations, and notes should be provided according to the *Chicago Manual of Style* (14th Edition) guidelines, chapters 15 and 16. For references, use the example on p. 648 as a guide. This is the humanities style, but dates immediately follow the authors' names. For text citations, use the examples on p. 641, 16.3 and p. 643, 16.10. For notes, use the example on p. 530. Notes that contain only bibliographic material should be incorporated into the references. Upon acceptance for publication, the final revised version of all manuscripts must be submitted by the author(s) on a three-and-one-half-inch high-density computer disk (with the platform and program clearly indicated).

Journal on Excellence in College Teaching

ADDRESS FOR SUBMISSION:

Gregg Wentzell, Managing Editor
Journal on Excellence in College Teaching
Miami University
Office for the Advancement of
  Scholarship and Teaching (OAST)
Oxford, OH 45056
USA
Phone: 513-529-7224
Fax: 513-529-3762
E-Mail: wentzeqw@muohio.edu
Web: ject.lib.muohio.edu
Address May Change:

PUBLICATION GUIDELINES:

Manuscript Length: 16-20
Copies Required: Six
Computer Submission: Yes
Format: MSWord
Fees to Review: 0.00 US$

Manuscript Style:
  American Psychological Association

CIRCULATION DATA:

Reader: Practicing Teachers, Academics
Frequency of Issue: 3 Times/Year
Copies per Issue: Less than 1,000
Sponsor/Publisher: Miami University
Subscribe Price: 43.00 US$ Print Copy
  49.00 US$ Non-US
  99.00 US$ Electronic Subscription

REVIEW INFORMATION:

Type of Review: Blind Review
No. of External Reviewers: 3
No. of In House Reviewers: 3
Acceptance Rate: 11-20%
Time to Review: 2 - 3 Months
Reviewers Comments: Yes
Invited Articles: 11-20%
Fees to Publish: 0.00 US$

MANUSCRIPT TOPICS:
Higher Education

MANUSCRIPT GUIDELINES/COMMENTS:

Call For Manuscripts
Manuscripts are solicited for publication in the *Journal on Excellence in College Teaching* a peer-reviewed journal published by and for faculty at universities and two- and four-year colleges to increase student learning through effective teaching, interest in and enthusiasm for the profession of teaching, and communication among faculty about their classroom experiences. The *Journal* provides a scholarly, written forum for discussion by faculty about all areas affecting teaching; and learning, and gives faculty the opportunity to share proven, innovative pedagogies and thoughtful, inspirational insights about teaching.

Manuscript Preparation Guidelines
Content
Accepted for publication are papers on college and university teaching that demonstrate scholarly excellence in at least one of the following categories:

- **Research**: Reports important results from own experience or research; describes problem clearly; provides baseline data; explains what researcher has done and why; and provides results.
- **Integration**: Integrates research of others in meaningful way; compares or contrasts theories; critiques results; and/or provides context for future exploration. Innovation
- **Innovation**: Proposes innovation of theory, approach, or process of teaching; provides original and creative ideas based on results of research by self or others; and outlines proposed strategy for testing effectiveness of ideas.
- **Inspiration**: Provides inspiration for teaching excellence; combines personal values, insight, and experience, to communicate enthusiasm and dedication to outstanding teaching.

Papers appearing in *the* Journal may be interdisciplinary or specific to one or a group of disciplines, and may address a general or specific audience.

Review Process

Manuscripts are reviewed first by the editorial staff. Those that are appropriate for the Journal are sent to at least two experts in teaching scholarship, particularly in the writer's discipline or subject area. All reviews are "blind," that is, without identifying the author(s) to the reviewers. Reviewers are encouraged to write comments for the author(s). Editorial feedback and/or reviews are provided to authors for all manuscripts.

Articles maybe rejected or accepted outright, or accepted with a request for revision. In some cases, articles requiring major revision (such as including an additional year's results) are not officially accepted or rejected, but will be reconsidered when revised.

Format

Please prepare your manuscript according; to *APA format* as described in the *Publication Manual e f the* American Psychological Association, Fifth Edition. The main points to remember are the *following:*

- Include in abstract of 100 words or less. See pages 8-11 of the *A13A Manual* for guidance on how to write a good abstract.
- Citations appear in a references section at the end of the manuscript. See pages 174-222 of the *MIA* for the formats for different types of reference material. Only and all sources cited appear in the references section. Suggested readings may be listed in a separate bibliography.
- In the text, sources are cited by author(s) and date, anti page numbers for direct quotations. See pages 9 5-99 and 168-174 of the *APA Manual* for citation formats.
- Headings, if they are used, are not numbered. See pages 90-93 of the *APA Manual* for guidance concerning headings.
- The proper physical appearance of the manuscript is described on pages 237-248 of the *APA Manual.*
- There are no length specifications; however, manuscripts submitted tend to average 20 to 25 double-spaced pages. Excessively long manuscripts usually can be reduced without damaging duality.

- Many reviewers tell us that tables, figures, and charts are effective ways to replace dull text and that examples and stories help capture the reader's interest.
- When you describe new approaches and programs, please include evaluative information. If you have not run a controlled study with pre- and post-tests, describe what next steps should be taken to confirm your findings.

Submission Requirements

Submit to the Managing Editor three copies of the Cover Sheet (attached), three copies of your complete manuscript, and three "blind" copies of the manuscript that omit your name and any reference to your institution. Indicate two or three key words for the manuscript that will be used for indexing. Mail your submission to: Gregg Wentzell; Managing Editor; *Journal on Excellence in College Teaching;* Office for the Advancement of Scholarship and Teaching; Miami University; Oxford, OH 45056

If your manuscript is accepted for, publication, we will ask you to send us the document on diskette. We can accept either PC or Mac formats on 3.5" diskettes. Do not send a diskette until requested.

If you have any questions, please contact the Managing Editor at (513) 529-7224 or at wentzegw@muohio.edu. Thank you for your interest in and support for the *Journal on Excellence in College leaching.*

Manuscript Cover Sheet

Title of manuscript_____

_____

Please enter the information requested below for all authors, listing the names in the order in which they should appear. Submit three copies of this sheet with three complete copies and three blind copies of your manuscript.

Name_____

Mailing address_____

_____

_____

Telephone_____Fax_____

Email address_____

[continue for all authors.]

Language, Culture and Curriculum

ADDRESS FOR SUBMISSION:

Eoghan MacAogain, Editor
Language, Culture and Curriculum
Linguistics Institute of Ireland
31 Fitzwilliam Place
Dublin 2,
Ireland
Phone: 353-1-6765489
Fax: 353-1-6610004
E-Mail: lcc@ite.ie
Web: www.multilingual-matters.com
Address May Change:

PUBLICATION GUIDELINES:

Manuscript Length: 21-25
Copies Required: Four
Computer Submission: No
Format: N/A
Fees to Review: 0.00 US$

Manuscript Style:
     American Psychological Association

CIRCULATION DATA:

Reader: Academics, Practicing Teachers
Frequency of Issue: 3 Times/Year
Copies per Issue: Less than 1,000
Sponsor/Publisher: Linguistics Institute of
   Ireland / Multilingual Matters Ltd.
Subscribe Price: 75.00 US$ Individual
   295.00 US$ Institution

REVIEW INFORMATION:

Type of Review: Blind Review
No. of External Reviewers: 2
No. of In House Reviewers: 1
Acceptance Rate: 50%
Time to Review: 2 - 3 Months
Reviewers Comments: Yes
Invited Articles: 0-5%
Fees to Publish: 0.00 US$

MANUSCRIPT TOPICS:
Bilingual/E.S.L.; Curriculum Studies; Languages & Linguistics; Teacher Education

MANUSCRIPT GUIDELINES/COMMENTS:

Aims of the Journal
This journal, published for the Linguistics Institute of Ireland provides a forum for the discussion of the many factors; social, cultural, cognitive and organizational which are relevant to the formulation and implementation of language curricula. Second languages, minority and heritage languages are a special concern. First-language and foreign language studies are also welcomed when they have implications for multiculturalism. The journal provides practical guidelines for the design and implementation of language curricula with cultural objectives, taking into account organizational factors in the school and community.

Guidelines
Articles should not normally exceed 7000 words. Note that it is our policy not to review papers that are currently under consideration by other journals. They should be typed, double-spaced on A4 (or similar) paper, with ample left and right-hand margins, on one side of the paper only, and every page should be numbered consecutively. A cover page should contain

only the title, thereby facilitating anonymous reviewing by two independent assessors. Authors may also wish to take precautions to avoid textual references which would identify themselves to the referees. In such cases the authors of accepted papers will have the opportunity to include any such omitted material before the paper is published.

Submissions for Work in Progress/ Readers' Response /Letters to the Editor sections should be approximately 500 words in length.

Main contact author should also appear in a separate paragraph on the title page.

An abstract should be included. This should not exceed 200 words (longer abstracts are rejected by many abstracting services).

A short version of the title (maximum 45 characters) should also be supplied for the journal's running headline.

To facilitate the production of the annual subject index, a list of keywords (not more than six) should be provided, under which the paper may be indexed.

Four copies of the article must be submitted.

Footnotes should be avoided. Essential notes should be numbered in the text and grouped together at the end of the article. Diagrams and Figures, if they are considered essential, should be clearly related to the section of the text to which they refer. The original diagrams and figures should be submitted with the top copy.

References should be set out in alphabetical order of the author's name in a list at the end of the article. They should be given in standard form, as in the Appendix below.

References in the text of an article should be by the author's name and year of publication, as in these examples: Jones (1997) in a paper on ...(commonest version); Jones and Evans (1997c:22) state that ...(where page number is required); Evidence is given by Smith et al. (1994)...(for three or more authors). Further exploration of this aspect may be found in many sources (e.g. Brown & Green, 1992; Jackson, 1993; White, 1991a) (note alphabetical order, use of & and semi-colons).

Once the refereeing procedures are completed, authors should, if possible, supply a word-processor disc containing their manuscript file(s). If presented on disc, we require files to be saved:

- on an IBM-PC compatible 3.5 inch disc (or CD-ROM) or on an Apple Mac high-density 3.5 inch disc.
- Text should be saved in the author's normal word-processor format. The name of the word-processor program should also be supplied. Tables and Figures should be saved in separate files.

The author of an article accepted for publication will receive page proofs for correction, if there is sufficient time to do so. This stage must not be used as an opportunity to revise the paper, because alterations are extremely costly; extensive changes will be charged to the author and will probably result in the article being delayed to a later issue. Speedy return of corrected proofs is important.

Contributions and queries should be sent to the Editors, Multilingual Matters Ltd., Frankfurt Lodge, Clevedon Hall, Victoria Road, Clevedon, BS21 7HH, England. A very large majority of authors' proof-corrections are caused by errors in references. Authors are therefore requested to check the following points particularly carefully when submitting manuscripts:

- Are all the references in the reference list cited in the text?
- Do all the citations in the text appear in the reference list?
- Do the dates in the text and the reference list correspond?
- Do the spellings of authors' names in text and reference list correspond, and do all authors have the correct initials?
- Are journal references complete with volume and pages numbers?
- Are references to books complete with place of publication and the name of the publisher?

It is extremely helpful if references are presented as far as possible in accordance with our house style. A few more typical examples are shown below. Note, especially, use of upper & lower case in paper titles, use of capital letters and italic (underlining can be used as an alternative if italic is not available) in book and journal titles, punctuation (or lack of it) after dates, journal titles, and book titles. The inclusion of issue numbers of journals, or page numbers in books is optional but if included should be as per the examples below.

Department of Education and Science (DES) (1985) *Education for All* (The Swann Report). London: HMSO

Evans, N.J. and Ilbery, B.W. (1989) A conceptual framework for investigating farm-based accommodation and tourism in Britain. *Journal of Rural Studies* 5 (3), 257-266.

Evans, N.J. and Ilbery, B.W. (1992) Advertising and farm-based accommodation: A British case-study. *Tourism Management* 13 (4), 415-422.

Laufer, B (2000) Vocabulary acquisition in a second language: The hypothesis of 'synforms'. PhD thesis, University of Edinburgh.

Mackey, W.F. (1998) The ecology of language shift. In P.H. Nelde (ed.) *Languages in Contact and in Conflict* (pp. 35-41). Wiesbaden: Steiner.

Marien, C. and Pizam, A. (1997) Implementing sustainable tourism development through citizen participation in the planning process. In S. Wahab and J. Pigram (eds) *Tourism, Development and Growth* (pp. 164-78). London: Routledge.

Morrison, D. (1999) Small group discussion project questionnaire. University of Hong Kong Language Centre (mimeo).

U.S. Census Bureau (1998) State profile: California. Online document: http/www.census.gov/statab/www/states/ca.txt.

Zahn, C.J. and Hopper, R (2000) The speech evaluation instrument: A user's manual (version 1.0a). Unpublished manuscript, Cleveland State University.

Zigler, E. and Balla, D. (eds) *Mental Retardation: The Developmental-Difference Controversy*. Hillsdale, N.J: Lawrence Erlbaum.

For more details, please e-mail us on multi@multilingual-matters com.

Leadership Magazine

ADDRESS FOR SUBMISSION:

Susan Davis, Editor
Leadership Magazine
Association of California School Admin.
1517 L. Street
Sacramento, CA 95814
USA
Phone: 916-444-3216
Fax: 916-444-1085
E-Mail: sdavis@acsa.org
Web:
Address May Change:

PUBLICATION GUIDELINES:

Manuscript Length: 8
Copies Required: One
Computer Submission: Yes
Format: Mac or IBM
Fees to Review: 0.00 US$

Manuscript Style:
    Associated Press Stylebook

CIRCULATION DATA:

Reader: Administrators
Frequency of Issue: 5 Times/Year
Copies per Issue: 10,001 - 25,000
Sponsor/Publisher: Association of
    California School Admin.
Subscribe Price: 50.00 US$

REVIEW INFORMATION:

Type of Review: Editorial Review
No. of External Reviewers: 0
No. of In House Reviewers: 2
Acceptance Rate: 31%
Time to Review: 4 - 6 Months
Reviewers Comments: No
Invited Articles: 11-20%
Fees to Publish: 0.00 US$

MANUSCRIPT TOPICS:

Adult Career & Vocational; Bilingual/E.S.L.; Counseling & Personnel Services; Curriculum Studies; Elementary/Early Childhood; Gifted Children; Health & Physical Education; Special Education; Teacher Education; Tests, Measurement & Evaluation; Urban Education, Cultural/Non-Traditional

MANUSCRIPT GUIDELINES/COMMENTS:

Leadership is a magazine, not a journal. We are interested in all topics that relate to practicing administrators' concerns. We encourage administrators to read across disciplines and special interests, so we prefer summaries of research and lay terminology. Busy administrators want to stay abreast of what is happening, but reading research articles is not the way to go about it.

For guidelines, write the editor.

Learning and Motivation

ADDRESS FOR SUBMISSION:

William A. Roberts, Editor
Learning and Motivation
University of Western Ontario
Department of Psychology
London
Ontario, N6A 5C2
Canada
Phone: 519-661-2111 xt 84686 or 88172
Fax: 519-661-3961
E-Mail: roberts@uno.ca
Web:
Address May Change: 12/31/03

PUBLICATION GUIDELINES:

Manuscript Length: 16-30
Copies Required: Four
Computer Submission: Yes Email
Format: MSWord or WordPerfect
Fees to Review: 0.00 US$

Manuscript Style:
    American Psychological Association

CIRCULATION DATA:

Reader: Academics
Frequency of Issue: Quarterly
Copies per Issue:
Sponsor/Publisher: Academic Press, Inc.
Subscribe Price: 425.00 US$ US, Canada
    550.00 US$ All Other Countries
    IDEAL Deep Discounts Avail.

REVIEW INFORMATION:

Type of Review: Blind Review
No. of External Reviewers: No Reply
No. of In House Reviewers: 2
Acceptance Rate: 40%
Time to Review: 1 - 2 Months
Reviewers Comments: Yes
Invited Articles: 0-5%
Fees to Publish: 0.00 US$

MANUSCRIPT TOPICS:
Basic Processes: Learning, Motivation, Cognition; Education Management/Administration

MANUSCRIPT GUIDELINES/COMMENTS:

Information for Authors
Learning and Motivation publishes original experimental papers addressed to the analysis of basic phenomena and mechanisms of learning and motivation, including papers on biological and evolutionary influences upon the learning and motivation processes. Studies involving either animal or human subjects are invited. Publication in *Learning and Motivation* is subject to the Editor's judgment that inclusion will make a substantial contribution to our understanding of basic principles of learning and motivation and to general behavioral theory. Monographic reports of an integrated series of experiments, as well as papers reporting a single experiment will be published. Preference is given to longer, more substantive papers.

Submission of Manuscripts.
Manuscripts must be written in English and should be submitted in quadruplicate (one original and three photocopies), including four sets of good-quality figures, to

598

Dr. William A. Roberts
Department of Psychology
University of Western Ontario
London, Ontario N6A 5C2
Canada
Tel: (519) 661-2111 ext. 84686
E-mail: roberts@julian.uwo.ca

There are no submission fees or page charges. Each manuscript should be accompanied by a letter outlining the basic findings of the paper and their significance.

Manuscripts are accepted for review with the understanding that no substantial portion of the study has been published or is under consideration for publication elsewhere and that its submission for publication has been approved by all of the authors and by the institution where the work was carried out. Manuscripts that do not meet the general criteria or standards for publication in *Learning and Motivation* will be immediately returned to the authors, without detailed review.

Authors submitting a manuscript do so on the understanding that if it is accepted for publication, copyright in the article, including the right to reproduce the article in all forms and media, shall be assigned exclusively to the Publisher. The Copyright Transfer Agreement, which may be copied from the journal home page listed here, should be signed by the appropriate person and should accompany the original submission of a manuscript to this journal. The transfer of copyright does not take effect until the manuscript is accepted for publication.

Authors are responsible for obtaining permissions to reprint previously published figures, tables, and other material. Letters of permission should accompany the final submission.

Electronic Transmission of Accepted Manuscripts.
Authors are requested to transmit the text and art of the manuscript in electronic form, via either computer disk, e-mail, or FTP, after all revisions have been incorporated and the manuscript has been accepted for publication. Submission as an e-mail attachment is acceptable provided that all files are included in a single archive the size of which does not exceed 2 megabytes (lm@acad.com). Hard-copy printouts of the manuscript and art must also be supplied. The manuscript will be edited according to the style of the journal, and authors must be read the proofs carefully. Complete instructions for electronic transmission can be found on the Electronic Submission page.

Digital Object Identifier.
Academic Press assigns a unique digital object identifier (DOI) to every article it publishes. The DOI appears on the title page of the article. It is assigned after the article has been accepted for publication and persists throughout the lifetime of the article. Because of its persistence, it can be used to query Academic Press for information on the article during the production process, to find the article on the Internet through various Web sites, including IDEAL, and to cite the article in academic references. When an Academic Press article is used in a reference section, it is important to include the article's DOI in the reference, as volume

and page information is not always available for articles published online. See References below for samples of DOIs included in references. Further information may be found at http://www.academicpress.com/doi.

Preparation of Manuscript.

Format and style of a manuscript should conform to the conventions specified in the most recent edition of the *Publication Manual of the American Psychological Association,* with the exceptions listed below. Please note that it is the responsibility of the author that manuscripts for *Learning and Motivation* conform to the requirements of this journal.

Manuscripts should be double-spaced throughout on one side of 8½ x 11-inch or A4 white paper. Pages should be numbered consecutively and organized as follows:

The **Title Page** (p. 1) should contain the article title, authors' names and affiliations, footnotes to the title, a running title of less than 50 characters, and the address for manuscript correspondence (including e-mail address and telephone and fax numbers).

The **Abstract** (p. 2) must be a single paragraph that summarizes the main findings of the paper in less than 150 words. After the abstract a list of up to 10 key words that will be useful for indexing or searching should be included.

The **Introduction** should be concise as possible, without subheadings.

Materials and Methods should be sufficiently detailed to enable the experiments to be reproduced.

Results and Discussion may be combined and may be organized into subheadings.

References should be cited in the text by surname of the author, followed by year of publication. Only articles that have been published or are in press should be included in the references. Unpublished results or personal communications should be cited as such in text. When citing an Academic Press journal, include the digital object identifier (DOI), if noted, from the article's title page. Please note the following examples, the second of which shows an article available on IDEAL but not yet assigned to a printed issue. Please use the following style:

Lloyd, P., & Beveridge, M. (1981). *Information and meaning in child communication.* New York: Academic Press.

Matthers, J. B. (2000). Learning tasks dependent on a variable reward. *Learning and Motivation,* doi:10.1006/lmot.1999.2007.

McSweeney, F. K., Swindell, S., & Weatherly, J. N. (1999). Within-session response patterns during variable interval, random reinforcement, and extinction procedures. *Learning and Motivation,* **30,** 221-240, doi:10.1006/lmot.1999.1032.

Miller, R.R., & Matzsel, L.D. (1988). The comparator hypothesis: A response rule for the expression of associations. In G. H. Bower (Ed.), *The psychology of learning and motivation: Advances in research and theory (Vol. 22).* New York: Academic Press.

Figures should be in finished form suitable for publication. and photographs. Number figures consecutively with Arabic numerals, and indicate the top and the authors on the back of each figure. Lettering on drawings should be professional quality or generated by high-resolution computer graphics and must be large enough to withstand appropriate reduction for publication.

Color figures can be accepted only if the authors defray the cost. Mounted color figures *must* be submitted on paper or flexible board due to the nature of the reproduction process.

Tables should be numbered consequently with Arabic numerals in order of appearance in the text. Type each table double-spaced on a separate page with a short descriptive title typed directly above and with essential footnotes below. Authors should submit complex tables as camera-ready copy.

Proofs will be sent to the corresponding author. To avoid delay in publication, only necessary changes should be made, and proofs should be returned promptly. Authors will be charged for alterations that exceed 10% of the total cost of composition.

Reprints. Fifty reprints will be provided to the corresponding author free of charge. Additional reprints may be ordered.

Learning Environments Research

ADDRESS FOR SUBMISSION:

Barry J. Fraser, Editor
Learning Environments Research
Journals Editorial Office LER
Kluwer Academic Publishers
PO Box 990
3300 AZ
Dordrecht,
The Netherlands
Phone: +61 8 9266 7896
Fax: +61 8 9266 2503
E-Mail: B.Fraser@curtin.edu.au
Web:
Address May Change: 12/12/03

PUBLICATION GUIDELINES:

Manuscript Length: 21-25
Copies Required: Four
Computer Submission: No
Format: N/A
Fees to Review: 0.00 US$

Manuscript Style:
American Psychological Association

CIRCULATION DATA:

Reader: Academics
Frequency of Issue: 3 Times/Year
Copies per Issue: Less than 1,000
Sponsor/Publisher: Kluwer Academic
Publishers
Subscribe Price: 97.00 US$ Individual
191.00 US$ Library

REVIEW INFORMATION:

Type of Review: Editorial Review
No. of External Reviewers: 2
No. of In House Reviewers: 0
Acceptance Rate: 21-30%
Time to Review: 4 - 6 Months
Reviewers Comments: Yes
Invited Articles: 0-5%
Fees to Publish: 0.00 US$

MANUSCRIPT TOPICS:

Curriculum Studies; Education Management/Administration; Educational Environment; Educational Psychology; Science Math & Environment; Tests, Measurement & Evaluation

MANUSCRIPT GUIDELINES/COMMENTS:

Aims & Scope

Learning Environments Research publishes original academic papers dealing with the study of learning environments, including theoretical reflections, reports of quantitative and qualitative research, critical and integrative literature reviews and meta-analyses, discussion of methodological issues, reports of the development and validation of assessment instruments, and reviews of books and evaluation instruments.

The scope of the journal deliberately is very broad in terms of both substance and methods. 'Learning environment' refers to the social, physical, psychological and pedagogical contexts in which learning occurs and which affect student achievement and attitudes. The aim of the journal is to increase our understanding of pre-primary, primary, high school, college and university, and lifelong learning environments irrespective of subject area. Apart from classroom-level and school-level environments, special attention is given to the many out-of-school learning environments such as the home, science centres, and television, etc. The influence of the rapidly developing field of Information Technology with its whole new range of learning environments is an important aspect of the scope of the journal.

A wide range of qualitative and quantitative methods for studying learning environments, and the combination of qualitative and quantitative methods, are strongly encouraged.

The journal has an affiliation with the American Educational Research Association's Special Interest Group on the Study of Learning Environments. However, having Regional Editors and an Editorial Board from around the world ensures that LER is a truly international journal.

Manuscript Submission
Kluwer Academic Publishers prefer the submission of manuscripts and figures in electronic form in addition to a hard-copy printout. The preferred storage medium for your electronic manuscript is a 3 1/2 inch diskette. Please label your diskette properly, giving exact details on the name(s) of the file(s), the operating system and software used. Always save your electronic manuscript in the word processor format that you use; conversions to other formats and versions tend to be imperfect. In general, use as few formatting codes as possible. For safety's sake, you should always retain a backup copy of your file(s). After acceptance, please make absolutely sure that you send us the latest (i.e., revised) version of your manuscript, both as hard copy printout and on diskette.

Kluwer Academic Publishers prefer articles submitted in word processing packages such as MS Word, WordPerfect, etc. running under operating systems MS DOS, Windows and Apple Macintosh, or in the file format LaTeX. Articles submitted in other software programs, as well as articles for conventional typesetting, can also be accepted.

For submission in LaTeX, Kluwer Academic Publishers have developed special LaTeX style files, KLUWER.STY (LaTeX 2.09) and KLUWER.CLS (LaTeX 2E), which are used for all Kluwer journals, irrespective of the publication's size or layout. The specific journal formatting is done later during the production process. KLUWER.STY and KLUWER.CLS are offered by a number of servers around the world. Unfortunately, these copies are often unauthorised and authors are strongly advised not to use them. Kluwer Academic Publishers can only guarantee the integrity of style files obtained directly from them. Authors can obtain KLUWER.STY and KLUWER.CLS and the accompanying instruction file KAPINS.TEX from the Kluwer Academic Publishers Information Service (KAPIS) at the following website: http://www.wkap.nl.

Technical support on the usage of the style files is given via the e-mail address: texhelp@wkap.nl.

Referee Process
Articles submitted to *Learning Environments Research* are reviewed by one of the Regional Editors and three referees. For the purpose of reviewing, articles for publication should be submitted as hard-copy printout (4-fold: 1 original and 3 copies) and on diskette to:

Learning Environments Research, Journals Editorial Office, Kluwer Academic Publishers, P.O. Box 990, 3300 AZ Dordrecht, The Netherlands

Manuscript Presentation

The journal's language is English. British English or American English spelling and terminology may be used, but either one should be followed consistently throughout the article. Manuscripts should range in length between 4000 and 7000 words (including references, tables and figures). Manuscripts should be printed or typewritten on A4 or US Letter bond paper, one side only, leaving adequate margins on all sides to allow reviewers' remarks. Please double-space all material, including notes and references. Quotations of more than 40 words should be set off clearly, by indenting the left-hand margin and using a smaller typeface. Use double quotation marks for direct quotations from the literature or from interviews, and single quotation marks for quotations within quotations and for words or phrases used in a special sense.

Number the pages consecutively with the first page containing:

- running head (shortened title, maximum of 50 characters including spaces)
- article type (if applicable)
- title
- author(s)
- affiliation(s)
- full address for correspondence, including telephone and fax number and e-mail address

Abstract

Please provide a short abstract of 100 to 250 words. The abstract should not contain any undefined abbreviations or unspecified references.

Key Words

Please provide 5 to 10 key words or short phrases in alphabetical order.

Figures and Tables

In addition to hard copy printouts of figures, authors are encouraged to supply the electronic versions of figures in either Encapsulated PostScript (EPS) or TIFF format. Many other formats, e.g. Microsoft Postscript, PiCT (Macintosh) and WMF (Windows), cannot be used and the hard copy will be scanned instead.

Figures should be saved in separate files *without* their captions, which should be included with the text of the article. Files should be named according to DOS conventions, e.g., 'figure1.eps'. For vector graphics, EPS is the preferred format. Lines should not be thinner than 0.25pts and in-fill patterns and screens should have a density of at least 10%. Font-related problems can be avoided by using standard fonts such as Times Roman and Helvetica. For bitmapped graphics, TIFF is the preferred format but EPS is also acceptable. The following resolutions are optimal: black-and-white line figures - 600 - 1200 dpi; line figures with some grey or coloured lines - 600 dpi; photographs - 300 dpi; screen dumps leave as is. Higher resolutions will not improve output quality but will only increase file size, which may cause problems with printing; lower resolutions can compromise output quality. Please try to provide artwork that approximately fits within the typeset areas of the journal. Screened originals i.e., originals with grey areas, may suffer badly from reduction by more than 10-15%.

Avoiding Problems with EPS Graphics

Please always check whether the figures print correctly to a PostScript printer in a reasonable amount of time. If they do not, simplify your figures or use a different graphics program.

If EPS export does not produce acceptable output, try to create an EPS file with the printer driver (see below). This option is unavailable with the Microsoft driver for Windows NT so, if you run Windows NT, get the Adobe driver from the Adobe site (www.adobe.com).

If EPS export is not an option, e.g. because you rely on OLE and cannot create separate files for your graphics, it may help us if you simply provide a PostScript dump of the entire document.

How to Set Up for EPS and PostScript Dumps Under Windows

Create a printer entry specifically for this purpose: install the printer 'Apple Laserwrite Plus' and specify 'FILE' as printer port. Each time you send something to the 'printer', you will be asked for a filename. This file will be the EPS file or PostScript dump that we can use.

The EPS export option can be found under the PostScript tab. EPS export should be used only for single-page documents. For printing a document of several pages, select 'Optimise for portability' instead. The option 'Download header with each job' should be checked.

Submissions of Hard Copy Figures

If no electronic versions of figures are available, submit only high-quality artwork that can be reproduced as is, i.e. without any part having to be redrawn or re-typeset. The letter size of any text in the figures must be large enough to allow for reduction. Photographs should be in black-and-white on glossy paper. If a figure contains colour, make absolutely clear whether it should be printed in black-and-white or in colour. Figures that are to be printed in black-and-white should not be submitted in colour. Authors will be charged for reproducing figures in colour.

Each figure and table should be numbered and mentioned in the text. The approximate position of figures and tables should be indicated in the margin of the manuscript. On the reverse side of each figure, the name of the (first) author and the figure number should be written in pencil; the top of the figure should be clearly indicated. Figures and tables should be placed at the end of the manuscript following the Reference section. Each figure and table should be accompanied by an explanatory legend. The figure legends should be grouped and placed on a separate page. Figures are not returned to the author unless specifically requested. In tables, footnotes are preferable to long explanatory material in either the heading or body of the table. Such explanatory footnotes, identified by superscript letters, should be placed immediately below the table.

Section Headings

First-, second-, third- and fourth-order headings should be clearly distinguishable.

Appendices
Supplementary material should be collected in an Appendix and placed before the Notes and Reference sections.

Author Note
Acknowledgements of people, grants, funds, etc. should be placed in a separate section before the References.

Notes
Please use endnotes rather than footnotes. Notes should be indicated by consecutive superscript numbers in the text and listed at the end of the article before the References. A source reference note should be indicated by an asterisk after the title. This note should be placed at the bottom of the first page.

Cross-Referencing
Please make optimal use of the cross-referencing features of your software package. Do not cross-reference page numbers. Cross-references should refer to, for example, equation numbers, figure and table numbers.

In the text, a reference identified by means of an author's name should be followed by the date of the reference in parentheses and page number(s) where appropriate. When there are three, four or five authors, cite 'all' authors the first time the reference occurs; in subsequent citations include only the surname of the first author followed by 'et al'. When a work has six or more authors, always cite only the surname of the first author followed by 'et al'. In the event that an author cited has had two or more works published during the same year, the reference, both in the text and in the reference list, should be identified by a lower case letter like 'a' and 'b' after the date to distinguish the works. Use alphabetical order for lists of references in parentheses.

Examples: Winograd (1986, p. 204); (Winograd, 1986a, 1986b); (Flores et al., 1988; Winograd, 1986); (Bullen & Bennett, 1990)

References
References should follow the American Psychological Association (APA) (Fourth Edition) style in alphabetical order (see examples below). Personal communications should not be included in the reference list but should only be mentioned in the article text, e.g. K. W. Schaie (personal communication, April 18, 1993).
Examples:
Journals.
Herman, L. M., Kuczaj, S. A., III, & Holder, M. D. (1993). Responses to anomalous gestural sequences by a language-trained dolphin: Evidence for processing of semantic relations and syntactic information. *Journal of Experimental Psychology: General, 122,* 184-194.

Books
Mitchell, T. R., & Larson, J. R., Jr. (1987). *People in organizations: An introduction to organizational behavior* (3rd ed.). New York: McGraw-Hill.

Edited Books
Gibbs, J. T., & Huang, L. N. (Eds.). (1991). *Children of color: Psychological interventions with minority youth.* San Francisco: Jossey-Bass.

Published Articles or Chapters in an Edited Book, Published Proceedings, Published Contributions to a Symposium
Massaro, D. (1992). Broadening the domain of the fuzzy logical model of perception. In H. L. Pick, Jr., P. van den Broek, & D. C. Knill (Eds.), *Cognition: Conceptual and methodological issues* (pp. 51-84). Washington, DC: American Psychological Association.

Technical and Research Reports
Mazzeo, J., Druesne, B., Raffeld, P. C., Checketts, K. T., & Muhlstein, A. (1991). *Comparability of computer and paper-and-pencil scores for two CLEP general examinations* (College Board Rep. No. 91-5). Princeton, NJ: Educational Testing Service.

Educational Resources Information Center (ERIC) Document (Report)
Mead, J. V. (1992). *Looking at old photographs: Investigating the teacher tales that novice teachers bring with them* (Report No. NCRTL-RR-92-4). East Lansing, MI: National Center for Research on Teacher Learning. (ERIC Document Reproduction Service No. ED 346 082)

Manuscripts in Progress or Submitted for Publication but Not Yet Accepted
McIntosh, D. N. (1993). *Religion as schema, with implications for the relation between religion and coping.* Manuscript submitted for publication.

Unpublished Manuscripts Not Submitted for Publication
Stinson, C., Milbrath, C., Reidbord, S., & Bucci, W. (1992). *Thematic segmentation of psychotherapy transcripts for convergent analyses.* Unpublished manuscript.

Unpublished Papers Presented at a Meeting
Lanktree, C., & Briere, J. (1991, January). *Early data on the Trauma Sympton Checklist for Children (TSC-C).* Paper presented at the meeting of the American Professional Society on the Abuse of Children, San Diego, CA.

Unpublished Doctoral Dissertations
Wilfley, D. E. (1989). *Interpersonal analyses of bulimia: Normal-weight and obese.* Unpublished doctoral dissertation, University of Missouri, Columbia.

Full Text Article From Electronic Database
Sale, P., & Carey, D. M. (1995). The sociometric status of students with disabilities in a full inclusion school [electronic database]. *Exceptional Children, 62*(1), 6-22. Available: Expanded Academic Index Electronic Collection: A17435391

World Wide Web Document
Land, T. (1996). *Web extension to American Psychological Association Style* (WEAPAS) [WWW document]. URL http://www.beadsland.com/weapas/

Proofs
Proofs will be sent to the corresponding author. One corrected proof, together with the original, edited manuscript, should be returned to the Publisher within three days of receipt by mail (airmail overseas).

Offprints
Twenty-five offprints of each article will be provided free of charge. Additional offprints can be ordered by means of an offprint order form supplied with the proofs.

Page Charges and Colour Figures
No page charges are levied on authors or their institutions. Colour figures are published at the author's expense only.

Copyright
Authors will be asked, upon acceptance of an article, to transfer copyright of the article to the Publisher. This will ensure the widest possible dissemination of information under copyright laws.

Permissions
It is the responsibility of the author to obtain written permission for a quotation from unpublished material, or for all quotations in excess of 250 words in one extract or 500 words in total from any work still in copyright, and for the reprinting of figures, tables or poems from unpublished or copyrighted material.
Additional Information
Additional information can be obtained from:

Learning Environments Research
Kluwer Academic Publishers
P.O. Box 17
3300 AA Dordrecht
The Netherlands
Tel: +31-78-6392183
Fax: +31-78-6392254
Internet: http://www.wkap.nl

Liberal Education

ADDRESS FOR SUBMISSION:

Bridget Puzon, Editor
Liberal Education
Association of American Colleges
    and Universities
1818 R Street, NW
Washington, DC 20009
USA
Phone: 202-884-7416
Fax: 202-265-9532
E-Mail: puzon@aacu.nw.dc.us
Web:
Address May Change:

CIRCULATION DATA:

Reader: Academics, Administration &
    Faculty, Public Policy
Frequency of Issue: Quarterly
Copies per Issue: 4,001 - 5,000
Sponsor/Publisher: Association of
    American Colleges and Universities
Subscribe Price: 42.00 US$
    36.00 US$ AAC&U Members

PUBLICATION GUIDELINES:

Manuscript Length: varies, 2,000 words
Copies Required: No Hard Copy Required
Computer Submission: Yes Email
Format: 3 1/2 disk; WP, MSWord PC
Fees to Review: 0.00 US$

Manuscript Style:
    Chicago Manual of Style

REVIEW INFORMATION:

Type of Review: Blind Review
No. of External Reviewers: 0-1
No. of In House Reviewers: 1-2
Acceptance Rate: 25%
Time to Review: 1-3 Months
Reviewers Comments: No
Invited Articles: 50% +
Fees to Publish: 0.00 US$

MANUSCRIPT TOPICS:
Curriculum Studies; Education Management/Administration; Faculty Matters; Global and Diversity Education; Higher Education; Institutional Reforms/Structures

MANUSCRIPT GUIDELINES/COMMENTS:

Readership includes academic administrators, faculty, public policy leaders in education.

The magazine is divided into three sections: Featured Topic (length 2,000-3,500 words or 11-12 pages); Perspectives (length 1,800-2,500 words or 10 pages); and My View (length 4-6 pages). Manuscript should cover some aspect of liberal education related to: curriculum, faculty development, intercultural education , administration, teaching and learning.

Lifelong Learning in Europe (LLINE)

ADDRESS FOR SUBMISSION:

Eeva Siirala, Editorial Manager
Lifelong Learning in Europe (LLINE)
KVS Foundation
Museokatu 18 A 2
Fin-00100
Helsinki,
Finland
Phone: +358 9 5491 8855
Fax: +358 9 5491 8811
E-Mail: eeva.siirala@kvs.fi
Web:
Address May Change:

PUBLICATION GUIDELINES:

Manuscript Length: 6-10
Copies Required: One
Computer Submission: Yes
Format: MSWord
Fees to Review: 0.00 US$

Manuscript Style:
   See Manuscript Guidelines

CIRCULATION DATA:

Reader: Academics
Frequency of Issue: Quarterly
Copies per Issue: 1,001 - 2,000
Sponsor/Publisher: KVS Foundation
Subscribe Price: 40.00 US$ Individual
     60.00 US$ Institution
     40.00 US$ European Countries

REVIEW INFORMATION:

Type of Review: Blind Review
No. of External Reviewers: 2
No. of In House Reviewers: 3
Acceptance Rate: No Reply
Time to Review: 1 - 2 Months
Reviewers Comments: No
Invited Articles: 50% +
Fees to Publish: 0.00 US$

MANUSCRIPT TOPICS:

Adult Career & Vocational; Educational Psychology; Educational Technology Systems;
Higher Education; Special Education; Teacher Education; Tests, Measurement & Evaluation

MANUSCRIPT GUIDELINES/COMMENTS:

LLinE offers adult educators and researchers in adult education a forum for exchanging ideas
and experiences. The journal introduces practical experiments and solutions in adult and
continuing education disseminating information and knowledge, practical and theoretical,
useful to practitioners and presenting cases interesting to researchers. The editors welcome
articles on successful undertakings in adult and continuing education, future developments
and changes in the field or values guiding adult and continuing education ranging from
training and development in enterprises to liberal adult education in all parts of Europe.

The readers represent both practitioners and researchers in adult and continuing education.
Therefore the style of the text should be clear and easy to read and have an anchoring to
concrete practice.

610

Manuscripts should be sent to Eeva Siirala, KVS Foundation, Museokatu 18 A 2, 00100 Helsinki, Finland, fax +358-9-5491 8811, email eeva.silrala@kvs.fi. Papers are accepted for publication if they have not been submitted to other publications in the English languages but Lifelong Learning in Europe.

Manuscripts should be submitted either by email or on a diskette as well as a paper copy. We can accept a variety of IBM compatible software packages including WPWordStar, MS Word. Also ASCII files are acceptable and for Macintosh compatible packages, the only possibility.

All papers submitted should be between 1000 and 5000 words in length and be prefaced, on a separate sheet, by an abstract of no more than 200 words. They must be written in English. Manuscripts should be typed, double spaced, including references, and on one side of the paper only. Articles will be sent to two referees for assessment.

The title page should carry the title, the authors' names and affiliations and current addresses. Authors must supply telephone and fax numbers and email addresses if available. The author to whom the correspondence should be addressed must be clearly indicated.

References
Whenever there is a direct quotation, short quotations must be placed in single quotation marks, but long quotations should form separate, indented and single-spaced paragraphs. All quotations should be referenced by: author, year of publication and page reference, e.g.Antikainen & al. (1996, 36) writes,... or quotation followed by (Antikainen & al. 1996, 36) argues,... or it has been argued... (Antikainen & al 1996, 50-54).

Bibliographic reference should be listed alphabetically at the end of the paper. Publisher and place of publication should always be given, and especially for conference proceedings where available.

Antikainen,A., Houtsonen, J., Kauppila, J & Huotelin H. (1996) Living in a Learning Society, London: Falmer Press. Habermas, J. (1983) Modernity: an incomplete project, in H. Foster (ed.) The Anti-Aesthetic. Essays on Postmodern Culture (PortTownsend, Bay Press), 3-15.

de Bruijn REM. (1992) Computer aided learning for adults: a new approach. Aikuiskasvatus, a Finnish journal, 4 (12), 203-215.

Brucke der Gefuhle. Unterschiede in Aufbau and Funktion mannlicher and weiblicher Gehirne. (1996). Der Spiegel, 19,122-123.

Groombridge Brian (1992) Learning from one another. LEIF magazine, 3, 2-5.

Stott, D.H. (1981). The school debate. Unpublished manuscript.

Montgomery, R. (1980, April). Training for the vital skills. In C.M. Bhatia (Chair), Education, the great debate. Symposium conducted at the meeting of the American Science Congress Association, Washington.

Reference to Internet sources
Email. Siirala, Eeva. [eeva.siirala@kvs.fi]."New version of instructions". Private email message to XX [email address]. date. Maillist: Fischer, Ben.[bdfischye@mailbox.syr.edu]. "Answer. Multiculturalism." In Maillist H-NET Intellectual History List. [h-ideas@uicvm.cc.uic.edu]. Feb 9, 1996

Notes n Contributors
Authors should supply brief autobiographical details, e.g. background and experience in adult and continuing education, position now, when they submit their paper, as well as field of research.

Photographs
The journal also publishes illustrated articles. If the character of the text allows or requires photographs, the author is requested to contact the editorial staff for closer information.

Referees
Texts classified as articles are submitted to our referee system. The referees for the year are listed in the last issue of the year.

Measurement and Evaluation in Counseling and Development

ADDRESS FOR SUBMISSION:

Patricia B. Elmore, Editor
Measurement and Evaluation in Counseling
    and Development
Southern Illinois University
Colllege of Education
Associate Dean
Mailcode 4624
Carbondale, IL 62901-4624
USA
Phone: 618-453-2415
Fax: 618-453-1646
E-Mail: pbelmore@siu.edu
Web:
Address May Change: 7/1/02

PUBLICATION GUIDELINES:

Manuscript Length: 21-25
Copies Required: Five
Computer Submission: Yes
Format: None Mandated
Fees to Review: 0.00 US$

Manuscript Style:
    American Psychological Association

CIRCULATION DATA:

Reader: Academics
Frequency of Issue: Quarterly
Copies per Issue: 3,001 - 4,000
Sponsor/Publisher: Assn. for Assessment in
    Counseling/ American Counseling Assn.
Subscribe Price: 55.00 US$

REVIEW INFORMATION:

Type of Review: Blind Review
No. of External Reviewers: 3-5
No. of In House Reviewers: 1
Acceptance Rate: 21-30%
Time to Review: 3-4 Months
Reviewers Comments: Yes
Invited Articles: 11-20%
Fees to Publish: 0.00 US$

MANUSCRIPT TOPICS:
Adult Career & Vocational; Assessment; Counseling & Personnel Services; Curriculum
Studies; Educational Psychology; Higher Education; Science Math & Environment; Tests,
Measurement & Evaluation

MANUSCRIPT GUIDELINES/COMMENTS:

Measurement and Evaluation in Counseling and Development invites manuscripts concerned
with research, theoretical issues, and practical applications in assessment, measurement, and
evaluation in a variety of settings including schools and colleges, public and private agencies,
business, industry, and government. All manuscripts must have clearly described implications
for the counseling field and for practitioners, educators, administrators, researchers, or
students in assessment, measurement, and evaluation.

The following guidelines should be used:

1. **Five copies** of manuscripts, typewritten and double-spaced, should be submitted. The submission should be accompanied by a **brief abstract no longer than 50 words**.

2. Authors are expected, upon acceptance, to submit an additional copy of manuscripts on a 3 1/2" microcomputer floppy diskette. The publisher prefers manuscripts to be submitted on IBM or IBM compatible diskettes using Microsoft Word 97 (or below) or Rich Text format. The author's name and the hardware and software used must be clearly labeled on the disk.

3. References both in the text and at the end of the manuscript should follow the style described in the *Publication Manual of the American Psychological Association* (4th ed., APA) Authors are responsible for the accuracy of references.

4. Author identification should appear only on the cover page so that it may be removed before blind review.

5. All artwork for figures should be submitted camera-ready - on white paper, with clear, professionally done drawings in black ink and text in 8-point type, or computer generated using a high quality printer. Authors should not submit more than three tables or two figures with each manuscript.

6. For lengthy quotations (generally 300-500 cumulative words or more from one source), it is the **author's responsibility** to secure written permission from the copyright holder for reproduction.

7. Authors are encouraged to use guidelines to reduce bias in language against persons on the basis of gender, sexual orientation, racial or ethnic group, disability or age by referring to the fourth edition of the *APA publication manual*.

8. Authors are requested to provide detailed descriptions of their samples (e.g., specification of gender, ethnicity, age range) to assist readers in generalizing from the results.

9. Authors are encouraged to assist readers in interpreting statistical significance of their results. For example, results may be indexed to sample size. An author may wish to say, "This correlation coefficient still would have been statistically significant even if sample size had been as small as $n = 33$," or "This correlation coefficient would have been statistically significant if sample size had been increased to $n = 138$."

10. Authors are **required** to provide readers with effect size estimates to accompany statistical significance tests that are reported. For example, in an analysis of variance, authors may wish to report R-squared, eta squared, or omega squared. Standardized effect size estimates (the difference between the intervention group mean minus control group mean divided by the control group standard deviation) also are helpful in interpretation.

11. Studies in which statistical significance is not achieved will still be considered seriously for publication if power estimates of protection against Type II error are reported and reasonable protection is available.

614

12. A manuscript that is currently being considered by another publication may not be submitted for concurrent consideration by *MECD*.

13. Submit manuscripts to the editor, Patricia B. Elmore, Associate Dean for Administrative Services, Southern Illinois University, College of Education, Dean's Office, Mailcode 4624, Carbondale, IL 62901-4624. The period between acknowledgment of receipt of the manuscript and notification of disposition is generally from 3 to 6 months.

Merrill-Palmer Quarterly: Journal of Developmental Psychology

ADDRESS FOR SUBMISSION:

Gary Ladd, Editor
Merrill-Palmer Quarterly: Journal of
   Developmental Psychology
University of Illinois/Urbana Champaign
Children's Research Center
Room 136
51 Gerty Drive
Champaign, IL 61820
USA
Phone: 217-333-4585
Fax: 217-333-4585
E-Mail: mpq@uiuc.edu
Web:
Address May Change:

PUBLICATION GUIDELINES:

Manuscript Length: 21-25
Copies Required: Five
Computer Submission: No
Format: N/A
Fees to Review: 0.00 US$

Manuscript Style:
   American Psychological Association

CIRCULATION DATA:

Reader: Academics
Frequency of Issue: Quarterly
Copies per Issue: 1,001 - 2,000
Sponsor/Publisher: Wayne State University
   Press
Subscribe Price: 42.00 US$ Individual
   82.00 US$ Institution

REVIEW INFORMATION:

Type of Review: Blind Review
No. of External Reviewers: 2
No. of In House Reviewers: 1
Acceptance Rate: 11-20%
Time to Review: 2 - 3 Months
Reviewers Comments: Yes
Invited Articles: 21-30%
Fees to Publish: 0.00 US$

MANUSCRIPT TOPICS:
Child Development; Educational Psychology; Elementary/Early Childhood;
Secondary/Adolescent Studies

MANUSCRIPT GUIDELINES/COMMENTS:

Empirical, theoretical, and review papers that are original and concerned with issues in human development are published in the *Merrill-Palmer Quarterly*. The primary focus of the journal is on infant, child, and adolescent development, and contexts of development, such as the family and school. There is a special interest in integrative papers that summarize an area of research or a topic in terms that are meaningful to professionals with a wide range of specializations. Occasional issues of the *Quarterly* are devoted entirely or in large part to a single theme. Persons interested in organizing a thematic collection of papers are asked to make preliminary inquiry to the Editor. Commentaries on papers published in the *Quarterly* are also invited.

616

The format and style of manuscripts should conform to the conventions specified in the *Publication Manual of the American Psychological Association*, 4th edition (1994). A submitted paper that does not comply with these conventions may be returned to the author.

Manuscripts that fit the objectives of the *Quarterly* will be submitted ordinarily to at least two reviewers for evaluation. Authors are invited to suggest names of potential reviewers for their manuscripts, with the understanding that present or former students, colleagues, or collaborators should not be suggested and that these recommendations are subject to the Editor's discretion. The identity of the author(s) will not be given to reviewers. Authors will receive an editorial decision usually within 3 months of manuscript submission. Publication of accepted papers is usually within 12 months of submission.

The *Quarterly* is regularly indexed in Child Development Abstracts and Bibliography, Currernt Contents/Social and Behavioral Sciences, Currernt Index to Journals in Education, Linguistics and Language Behavior Abstracts, Psychological Abstracts, PsycSCAN: Developmental Psychology, Sage Family Studies Abstracts, Social Work Research and Abstracts, Sociological Abstracts, and Sociology of Education Abstracts (British).

Style Requirements
A, manuscript must conform completely with the specifications of the 2001 *American Psychological Association Publication Manual*, Fourth Edition, before it is sent to the typesetter. This manual can be purchased from the Order Department of the American Psychological Association, P.O. Box 2710, Hyattsville, MD 20784.

The checked items below need your attention. Refer to the 2001 *Publication Manual* for complete information:

1. Double space everything in the manuscript. There should be no single-spacing anywhere. One-and-one-half spacing is not acceptable either. Do not use dot matrix typeface.

2. There should be margins of 1 inch on every page of the manuscript, top, bottom, and sides. Do not divide words at the end of a line, and do not use "justified" lines.

3. Provide a footnote with the author's name and address for correspondence.

4. Provide a 120 word abstract on a separate page.

5. Title page, abstract, tables, figure captions, figures footnotes, content footnotes, and references should be on separate pages.

6. Number and identify every page; the title page is page 1.

7. Statistical symbols should be underlined so that they will be set in italics; identify Greek letters for typesetter.

8. Numbers less than 10 should be spelled out except in special cases. These are noted in the Manual.

9. Avoid combinations of inanimate noun and animate verb, e.g., "these hypotheses state, 11 this study examined," 11 Table 1 shows."

10. References in the text must be cited in the Reference list and conform to the described style.

11. References inside parenthesis in the text must be alphabetized (i.e., Adams, 1984; Boyd, 1970 etc.)

12. Reference list items must be cited in the text and conform to the described style.

13. Dates must agree between the citations in the text and the Reference list.

14. Tables should conform to the described style; only pencil lines in table.

15. Provide figure(s) in finished form (glossy).

16. Do not staple pages together. Submit original typewritten manuscript and three machine copies.

SCHOOL OF EDUCATION
CURRICULUM LABORATORY
UM-DEARBORN

Migration World

ADDRESS FOR SUBMISSION:

Lydio F. Tomasi, Editor
Migration World
Center for Migration Studies
209 Flagg Place
Staten Island, NY 10304-1199
USA
Phone: 718-351-8800
Fax: 718-667-4598
E-Mail: cmslft@aol.com
Web: www.cmsny.org
Address May Change:

PUBLICATION GUIDELINES:

Manuscript Length: 11-15
Copies Required: Two
Computer Submission: Yes
Format: Wordperfect, IBM
Fees to Review: 0.00 US$

Manuscript Style:
   See Manuscript Guidelines

CIRCULATION DATA:

Reader: Academics, Government or
   Voluntary Agency
Frequency of Issue: 5 Times/Year
Copies per Issue: 1,001 - 2,000
Sponsor/Publisher:
Subscribe Price: 31.00 US$ Individual
   50.00 US$ Institution
   46.00 US$ Indv.& $61 Inst. Foreign

REVIEW INFORMATION:

Type of Review: Blind Review
No. of External Reviewers: 3
No. of In House Reviewers: 2
Acceptance Rate: 21-30%
Time to Review: 2 - 3 Months
Reviewers Comments: Yes
Invited Articles: 6-10%
Fees to Publish: 0.00 US$

MANUSCRIPT TOPICS:
Adult Career & Vocational; Migration and Refugee Studies; School Law; Social Studies/Social Science

MANUSCRIPT GUIDELINES/COMMENTS:

Editorial Procedures:
In order to provide impartiality in the selection of manuscripts for publication, all papers deemed appropriate for MW are sent out anonymously to readers. To protect anonymity, the author's name and affiliation should appear only on a separate cover page. MW has the right to first publication of all submitted manuscripts. Manuscripts submitted to MW cannot be submitted simultaneously to another publication. Submit four copies and retain a copy for your own files. Submission of a manuscript to the MW is taken to indicate the author's commitment to publish. No paper known to be under jurisdiction by any other journal will be reviewed by MW. Manuscripts submitted to MW are not returned. Authors are not paid for accepted manuscripts. If manuscripts are accepted and published all rights, including subsidiary rights, are owned by the Center for Migration Studies. The author retains the right to use his/her article without charge in any book of which he/she is the author or editor after it has appeared in the *Migration World.*

Preparation of Copy:
1. Type all copy--including indented matter, footnotes and references-- double spaced on white standard paper.

2. Type each table on a separate page. Insert a location note, e.g., "Table 2 about here," at the appropriate place in the text.

3. Type footnotes (double spaced) on separate sheets. Footnotes should never be placed in the body of the text. Footnotes should include grant numbers or credits but not author's affiliation.

4. Draw figures on white paper with India ink Send the original drawings with the manuscripts; they will be returned to the author if the manuscript is not published.

5. Number all pages consecutively including those with tables and footnotes.

6. Two copies of the manuscript on white paper, and a diskette, if your manuscript has been created using a word processor, must be submitted. Please indicate in the cover letter the format and type of the diskette. Manuscripts should be addressed to the Editor of Migration World Magazine, Center for Migration Studies, 209 Flagg Place, Staten Island, NY 10304-1199 Tel: (718) 351-8800.

Format of Text:
All references to monographs, articles and statistical sources are to be identified at an appropriate point in the text by last name of author, year of publication and pagination where appropriate, all within parentheses. Footnotes are to be used only for substantive observations and not for the purpose of citation. However, footnotes are discouraged. There is no need for "Ibid.," "op cit.," or "loc cit"; specify subsequent citations of the same source in the same way as the first citation. Examples follow:

1. If author's name is in the text, follow it with year of publication in parentheses ["...Duncan (1969) had proven that..."]. If author's name is not in the text, insert at an appropriate point the last name and year, separated by a comma ["...some have claimed (cf., Gouldner, 1943) that..."].

2. Pagination (without "p" or "pp") follows year of publication separated by a colon ["...it has been noted (Lipset, 1964:61-4) that..."]. Incorporate within parentheses any brief phrase associated within the reference ["...have claimed that this is so (See, Jones, 1952:99 for conflicting view)..."].

3. With dual authorship, give both last names; for more than two, use "et al." For institutional authorship supply minimum identification from the beginning of the complete citation ["...occupational data (U.S. Bureau of the Census, 1963:117) revealed..."].

4. If there is more than one reference to the same author and year, distinguish them by use of letters (a, b) attached to year of publication, in text and in reference appendix ["...as was previously suggested (Levy, 1965a: 311)...]".

620

5. Enclose a series of references within a single pair of parentheses and separate by semicolons ["...as many have noted (Johnson, 1942; Perry, 1947; Linguist, 1984)..."].

Forms of References in Appendix:
List all items alphabetically by author and, within author(s), by year of publication beginning with the most recent year, in an appendix titled "REFERENCES." For multiple authors or editors listings (more than two), give the first author only and add 'let al." Use italics for titles of books and journals. For typing format, see the following examples:

Barakat, H.l.
1973   "The Palestinian Refugee: An Uprooted Community Seeking Repatriation", International Migration Review, 7(2):147-160. Summer.

Fawcett, J.T. and B.V. Carino, eds.
1987   Pacific Bridges: The New Immigration from Asia and the Pacific Islands. Staten Island, NY: Center for Migration Studies.

Fragomen, A.T.
1974   "Regulating the Illegal Aliens," International Migration Review, 8(4):567-572. Winter.

1973a   "Constitutional Rights of Aliens upon Arrest," International Migration Review, 7(1):67-71. Spring.

1973b   "Judicial Decisions of Interest," International Migration Review, 7(4):457-459. Winter.

Scammon, R.M.
1972   "Ethnic Circumstances: America at the Polls." In Pieces of a Dream. Edited by W. Wenk, et al. Staten Island, NY: Center for Migration Studies.

Multicultural Perspectives

ADDRESS FOR SUBMISSION:

Penny Lisi, Co-Editor
Multicultural Perspectives
Central Connecticut State University
1615 Stanley Street
New Britain, CT 06050
USA
Phone: 860-832-2137
Fax: 860-233-0759
E-Mail: lisip@ccsu.edu
Web: www.earlbaum.com
Address May Change:

PUBLICATION GUIDELINES:

Manuscript Length: 21-25
Copies Required: Five
Computer Submission: No
Format: N/A
Fees to Review: 0.00 US$

Manuscript Style:
    American Psychological Association

CIRCULATION DATA:

Reader: Practicing Teachers, Academics
Frequency of Issue: Quarterly
Copies per Issue: 1,001 - 2,000
Sponsor/Publisher: Lawrence Erlbaum
    Associates; National Association for
    Multicultural Education
Subscribe Price: 50.00 US$ Individual
    145.00 US$ Institution

REVIEW INFORMATION:

Type of Review: Blind Review
No. of External Reviewers: 3
No. of In House Reviewers: 1
Acceptance Rate: 21-30%
Time to Review: 4 - 6 Months
Reviewers Comments: Yes
Invited Articles: 0-5%
Fees to Publish: 0.00 US$

MANUSCRIPT TOPICS:
Bilingual/E.S.L.; Curriculum Studies; Languages & Linguistics; Multicultural Education; Social Justice, Equity; Special Education; Teacher Education; Urban Education, Cultural/Non-Traditional

MANUSCRIPT GUIDELINES/COMMENTS:

Editorial Scope
This publication promotes the philosophy of social justice, equity, and inclusion. It celebrates cultural and ethnic diversity as a national strength that enriches the fabric of society. The journal encourages a range of material from academic to personal perspectives, poetry, and art; articles of an academic nature illuminating the discussion of cultural pluralism and inclusion; articles and position papers reflecting a variety of disciplines; and reviews of film, art, and music that address or embody multicultural forms.

Audience
K-12 educators; social scientists; governmental social service personnel; teacher educators, and those involved in multicultural education.

622

Instructions to Contributors
The length for articles for the "Advancing the Conversation" section is 2,000-4,000 words. Manuscripts for "Advancing the Conversation" should include an abstract of approximately 80-100 words. Reviews and essays for other sections should be kept to 500-1,500 words. All pages should be double-spaced and numbered. The title of the manuscript, word count, and the author's name, affiliation, address, telephone number, and e-mail address should appear on the cover page only. Since reviews are blind, no author identification should appear on other pages. *Multicultural Perspectives* follows the *Publication Manual of the American Psychological Association (4th ed.)* style guidelines for publication.

Send your article on a 3.5-inch IBM- or Macintosh-formatted disk using MSWord or WordPerfect word processing software. Multicultural Perspectives publishes a range of materials, including full-length scholarly/research articles in the "Advancing the Conversation" section, and shorter essays, position papers, poetry, art, and reviews in other sections. Please send five printed copies of full-length articles for "Advancing the Conversation" to Philip C. Chinn. Send two printed copies when submitting to other sections of the journal to Penelope L. Lisi. Indicate on the label which software program you used, your name, address, and article title. Authors are responsible for all statements made in their work. If you use tables, graphics, or excerpts from another source, provide a signed agreement from the copyright holder that allows us to reprint the material. Include copies of all permissions and credit lines with the manuscript.

How to Write for Multicultural Perspectives
Multicultural Perspectives (MCP) is published four times a year by the National Association for Multicultural Education. Many more manuscripts are submitted each year than can be published. Following the guidelines below will enhance the likelihood of your manuscript's acceptance. Articles are reviewed by a panel of reviewers under a bind review process.

Length The length for articles for the section "Advancing the Conversation" is 2 000 to5,000-words. Articles that exceed 5,000 words will be returned unread. Reviews and essays for other sections should be kept to 500 to 1,500 words. The maximum word count will be strictly enforced.

Format All pages should be double-spaced, including references and any other material. The title of the manuscript, a word count, and the author's name, affiliation, address, telephone number, fax number, and E-mail must appear on the title page only. All subsequent pages must be numbered and include the manuscript title. Do not include author identification on any pages other than the title page. MCP follows the *Publication Manual of the American Psychological Association* (4th ed., 1994) style guidelines for publication, Compile references alphabetically (see *APA* Manual for multiple-author citations arid references). Spell out the names of journals, Provide page numbers of chapters in edited books. Text citations must correspond accurately to the reference list.

Authors are responsible fox all statements made in their work. If you use tables, graphics, poetry, or a lengthy quotation (500 words or move) from another source, provide a signed agreement from the copyright holder that allows us to reprint the material. Authors should write to original author(s) and original publisher to request nonexclusive world rights in all languages to use the material in the article and in future editions. Include copies of all permissions and credit lines with the manuscript. Material cannot be published without permission.

What To Send We will need a final version of your article on a 3.5-inch IBM- or Macintosh-formatted disk using MSWord or WordPerfect word-processing software. Please also send FIVE (5) printed copies of full-length articles for the "Advancing the Conversation" section to send to our reviewers or TWO (2) printed copies when sending articles for other sections. Please indicate on the disk label which software program you used, your name, address, and article title. Disks sent in other formats cannot be accepted, and your submission packet will be returned unread.

Our publisher, Lawrence Erlbaurn Associates, Inc. (LEA), will be the copyright holder of the magazine and its contents. After acceptance of your article, you will be sent a "Publication Agreement" assigning copyright to LEA; the agreement specifically gives you personal and proprietary rights over the use of your article and its information for other purposes.

Authors' files are copyedited and typeset into page proofs. Authors read proofs to correct errors and answer editors' queries.

Where To Send It Articles and reviews should be sent to the co-editor for each section of MCP indicated here:

"Advancing the Conversation"
Francisco Rios, Senior Associate Editor
Multicultural Perspectives
Department of Educational Studies
College of Education, University of Wyoming
202 McWhinnie Hall, PO Box 3374
Laramie, WY 82071-3374

"Creating Multicultural Classrooms" and **"Personal Perspectives"**
Penelope L. Lisi, Editor
Multicultural Perspectives
Department of Educational Leadership
Central Connecticut State University
New Britain, CT 06050

If you aren't sure, send your submission to Penelope L. List: Editor, Multicultural Perspectives, Department of Educational Leadership, Central Connecticut State University, New Britain, CT 06050.

Writing The Article

Articles and research papers written for "Advancing the Conversation" (feature articles) will be more formal and must include abstracts, Position papers and essays acid reviews may be written in a more informal journal style. Here are sortie additional tips:

- Explain the meaning of all words that may not be understood by the general reader. Remember some readers are new to the education field or may work in a. different area of education or discipline. Write out the meaning of acronyms you use every day.
- Use practical examples to support key points.
- Our goal is to provide useful, interesting information about multicultural issues to a broad range of readers in a variety of academic disciplines and educational and work settings.
- We only accept manuscripts that have not been published elsewhere. If your article was submitted to another journal and is accepted for publication, let us know immediately.

Graphics/Photographs/Art
Charts, high-quality photographs, arid original art that would complement your article are welcome Please submit them on separate pages at the end of the manuscript. Consecutively number all graphics/photographs/art and captious and provide callouts in the text. In your captions, provide the names of the people in the photos and explain where the people are and what they are doing. Please provide useful biographical information of the artists and their names and addresses. If you are using the work of another person, please supply us with a signed agreement from the copyright holder that allows us to reprint the material. Material cannot be published without permission.

What Gets Published A goad manuscript may be accepted for publication, but may not be published immediately because the policy of the journal is to offer range of articles in each issue. If your article is accepted but riot published immediately, we will inform you that we are holding it for a future issue. Manuscripts requiring extensive revisions will be rejected. We may return your article for revision if we feel that it has promise. You will then have an opportunity to resubmit after making the suggested changes.

What Gets Edited: Most manuscripts are edited, Our reviewers may ask for content and style changes. Lawrence Erlbaum Associates Inc,, publisher of MCP, will: copyedit for grammar, punctuation, and format. LEA will send each author a copy of the edited article proofs for approval before publication.

Questions Contact Francisco Rios with questions regarding "Advancing the Conversation." Contact Penelope T,. Lisi with all other questions.

Multivariate Behavioral Research

ADDRESS FOR SUBMISSION:

Roger E. Millsap, Editor
Multivariate Behavioral Research
Arizona State University
Dept. of Psychology
Box 871104
Tempe, AZ 85287-1104
USA
Phone: 480-965-2584
Fax: 480-965-8544
E-Mail: millsap@asu.edu
Web: www.erlbaum.com
Address May Change:

PUBLICATION GUIDELINES:

Manuscript Length: 40 Max
Copies Required: Four
Computer Submission: No
Format: N/A
Fees to Review: 0.00 US$

Manuscript Style:
    American Psychological Association

CIRCULATION DATA:

Reader: Academics
Frequency of Issue: Quarterly
Copies per Issue: Less than 1,000
Sponsor/Publisher: Lawrence Erlbaum
    Associates
Subscribe Price: 45.00 US$ Individual
    340.00 US$ Institution

REVIEW INFORMATION:

Type of Review: Blind Review
No. of External Reviewers: 3
No. of In House Reviewers: 1
Acceptance Rate: 20%
Time to Review: 4 - 6 Months
Reviewers Comments: Yes
Invited Articles: 11-20%
Fees to Publish: 0.00 US$

MANUSCRIPT TOPICS:
Educational Psychology; Multivariate Statistics and Behavior

MANUSCRIPT GUIDELINES/COMMENTS:

This Journal publishes substantive, methodological and theoretical articles. Substantive articles report results of behavioral research employing multivariate methods. Methodological articles present flew multivariate mathematical-statistical procedures or definitive critical contributions of methodological or substantive interest. Theoretical articles may convey new insight into the historical development of multivariate scientific approaches, Formulate meta-theoretical principles governing programmatic research or provide new conceptual multivariate models for researchable systems. Additionally, shorter paper will be considered For the Notes and Commentary section of the Journal. The Editor should bee consulted regarding the appropriateness, for the Journal, of papers which do not clearly fit any of the preceding descriptions.

Manuscripts up to 40 typed, double-spaced pages are invited. Submit 4 copies. They should be prepared according to the *Publication Manual of the American Psychological Association,*

Fifth Edition except that equations should be triple-spaced and numbered in parentheses to the left. Provide a title page that specifics title, names and institutional affiliations of all authors exactly as they are to be printed, and name and address of person to whom requests for reprints should be addressed. A 120-word abstract in English should follow the title page. Authors are referred to the Statement of Editorial Policy which appeared in Volume 31, Number 3 (1996) issue of the Journal for more information about manuscript policies.

Reprints

Reprints may be obtained at rates supplied only at the tithe the author receives page proofs.

Instructions for Authors

In view of the page limitations of this journal, and in order to publish as many good papers as possible, we ask that manuscripts be kept to a reasonable length (not over 40 double-spaced typewritten pages).

Contributors are responsible for all statements made in their work and for obtaining permission from copyright owners if they use an illustration or lengthy quote (over 100 words) that has been published elsewhere. Contributors should write to both publisher and author of such material, requesting nonexclusive world right, in all languages for such use in the article and all future editions of it.

Submission of an article to this journal will be taken to imply that it represents original work not previously published, and that it is not being considered elsewhere for publication. Authors submitting a manuscript do so on the understanding that if it is accepted for publication, copyright on the article, including the right to reproduce the article in all forms and media, shall be; assigned exclusively to the Publisher- Author's reasonable requests for permission to reproduce contributions may be approved by contacting the Permission Department Lawrence Erlbaum Associates, Inc., 10 Industrial Avenue, Mahwah, NJ 07430-2262.

Authors have an option of "open" reviewing (authors identified) or "blind" reviewing (authors not identified). Article reviews will be "blind" unless the author specifically requests "open" review when the manuscript is submitted, and the manuscript is prepared in a format suitable for "blind" reviewing.

Once a contribution is approved for publication, author will be asked to submit the manuscript in word-processed form on diskette. Most IBM compatible formats present few problems; if Macintosh format is used, check for a "MS-DOS format" save option. (In Microsoft Word, make sure Full Menu option under Edit is chosen; choose Save, the File Format, then MS-DOS-) **Do not** use the "Fast Save' option available in many word processors. Submit a letter with your diskette indicating which ward processor (and other software) and version were used and a list/chart of any character substitutions made for Greek lettering and/or unusual characters. Mention of any little known macros, printer or other distinctive commands used would be appreciated Indications of preferred placement should be included in the word processed manuscript for all tables and/or figures. When formatting text and, particularly tables, use of tabs rather than spaces is urgently requested. Refer to the *Publication Manual of the American Psychological Association*, Fourth Edition, for exact instructions regarding table/figure format, numbering, titling, footnoting, underlining, etc. Tables should be included in the word-processed document following the references, with each table on a separate page. Figures should be submitted in camera-ready form and, if possible, on diskette in EPS or TIF format.

Uncertainties and questions regarding preferred format and magnetic media submission should be directed to Editor Roger E. Millsap (see above address).

NACADA Journal

ADDRESS FOR SUBMISSION:

Thomas J. Kerr, Editor
NACADA Journal
Kansas State University
2323 Anderson Avenue, Suite 225
Manhattan, KS 66052-2912
USA
Phone: 201-692-7317
Fax: 201-692-7309
E-Mail: kerrtj@fdu.edu
Web:
Address May Change:

PUBLICATION GUIDELINES:

Manuscript Length: 21-25
Copies Required: Five
Computer Submission: No
Format: Final Accepted Only, IBM
Fees to Review: 0.00 US$

Manuscript Style:
    American Psychological Association

CIRCULATION DATA:

Reader: , Academic Advisors
Frequency of Issue: 2 Times/Year
Copies per Issue: 5,001 - 10,000
Sponsor/Publisher: Professional
    Organization
Subscribe Price: 50.00 US$

REVIEW INFORMATION:

Type of Review: Blind Review
No. of External Reviewers: 0
No. of In House Reviewers: 3
Acceptance Rate: 40%
Time to Review: 4 - 6 Months
Reviewers Comments: Yes
Invited Articles: 0-5%
Fees to Publish: 0.00 US$

MANUSCRIPT TOPICS:

Adult Career & Vocational; Counseling & Personnel Services; Curriculum Studies; Education Management/Administration; Educational Psychology; Higher Education; School Law; Tests, Measurement & Evaluation

MANUSCRIPT GUIDELINES/COMMENTS:

Purpose of NACADA

The National Academic Advising Association (NACADA), founded in 1979, promotes the quality of academic advising in institutions of higher education. NACADA is dedicated to the support and professional growth of academic advisors and the advising profession. Through its publications and meetings, NACADA provides a forum of discussion, debate, and the exchange of ideas regarding the role of academic advising in higher education.

The *NACADA Journal* is published twice yearly. It seeks to enrich the knowledge, skills, and the professional development of persons involved in academic advising in higher education.

The *NACADA Journal* considers articles from a wide variety of interest areas and from a wide spectrum of disciplines. Although the below-listed categories are non-inclusive of the types of articles solicited by the *Journal*, authors may find these categories useful in guiding the preparation of manuscripts.

1. Research: Quantitative, data-based research reports reflect thoughtfully and carefully designed research on topics relevant to the field of academic advising. Authors are encouraged to relate data to general, theoretical bases and to interpret data beyond the specific nature of individual institutions.

2. Theoretical, conceptual, and literature review articles: Articles address concepts and ideas about academic advising. Articles in this section could, for instance, discuss academic advising models (and the theoretical foundation for these models), concepts about intellectual and personal development, foundations of career/academic advising issues, literature reviews, and issues specific to advising special populations.

3. Critical issues: Articles that take a specific stand on an issue will appear in this section. Editorials are welcome, as are full-length articles that discuss particular issues. Depending on the importance and complexity of the issue, the editors may, with the permission of the author(s), solicit responses and rejoinder, which will appear in the same issue as the original manuscript.

4. Brief reports: Articles include descriptions of specific systems of advising and practical, working ideas. Articles in this section need not be rigorous, but they cannot be so specific to the authors own experiences that they are not useful to other advisors or advising systems. Articles that are strictly show-and-tell are discouraged. This section is meant to encourage authors to submit working ideas and suggestions without having to engage in the formal kind of paper writing that is required in other sections.

5 From other fields: Advisors have eclectic interests. Much of what they must know to be effective advisors is taken from a wide variety of fields. Examples include motivation theory, the integration of noncognitive variables into the advising scheme, issues of special populations, math anxiety, and career development.

6 Book reviews: Book reviews should be no longer than 400 words. They should include author, title, date of publication, publisher, city of publication, page length, price, ISBN number, and phone numbers for orders. The review should include a brief description of the book's contents as well as the reviewer's impressions and opinions of the book's applicability and usefulness to advisors. Members may request that the editors supply complimentary copies of books for review. These requests may include books listed in the *NACADA Journal* Books Received section.

7 Advisor's Toolbox: Very short research reports or conceptual articles based in the literature. Note that these contributions differ from the short speculative pieces and advising hints published in the *Newsletter*.

Manuscript Guidelines

Prospective authors should follow the guidelines below before submitting a manuscript for consideration. Please send five copies of the manuscript to the editor at the following address:

Dr. Thomas Kerr, Editor; *NACADA Journal;* 2323 Anderson Avenue, #225; Manhattan, KS 66502-2912.

The editor will send an acknowledgment to the author and send copies to editorial board members for review. Authors will be contacted after the review process, which generally takes between 30 and 45 days. Authors whose articles have been accepted will need to send a hardcopy and an IBM-compatible disk containing a manuscript identical to the hardcopy. Additional information on the nature of the disk and other publication procedures will be sent to the author at that time.

Text Style
Because the *NACADA Journal* publishes a variety of articles, no one type of organization will be appropriate for all manuscripts. However, general writing and *American Psychological Association (APA)* format guidelines apply to all submissions. Some *APA* format rules are highlighted below. Numbers in brackets refer to specific sections of the *American Psychological Association Publication Manual* (1994). To see a sample research paper in proper format, please see www.ksu.edu/nacada/profres/pubguide.htm

The *APA Manual* (pp. 120B41) gives excellent instructions for the use and proper styling of tables and should be followed. Some points of particular importance are included in the following.

- Do not allow tables to exceed 35 picas (5☐ in) in width or 51 picas (8☐ in) in length.
- Use Times New Roman Font.
- Double-space all tables for easy editing. Number all tables in the order that they are mentioned in the text. Make sure that all tables are mentioned in text.
- Define all measurements used for values in tables. Define the measurements in headings explained in footnotes. Do not include those labels in the body of the table.
- Define or avoid using all abbreviations. Do not use material, such as graphics or photographs, in tables that should be placed in figures.
- Do not print a table in a visible cellular format. Avoid vertical and horizontal rules within the body of the table.

Figures
- Do not allow tables to exceed 35 picas (5☐ in) in width or 51 picas (8☐ in) in length.
- Supply a printed and electronic version of the figure.
- Ensure that figure is of professional quality; that is, the original should be a sharp, in-focus photograph print, a PMT stat, or a clear laser print.
- Identify all figures on the back of the page by number and author name. Include a list of figure captions on a separate sheet. Do not place the caption on the figure.

If you have questions about manuscript preparation or submission guidelines, please contact Nancy Vesta; Copy Editor; PO Box 51; Leonardville, KS 66449; Phone: 785.293.4919; FAX: 785.293.5281; E-mail: NJV@Compuserve.com.

NASAP Journal

ADDRESS FOR SUBMISSION:

Melvin C. Terrell, Editor
NASAP Journal
Northeastern Illinois University
V.S.P.A.
5500 N. St. Louis Avenue
Chicago, IL 60625
USA
Phone: 773-442-4603
Fax: 779-442-4605
E-Mail: M-Terrell@neiu.edu
Web: www.angelfire.com/ga/nasap
Address May Change:

PUBLICATION GUIDELINES:

Manuscript Length: 11-15
Copies Required: Two
Computer Submission: Yes Disk, Email
Format: WordPerfect, rtf
Fees to Review: 0.00 US$

Manuscript Style:
   American Psychological Association

CIRCULATION DATA:

Reader: Administrators, Academics
Frequency of Issue: Yearly
Copies per Issue: Less than 1,000
Sponsor/Publisher: National Association of
   Student Affairs Professionals
Subscribe Price: 10.00 US$

REVIEW INFORMATION:

Type of Review: Blind Review
No. of External Reviewers: 2
No. of In House Reviewers: 1
Acceptance Rate: 11-20%
Time to Review: 1 - 2 Months
Reviewers Comments: Yes
Invited Articles: 0-5%
Fees to Publish: 0.00 US$

MANUSCRIPT TOPICS:
Counseling & Personnel Services; Educational Management/ Administration

MANUSCRIPT GUIDELINES/COMMENTS:

Manuscript Guidelines
The National Association of Student Affairs Professionals (NASAP) invites articles dealing with student affairs research and development for inclusion in the NASAP Journal. Please follow this format in preparing your contribution on disk and hard copy. These guidelines preempt and supercede those listed in the *APA* Guidelines. The *Journal* reserves the right to return manuscripts if they do not conform to these requirements.

The 2002 Edition of the *NASAP Journal* will focus on the examination of the current trend to renew higher education's minority student retention and recruitment mission, and the educational strategies used by colleges and universities making a major commitment to minority student development. Do not submit manuscripts that are under consideration by another publisher.

Formatting Instructions

We are **NOT** using *APA* Guidelines for formatting, except where otherwise noted below. However, as far as style and quality, (how the article is written) and the references, follow *APA* Guidelines.

Eliminate all extra formatting and codes, including running heads/headers, footers, tab settings, font changes, margin changes, pre-formatted styles. Do not use bold face. Page numbering should be only in the upper right hand corner.

Cover Letter

With your submission, please send a cover letter that includes contact information for **ALL** authors, and indicate who will be the primary contact person (to appear in the Journal). Give a brief summary of your article in the cover letter and include the title.

Cover Page

Include a cover page that lists the title of the manuscript and the authors' names and university affiliations **ONLY** (no author titles or contact information). Title of manuscript should also appear at top of first page in Times New Roman 12 pt. font. Manuscript title should be as brief as possible. Author(s) name(s) should appear only on the cover sheet. Names should be typed as you wish them to appear in print. Also include, on a separate sheet, a brief statement (one or two sentences) indicating your title, your institutional affiliation, and any acknowledgments you would like included.

Title and Abstract

Title should also appear on the first page of your article, as well as an abstract of 100 words or less. Abstract should appear directly below title, with the rest of the manuscript following. The abstract should be indented. Please make the abstract concise (one paragraph only) and be aware that it is what people will see when searching databases such as ERIC for articles.

Manuscript

Manuscripts should reflect logical, concise, and creative thinking. Authors must present their ideas in a cohesive and interesting manner. No reference to the author's identity or institutional affiliation should appear within the manuscript.

- Margins on all sides should be 1 inch.
- Use Times New Roman 12 pt. or Courier 12 pt. font. Do not change font or font size. Automatic hyphenation should be off.
- The entire manuscript should be double spaced, including quotations, tables, abstract and references.
- Do not change line spacing within the manuscript.
- Select left justification. Do not indent the first line of each paragraph; put two blank lines between paragraphs.

Sources

All sources cited in the text must be listed in the references; conversely, all sources cited in references must appear in the text. Provide complete bibliographic information, using *APA* format. Include all authors' names (do **NOT** use "and others" or "et al."). List complete journal titles. Authors are responsible for accuracy of references.

Headings
Use headings to outline the structure of your chapter. As per the *APA*, avoid putting more than one heading in a row. Make headings brief but compelling rather than simple. (Instead of "Review of the Literature" you might use "Conflict in Ideology" if applicable.) As noted above, headings should be left justified and do not use bold or italics. Separate them from text by adding an extra line space above and below the heading.

Reprinting Information
If you reprint information or tables from a source, be sure you have the correct permissions. Usually this will mean requesting permission from the author or publisher through a letter of permission to reprint. The source information is included in the Note (refer to *APA*). The original of the permission letter must be received with the manuscript submission.

Length
Manuscripts should be at least 2,000 words but not more than 3,000 words (approximately 12-15 typed, double-spaced pages with 1" margins).

References
References must be in accordance with the Publication Manual of the American Psychological Association, Fourth Edition as far as their content and arrangement. In this section, italics are included (the APA shows them as underlined titles, etc.). However, do **NOT** indent either the first or subsequent line(s) of each reference. Insert an extra line space in between each reference.

Tables
Tables should be brief and include only essential data. The articles' authors are responsible for accuracy of data, references, quotations and tables.

Submissions
Always keep backup copies of your files (hard copies and copies on disk) for your own protection. Manuscripts must be accompanied by three (3) copies of the article for consideration as well as a 3.5" disk (IBM formatted). Label the disk with your name and the word processing program you used. It should be a 3.5" diskette, formatted in WordPerfect or in IBM Rich Text Format (RTF). We prefer to receive documents in WordPerfect, any version from DOS through WordPerfect 8. Indicate in the cover letter and on the disk what format was used. **As stated above, eliminate all extra formatting and codes, such as tab settings, font changes, or any running head other than the page number. Do not follow *APA* guidelines for this formatting.**

Submissions by E-mail are acceptable. Address the message to m-terrell@neiu.edu with a copy to editors_aide@iwon.com. We will send you a message confirming receipt of your article by E-mail. You will still need to submit copies and a diskette by mail. As above, be sure all codes/formatting are removed from your document.

634

Book Reviews

If you would like to write an informative book review, contact the editor about having a topic assigned to you, or submit a manuscript for consideration. The chosen book must be of interest to student affairs professionals and reflect the focus of the journal. Reviews should be 500-800 words and include three copies as well as a 3.5" diskette formatted as indicated in these guidelines (WordPerfect, all extra formatting and codes eliminated). Please include quotes in your review and indicate the page number for each. Include the following information about the book in the heading: title, author, publisher, date, number of pages, price (If known). List your name and college/university affiliation in the book review. Follow the above guidelines for formatting and for E-mail submissions. Reviewers receive two (2) copies of the *Journal* in which the review appears.

If you do not adhere to the above guidelines, your article will be returned to you unread. The *Journal* is refereed and manuscripts are evaluated through a blind review system. All manuscripts approved for publication become the property of the Association. The editor reserves the right to edit or rewrite accepted articles to meet the *Journal's* standards.

The *NASAP Journal* is published yearly (Winter) and is usually available for the NASAP Conference in February. The deadline for submitting articles is September 1. Upon publication, authors are supplied gratis four (4) copies of the Journal in which their article appears. Additional copies are available at a nominal cost.

Address manuscripts, queries and correspondence to:

Melvin C. Terrell, Ph.D. Editor
NASAP Journal
and Vice President for Student Affairs
Northeastern Illinois University
5500 North St. Louis Ave., P.E. #1124
Chicago, IL 60625-4699
773-794-2867, Fax: 773-794-6515
E-mail: M-Terrell@neiu.edu

Fred A. Bonner, II, Ph.D.
NASAP Journal Co-Editor
Assistant Professor, Education Department
University of Texas at San Antonio
6900 North Loop 1604 West
San Antonio, TX 78249
210-458-7287, Fax: 210-458-5848
E-mail: FBonner@utsa.edu

NASPA Journal

ADDRESS FOR SUBMISSION:

Larry Roper, Editor
NASPA Journal
Oregon State University
Vice Provost of Student Affairs
632 Kerr Administration Bldg.
Corvallis, OR 97331-2154
USA
Phone: 541-737-2759
Fax: 541-737-3033
E-Mail: larry.roper@orst.edu
Web:
Address May Change:

PUBLICATION GUIDELINES:

Manuscript Length: 16-20
Copies Required: Four
Computer Submission: No
Format: N/A
Fees to Review: 0.00 US$

Manuscript Style:
    American Psychological Association

CIRCULATION DATA:

Reader: Administrators
Frequency of Issue: Quarterly
Copies per Issue: 5,001 - 10,000
Sponsor/Publisher: National Association of
    Student Personnel Administrators
Subscribe Price: 35.00 US$
    40.00 US$ Foreign

REVIEW INFORMATION:

Type of Review: Blind Review
No. of External Reviewers: 3
No. of In House Reviewers: 0
Acceptance Rate: 35%
Time to Review: 1 - 2 Months
Reviewers Comments: Yes
Invited Articles: 0-5%
Fees to Publish: 0.00 US$

MANUSCRIPT TOPICS:

Education Management/Administration; Higher Education; Leadership in Education

MANUSCRIPT GUIDELINES/COMMENTS:

Purpose

Manuscripts should be written for the student affairs generalist who has broad responsibility for educational leadership, policy, staff development, and management. Articles on specialized topics, such as residence hall programming, should be written to provide the generalist with an understanding of the importance of the program to student affairs areas; such an article should not take the form of a program specialist writing to a program specialist.

Research articles for the *NASPA Journal* should stress the underlying issues or problems that stimulated the research; treat the methodology concisely; and most important, offer a full discussion of the results, implications, and conclusions. In the belief that *NASPA* readers have much to learn from one another, we encourage the submission of thoughtful, documented essays or historical perspectives.

Language

Authors are reminded that language is a powerful tool; use language precisely to communicate ideas and concepts accurately. Consider if any words can be read as biased, oppressive, or pejorative by reasonable people. For assistance in finding appropriate language, use sources such as *The Nonsexist Word Finder: A Dictionary of Gender-Free Usage and The Dictionary for Bias-Free Usage: A Guide to Nondiscriminatory Language.*

Procedure

1. Manuscripts should be at least 2,000 but not more than 3,000 words (approximately 12 pages of double-spaced, typewritten copy, including references, tables and

2. figures). Exceptions should be discussed with the editor prior to submission. Before submitting an article:

3. Prepare the manuscript, including page numbering, in accordance with the Publication Manual of the American Psychological Association, Fourth Edition.

4. Send the original and three copies of manuscript to the NASPA Journal editor.

5. Place the name of the author(s), position(s), and institutional affiliation(s) on a separate title page.

6. Double-space all portions of the manuscript, including references, tables, figures, and quotations.

7. Avoid sexist terminology (see pp. 50-52 of the publication manual).

8. Do not use footnotes; incorporate the information in the text.

9. Use the APA reference style, listing only references cited in the text.

10. Use the active voice to the largest extent possible.

11 Use verb tense appropriately: past tense for the literature review and description of procedures, and present tense for the results and discussion.

12. Proofread and double check the references before submitting your manuscript.

13. Submit only manuscripts not under consideration by other journals.

All manuscripts and inquiries about manuscripts should be sent to:
NASPA Journal Editor, Larry Roper, Vice Provost, Student Affairs, Oregon State University, 632 Kerr Administration Building, Corvallis, OR 97331-2154, Phone: (541) 737-2759, Fax: (541) 737-3033, Email: larry. roper@orst. edu

NASSP Bulletin

ADDRESS FOR SUBMISSION:

Amy Ciliberto, Editor
NASSP Bulletin
1904 Association Drive
Reston, VA 20191-1537
USA
Phone: 703-860-0200
Fax: 703-476-5432
E-Mail: cilibertoa@principals.org
Web:
Address May Change:

PUBLICATION GUIDELINES:

Manuscript Length: 4,000 words (14-16)
Copies Required: Two
Computer Submission: Yes
Format: MSWord
Fees to Review: 0.00 US$

Manuscript Style:
        American Psychological Association

CIRCULATION DATA:

Reader: Administrators
Frequency of Issue: 9 Times/Year
Copies per Issue: 37,000
Sponsor/Publisher: National Association of
    Secondary Principals
Subscribe Price: 65.00 US$ Library

REVIEW INFORMATION:

Type of Review: Peer Review
No. of External Reviewers: 3+
No. of In House Reviewers: 2
Acceptance Rate: 11-20%
Time to Review: 4 Months
Reviewers Comments: Yes
Invited Articles: Yes
Fees to Publish: 0.00 US$

MANUSCRIPT TOPICS:
Education Management/Administration; Instructional Leadership; Research Into Practice;
Secondary/Adolescent Studies

MANUSCRIPT GUIDELINES/COMMENTS:

Bulletin is a scholarly journal that informs practice, supports data-driven decisions, and advances vision and performance of middle level and high school principals. *Bulletin* articles are timely, thought provoking, and emphasize effective administration and leadership. As Bulletin is a scholarly resource, manuscript, that discuss opinions and best practices are more appropriately submitted to NASSP's magazine *Principal Leadership.*

Resource Reviews: *Bulletin* welcomes general interest inquiries from readers who would like to review books, videos. or software. Resource reviews are commissioned by the Editor. Unsolicited reviews will not be accepted.

Submission
Manuscripts should be double-spaced on 8 ½ x 11" white paper, with any supporting information placed on separate pages. Manuscripts must be accompanied by an abstract, and should follow the *Publication Manual of the American Psychological* Association, Fifth

Edition. All copses should be clear and readable. Poor quality faxed or photocopied submissions will not be accepted. Manuscripts should have a cover sheet indicating the title, authors' names and affiliations, and the date the manuscript is submitted. The first page of the manuscript should contain only the title of the manuscript and date submitted. Authors should keep a copy of their manuscript to guard against loss. The submission package should contain the following:

- Two copies of the manuscript bound by a paper clip. Please do not staple.
- A cover letter that briefly describes the article and other important information (presented at a conference, if the article has been submitted elsewhere, etc.), The letter *should* contain complete address, telephone, fax, e-mail, and affiliation information.
- An electronic version of the manuscript on 3 ½ " disk, MS Word 7.0 preferred.
- Letters of permission to use copyrighted material.

Send the complete package to Bulletin Editor, NASSP, 1904 Association Drive, Reston. VA 20191. Electronic submission via e-mail to Bulletin@principals.org is also acceptable.

Copyright
Authors are asked to sign a statement of original work and copyright release. As publisher, NASSP protects its rights and those of its authors from copyright infringement. Authors who request permission to republish their Bulletin article generally receive it, providing that NASSP is cited as the original publisher.

Previously Copyrighted Work
Authors are responsible for the accuracy of references, quotations, and tables, and must obtain all necessary permission to use previously copyrighted work.

Peer Review
Manuscripts submitted to *Bulletin* will go through several stages of masked review. Authors should make even effort to see that the manuscript itself contains no identification.

Acknowledgment and Decision
All manuscripts will be acknowledged upon receipt. Decisions to accept or reject a manuscript are made within sic weeks after receipt in the editorial office; however, authors should allow up to four months for publication assignment. Each author will receive two copies of the issue that contains their published article.

National Forum of Educational Admin. and Supervision Journal (NFEAS Journal)

ADDRESS FOR SUBMISSION:

William Kritsonis, Editor
National Forum of Educational Admin. and
  Supervision Journal (NFEAS Journal)
National Forum Journals
4000 Lock Lane, Suite 9
Lake Charles, LA 70605
USA
Phone: 337-477-0008
Fax: 337-562-2848
E-Mail:
Web: www.nationalforum.com
Address May Change:

PUBLICATION GUIDELINES:

Manuscript Length: 10-50
Copies Required: Five
Computer Submission: Yes
Format: MSWord
Fees to Review: 0.00 US$

Manuscript Style:
  American Psychological Association

CIRCULATION DATA:

Reader: Practicing Teachers, Academics,
  Administrators
Frequency of Issue: 3 Times/Year
Copies per Issue: 10,001 - 25,000
Sponsor/Publisher: National Forum
  Journals
Subscribe Price: 36.00 US$
  72.00 US$ Library/Institution

REVIEW INFORMATION:

Type of Review: Blind Review
No. of External Reviewers: 3+
No. of In House Reviewers: 2
Acceptance Rate: 21-30%
Time to Review: One Month or Less
Reviewers Comments: Yes
Invited Articles: 0-5%
Fees to Publish: 0.00 US$

MANUSCRIPT TOPICS:

Curriculum Studies; Education Management/Administration; Educational Psychology; Educational Technology Systems; Gifted Children; Higher Education; School Law; Teacher Education; Urban Education, Cultural/Non-Traditional

MANUSCRIPT GUIDELINES/COMMENTS:

The *National Forum of Educational Administration and Supervision Journal* was founded in 1983 by Dr. William Kritsonis, Editor-in-Chief. The Journal is sponsored by California State University, Los Angeles, Charter School of Education Program in Educational Administration. The Journal is the flagship publication of the family of National Forum Journals On-line Scholarly Electronic Publishing Journal and Monograph Division which publishes original refereed, blind-reviewed, peer-evaluated, juried manuscripts intended for national and international dissemination. Readers from around the world will have access to your published article(s) by contacting our website as: www.nationalforum.com.

All of the family of *National FORUM Journals* require that writers who submit manuscripts follow the latest technical specifications set in the *Publication Manual of the American Psychological Association*, 5th Edition.

Manuscripts must be typed double-spaced in a fixed-pitch font (ex. Courier). The writer's name, title affiliation, telephone, complete address, and date of submission should be on a separate cover page, and only this page to ensure anonymity in the reviewing process. Writers must include on separate pages an abstract of 75-150 words, and on another separate page a brief biographical summary of 50-75 words. Submit five hard copies.

Processing Fee. At the time a manuscript is submitted for consideration for national publication in any *National FORUM Journal*, the writer, institution, or agency must include a non-refundable processing fee of $30. This fee covers the initial screening and evaluation of the manuscript by the editorial staff.

Professional Service Fee. Most professional journals are financed by associations as part of their dues structure. We have no such luxury. Each *National FORUM Journal* publication is a self-supported journal. The costs of publishing and printing continue to increase. We pledge to our authors, readers, referees, and friends the highest possible quality journal.

When a manuscript is recommended for national publication by members of our national board, the author, associated institution, school, or agency is expected to submit a pre-specified nominal professional service fee. This is NOT a publication fee. This fee simply helps cover expenses relative to processing, evaluating, examining, and communicating about the manuscript, along with other escalating costs of advertising, marketing, and promoting the particular issue at the national and international levels.

How To Determine Your Professional Service Fee
The professional service fee is determined by the number of authors and the length of manuscript. The first author is assessed $100, second author $90, third author $80, fourth author $70, fifth author $60. Also, $15.00 per double-spaced page, typed in a fixed-pitch (ex: Courier), is assessed each manuscript. Each author receives two (2) complimentary issues wherein their article is published. Authors may supply labels of a list of six names of persons they wish to receive complimentary copies of the issue.

Our goal is to help in the global circulation of ideas to promote the kind of professional articulation that will move our profession forward. We appreciate your support.

Submit manuscripts to the appropriate *National FORUM Journal* and forward to:
Dr. William Kritsonis, Editor-in-Chief, National FORUM Journals Online, 4000 Lock Lane - Suite 9/KL, Lake Charles, LA 70605, Phone: 318-477-0008

A Note To Our Authors About The Review Process And Fee Structure
Some journals like to brag about the number of manuscripts they reject as a badge of quality. *National Forum Journals* doesn't follow that pattern. Rejecting a manuscript is never easy and it is always accompanied by some stress. We try to make the review process pleasant and beneficial, although we certainly can't and don't accept all manuscripts we receive.

Each manuscript is treated with the respect and consideration you would expect if you gave it to a friend. We also demand that our national reviewers get materials back to us on time. Over the past 11 years, we have learned that some reviewers take too much time or are not thorough in their work. We don't use them if they are not conscientious. And we don't use them if they are not timely. It is a measure of arrogance and disrespect to keep an author waiting our or five months for an answer regarding publication. We take great pride in our timeliness on this matter in dealing with our authors. We also believe in working with authors on manuscript details. If your manuscript shows promise, we won't give up if you don't.

We believe that the fields of educational administration, educational research special education, and teacher education have for too long been stagnant. We believe that many ideas have been lost because of excessive rigidities imposed in the review process. Our national review process is flexible and we welcome innovative approaches and ideas. The field is open. We believe that all ideas that look promising deserve wider attention. Like some journals, we don't impose any a prior conceptual model on articles or papers. We believe in the legitimacy of all approaches.

So, the bottom line is that your article is part of a process that is author friendly without sacrificing anything such as scholarly standards. Too often, those words are used to hide a conceptual preference for some kinds of articles or approaches. This is simply not the case with all *National Forum Journals*.

Let me briefly explain a bit out our fee structure. Most professional journals are financed by associations as part of their dues structure. We have no such luxury. Each journal is affiliated with a sponsor. Each journal is financial) self-supporting. To be effective, *National Forum Journals* must be financially healthy. That is the last of three legs of successful journal publishing, which are quality of articles, integrity of the review process, and fiscal strength. The costs of publishing and printing continue to increase. We pledge to our authors, reviewers, and national and international readership professional journals of the highest quality that are open to new ideas, sound in approach and secure in the knowledge that fields belong to those bold enough to lead it with vision. Thank you for your confidence in us. We will continue working to earn it.

William Kritsonis, Ph.D.
Founder, Publisher, Editor --NATIONAL FORUM JOURNALS

NEA Today

ADDRESS FOR SUBMISSION:

William Fischer, Editor
NEA Today
1201 16th Street, NW
Washington, DC 20036
USA
Phone: 202-822-7288
Fax: 202-822-7206
E-Mail: neatoday@nea.org
Web: www.nea.org
Address May Change:

PUBLICATION GUIDELINES:

Manuscript Length:
Copies Required: N/A
Computer Submission:
Format: N/A
Fees to Review: 0.00 US$

Manuscript Style:

CIRCULATION DATA:

Reader:
Frequency of Issue:
Copies per Issue:
Sponsor/Publisher: National Education
  Association
Subscribe Price: 0.00 US$

REVIEW INFORMATION:

Type of Review:
No. of External Reviewers:
No. of In House Reviewers:
Acceptance Rate:
Time to Review:
Reviewers Comments:
Invited Articles:
Fees to Publish: 0.00 US$

MANUSCRIPT TOPICS:
Education Management/Administration

MANUSCRIPT GUIDELINES/COMMENTS:

NEA Today is mostly staff-written and we no longer accept unsolicited manuscripts.
Thanks.

New Directions for Student Services

ADDRESS FOR SUBMISSION:

John H. Schuh, Editor
New Directions for Student Services
Iowa State University
N243 Lagomarcino Hall
Ames, IA 50011
USA
Phone: 515-294-6393
Fax: 515-294-4942
E-Mail: jschuh@iastate.edu
Web: www.interscience.wiley.com/jpages
Address May Change:

PUBLICATION GUIDELINES:

Manuscript Length: 30+
Copies Required: One
Computer Submission: No
Format: N/A
Fees to Review: 0.00 US$

Manuscript Style:
    American Psychological Association

CIRCULATION DATA:

Reader: Academics
Frequency of Issue: Quarterly
Copies per Issue: 1,001 - 2,000
Sponsor/Publisher: Jossey-Bass (Wiley
    Publishers)
Subscribe Price: 65.00 US$ N. America
    89.00 US$ Rest of World

REVIEW INFORMATION:

Type of Review: Editorial Review
No. of External Reviewers: 0
No. of In House Reviewers: 2
Acceptance Rate: No Reply
Time to Review: 2 - 3 Months
Reviewers Comments: Yes
Invited Articles: 50% +
Fees to Publish: 0.00 US$

MANUSCRIPT TOPICS:
Higher Education; Student Affairs Administration

MANUSCRIPT GUIDELINES/COMMENTS:

Aims and Scope
An indispensable resource for vice presidents of student affairs, deans of students, student counselors, and other student services professionals, *New Directions for Student Services* offers guidelines and programs for aiding students in their total development: emotional, social, physical, and intellectual. The Journal is now in its twenty-second year.

This is a monograph series. Proposal guidelines follow.

Prospectus Preparation
Jossey-Bass Publishers, Inc publishes the New Directions for Student Services Sourcebook Series. As a commercial publisher, Jossey-Bass is committed to publishing high quality materials that are contemporary in thought and attractive to a wide market. The New Directions Series is published on a quarterly basis. John Schuh and Elizabeth Whitt provide the general editorial leadership for the series.

Elements of a proposal for a potential Sourcebook include the following items:

1. The tentative title.

2. The names of the guest editors along with a brief paragraph or two describing the following:
   a) Their expertise as editors
   b) Their knowledge about the topic of the Sourcebook

3. The need for the Sourcebook.

4. The potential market for the publication beyond the annual subscribers to the Sourcebook series.

5. A chapter by chapter discussion of the book. For each chapter the following should be provided:
   a) The title
   b) The potential author(s)
   c) A paragraph describing the content of the chapter.

6. For all contributors, a listing of their address, telephone number, facsimile number and electronic mail address should be provided.

7. Decisions about publishing sourcebooks are made at least one year in advance of the publication date. For best consideration, proposals should be submitted by December 1 of each calendar year.

8. Compensation. Compensation is provided to the editors and authors in the form of Jossey-Bass publications. This is arranged directly by Jossey-Bass with the contributor.

If you have further questions, please feel free to contact either editor.

John H. Schuh, Editor or Elizabeth J. Whitt, Associate Editor
515-294-6393 (office) 515-294-4942 (facsimile)
N 243 Lagomarcino Hall Iowa State University Ames, Iowa 50011
jschuh@ iastate.edu (Internet)

Nurse Educator

ADDRESS FOR SUBMISSION:

Suzanne P. Smith, Editor
Nurse Educator
4301 32nd Street W., Suite C12
Bradenton, FL 34205-2748
USA
Phone: 941-753-5662
Fax:
E-Mail:
Web: www.nursingcenter.com
Address May Change:

PUBLICATION GUIDELINES:

Manuscript Length: 11-15
Copies Required: Three
Computer Submission: No
Format: N/A
Fees to Review: 0.00 US$

Manuscript Style:
, AMA

CIRCULATION DATA:

Reader: Academics
Frequency of Issue: Bi-Monthly
Copies per Issue: 4,001 - 5,000
Sponsor/Publisher: Lippincott, Williams &
 Wilkins
Subscribe Price: 74.00 US$

REVIEW INFORMATION:

Type of Review: Blind Review
No. of External Reviewers: 2
No. of In House Reviewers: 1
Acceptance Rate: 11-20%
Time to Review: 1 - 2 Months
Reviewers Comments: Yes
Invited Articles: 6-10%
Fees to Publish: 0.00 US$

MANUSCRIPT TOPICS:

Adult Career & Vocational; All Topics Related to Nursing; Counseling & Personnel Services; Curriculum Studies; Education Management/Administration; Educational Psychology; Educational Technology Systems; Higher Education; Teacher Education; Tests, Measurement & Evaluation

MANUSCRIPT GUIDELINES/COMMENTS:

Nurse Educator, edited for academic educators and administrators, provides information on both the theories and practice of nursing education, including education, including educational philosophy, research, curriculum and program development, teaching methods, instructional materials, testing and measurement, and administration.

Editorial Procedures

Query letters are not required; however, they allow the editor to give advice on proposed manuscript topics. Responses to query letters prevent manuscript rejection by providing authors with pertinent information: the journal has recently published or accepted an article on the topic; the topic has been covered widely in the nursing literature; or the topic or focus is inappropriate for *Nurse Educator's* readers.

The main reasons for rejection of manuscripts with appropriate topics are: the topic is not made explicitly relevant to the needs of nurse educators, content does not address significant problems and needs; the topic is developed poorly; the content is too basic; the research design is inadequate; and/or the writing style is poor.

Manuscripts are reviewed by at least two members of *Nurse Educator's* editor advisory board for relevance, accuracy, and usefulness of the content to educators. The review process for manuscripts received during any particular month starts on the first day of the following month. Publication decisions and author notification are made within 8 weeks from the beginning of the review process.

Manuscript Preparation
Submit the original and two copies, along with a stamped, self-addressed business-size envelope if you want receipt of your manuscript acknowledged. if you want your original manuscript returned after the review process, enclose self-addressed 9 1/2 X 12 1/2 envelope with sufficient postage affixed.

The maximum length of a manuscript is 14 pages including figures, tables, and references. Leave 1 1/2" margins and double space throughout (including tables, figures, and references). Number pages in the upper right corner, starting on the first page of text and continuing through the end of the reference list.

In addition to the manuscript, submit: (1) a 50-75 word abstract that stimulates readers' interest in the topic and states the benefits of the article to academic educators, (2) a title/author biography page that lists the article title and authors (as they should be listed in the journal), their credentials, position, place of employment, city, and state. EXAMPLE: Alice M. Jones, PhD, RN, is Associate Professor, Green University, College of Nursing, Smithfield, Ohio.

Tables And Figures
Each table (detailed data in tabular form) should be typed double-spaced on a page by itself. Tables must have an Arabic numeral (numbered consecutively) and a caption (title) typed in at the top. Place footnotes at the bottom, using the following symbols: *, etc. Figures (line drawings or photographs) should be unmounted black-ink drawings or black-and-white glossy photographs. A separate list of captions must be submitted. Figures and tables must be referred to in number order in the text.

Each figure and table should be on a separate page, numbered as if a narrative page, and inserted after the reference list.

Headings
Subdivide the article into main sections by inserting subheads in the text. Subheads should be short, succinct, meaningful, and similar in sense and tone.

Authorship Responsibility
All people designated as authors should qualify for authorship. Each author should have participated significantly in the conception and design of the work and the writing of the

manuscript to take public responsibility for it. The editor may request justification of assignment of authorship. Names of those who contributed general support or technical help may be listed in an acknowledgement.

Permissions

It is the authors responsibility to request any permission required for the use of material owned by others such as any copyrighted material that is complete in itself: tables, charts, forms, figures. Written permission must also be obtained from people mentioned in an acknowledgement or the narrative and from the head of an institution mentioned in the manuscript. All letters of permission should be submitted with the manuscript. Where permission has been granted, the author should follow any special wording stipulated by the grantor.

References

References are placed at the end of the article and typed double-spaced. References are cited in the narrative by an Arabic number and listed in citation order in the reference list. If a reference is cited more than once, it should have the same number. Follow the *Index Medicus* for style and,.abbreviations of journal name; if the journal names does not appear, use full journal names. A few examples are listed below.

(Journal)   Bailey PA. Cheating among nursing students. Nurs Educ 1990; 15(3):32-35.

(Book)   Rankin SH, Stallings KD. Patient education: Issues, principles, practices. Philadelphia: J.B. Lippincott, 1990.

(Chapter
in Book)   Greco S. Vasoactive drugs. In: Underhill SL, Froelicher ES, Halpenny CJ. Cardiovascular medications for cardiac nursing. Philadelphia: J.B. Lippincott, 1990.

Perspectives: The New York Journal of Adult Learning

ADDRESS FOR SUBMISSION:

Kathleen P. King, Editor
Perspectives: The New York Journal of
   Adult Learning
Fordham University
Graduate School of Education
113 W. 60th Street, Room 1102
New York, NY 10023
USA
Phone: 212-636-6472
Fax: 212-636-6452
E-Mail: perspectives@fordham.edu
Web: www.fordham.edu/gse/aded/...
Address May Change:

PUBLICATION GUIDELINES:

Manuscript Length: 16-20
Copies Required: Four , Include disk
Computer Submission: Yes by disk
Format: Word or Rtf with Hardcopy
Fees to Review: 0.00 US$

Manuscript Style:
   American Psychological Association

CIRCULATION DATA:

Reader: Practicing Teachers, Academics,
   Administrators
Frequency of Issue: 2 Times/Year
Copies per Issue: Less than 1,000
Sponsor/Publisher: New York Assn. of
   Adult Continuing Community Education,
   Fordham U. Grad. Sch. of Education
Subscribe Price: 40.00 US$ Individual
   100.00 US$ Institution

REVIEW INFORMATION:

Type of Review: Blind Review
No. of External Reviewers: 2
No. of In House Reviewers: 1
Acceptance Rate: New J
Time to Review: 2 - 3 Months
Reviewers Comments: Yes
Invited Articles: New J
Fees to Publish: 0.00 US$

MANUSCRIPT TOPICS:
Adult Career & Vocational; Adult Literacy; Bilingual/E.S.L.; Higher Education; Workforce
Development

MANUSCRIPT GUIDELINES/COMMENTS:

Mission
Perspectives: The New York Journal of Adult Learning seeks to publish articles that will
address the needs and interests of those involved in educating adults in the specific areas of
adult literacy, adult education, community education, continuing education and higher
education. The ultimate goal is to improve understanding and practice of adult education
through careful consideration and reflection of timely research and issues. The journal is
intended to be a source of adult education articles that are practical, substantial, and scholarly.
Articles may be submitted for consideration in the following areas: refereed articles, book
reviews, issues and trends, invited research summaries and best practice. (This journal will be
published twice a year with its inaugural issue scheduled for late 2002.)

General Guidelines
(1) Articles should readily address the readership of the journal in content, interest, and readability.

(2) All submissions must conform to the *Publications Manual of the American Psychological Association* (5th Ed.) except where modified in these guidelines. See website 'Guidelines for Authors' for a brief summary of citation and reference list formatting.

(3) Four typed copies of the manuscript should be submitted (double-spaced, 12-point font, with 1" margins at top, bottom and sides).

(4) Four printed copies of the article should be submitted to the editor. Articles cannot be submitted by e-mail. Please keep an original copy, because no copies will be returned.

(5) Tables, graphs, and figures should be kept to a minimum and must be submitted on separate pages as camera ready.

(6) All submissions will include a Word or RTF file on disk.
   a. Label your disk with the following information: your name, name of the article, computer (i.e., PC, Mac) type and file type (doc or rtf).
   b. Use Times New Roman (or similar font) 12-point type and double-space the entire document.
   c. Do not insert headers, footers, or specified page numbers.
   d. Do not use any special commands for spacing or other formatting commands.
   e. Do not use any special features to configure tables within your article. Tables should be configured using APA 5th Edition guidelines and can be drawn using underline feature to make horizontal lines.
   f. Figures should be placed in a separate file on the disk and not placed in the manuscript. We recommend jpg, gif, bmp or pcx formats for graphics, with jpg being the preferred format. The graphic file should be in black and white or gray scale, NOT color. Please enclose a black and white or gray scale camera-ready copy of any figure.

(7) Evaluation of manuscripts is based upon value of the topics to the field, clarity of purpose and theoretical and conceptual base, soundness of the approach (e.g., research methodology, logic of analyses, etc.), strength of conclusions, implications for practices, quality of writing and readability.

Refereed Articles
Articles that relate to theory, research and practice of adult education are welcomed in this journal. The purposes of this section are to improve practice and encourage research and theory development. Refereed articles are subject to a blind peer review process.
- The General Guidelines above must be followed.
- Articles should be no more than 5,000 words in length, including, charts, appendices and references. Articles should comply with the American Psychological Association (APA)

Publication Manual (5th ed.). (This should include 12-point font, 1" margins and the specified format of citations and reference list).

- Submissions should include a single cover page with article title, author/s name, institutional affiliation, address, and telephone, fax, email, and the signed warranty statement (See below).
- All other pages of the manuscript should have no information that identifies the author.
- The first page of the manuscript should repeat the title, along with a 50 word abstract.

Book Review Guidelines

Book reviews that pertain to the theory, research and practice of adult education are welcomed. The purpose of the book reviews is to provide adult educators with insight into the literature of adult education. Book reviews are subject to a review process that includes the journal's book review editor and the editorial staff.

- The General Guidelines above must be followed.
- Book reviews should be no more than 1,000 words in length, total. Submissions should comply with the American Psychological Association (APA) Publication Manual (5th ed.). (This should include 12-point font, 1" margins and the specified format of citations and reference list).
- Submissions should include a cover page with the title and publication information of the reviewed book, author/s name, institutional affiliation, address, and telephone, fax, email, and the signed warranty statement (See below).

Issues and Trends, Research Summaries and Best Practice Guidelines

Articles that relate to current issues and trends, as well as available resources for adult education. The Issues and Trends section will provide the readership with timely discussions of issues and developments in the field. The Research Summaries will present brief synopses of the background, research method, data and conclusions of a completed research project and Best Practices articles will highlight instructional strategies and programs that are valuable for adult educators, adult learners and adult education programs. Submissions from this category will be subject to review by the journal's resources editor and the journal's editorial staff.

- The General Guidelines above must be followed.
- Submissions for this category should be no more than 750 words in length, including, charts, appendices and references. Articles should comply with the American Psychological Association (APA) Publication Manual (5th ed.). (This should include 12-point font, 1" margins and the specified format of citations and reference list).
- Submissions should include a single cover page with article title, author/s name, institutional affiliation, address, and telephone, fax, email, and the signed warranty statement (See below).

Warranty Statement (To be signed and included with all submissions to the journal.)

"I hereby confirm the assignment of first publication rights to the manuscript named above in all forms to the New York Association of Continuing, Community Education, effective if and when it is accepted for publication in *Perspectives: The New York Journal of Adult Learning.* I warrant that my manuscript is original work and has not been accepted for publication by another periodical. I further warrant that my work does not infringe upon any copyright or

651

statutory rights of others, does not contain libelous statements, and that editorial board members, staff, and other officers of the New York Association of Continuing, Community Education and Fordham University are indemnified against all costs, expenses, and damages arising from any breach of the fore going in regard to this manuscript. Finally, I acknowledge that the New York Association of Continuing, Community Education is relying on this statement in any publishing of the manuscript's information." *(Signature and date)*

Submissions to the Journal May Be Sent to:
Perspectives: The New York Journal of Adult Learning
Dr. Kathleen King, Editor,
Fordham University
113 W. 60th St., Rm. 1102
New York, NY 10023

For Additional Information, Contact Us by Email: Perspectives@fordham.edu

Journal Homepage: http://www.fordham.edu/gse/adcd/perspectives

Planning and Changing

ADDRESS FOR SUBMISSION:

Judith Mogilka, Editor
Planning and Changing
Illinois State University
Department of Education Administration
    and Foundations
Campus Box 5900
Normal, IL 61790-5900
USA
Phone: 309-438-2399
Fax: 309-438-8683
E-Mail: ljmEine@ilstu.edu
Web: coe.ilstu.edu/eafdept/pandc.htm
Address May Change:

PUBLICATION GUIDELINES:

Manuscript Length: 2500-4000 words
Copies Required: Three
Computer Submission: No
Format: N/A
Fees to Review: 0.00 US$

Manuscript Style:
    American Psychological Association

CIRCULATION DATA:

Reader: Academics, Administrators
Frequency of Issue: Quarterly
Copies per Issue: Less than 1,000
Sponsor/Publisher: Illinois State University
Subscribe Price: 18.00 US$

REVIEW INFORMATION:

Type of Review: Blind Review
No. of External Reviewers: Varies
No. of In House Reviewers: 17
Acceptance Rate: 45%
Time to Review: 2 - 3 Months
Reviewers Comments: No
Invited Articles: 6-10%
Fees to Publish: 0.00 US$

MANUSCRIPT TOPICS:
Education Management/Administration; Higher Education; Rural Education & Small Schools; Topical Issues in Educational Practice & Policy; Urban Education, Cultural/Non-Traditional

MANUSCRIPT GUIDELINES/COMMENTS:

1. Manuscripts are judged by their contribution to the understanding of educational leadership and policy issues.

2. Manuscripts should be prepared according to the style recommendation in the *Publication Manual of the American Psychological Association,* Fifth Edition. No abstract is needed.

3. Manuscripts of 2500-4000 words should be submitted in triplicate. Upon receipt, the principal author will receive notification.

4. One manuscript should have a cover sheet including a brief statement of each author's current title, position, and institutional affiliation and the address of the principal author. No

other author identification should be included in the manuscript. The two remaining copies should have no author identification.

5. Each accepted manuscript will ordinarily have been reviewed by three independent reviewers. The blind review process normally takes six to eight weeks.

6. Authors will be asked for a computer diskette containing the manuscript if it is accepted for publication.

7. Authors may be requested to make revisions prior to final acceptance. The editor reserves the right to make editorial changes which do not materially affect the meaning of the text. Authors will receive a final copy to proof and approve.

8. Manuscripts and correspondence should be addressed to the Editor; correspondence about subscriptions and change of address should be sent to Business Manager, *Planning and Changing*, Illinois State University, Department of Educational Administration and Foundations, Campus Box 5900, Normal, IL 61790-5900. Tel: 309-438-5422, Fax: 309-438-8683.

654

Planning for Higher Education

ADDRESS FOR SUBMISSION:

Sharon Morioka, Managing Editor
Planning for Higher Education
Society for College and Univ. Planning
311 Maynard Street
Ann Arbor, MI 48104-2211
USA
Phone: 770-643-4785
Fax: 770-643-4785
E-Mail: smorioka@scup.org
Web: www.scup.org/phe.htm
Address May Change:

PUBLICATION GUIDELINES:

Manuscript Length: 4000 words or less
Copies Required: Three
Computer Submission: Yes
Format: MSWord
Fees to Review: 0.00 US$

Manuscript Style:
  Chicago Manual of Style

CIRCULATION DATA:

Reader: Administrators, Planners
Frequency of Issue: Quarterly
Copies per Issue: 4600-4800
Sponsor/Publisher: Society for College and
  University Planning
Subscribe Price: 50.00 US$
  62.00 US$ Canada & Mexico
  155.00 US$ Membership (Journal free)

REVIEW INFORMATION:

Type of Review: Blind Review
No. of External Reviewers: 3
No. of In House Reviewers: 1
Acceptance Rate: 50%
Time to Review: 2 - 3 Months
Reviewers Comments: Yes
Invited Articles: 31-50%
Fees to Publish: 0.00 US$

MANUSCRIPT TOPICS:
Higher Education

MANUSCRIPT GUIDELINES/COMMENTS:

Planning for Higher Education is a quarterly publication of the Society for College and University Planning, an association of professionals devoted to planning at academic institutions. This journal seeks to transmit the knowledge, ideas, research, and experience mostlikely to advance the practice of higher education planning and policy making. SCUP members receive a complimentary subscription. The Society offers both individual and institutional memberships.

Editors
Executive Editor: Rod Rose, The JCM Group
Associate Editors: Carol Everly Floyd, Education Consultant,
  Sandra Gleason, Pennsylvania State University
  Frank Schmidtlein, University of Maryland at College Park
  Albert A. Dekin, Jr., Binghamton University
  Andrea Serban, Santa Barbara City College

For Contributors

Planning for Higher Education invites well-written articles about important trends and issues that could influence academic planning and management, about novel or effective planning techniques, and about applied research of relevance to educational decision making.

Contributors should submit three copies of their paper. Articles should be typed, double spaced with large margins, and should not exceed 15 pages (approximately 4,000 words). Papers should have a cover page with the article title and the name, title, address, and telephone and fax numbers of each contributor. The article's first text page should include the manuscript title, but not the author's name. A copy of the article should be included on a disk in Microsoft Word 6.0 format. Charts, tables, or maps can be included on the disk or attached on hard copy. For photographs, black and white (at least four-by-five-inch) glossy prints should be provided. Also include eight to ten key words or phrases, a two-to four-sentence summary of the article, and a one-paragraph author biography. Authors of all articles accepted for publication will receive two complimentary issues of the journal.

To cite references and sources use the author-date style, e.g. (Keller 1994), in the text and a list of all citations, alphabetically by author, at the end. For style in listing references, consult the *Chicago Manual of Style*, 14th edition, chapters 15 and 16. When possible, include citations to pertinent on-line resources.

Be sure to proofread the article and to check the accuracy of assertions and documentation. Avoid references to gender unless referring to specific individuals. Three members of the Editorial Review Board read submitted articles and make recommendations regarding rejection or acceptance. an editor then reviews the article and, upon acceptance, may request that an author edit a manuscript before accepting it for publication. The executive editor reserves the right to edit accepted articles to meet the journal's standards.

Articles should be sent to the Managing Editor; for queries, call or e-mail. (See 'Address for Submission' above.)

Practical Assessment, Research and Evaluation

ADDRESS FOR SUBMISSION:

Lawrence Rudner, Editor
Practical Assessment, Research and
    Evaluation
ERIC Clearinghouse
    on Assessment and Evaluation
1131 Shriver Laboratory
College Park, MD 20742
USA
Phone: 301-405-7449 or 800-464-3742
Fax: 301-405-8134
E-Mail: pare2@ericae.net
Web: www.ericae.net/pare
Address May Change:

PUBLICATION GUIDELINES:

Manuscript Length: 6-10
Copies Required: No Paper Copy Required
Computer Submission: Yes Email
Format: Any
Fees to Review: 0.00 US$

Manuscript Style:
    American Psychological Association

CIRCULATION DATA:

Reader: , Measurement Practitioners
Frequency of Issue: 12 Times/Year
Copies per Issue: 10,001 - 25,000
Sponsor/Publisher: ERIC Clearinghouse on
    Assessment & Dept. of Measurement,
    Statistics & Evaluation, Univ. of MD
Subscribe Price: 0.00 US$

REVIEW INFORMATION:

Type of Review: Blind Review
No. of External Reviewers: 3+
No. of In House Reviewers: 2
Acceptance Rate: 11-20%
Time to Review: 1 Month or Less
Reviewers Comments: Yes
Invited Articles: 0-5%
Fees to Publish: 0.00 US$

MANUSCRIPT TOPICS:
Education Management/Administration; Educational Psychology; Tests, Measurement &
Evaluation

MANUSCRIPT GUIDELINES/COMMENTS:

Practical Assessment, Research and Evaluation (PARE) is an on-line journal published by the
ERIC Clearinghouse on Assessment and Evaluation (ERIC/AE) and the Department of
Measurement, Statistics, and Evaluation at the University of Maryland, College Park. Its
purpose is to provide education professionals access to refereed articles that can have a
positive impact on assessment, research, evaluation, and teaching practice, especially at the
local education agency (LEA) level.

Manuscripts published in *Practical Assessment, Research and Evaluation* are scholarly
syntheses of research and ideas about issues and practices in education. They are designed to
help members of the community keep up-to-date with effective methods, trends and research
developments. While they are most often prepared for practitioners, such as teachers,

administrators, and assessment personnel who work in schools and school systems, *PARE* articles can target other audiences, including researchers, policy makers, parents, and students.

Manuscripts to be considered for *Practical Assessment, Research and Evaluation* should be short, 1500-2000 words or about four pages in length, exclusive of tables and references. They should conform to the stylistic conventions of the *American Psychological Association (APA)*. See the Policies section of this web site for technical specifications and a list of suggested topics. Manuscripts should be submitted electronically to pare2@ericae.net. Articles appearing in *Practical Assessment, Research and Evaluation* also become available in the ERIC database through the ERIC Digest Series. Many articles published in *PARE* were previously published as part of the *ERIC/AE Digest Series.*

Permission is granted to distribute any article in this journal for nonprofit, educational purposes if it is copied in its entirety and the journal is credited. Please notify the editor if an article is to be used.

Practical Assessment, Research and Evaluation is listed among the ejournals in education at the website for the AERA SIG "Communications Among Researchers".

Professional Standards
Manuscripts submitted to *Practical Assessment, Research & Evaluation* should adhere to

The authorship standards outlined in the *Uniform Requirements for Manuscripts Submitted to Biomedical Journals.*

The *Uniform Requirements* addresses criteria for authorship, acknowledgments, redundant publication, competing manuscripts, and conflict of interest. A concise summary of the *Uniform Requirements* can be found in Syrett and Rudner (1996).

A key concept in the *Uniform Requirements* is that individuals identified as authors should have made significant contributions to the conception and design, or analysis and interpretation of data, or both; to drafting of the manuscript or revising it critically for intellectual content; and on final approval of the version of the manuscript to be considered for publication. Being an advisor or head of a research group, does not, in itself, warrant authorship credit.

Publication Manual of the American Psychological Association (4th ed.)
The *Publication Manual* provides detailed information about the entire process of publication --from organizing, writing, keying, and submitting your manuscript, to seeing the accepted manuscript through production and publication. Of special interest in the fourth edition are updated sections on reporting statistics; writing without bias; preparing manuscripts with a word processor for electronic production; and publishing research in accordance with ethical principles of scientific publishing.

Content
Practical Assessment, Research & Evaluation publishes the following types of papers

- *Overviews* serve as in introduction to a topic. Its audience is individuals, whether professional or general, who wish to acquire introductory information on the topic treated in the paper.
- *Fact sheets* which provide current information of a factual nature related to a topic.. As appropriate, it also interprets and discusses the facts presented. Its primary audience is policymakers, administrators, and other decision makers; its secondary audience is other professionals and members of the general public who are interested in factual information on the topic.
- *Issue Papers* which define and describe a controversial topic. It does not resolve controversies in the literature or practices, but it delineates the various perspectives related to the topic. Its audience is individuals, both professional and general, who wish to become informed about alternative perspectives on educational issues.
- *Practice Applications* which provide specific, concrete examples of how practitioners can apply research results in practical settings. Its primary audience is educational practitioners, while its secondary audience is other educators interested in the topic.
- *Research Findings* which present the current status of research in an area. It summarizes and synthesizes recent findings from relevant research. Its primary audience is those individuals who wish to become informed about research findings, including researchers, graduate students, policymakers, administrators, and teachers.
- *Synopsi of Synthesis* Papers which summarize an existing review and synthesis publication. This type of paper is based on one primary publication, which is itself a review and synthesis of many publications. Its audience is individuals, both professional and general, who wish to become informed about the topic.

Topics
We are particularly interested in papers that address the following hot topics. This list is intended to be suggestive, the topics are not in any kind of rank order. Authors should feel free to submit papers on any topic within the scope of the journal.

- History of Educational and Psychological Testing
- National Tests in America - Precedents, The Executive Proposal and its Rebuttals
- Resources for Education Statistics - including International, National, and Local Levels
- State Assessment Practices - Extant Practices and Emerging Trends
- Qualitative and Quantitative Research Methods - an overview; types and their proper roles and appropriate audiences, i.e., their proper application and interpretation
- Meta Analysis - definition, methodology, recent critiques and, perhaps, response/rebuttal to critiques
- Meta Evaluation - definition, methodology
- Pedagogy of Educational Research & Educational Measurement
- Testing Accommodations for Students with Disabilities - current state of the research and practice (including commentary on apparent abuses); trends to anticipate
- Computer Adaptive Testing - state of the research and practice; trends to anticipate
- Report Cards/Reporting to Parents - types [format & content], policies, appropriate intervals of reporting
- Program Evaluation Primers
- Ability Grouping/Tracking (in Education) - pros & cons; demonstrated outcomes

- Test Selection - process and important sources, for administrators and committees
- Current Educational Indicators - definition(s); their role in School Accountability; factors for parents to consider in school selection; the School Report Card trend
- Benchmarking Effective School Practices - sources of benchmarks; benchmarking process
- Benchmarking Curriculum to National/Subject Standards - sources of the standards; benchmarking process; a.k.a. "curriculum alignment"
- Parents' Guide to Test Score Interpretation - including explanations about equated scores and factors other than test scores to consider in child's achievement and in deciding upon school enrollment [i.e., scores as ed. indicators]; advisement re: test takers' rights/test administrators' responsibilities [the Standards]; definitions/explanations of types of scores
- Home Schooling - sources of standardized assessment instruments; sources of states' policies; available documentation, and the rising trend
- Grade Retention - pros and cons; demonstrated outcomes
- Cognitive Style - definition, types, assessment thereof, incorporation into instruction
- Difference between Assessment & Evaluation
- Legal Research in Education - standard sources and processes; explanation of authoritative entities for education law and education policy at various levels
- Time of Day and Achievement [i.e., Environmental and Biological Factors in Learning]
- Performance Based Assessment - definition, types, rationale, current Practices, trends to anticipate; comparative analyses to traditional assessment; esp. definitions/apps of:
- Scoring Rubrics; Portfolios, including Electronic Portfolios; Observation & Anecdotal Records; Student Led Conferences; Multiple Assessments [w/performance based assessment as a component]; also, validity, reliability, and cost concerns in their development & application
- Demonstrating Statistical and Practical Equivalence
- Demonstrating Growth

Technical specifications

All *Practical Assessment Research & Evaluation* articles adhere to the following technical specifications:

Length -- 1,500 to 2,000 words.

Style -- Articles should have information subheadings and should be written clearly and concisely. For the most part, keep your sentences short and to the pointy. Short lists help to break up the text and to focus attention on series of items. Online constraints currently restrict our use of a wide range of type sizes, fonts, and other printing devices.
Introduction -- We like to see a short, two or three paragraph introduction that clearly indicates what is covered in the article and the intended audience. We like to see the second paragraph start with "This article ..."

Content -- Articles should be substantive, informative, and based on well-documented sources. Bibliographies, directories, and extensive lists of organizations are inappropriate.

660

References -- List four to six references to journal articles, commercial publications, and other resources that you used as supporting material for your digest and/or will point to key literature in the field.

Reference and additional reading

American Psychological Association (1992). Ethical principles of psychologists and code of conduct. *American Psychologist*, *47*, 1597-1611. [Available online http://www.apa.org/ethics/code.html].

American Psychological Association (1994). *Publication Manual of the American Psychological Association* (4th ed.). Washington, DC: Author.

Uniform requirements for manuscripts submitted to biomedical journals. [Available online at http://jama.ama-assn.org/info/auinst_req.html]

Syrett, Kristen L. & Rudner, Lawrence M. (1996). Authorship Ethics. *Practical Assessment, Research & Evaluation*, 5(1). [Available online: http://ericae.net/pare/getvn.asp?v=5&n=1].

Thompson, B. (1995). Publishing your research results: Some suggestions and counsel. *Journal of Counseling and Development, 73*, 342-345.

Wilkinson, L. and Task Force on Statistical Inference (1999). Statistical Methods in Psychology Journals: Guidelines and Explanations. *American Psychologist, 54* (8), 594B604. [Available online: http://www.apa.org/journals/amp/amp548594.html].

Professional School Counseling

ADDRESS FOR SUBMISSION:

Kenneth Hughey, Editor
Professional School Counseling
Kansas State University
Counseling & Educational Psychology
329 Bluemont
Manhattan, KS 66505-7801
USA
Phone: 785-532-6445
Fax: 785-532-7304
E-Mail: khughey@ksu.edu
Web: www.schoolcounselor.org
Address May Change: 5/1/02

PUBLICATION GUIDELINES:

Manuscript Length: 21-25
Copies Required: Three
Computer Submission: No
Format: N/A
Fees to Review: 0.00 US$

Manuscript Style:
    American Psychological Association

CIRCULATION DATA:

Reader: Counselors, Counselor Educators
Frequency of Issue: 5 Times/Year
Copies per Issue: 10,001 - 25,000
Sponsor/Publisher:
Subscribe Price: 90.00 US$ Member Dues
    Free w/ Membership to ASCA

REVIEW INFORMATION:

Type of Review: Blind Review
No. of External Reviewers: 2
No. of In House Reviewers: 1
Acceptance Rate: 21-30%
Time to Review: 2 - 3 Months
Reviewers Comments: No Reply
Invited Articles: 6-10%
Fees to Publish: 0.00 US$

MANUSCRIPT TOPICS:
Counseling & Personnel Services

MANUSCRIPT GUIDELINES/COMMENTS:

The *Professional School Counseling* journal welcomes original manuscripts on school counseling research, practice, theory, and contemporary issues in the field.

Writing Your Manuscript for One of the Following Sections

Features. These articles are largely research-oriented. Theoretical, philosophical, and literature reviews or meta-analyses will be considered. Manuscripts should include implications or practical applications for school counselors.

Perspectives from the Field (1,500-2,000 words). These short articles or opinion pieces focus on beneficial school-based practices or contemporary issues and concerns related to school counselors. School counselors are especially encouraged to submit their views.

662

Resource Reviews. These are reviews of current books and other resources of interest to school counselors. For consideration please contact: Dr. Toni Tollerud, Department of CAHE, Northern Illinois University, DeKalb, IL 60115.

Submitting Your Preliminary Manuscript for Committee Review
Do not submit material under consideration by another periodical.

Manuscripts must conform to the guidelines in the 1994 edition of the *American Psychological Association (APA) Publication Manual* (4th ed.). The manual is in most libraries and major bookstores. You may also contact APA Order Department, 750 First St., NE, Washington, DC 20002-4242 or call 1.800.374.2721.

Refer to the *APA* guidelines to eliminate bias based on gender, sexual orientation, racial or ethnic group, disability, or age. Avoid using passive voice.

Keep article titles and headings within the article as short as possible.

For the reviewers' benefit, double space all material, including references and quotations, and allow wide margins.

- Place the article's title on a separate page accompanying the manuscript. Include the author(s) name(s), contact information, and institutional affiliation(s).
- Send one original plus two copies of all material.
- On a separate page in all three copies, include an abstract of no more than 75 words. Place the article title on top of the page.
- Mail the package to Dr. Kenneth F. Hughey, Counseling and Educational Psychology, Kansas State University, 1100 Mid-Campus Dr., 369 Bluemont Hall, Manhattan, KS 66506-5312.

Preparing the Final Version
Upon article acceptance for publication, the editor will send you
- Edited remarks
- A copyright release form
- An author information form
- A diskette description form

The author must secure written permission(s) from the copyright holder for reproducing lengthy quotation (generally 300-500 words or more from one source) and for reprinting and/or adapting tables and figures. The author must provide the journal editor a copy of those copyright holder's written permission(s).

The author should check all references for the most available source and completeness according to *APA style*. All references cited in the text should also appear in the reference section and vice versa.

Place each table and figure on a separate page following the reference section. Final placement of the tables and figures is at the discretion of the production editor. In all cases, tables and figures will appear after the first reference in the text. Type font should be no smaller than 9 point.

- Provide the final version in hard copy **and** on a disk (3.5 inch) high density (HD), IBM format. Macintosh users must save the manuscript electronic file in Microsoft Word 6.0 or higher and WordPerfect 5.0. PC or IBM users must save the electronic file in Microsoft Word 6.0 or higher, WordPerfect 5.0 or in ASCII (text only). Do not worry about format as the hard copy will show format. On the disk label, write the author's name, the file name(s) and the software name.

- Supply tables in a separate file on the disk and indicate file name and software on the label. Keep tables to a minimum. Include only essential data and combine tables wherever possible. Recent journal issues show styles of table presentations.

- Supply figures (graphs illustrations, line drawings) as camera ready art (laser or glossy print or velox) or on disk in separate TIFF or EPS files and indicate the file name(s) on disk label.

ASCA will assign your article to an issue and mail you a copy of the final edited article for your review before press time.

Psychology in the Schools

ADDRESS FOR SUBMISSION:

LeAdelle Phelps, Editor
Psychology in the Schools
SUNY Buffalo
Department of Counseling and
    Educational Psychology
409 Baldy Hall
Buffalo, NY 14260
USA
Phone: 716-645-2484 ext 1075
Fax: 716-645-4501
E-Mail: phelps@acsu.buffalo.edu
Web: www.wiley.com
Address May Change:

PUBLICATION GUIDELINES:

Manuscript Length: 20-25 pages
Copies Required: Four
Computer Submission: No
Format: N/A
Fees to Review: 0.00 US$

Manuscript Style:
    American Psychological Association

CIRCULATION DATA:

Reader: Academics, School Psychologists
Frequency of Issue: 6 Times/Year
Copies per Issue: 10,001 - 25,000
Sponsor/Publisher: John Wiley & Sons
Subscribe Price: 35.00 US$ Individual
    100.00 US$ Institution

REVIEW INFORMATION:

Type of Review: Blind Review
No. of External Reviewers: 2
No. of In House Reviewers: 1
Acceptance Rate: 21-30%
Time to Review: 1 - 2 Months
Reviewers Comments: Yes
Invited Articles: 0-5%
Fees to Publish: 0.00 US$

MANUSCRIPT TOPICS:
Counseling & Personnel Services; School Psychology; Special Education

MANUSCRIPT GUIDELINES/COMMENTS:

This Authors' Guide has been prepared to facilitate the production process and to insure the completeness and accuracy of material published in this Journal. By following this Guide, authors are assured that their manuscripts will receive prompt attention and publication at the earliest possible date.

Acceptable manuscripts include research, opinion, and review articles, as well as those relating to practice. This includes a range from those that deal with theoretical and other problems of the school psychologist to those directed to the teacher, counselor, administrator, and other personnel workers in schools and colleges. Articles are published in the following areas: evaluation and assessment, educational practices and problems, strategies in behavioral change, and topics of general impact on schools.

Manuscripts received are reviewed by the editor for general qualities of writing, conciseness, and appropriateness. They are then sent to reviewers for an evaluation of originality, timeliness, validity, and interest to the profession.

All manuscripts accepted for publication are subject to copyediting. The author(s) assumes final responsibility for the content of the manuscript, including any copyediting. Please bear in mind that a manuscript prepared in accordance with the journal style appears in print with less delay than one that requires extensive editorial attention. Manuscripts should not exceed 14-16 typed, double-spaced pages, including tables and figures.

Copyright. Manuscripts published in the journal are copyrighted John Wiley & Sons and may not be published elsewhere without written permission. All authors are required to sign a Copyright Assignment Form, which explicitly transfers copyright ownership from the author to the publisher of the journal.

Permission, however, is not required to photocopy or to reproduce up to ten copies of an article which appears in *Psychology in the Schools*, if such reprints are distributed without charge for educational purposes and if copyright ownership is indicated on each copy reproduced.

Submission of Manuscript. Manuscripts are received with the explicit assurance that they are not simultaneously under consideration by any other publication. A letter of manuscript transmittal should designate the senior author or other person as correspondent.

The original and two copies of the manuscript, typed double-spaced on standard 8 1/2" x 11" bond paper should be sent to the editor. Authors are requested to retain a copy of their original manuscript to aid them when correcting galley proofs.

Title Page. Titles should be short, specific, informative, and should summarize the main idea of the paper. Authors' names should appear as they are customarily used. Affiliations should be given for each author. A short title, or running head, should be designated on this page.

Abstracts. Each article, except for very short notes, should begin with an abstract (maximum 150 words). An abstract should be factual and complete in itself so that the reader may quickly obtain the essence of the paper. Avoid abbreviations in the abstract and cite any reference material in its entirety. Abstracts should not begin with a paragraph indent. The abstract should be typed on a separate page.

Style Guide. *Psychology in the Schools* follows the stylistic guidelines of the *Publication Manual of the American Psychological Association*, fourth edition (Washington, D.C.: APA, 1994).

Tables. Tables should be self-explanatory and supplement the text. The journal, however, prefers that tables be avoided unless absolutely necessary for a clear presentation. If possible, the information contained in tables should be presented in-text. Tables should be typed one to a page and attached to the end of the manuscript. It should be noted in-text where the table is to be printed.

Figures. All figures must be submitted in camera-ready form. Figure captions should be typed on a separate page and attached to the manuscript.

Galley Proofs. Authors will receive galley proofs for review and correction. Proofs must be returned to the managing editor within three days of receipt. Alterations should be kept to a minimum, since authors will be charged for all authors' alterations. Since galleys are not read against original manuscripts by the managing editor, authors are responsible for making sure that all necessary corrections have been made. Page proofs are not sent to authors.

Reprints. Free copies of reprints are not sent to authors. A reprint order form will accompany the galley proofs. Payment or purchase orders must accompany all reprint orders. Ordinarily reprints are delivered to authors within 30 days of the publication of the issue in which the article appears.

References. References should be typed double-spaced in alphabetical order according to the last names of first authors. Do not abbreviate journal names. Authors should review and verity references before manuscripts are submitted for consideration, since they alone are responsible for accuracy and completeness.

In-text references should not employ superscripts. Examples of the proper style for in text references are given below:
a) Kaufman and Kaufman (1977) stated that...
b) These differences are to be expected (Wallbrown, Blaha, & Wherry, 1973) and are attributable to the different samples...

A sampling of the most common entries in reference lists appears below. Entries not exemplified below are modeled in the *APA Publications Manual*.

References
Kaufman, A. S., & Kaufman, N. L. (1977). Clinical evaluation of young children with the McCarthy Scales. New York: Grune & Stratton.

Wall brown, F., Blaha, J., & Wherry, R. J. (1973). The hierarchical factor structure of the Wechsler Preschool and Primary Scale of Intelligence. Journal of Consulting and Clinical Psychology, 41, 356-362.

Public Personnel Management

ADDRESS FOR SUBMISSION:

Karen D. Smith, Editor
Public Personnel Management
International Personnel Management Assn.
1617 Duke Street
Alexandria, VA 22314
USA
Phone: 703-549-7100
Fax: 703-684-0948
E-Mail: ksmith@ipma-hr.org
Web: www.impma-hr.org
Address May Change:

PUBLICATION GUIDELINES:

Manuscript Length: 16-20
Copies Required: Five
Computer Submission: Yes
Format: WordPerfect or ASCII only
Fees to Review: 0.00 US$

Manuscript Style:
, Kate L. Turabian's Style

CIRCULATION DATA:

Reader: , Public Administrators
Frequency of Issue: Quarterly
Copies per Issue: 7,000
Sponsor/Publisher: International Personnel
  Management Association (IPMA)
Subscribe Price: 50.00 US$

REVIEW INFORMATION:

Type of Review: Blind Review
No. of External Reviewers: 3
No. of In House Reviewers: 1
Acceptance Rate: 50%
Time to Review: 2 - 3 Months
Reviewers Comments: Yes
Invited Articles: 11-20%
Fees to Publish: 0.00 US$

MANUSCRIPT TOPICS:

Adult Career & Vocational; Counseling & Personnel Services; Educational Technology Systems; Elementary/Early Childhood; Social Studies/Social Science; Tests, Measurement & Evaluation

MANUSCRIPT GUIDELINES/COMMENTS:

As a leading journal in public sector human resources, *Public Personnel Management* particularly encourages manuscripts from a practitioner's perspective, as well as submissions on emerging national and international trends in public personnel management. Articles in response to previously published manuscripts are also welcome.

1. *Public Personnel Management*, the journal of the International Personnel Management Association, encourages contributions on all aspects of personnel management in the public sector. Manuscripts for publication should be sent to the editor. Authors are strongly advised to consult one or more recent issues of the journal before submitting manuscripts for publication.

2. Manuscripts are subject to a blind review process. Reviewers submit their recommendations as to acceptance, revision or rejection. In the cases of revision or rejection, the unidentified reviewers comments will be sent to the author.

3. Contributions should be accompanied by a statement that they have not already been published, and that if accepted for publication in *Public Personnel Management* they will not be published elsewhere without the agreement of the editor.

4. Articles are accepted for publication on the understanding that they are subject to editorial revision and that the right of publication in any form or language is reserved by the Association.

5. Manuscripts should be in English. Submit five copies of the manuscript. If less than five are submitted, you will be requested to send the additional copies. Manuscript copies must be double spaced throughout, and submitted on 8 1/2" x 11" white paper, single sided. Manuscripts must also be submitted on 3 1/2" diskette in WordPerfect 5.1 or ASCII format. Authors should keep the original of the manuscript. Pages must be numbered consecutively.

6. Place the title of the manuscript, the author's name, address, telephone number and a biographical sketch of no more than 50 words on a separate cover page--please **do not** send complete resumes for a biographical sketch. In the case of co-authors, respective addresses and telephone numbers should be clearly indicated, as well as the author who is to receive correspondence (primary author). Please notify the editor of any change of address which occurs while a paper is under review, or in the process of publication. Biographical sketches must be provided for co-authors on the separate cover page.

7. The essential contents of the manuscript should be summarized in a single-paragraph abstract on a separate sheet following the cover page. The title of the article should appear again above the abstract, without the author's name, as a means of identification. Manuscripts are circulated for review without identifying the author.

8. The title of the article should appear again on the first text page of the manuscript, without the author's name, as a means of identification.

9. All tables, photographs, maps, charts and diagrams should be referred to as "Figures or Tables" and should be presented at the end of the manuscript. They should be numbered consecutively (in Arabic numerals) as they appear in the text and should have informative titles. Their positions in the manuscript should be indicated. All tables, charts, etc. must be provided on computer diskette as an .eps, .pcx, or .wpg file.

10. *Public Personnel Management* does not accept manuscripts that use the author/date style of references. Endnotes should be numbered consecutively in superscript and should be presented in a **separate**, double-spaced listing at the end of the article. The bibliography should be presented after the endnotes at the end of the article. *Public Personnel Management* subscribes to the style of references presented in the most recent edition of Kate L. Turabian's *A Manual for Writers of Term Papers, Theses and Dissertations*. The editor strongly urges

contributors to consult the Manual regarding style of references before they submit manuscripts--they will be returned if they do not conform to Turabian's style.

11. Because of the difficulties of scheduling and transmission delays, proofs of articles accepted for publication cannot be sent to authors.

12. Articles may be reproduced for internal, non-commercial use without authorization, provided the source is identified. Requests for permission to publish, reproduce, or translate articles should be made to the editor.

13. *Public Personnel Management* will also publish appropriate book reviews. Reviews should be between 500 and 1,000 words in length and the reviewer's full name and identification should be provided.

670

Reading Professor (The)

ADDRESS FOR SUBMISSION:

Larry Kenney, Editor
Reading Professor (The)
University of Wisconsin-Whitewater
800 W Main Street
Whitewater, WI 53190
USA
Phone: 262-472-4677
Fax: 262-472-5716
E-Mail: kenneyl@mail.uww.edu
Web:
Address May Change:

PUBLICATION GUIDELINES:

Manuscript Length: 16-20
Copies Required: Four
Computer Submission: No
Format: N/A
Fees to Review: 0.00 US$

Manuscript Style:
    American Psychological Association

CIRCULATION DATA:

Reader: Academics
Frequency of Issue: 2 Times/Year
Copies per Issue: Less than 1,000
Sponsor/Publisher: Professors of Reading
    Teacher Educators (PRTE)
Subscribe Price: 15.00 US$ PRTE Dues

REVIEW INFORMATION:

Type of Review: Blind Review
No. of External Reviewers: 3
No. of In House Reviewers: 1
Acceptance Rate: 60%
Time to Review: 1 - 2 Months
Reviewers Comments: Yes
Invited Articles: 0-5%
Fees to Publish: 0.00 US$

MANUSCRIPT TOPICS:
Reading

MANUSCRIPT GUIDELINES/COMMENTS:

Reviewers Comments. Mailed regularly to all submitting manuscripts.
Reader. International reading audience, especially US., Canada, and UK.

Sponsorship. *Professors of Reading Teacher Educators (PRTE), a special interest group of* IRA. Professors of Reading Teacher Educators hold an annual program at the International Reading Association in convention each spring (2002, San Francisco).

Additional Comments. After manuscript is renewed and accepted a disk using Word Perfect is required to make material camera ready for printing.

Guidelines For Authors
The Reading Professor seeks manuscripts dealing with topics, issues and events of interest to professors of reading. Authors are encouraged to submit articles and/or research studies that

are directed toward the improvement of reading instruction at all levels of education. All authors must be members of both IRA and PRTE.

Preparing and Submitting Manuscripts

Manuscripts should be typed and double-spaced (including references). The author's name, full address, and the date of the manuscript is submitted should appear only on the cover page of each manuscript. Every effort should be made to avoid inclusion of the author's identity in any portion of the manuscript in order to secure an impartial view.

Send four copies of each manuscript to the editor. A word processor should be used; Word Perfect 6.1 in IBM format is preferred. Please print final copies using a letter-quality printer. If the manuscript is returned; in that case, stamps for the return of the manuscript should be sent. If references are included, they should be cited in the article by name and date, for example, (Shantz, 1993). References at the end of the article should follow the format used in the International Reading Association journals, i.e., *APA style*, 1994.

Evaluation of Manuscripts Upon receipt of a manuscript, the editor first prescreens it and sends an acknowledgment to the author. Manuscripts are evaluated by at least three reviewers who are uninformed as to the identity of the author. Manuscripts are evaluated in terms of interest, quality of writing, appropriate documentation of ideas, uniqueness, and needs of the journal. A decision on the manuscript is usually reached within two months. Manuscripts submitted are assumed to be previously unpublished and not under consideration by any other publication. Accepted manuscripts may be edited to promote clarity and to improve organization.

Manuscripts and correspondence regarding editorial matters should be addressed to Dr. Kenney, Editor.

672

Rehabilitation Counseling Bulletin

ADDRESS FOR SUBMISSION:

Douglas C. Strohmer, Editor
Rehabilitation Counseling Bulletin
LSU Health Sciences Center
School of Allied Health Professions
Department of Rehabilitation Counseling
1900 Gravier St., Room 8C1, Box G6-2
New Orleans, LA 70112-2262
USA
Phone: 504-568-4315
Fax: 504-568-4324
E-Mail: sdstroh@communique.net
Web:
Address May Change:

PUBLICATION GUIDELINES:

Manuscript Length: 16-20
Copies Required: Five
Computer Submission: Yes
Format: Mac or PC
Fees to Review: 0.00 US$

Manuscript Style:
    American Psychological Association

CIRCULATION DATA:

Reader: Academics
Frequency of Issue: Quarterly
Copies per Issue: 4,001 - 5,000
Sponsor/Publisher: Professional Association
Subscribe Price: 18.00 US$

REVIEW INFORMATION:

Type of Review: Blind Review
No. of External Reviewers: 3
No. of In House Reviewers: 1
Acceptance Rate: 40%
Time to Review: 1-3 Months
Reviewers Comments: Yes
Invited Articles: 0-5%
Fees to Publish: 0.00 US$

MANUSCRIPT TOPICS:
Adult Career & Vocational; Counseling & Personnel Services; Disability Related;
Rehabilitation Counseling; Higher Education; Tests, Measurement & Evaluation

MANUSCRIPT GUIDELINES/COMMENTS:

Rehabilitation Counseling Bulletin seeks research articles illuminating the theory and practice
of rehabilitation counseling and exploring innovations in the field. If you wish to contribute to
the journal, follow these guidelines. All manuscripts not meeting the specifications detailed
below will be returned to the authors before review 'or publication.

In general, guidelines specified in the *APA Publication Manual* (4th ed., 1994) should be
followed. Pay particular attention to sections concerning and reducing bias in language.

According to ACA publication policy, the term subject should not be used when referring to a
sample of research participants or to an individual participant. Usually a nor specific term

should be used (e.g., clients, students) or if a more general term is desired participants should be used.

Avoid footnotes wherever possible.

Tables should be kept to a minimum. Include only essential data and combine tables where possible. Refer to recent issues of this journal for table style. Double-space all tables. Each table should be on a separate page following the reference section of the article. Final placement of tables is at the discretion of the production editor.

Lengthy quotations (generally 300-500 cumulative words or more from one source) require written permission from the copyright holder for reproduction. Adaptation of tables and figures also required reproduction approval from the copyrighted source. It is the author's responsibility to secure such permission and a copy of the publisher's written permission must be provided the journal editor upon acceptance for publication.

References should follow the style of recent issues of the journal. Check all references for completeness, including year, volume number and pages for journal citations. Make sure that all references mentioned in the text are listed in the reference section and vice versa. For other questions of style consult the *APA Publication Manual* (5th ed., 1994). Double-space all references.

Article title and headings should be as short as possible. On a separate page place the title of the article, the names of the authors, their professional titles, and their institutional affiliations. Double-space all title page material.

Articles should include an abstract of not more than 100 words and one of not more than 25 words with each copy of the manuscript. The abstracts should express the central idea of the article in non-technical language and should appear on separate pages.

Double-space all material (including references) all lines of tables (including heads) and extensive quotes. Allows wide margins (at least one inch on all four sides).

Never submit material for concurrent consideration by another publication.

Research in Higher Education

ADDRESS FOR SUBMISSION:

John C. Smart, Editor
Research in Higher Education
University of Memphis
Center for the Study of Higher Educaiton
308 Browning Hall
Memphis, TN 38152
USA
Phone: 901-678-4145
Fax: 901-678-4291
E-Mail: jsmart@memphis.edu
Web: www.wkap.nl
Address May Change:

PUBLICATION GUIDELINES:

Manuscript Length: 21-25
Copies Required: Three
Computer Submission: No , not initially
Format: After Acceptance Only
Fees to Review: 0.00 US$

Manuscript Style:
American Psychological Association

CIRCULATION DATA:

Reader: Academics
Frequency of Issue: 6 Times/Year
Copies per Issue: 1,001 - 2,000
Sponsor/Publisher: Kluwer Academic
  Publishers
Subscribe Price: 59.00 US$

REVIEW INFORMATION:

Type of Review: Blind Review
No. of External Reviewers: 2
No. of In House Reviewers: 0
Acceptance Rate: 11-20%
Time to Review: 2 - 3 Months
Reviewers Comments: Yes
Invited Articles: 0-5%
Fees to Publish: 0.00 US$

MANUSCRIPT TOPICS:
Higher Education

MANUSCRIPT GUIDELINES/COMMENTS:

Research in Higher Education is directed to those concerned with the functioning of post-secondary education, including two-year and four-year colleges, universities, and graduate and professional schools. It is of primary interest to institutional researchers and planners, faculty, college and university administrators, student personnel specialists and behavioral scientists. Generally, empirical studies are sought which contribute to an increased understanding of an institution or allow comparison between institutions, which aid faculty and administrators in making more informed decisions about current or future operations, and which improve the efficiency or effectiveness of the institution. Of particular interest are topics such as: administration and faculty; curriculum and instruction; student characteristics; alumni assessment; recruitment and admissions; prediction and student academic performance; campus climate; retention, attrition and transfer. Brief notes of a methodological nature will also be considered for publication.

Manuscripts will be evaluated according to (a) significance in contributing new knowledge, (b) technical adequacy, (c) appropriateness for *Research in Higher Education*, and (d) clarity of presentation. When published, manuscripts will be part of the journal copyright filed by the publisher.

All manuscripts should be sent, in triplicate, to the Editor.

Manuscripts should be typed double-spaced throughout, including the reference list. If the manuscript is produced on a word processor, please use a letter-quality printer. The first page should contain the article title, author's name, affiliation, and address to which correspondence and proofs should be sent. The author should **not** place his name on the other manuscript pages. A brief abstract of about 150 words should be included. Tables should be typed on separate pages at the end of the manuscript. Figures must be originals, or sharp and clear photostats. Figure legends should be typed on a separate page.

References are cited by name and year in the text and listed alphabetically in the reference list. Be sure that all references listed are cited in the text, and all those cited are listed. Check that spellings of names and years in the text agree with the list. References should be styled according to the following examples:

Journal. Saunier, Margaret Ellen (1985). Objective measures as predictors of reputational ratings. Research in Higher Education 23 (3): 227-244.
Book. Astin, A.W. (1982). Minorities in Higher Education. San Francisco: Jossey-Bass.
Chapter in edited book. Morgan, Anthony W., and Mitchell, Brad L. (1985). The quest for excellence: underlying policy issues. In John C. Smart (ed.), Higher Education: Handbook of Theory and Research, Vol. 1, pp. 309-348. NewYork: Agathon Press.
Reports, theses, etc. Style title like that of an article, with as much source information as possible.

In other style matters, please consult the *Publication Manual of the American Psychological Association*, 3rd ed.

After a manuscript has been accepted for publication and after all revisions have been incorporated, manuscripts may be submitted to the Editor's Office on Personal-Computer Disks. Label the disk with identifying information – kind of computer used, kind of software and version number, disk format and file name of article, as well as abbreviated journal name, authors' last names, and (if room) paper title. Package the disk in a disk mailer or protective cardboard. **The disk must be the one from which the accompanying manuscript (finalized version) was printed out.** The Editor's Office cannot accept a disk without its accompanying, matching hard-copy manuscript. Disks will be used on a case-by-case basis – where efficient and feasible.

For information about The Association for Institutional Research, write the AIR Administrative Director, 314 Stone Building, Florida State University, Tallahassee, FL 32306: or telephone (904) 644-4470.

Research in Post-Compulsory Education

ADDRESS FOR SUBMISSION:

Catherine Emanuelli, Editor
Research in Post-Compulsory Education
University College of Worcester
Henwick Grove
Worcester, WR2 6AJ
UK
Phone: +44 (0) 1905 855145
Fax: +44 (0) 1905-855000
E-Mail: c.emanuelli@worc.ac.uk
Web:
Address May Change:

PUBLICATION GUIDELINES:

Manuscript Length: 21-25
Copies Required: Three
Computer Submission: Yes
Format: MSWord
Fees to Review: 0.00 US$

Manuscript Style:
  See Manuscript Guidelines

CIRCULATION DATA:

Reader: Academics, Practicing Teachers
Frequency of Issue: 3 Times/Year
Copies per Issue: Less than 1,000
Sponsor/Publisher: Further Education
  Research Association; Triangle Journals,
  Ltd.
Subscribe Price: 200.00 US$

REVIEW INFORMATION:

Type of Review: Blind Review
No. of External Reviewers: 2
No. of In House Reviewers: 2
Acceptance Rate: 21-30%
Time to Review: 2 - 3 Months
Reviewers Comments: Yes
Invited Articles: 6-10%
Fees to Publish: 0.00 US$

MANUSCRIPT TOPICS:
Adult Career & Vocational; Curriculum Studies; Education Management/Administration; Educational Psychology; Higher Education; Teacher Education; Urban Education, Cultural/Non-Traditional

MANUSCRIPT GUIDELINES/COMMENTS:

Contributions, to this. new journal are welcome. To ensure the highest standards all submitted articles will be scrutinised by two independent referees before being accepted for publication. Manuscripts (three copies please) should be sent to Dr Geoffrey Elliott Director of External Affairs, University College Worcester, Oldbury Road, Worcester WR2 6AJ, United Kingdom c.emanuelli@worc.ac.uk

Unless agreed, all accepted papers become the copyright of the journal. All contributors should be aware they are addressing an international audience.

Manuscripts should be in the following form: (a) full length articles normally of 5,000 to 8,000 words in length, plus any necessary attachments, or (b) shorter articles (up to 3,000 words plus attachments) in the form of contributions to a 'debates' or 'ongoing research' section of the journal

Review articles on suitable areas of post-compulsory education will normally be commissioned by the Editors. Review articles will be subject to peer review and will normally not exceed 5,000 words.

Book and software reviews are also commissioned but are not subject to the full review process. Reviews will be between 500 and 1,000 words in length.

Reviews

If you are interested in reviewing books and/or software, send or email Neil Moreland with the following information:

* Your full name (and institutional affiliation)
* Your full postal and email addresses
* A paragraph outlining your main areas of post-compulsory research interests

Three complete copies of the manuscript should be submitted, typed double-spaced on one side of the paper. It is essential the full postal address be given of the author who will receive editorial correspondence, offprints and proofs

Figures and tables should have their positions clearly marked and be provided on separate sheets that can be detached from the main text. The captions to figures should be listed in one group and be provided on a separate sheet. Figure numbers should be shown as Arabic numerals, table numbers as Latin numerals,

References should be indicated in the text by giving the author's name followed by the year in parentheses, e.g. '... early research by Smith & Jones (1975) showed...'; alternatively this could be shown as '... early research (Smith & Jones, 1975) showed...'. The full references should be listed in alphabetical order at the end of the paper using the following style:

Book: Dale, Roger (1989) *The State and Education Policy*, pp- 107-109. Milton Keynes: Open University Press.

Article in a journal: Brehony, K.J. & Deem, R (1990) Charging for free education: art exploration of a debate in school governing bodies, *Journal of Education Policy, 5, pp. 333-345.*

Chapter in a book: Bernstein, B. (1971) On the classification and framing of sociological knowledge, in M_ F. D. Young (Ed.) Knowledge and Control. London: Collier Macmillan.

Please note that journal titles must be given in full and that authors' full first names or initials nay be used. Particular care in the presentation of references would be greatly appreciated by the Editorial Board and the publisher

Proofs will be sent to the author designated to receive them, and should be corrected and returned immediately to the Editor. Fifty offprints of each article will be supplied free of charge; they are normally sent by accelerated surface post, together with a complete copy of the journal issue, shortly after publication.

Rhetoric Review

ADDRESS FOR SUBMISSION:

Theresa Enos, Editor
Rhetoric Review
c/o Derek B. Fiore
Lawrence Erlbaum Associates, Inc.
Advertising Coordinator
10 Industrial Avenue
Mahwah, NJ 07430
USA
Phone: 520-621-3371
Fax: 520-621-7397
E-Mail: enos@u.arizona.edu
Web: www.erlbaum.com
Address May Change:

PUBLICATION GUIDELINES:

Manuscript Length: 26-30
Copies Required: Three
Computer Submission: No
Format: N/A
Fees to Review: 0.00 US$

Manuscript Style:
, MLA

CIRCULATION DATA:

Reader: Academics
Frequency of Issue: Quarterly
Copies per Issue: Less than 1,000
Sponsor/Publisher: Lawrence Erlbaum
  Associates
Subscribe Price: 17.00 US$ Individual
  60.00 US$ Institution
  14.00 US$ Student

REVIEW INFORMATION:

Type of Review: Blind Review
No. of External Reviewers: 2
No. of In House Reviewers: 2
Acceptance Rate: 11-20%
Time to Review: 1 - 2 Months
Reviewers Comments: Yes
Invited Articles: 0-5%
Fees to Publish: 0.00 US$

MANUSCRIPT TOPICS:
Adult Career & Vocational; Higher Education; Rhetoric and Composition; Urban Education, Cultural/Non-Traditional

MANUSCRIPT GUIDELINES/COMMENTS:

Rhetoric Review is a scholarly interdisciplinary journal publishing in all areas of rhetoric and writing and providing a professional forum for its readers to consider and discuss current topics and issues. The journal publishes manuscripts that explore the breadth and depth of the discipline, including history, theory, writing, praxis, technical/professional communication, philosophy, rhetorical criticism, cultural studies, multiple literacies, technology, literature, public address, graduate education, and professional issues.

Rhetoric Review also invites readers to contribute to the Burkean Parlor, a discourse forum for discussion of the journal's published articles as well as professional issues. Essay reviews, commissioned by the editor, are included as a regular feature. Book reviews are assigned by the editor.

680

Submission: Submit three copies of the manuscript to the Editor, Theresa Enos, Department of English; The University of Arizona, Tucson, AZ 85721 (phone: 520-621-3371; fax: 520-621-7397; e-mail: enos@u.arizona.edu).

Enclose an envelope with a return address to which return postage - and postage sufficient for mailing two copies to peer reviewers - has been paper clipped.

Cover Letter: The cover letter should include the contact author's complete mailing address, e-mail address, and telephone and fax numbers. In the cover letter, the author(s) should request publication of the manuscript in *Rhetoric Review* and should include a statement that the manuscript is not previously published or simultaneously submitted elsewhere (manuscripts copyrighted electronically or online will also not be considered).

Manuscript Preparation: Manuscripts should be prepared according to the guidelines of the *MLA Style Manual and Guide to Scholarly Publishing* (2nd ed.). Double-space all material and place in the following order: title page, text, notes, works cited, appendixes, biographical blurb, tables, and figures. Because all manuscripts are blind reviewed, author identification should appear on the title page of one manuscript copy, only. Author identification includes the names and affiliations of all authors; the name, mailing address, e-mail address, and telephone and fax numbers of the corresponding author; and a running head of no more than 48 letters and spaces. Number all manuscript pages, including the figures. All figures must be camera-ready black-and-white originals.

Length: Manuscripts should be no longer than 7,500 words, including notes, works cited, and appendixes. Biographical blurbs should be no longer than 100 words. Contributions to the Burkean Parlor should be no longer than 500 words.

Permissions: Authors are responsible for all statements made in their work and for obtaining permission from copyright owners to use a lengthy quotation (500 words or more) or to reprint or adapt a table or figure published elsewhere. Authors should write to original authors) and publisher of such material to request nonexclusive world rights in all languages for use in the article and in future print and nonprint editions. Provide copies of all permissions and credit lines obtained.

School Administrator (The)

ADDRESS FOR SUBMISSION:

Jay Goldman, Editor
School Administrator (The)
1801 North Moore Street
Arlington, VA 22209
USA
Phone: 703-875-0745
Fax: 703-528-2146
E-Mail: jgoldman@aasa.org
Web: www.aasa.org
Address May Change:

CIRCULATION DATA:

Reader: Administrators
Frequency of Issue: Monthly
Copies per Issue: 10,001 - 25,000
Sponsor/Publisher: American Association
of School Administrators
Subscribe Price: Varies

PUBLICATION GUIDELINES:

Manuscript Length: 1-10
Copies Required: One
Computer Submission: Yes
Format: MSWord, Wordperfect
Fees to Review: 0.00 US$

Manuscript Style:
American Psychological Association

REVIEW INFORMATION:

Type of Review: Editorial Review
No. of External Reviewers: 0
No. of In House Reviewers: 2
Acceptance Rate: 21-30%
Time to Review: 2 - 3 Months
Reviewers Comments: No
Invited Articles: 50% +
Fees to Publish: 0.00 US$

MANUSCRIPT TOPICS:
Education Management/Administration; Elementary/Early Childhood; Gifted Children; Rural Education & Small Schools; Special Education; Tests, Measurement & Evaluation

MANUSCRIPT GUIDELINES/COMMENTS:

About our magazine and audience...
The School Administrator, the official magazine of the American Association of School Administrators, is published 11 times a year and generally organized around a theme (see Editorial Calendar on our website). The primary audience is district-level school administrators nationwide. In recent years, we have accepted for publication about 30 percent of all unsolicited manuscripts.

What we look for...
The School Administrator reaches a national audience so we seek timely articles about school system practices, policies and programs that have widespread appeal. Articles typically emphasize actual experiences--some successful, some not. Articles may be written in the first person and should include insightful reflections that might help other administrators.

We seek articles written in a journalistic rather than academic style--short paragraphs and clear, concise jargon-free language. Potential authors are urged to examine past issues of the magazine to note how topics are covered as well as the tone and voice of the articles.

The School Administrator regularly invites experts in various fields and hires professional education reporters as free-lancers to write the major feature articles, but we also welcome contributions for various sections of the magazine. The sections are as follows:

Features
These major articles typically are written on assignment by experts in their field or professional education writers. Often the lead article is an investigative piece or an in-depth examination with several articles clustered around a similar topic. Most issues of *The School Administrator* are based on themes, such as school safety, privatization, superintendent-board relations or testing and assessment. We welcome detailed query letters or manuscripts. Feature articles generally run from 1,500 to 3,000 words.

Focus
These short instructive articles cover aspects of school management, programs or policies. Focus articles, usually written by practitioners and professors of educational leadership, are based on the actual experiences of school administrators and school systems. Topics include community relations, personnel management, instruction, technology, school law, school safety, board relations, shared decision making and staff development. Focus articles run about 750-850 words (2½ to 3 double-spaced pages). Focus articles run with a photograph (black and white headshot) of each author.

Guest Columns
Guest columns present informed opinions on timely issues relevant to local school leaders. We seek provocative points of view, similar to op-ed pieces in a newspaper. We also welcome humorous commentaries. Guest columns run about 750 words (2½ to 3 double-spaced pages).

Leadership Lite
The Leadership Lite page welcomes short humorous anecdotes, quips, quotations and malapropisms relating to school district administration and school board governance. Upon request, names may be withheld in print. Submissions typically are three to four paragraphs and may be sent by mail, facsimile (703-528-2146) or electronic mail (magazine@aasa.org).

Book Reviews
School administrators interested in writing brief reviews (250-300 words) of new books on educational leadership should send a letter to the editor indicating their interest and enclosing a sample of their critical writing. Only AASA members can be considered for reviewing.

Profiles
Written by *The School Administrator* staff members, these profiles of outstanding educational leaders are members of the American Association of School Administrators. We welcome reader nominations of individuals to be featured in this section. We seek educational leaders who are distinctive in their style of management, their career path or their contribution to the field.

People
The People page seeks brief news items (one or two paragraphs, 50-70 words) about AASA members--promotions, retirements, deaths and significant honors. Black and white or color headshots are welcomed.

Resource Bank
The Resource Bank includes short items related to new research and new resources available to school leaders.

Letter to the Editor
The School Administrator welcomes letters from its readers commenting on an article, series of articles or points of view published in our magazine. We prefer typewritten letters up to 250 words. We reserve the right to edit letters for clarity and space. Letters may be sent by facsimile (703.528.2146) or electronic mail (magazine@aasa.org).

Our writing style...
Articles accepted for publication are selected on the basis of their relevancy to our readers, originality, readability, interest level, soundness, timeliness and freshness of viewpoint.

We are not looking for scholarly term papers or dissertation reports. We do not use footnotes or endnotes. See Editing Yourself on our website for tips on tightening and strengthening your writing.

How to prepare your manuscript...
1. Prepare a cover page for your manuscript that includes the following: proposed title of article, writer's name, complete contact information (address, telephone, facsimile, e-mail), writer's current professional position.

2. Prepare your manuscript double-spaced, with margins of at least one inch. Please do not single-space your article or crowd the pages.

3. Use capital and lowercase letters, in 11- or 12-point type.

4. Number all pages and print on only one side of the page.

5. If you want us to consider tables, graphs and charts, submit them on separate pages. We do not routinely use them.

6. Cite research literature by making attributions within the narrative (e.g., Sally Smith, in her 1998 book *Back to Basics*, indicated that ...). Do not cite scholarly references inside parentheses or through endnotes.

7. Give your article a possible headline as well as suggested subheads (two to three words) when a new topic begins.

8. For longer articles, provide supporting articles (250-750 words) that suggest possible action steps by the reader. Include data or examples or elaborate on a major point that might get lost

in the main article. Also consider including suggested readings, Web sites and additional resources on your subject.

Include a cover letter with your manuscript...
1. Include in your cover letter whether your article has been published elsewhere and whether you are submitting it simultaneously to several publications. If it is accepted for publication, *The School Administrator* will ask you to sign a form indicating that you do not plan to publish this article elsewhere before its publication in AASA's magazine.

2. Please indicate in your cover letter about the availability of photos of professional quality relating to your article or of the author. Give us the name and contact information of the person who can provide them.

3. Include in your cover letter sufficient information about yourself for a standard author identification paragraph. Please include your postal and e-mail address.

How to submit your manuscript...
1. You may submit your manuscript by one of three ways:
- Send a single copy by mail;
- Send a copy of your article on a 3½-inch IBM-compatible diskette using Word 6.0 (write this information on the diskette: the file name of your manuscript and your name and phone number);
- Send your material as an attached file by e-mail to magazine@aasa.org.

2. Do not send material by facsimile.

What happens after your manuscript is submitted...
1. Within 10 days, the author should receive a postcard or e-mail from the editors acknowledging receipt of the article.

2. Two to three magazine staff members typically evaluate each manuscript and recommend whether it should be considered for publication. The author generally receives a letter on the status of the article within eight to 10 weeks. If two months pass and the author has not received a final decision, he or she should call the magazine staff at 703.875.0772.

3. Articles not accepted for publication are returned to the author.

If your manuscript is accepted...
You will receive a letter from the editor and your article will be edited. An edited version will be returned for you to review and revise. Articles accepted for publication are edited by magazine staff members, who strive to preserve the author's writing style. We work with authors to make every article as lively, clear and concise as possible. Articles also are edited to fit space allotments.

You also will be sent an Agreement of Publication to sign and return to *The School Administrator*, granting your permission to publish the article and providing for copyright transfer.

No financial compensation is provided; however you will be given five complimentary copies of *The School Administrator* in which your article appears.

Send manuscripts to...
Editor, *The School Administrator*, AASA, 1801 N. Moore St., Arlington, Va. 22209-1813 or as an attached file to magazine@aasa.org.

The School Administrator staff welcomes feedback, including constructive criticism, to help us improve the magazine. We look forward to your letters and comments.

School Business Affairs

ADDRESS FOR SUBMISSION:

Kari Baer, Editor
School Business Affairs
1140 North Shore Dr.
Reston, VA 20190
USA
Phone: 703-478-0405
Fax: 703-478-0205
E-Mail: kbaer@asbointl.org
Web: www.asbointl.org
Address May Change:

PUBLICATION GUIDELINES:

Manuscript Length: 6-15
Copies Required: One
Computer Submission: Yes
Format: MSWord preferred
Fees to Review: 0.00 US$

Manuscript Style:
American Psychological Association

CIRCULATION DATA:

Reader: Administrators
Frequency of Issue: Monthly
Copies per Issue: 5,001 - 10,000
Sponsor/Publisher: Association of School
   Business Officials International
Subscribe Price: 68.00 US$

REVIEW INFORMATION:

Type of Review: N/A
No. of External Reviewers: 3+
No. of In House Reviewers: 2
Acceptance Rate: No Reply
Time to Review: 1 - 2 Months
Reviewers Comments: Yes
Invited Articles: 31-50%
Fees to Publish: 0.00 US$

MANUSCRIPT TOPICS:

Education Management/Administration; Educational Psychology; School Law

MANUSCRIPT GUIDELINES/COMMENTS:

About the Magazine. *School Business Affairs* is the professional journal of the Association of School Business Officials International, a non-profit organization. The monthly magazine provides information on all phases of school business management, including data processing, communications, building materials, budget and finance, insurance, security, maintenance, food service and transportation, among others.

School Business Affairs provides the latest information on methods, ideas and examples of what works for school business affairs.

Benefits. What are the benefits of having an article published in *School Business Affairs*? Having an article appear in *School Business Affairs* establishes your credentials in the school business profession, gets your name recognized and provides members with an opportunity to earn points toward ASBO's Professional Registration Program.

Communicate. Authors are invited to submit ideas for articles, preferably with a brief outline of the proposed article and a sample of the author's published work(s), if available.

Subject and Style

Features - When preparing your article, keep your audience in mind. It is school business officials who want to hear about practical, cost-saving efficiency producing ideas and methods, laws, practices, policies, etc.

Use concrete, everyday vocabulary and avoid theoretical or "teachy" material.

The length should be 10-15 **double spaced** typewritten pages (2,500-3,000 words) although this standard is flexible depending on the subject.

Your article is a tool for school business officials and should not promote products or services.

Use an attention-getting headline and any appropriate art, charts, tables, graphs or action/candid photos.

If accepted, articles are scheduled for publication on a "space available" basis, unless otherwise specifically indicated.

Submitted manuscripts will be acknowledged as soon as possible and authors will be notified of intended publication date.

Articles are usually edited for length and style. The editors will try to work closely with the author if there are substantial changes.

Columns – Specialized columns currently include the following topics: Management, Ethics, Educational Perspectives, Legal Perspectives, and Technology. These are usually written by assigned writers. However, if you are interested in writing one of these columns, and have a specific idea, please contact the editor. Column articles run 3-5 double-spaced typewritten pages (700-1,500 words).

Manuscript Preparation

1. Submit your manuscript via email.

2. Begin your article with a suggested title and your byline underneath.

3. Use subheads and bullets for easier reading. However, please avoid outlining. Please do not use headers, footers or automatic page numbers.

4. Do not use automatic footnotes or endnotes which are imbedded with text. In fact, footnotes are discouraged. Reference lists for cited works or any necessary endnotes should be typed at the end of the article.

5. For graphs or bar charts, include numerical data points, as well as the numerical range of the horizontal and vertical axis labels.

6. Put "-30-" at the bottom of the last page to signify the end of the article and attach biographical information.

7. Please proofread carefully and check data before submitting.

Letters to the Editor. The editors of *School Business Affairs* want to hear from you. Letters to the Editor help broaden the perspective our readers have on current events in school business administration. Letters are usually edited only for length and we attempt to let the writer known that we are using a letter. We want to hear from you.

2001-2002 Editorial Calendar
If you are interested in writing for School Business Affairs, please read SBA's writer guidelines and contact the shepherd of the issue you're interested in to discuss your idea.

February 2002: Technology – Articles Due: November 1
Shepherd: Philip Geiger, pgeiger@sfb.state.az.us

March 2002: Membership Directory – Content produced by staff

April 2002: Collective Bargaining – Articles Due: January 1
Shepherd: Dan Brown, dan.brown@ubc.ca

May 2002: School Finance – Articles Due: February 1
Shepherd: Catherine Sielke, csielke@coe.uga.edu

June 2002: Business Operations – Articles Due: March 1
Shepherd: Michael Jacoby, mjacoby@geneva.k12.il.us

July 2002: Safe Schools – Articles Due: April 1
Shepherd: Richard Griffin, RAGriffin@msn.com

August 2002: Legal and Legislative – Articles Due: May 1
Shepherd: Frank Brown, fbrown@email.unc.edu

September 2002: Planning – Articles Due: June 1
Cecilia DiBella, cdibella@johnsonschool.org

October 2002: Management and Human Resources – Articles Due: July 1
Contact: Kari Baer, kbaer@asbointl.org

November 2002: Accounting and Budgeting – Articles Due: September 1
Shepherd: Denny Bolton, dbolton@ojr.k12.pa.us

December 2002: School Operations and Facilities – Articles Due: September 1
Shepherd: Philip Geiger, pgeiger@sfb.state.az.us

School Foodservice & Nutrition

ADDRESS FOR SUBMISSION:

Patricia Fitzgerald, Managing Editor
School Foodservice & Nutrition
American School Food Service Association
1600 Duke Street, 7th Floor
Alexandria, VA 22314-3436
USA
Phone: 703-739-3900
Fax: 703-739-3915
E-Mail: pfitzgerald@asfsa.org
Web: www.asfsa.org
Address May Change:

PUBLICATION GUIDELINES:

Manuscript Length: 6-10
Copies Required: One
Computer Submission: Yes Disk
Format: MSWord
Fees to Review: 0.00 US$

Manuscript Style:
See Manuscript Guidelines

CIRCULATION DATA:

Reader: Administrators
Frequency of Issue: 11 Times/Year
Copies per Issue: More than 25,000
Sponsor/Publisher: American Society of
   Food Service Assocation
Subscribe Price: 75.00 US$ Non Member
   125.00 US$ Foreign

REVIEW INFORMATION:

Type of Review: Editorial Review
No. of External Reviewers: 0
No. of In House Reviewers: 0
Acceptance Rate: No Reply
Time to Review: Over 6 Months
Reviewers Comments: No
Invited Articles: 50% +
Fees to Publish: 0.00 US$

MANUSCRIPT TOPICS:

All Topics as Related to Child Nutrition; Education Management/Administration;
Elementary/Early Childhood; Gifted Children; Health & Physical Education; Special
Education; Urban Education, Cultural/Non-Traditional

MANUSCRIPT GUIDELINES/COMMENTS:

School Foodservice & Nutrition (SF&N) welcomes articles for possible publication. The
following are specific recommendations to increase the chances of articles being accepted.

In addition to these guidelines, please read "12 Tips for Contributing to *School Foodservice &
Nutrition"* or "Industry Tips for Contributing to *School Foodservice & Nutrition"* before
submitting your piece. See 'Related Links' on our website to view these articles.

Article Requirements

Query. Send us a query letter and/or outline that describes the proposed article so *SF&N* can
be sure the idea is on target with the Magazine's editorial needs.

Length. Feature articles should average between 1,500 and 2,500 words (or more if the topic requires greater detail). Regular departments (such as "At Your Service," "Playing it Safe," or "Food Focus") should be a minimum of 800 words and not exceed 1,700 words. Member news items for "Marketing Notebook" and "Cafeteria Classroom" should average between 50 and 200 words.

Specifications. Articles may be submitted via e-mail to sfn@asfsa.org. A paper copy also should be faxed to 703-739-3915. When submitting through regular mail, submit articles on 3 1/2-inch diskettes or typed, hard-copy manuscripts. (Even if you send a diskette, be sure to include a laser printed copy. This is helpful in case the diskette is damaged, incompatible or in some way unusable.) The Magazine staff prefers Microsoft Word for Windows, but can convert from a number of other formats. Always include your name, title, business mailing address, phone number and fax number with your article. *Handwritten articles will be rejected without review.*

Tone. Write in a personal, direct tone in an active voice. Whenever possible, give specific examples from an actual school foodservice environment, preferably by an ASFSA member school or district. Quotes are encouraged. Charts, tables and sidebars (short accompanying pieces of tips, pointers or resources) are helpful if they illustrate points in the article.

Artwork. The Magazine staff prefers color slides, photos and transparencies and encourage charts, graphs and other artwork. Include captions, but do not write on the backs of photos; ink can smear when used on photographic paper. Identify people and the activity in the photo on a separate sheet of paper or on a paper label attached to the back. Indicate if pictures must be returned. Photos accompanying accepted articles may be kept for several months. ht this time, most scanned photos submitted electronically are not at a high enough resolution for use in the Magazine, so please do not submit jpegs or other electronic formats unless there is no other alternative.

Topic Areas
The editorial in *School Foodservice & Nutrition* is divided into feature articles, food articles and regular departments. The Editorial Calendar lists feature topic areas that are currently planned for a specific issue. See the table at the bottom of this page to view the Editorial Calendar.

Feature articles. These are usually written by the editorial staff or assigned by the editors to writers or experts in the industry. If you are interested in writing on a specific topic, you can submit your name as a potential writer or expert, or send us a query and outline of your article idea.

Food articles. These are short pieces about a specific food topic, often accompanied by recipes and photographs. Separate contributor guidelines for the *Food Focus* section are available. Please request them from the editorial office at *703-739-3900.*

Regular departments. Although many of these departments are assigned to regular contributors, if your article idea is particularly appropriate for "Marketing Notebook," "Cafeteria Classroom," "It's Your Business," "Partners for Progress," "Nutrition Matters," "At

Your Service," "Ideas at Work," "Playing it Safe" or "Tools of the Trade," it will be considered for publication. "On the Market" features new product releases selected at the sole discretion of the editorial staff.

Editorial Policies

Review and acceptance. For features and departments, the editorial staff will review all articles for timeliness and appropriateness and will attempt to notify authors of the decision within 12 weeks of receipt. Note, however, that your article may not be scheduled for publication at the time of its acceptance. In addition, advertising and space considerations may "bump" your article to a different issue. Published authors will receive two complimentary copies of the magazine in which their article appears, as well as return of diskettes and artwork. Because of the volume of submissions for the member news items in "Marketing Notebook" and "Cafeteria Classroom," preference is given to those items that describe unusual activities and include complete facts. Press releases submitted for "On the Market" will be reviewed for appropriateness to the school foodservice market. Advertisers with regular schedules also are frequently given preference, but duplication of releases will not be permitted.

Product endorsements. Feature articles must be nonpromotional and generic in nature. The editors will delete references to product brand names in articles or recipes. However, authors do receive bylines, and the Magazine credits all photographs, artwork and recipes.

Originality. Aside from occasional book or magazine excerpts, adaptations or reprints, *SF&N* accepts only previously unpublished manuscripts.

Copyright. All published material is copyrighted by the American School Food Service Association under the "work made for hire" provision. Article submission implies author agreement with this policy.

Proof review. *SF&N* reserves the right to alter any accepted manuscript for clarity and adherence to *School Foodservice & Nutrition's* editorial style. Manuscript submission implies author agreement with this policy. With certain exceptions, *SF&N* does not provide authors with proofs of edited versions of their manuscripts.

School Leadership & Management

ADDRESS FOR SUBMISSION:

Brian Fidler, Editor
School Leadership & Management
University of Reading
Centre for Education Management
School Education
Bulmershe Court, Early
Reading, RG6 1HY
UK
Phone: +44 1189 318632
Fax: +44 1189 938863
E-Mail: F.B.Fidler@rdg.ac.uk
Web: www.tandf.co.uk/journals
Address May Change:

CIRCULATION DATA:

Reader: Academics, Administrators
Frequency of Issue: Quarterly
Copies per Issue: Less than 1,000
Sponsor/Publisher: Carfax Publishing
    (Taylor & Francis Group)
Subscribe Price: 116.00 US$ Individual
    578.00 US$ Institution

PUBLICATION GUIDELINES:

Manuscript Length: up to 6,000 words
Copies Required: Three
Computer Submission: Yes
Format: N/A
Fees to Review: 0.00 US$

Manuscript Style:
    Uniform System of Citation (Harvard
    Blue Book)

REVIEW INFORMATION:

Type of Review: Blind Review
No. of External Reviewers: 2
No. of In House Reviewers: 1
Acceptance Rate: 50%
Time to Review: 1 - 2 Months
Reviewers Comments: Yes
Invited Articles: 11-20%
Fees to Publish: 0.00 US$

MANUSCRIPT TOPICS:
Education Management/Administration

MANUSCRIPT GUIDELINES/COMMENTS:

Editor's Comments
Articles need to make a worthwhile contribution for international readers. They should be written for academics but be accessible to practitioners. Publication guidelines are based on Harvard.

Notes for Contributors
Papers will be accepted on the recommendation of two specialist referees.

Authors submitting their first article to the journal are invited to discuss their ideas with the Editor. Inexperienced authors may request assistance from a designated member of the Editorial Board under the Journal's author support and guidance service.

Manuscripts. Three copies of manuscripts should be sent to the Editor, Brian Fidler, School Improvement and Leadership Centre, School of Education, The University of Reading, Bulmershe Court, Earley, Reading RG6 1 HY, UK. They should be typed on one side of the paper, double spaced, with ample margins and bear the title of the contribution, name(s) of the author(s) and the address where the work was carried out. Each article should be up to 6000 words in length (an estimation of the length should be given), and be accompanied by an abstract of 50-100 words on a separate sheet. All pages should be numbered. Footnotes to the text should be avoided where possible. A brief description of the professional work of the author(s) of and up to 30 words should be given and an E-mail address (if applicable). The full postal address of the author who will check proofs and receive off-prints should also be included together with phone and fax numbers for speed of communication.

Disk. Authors should send the final, revised version of their articles in both hard copy paper and electronic disk forms. It is essential that the hard copy (paper) version exactly matches the material on disk. Please print o include out the hard copy from the disk you are sending. Submit three printed copies of the final version with the disk to the journal's editor. Save all files on a standard 3.5 inch high-density disk. We prefer to receive disks in Microsoft Word in a PC format, but can translate from most other common word-processing programs as well as Macs. Please specify which program you have used. Do not save your files as "text only" or "read only". For further details on Electronic Submission, please visit the Taylor & Francis Website at: http://www.tandf.co.uk/journalstcarfax113632434.html.

Tables and captions to illustrations should be typed out on a separate sheet and not included as part of the text. The captions to illustrations should be gathered together and also typed out on a separate sheet. Tables should be numbered by Roman numerals, and figures by Arabic numerals. The approximate position of tables and figures should be indicated in the manuscript. Captions should include keys to symbols.

Figures Please supply one set of artwork in a finished form, suitable for reproduction. If this is not possible, figures can be redrawn by the publishers.

References should be indicated in the typescript by giving the author's name, with the year of publication in parentheses. If several papers by the same author and from the same year are cited, a, b, c, etc., should be placed after the year of publication. The references should be listed in full, including page numbers, at the end of the paper in the following standard form:

For books: Bliss JR, Firestone WA & Richards CE (eds) (1991) *Rethinking Effective Schools Research and Practice*, Englewood Cliffs, NJ: Prentice Hall.

For articles: Louis KS, (1994) Beyond `managed change': rethinking how schools improve, *School Effectiveness and School Improvement*, 5(1), 2-24.

For chapters within books: Hopkins D (1996) Towards a theory for school improvement in Gray J, Reynolds D, Fitz-Gibbon C & Jesson D (eds) *Merging Traditions: the future of research on school effectiveness and school improvement*, London: Cassell.

Titles of journals should nor be abbreviated.

694

Proofs will be sent to authors if there is sufficient time to do so. They should be corrected and returned to the Editor within three days. Major alterations to the text cannot be accepted.

Offprints Fifty offprints of each paper are supplied free of charge. Additional copies may be purchased and should be ordered when the proofs are returned. Offprints, together with a complete copy of the relevant journal issue, are sent by accelerated surface post about three weeks after publication.

School Psychology International

ADDRESS FOR SUBMISSION:

Caven S. Mcloughlin, Editor
School Psychology International
Kent State University
School of Psychology Program
405 White Hall
Kent, OH 44240
USA
Phone: 330-672-2928
Fax: 330-672-2675
E-Mail: caven@kent.edu
Web: www.sagepub.com
Address May Change:

PUBLICATION GUIDELINES:

Manuscript Length: 11-15
Copies Required: Three
Computer Submission: No
Format: MSWord
Fees to Review: 0.00 US$

Manuscript Style:
    American Psychological Association

CIRCULATION DATA:

Reader: , School Psychologists
Frequency of Issue: Quarterly
Copies per Issue: Less than 1,000
Sponsor/Publisher: International School
    Psychology Association / Sage
    Publications
Subscribe Price: 74.00 US$ Individual
    620.00 US$ Institution

REVIEW INFORMATION:

Type of Review: Blind Review
No. of External Reviewers: 3
No. of In House Reviewers: 1
Acceptance Rate: 21-30%
Time to Review: 1 - 2 Months
Reviewers Comments: No
Invited Articles: 0-5%
Fees to Publish: 0.00 US$

MANUSCRIPT TOPICS:
Counseling & Personnel Services; Educational Psychology; School Psychology; Special
Education

MANUSCRIPT GUIDELINES/COMMENTS:

Published quarterly, *School Psychology International* highlights the concerns of those who
provide quality mental health, educational, therapeutic and support services to schools and
their communities throughout the world. It offers articles reflecting high quality academic
research in the field as well as examples of proven best practice.

School Psychology International aims to promote good practice in school and educational
psychology throughout the world. Your subscription to this valuable resource will provide you
with a forum for sharing ideas and solutions in current school psychology. The journal
encourages innovation among all professionals in the field and presents descriptions of best
practice with research studies and articles which address key issues and developments in
school psychology world-wide.

School Psychology International publishes speculative "work in progress" and emergent new methods and techniques which reflect the most innovative developments in the field. The journal is an indispensable resource for policy makers, researchers and practitioners of school psychology.

Submission Guidelines

Editorial Policy: *School Psychology International* publishes critical and descriptive review articles and empirical contributions of international interest in all practical and academic areas of school and educational psychology. Many issues will contain review articles based on defined themes. Review article manuscripts should normally be between 3000 and a maximum of 6000 words in length, including tables, figures and references, and will be evaluated by anonymous referees. Book reviews will also be published.

Submission of manuscripts: A manuscript will be accepted only on the understanding that it is an original contribution that has not been published previously. Papers should be submitted to one of the following:

Prof. R.L. Burden, School of Education, University of Exeter, Exeter EX4 4QJ.

Authors in *North America* should submit manuscripts to:
Dr C.S. Mcloughlin, School Psychology Program, 412 White Hall, Kent State University, Kent, OH 44242, USA.

Manuscript Specification: Manuscripts should be submitted in English as A4 double-spaced typescript with generous margins, complete in all respects including a title and the name and address of the author(s). Original typescripts and figures should be submitted together with two photocopies.

Style: Each of the following parts of a manuscript should begin on a new page and should appear in the order shown: (a) Manuscript title and author(s) affiliation(s); (b) Abstract, not exceeding 200 words; (c) Text with appropriate headings, followed by address to which requests for offprints may be addressed; (d) Tables; (e) Figure captions; (f) Figures.

Spelling should follow the *Oxford English Dictionary*, and punctuation should conform to British orthographic conventions, including the use of single rather than double quotation marks except for quotations within quotations. Footnotes should be avoided. The text should be organized conventionally: a typical experimental report is divided into Introduction, Method, Results and Discussion; review articles require a different structure which depends upon the nature of the material discussed. Apart from the details mentioned above, the style of manuscripts should follow the guidelines laid down in either the *Suggestions to Contributors* published by the British Psychological Society or the *American Psychological Association's Publication Manual.*

Tables: Tables should be numbered consecutively and given titles which are comprehensible without reference to the text. Each table should be typed, double-spaced, on a separate sheet, and its approximate location should be indicated by a separate line in the text, e.g. '-Table 1 about here'.

Illustrations: Graphs, diagrams, and other illustrations on separate sheets should be numbered consecutively 'Figure 1', 'Figure 2', etc., and their approximate location in the text indicated in the manner shown above for Tables. Only high quality artwork can be satisfactorily reproduced. Labeling should be done with stencils or instant lettering of sufficient size to remain legible when reduced for reproduction. The figure number and author(s) names should be written in pencil on the back of each illustration, and the top indicated with an arrow. Figure captions should be typed on a separate sheet.

Permission to Reproduce: If illustrations are borrowed from published sources, written permission must be obtained from both publisher and author, and a credit line giving the source added to the legend. If text material totaling 250 to 300 words, or any tables, are borrowed verbatim from published sources, written permission is required from both publisher and author. With shorter quotations, it is sufficient to add a bibliographic credit. Permission letters for reproduced text or illustration must accompany the manuscript. If you have been unable to obtain permission, please point this out.

References: References should be cited in the text in the usual way, thus: Smith (1963); Smith and Jones (1965).

If a work has three or more authors use the 'et al.' form throughout, e.g. Smith et al. (1980). The list of references following the text, and the acknowledgements, should accord with the British conventions illustrated by the examples below:

1. *Journal articles*
Acker, W. and Toone, B. (1978) 'Attention, Eye Tracking and Schizophrenia', *British Journal of Social and Clinical Psychology* 17: 173-81.

2. *Books*
McGee, M.G. (1979) *Human Spatial Abilities*, New York: Praeger.

3. *Articles in books*
Coleite, G. and Hoffman, L.R. (1979) 'Valence, Satisfaction, and Commitment of the Group's Solution', in L.R. Hoffman (ed.) *The Group Problem Solving Process*, pp. 113-20. New York: Praeger.

Proofs: Page proofs will be returned to authors to allow for **essential corrections**. Changes other than corrections of printer's errors will not normally be allowed.

Copyright: Authors submitting a manuscript do so on the understanding that if it is accepted for publication, copyright of the paper shall be assigned to the Publisher. The Publisher will not place any limitation on the personal freedom of the author(s) to use material contained in the paper in any subsequent publications.

School Public Relations Journal

ADDRESS FOR SUBMISSION:

Albert E. Holliday, Editor
School Public Relations Journal
Educational Communication Center
PO Box 657, 1830 Walnut Street
Camp Hill, PA 17011
USA
Phone: 717-761-6620
Fax:
E-Mail: aholliday@earthlink.net
Web:
Address May Change:

PUBLICATION GUIDELINES:

Manuscript Length: 11-20
Copies Required: Five
Computer Submission: Yes
Format: N/A
Fees to Review: 0.00 US$

Manuscript Style:
    See Manuscript Guidelines

CIRCULATION DATA:

Reader: Academics, Administrators
Frequency of Issue: Quarterly
Copies per Issue: 1,001 - 2,000
Sponsor/Publisher:
Subscribe Price: 48.00 US$ Individual
    60.00 US$ Library / Institution
    4.00 US$ Add for Foreign

REVIEW INFORMATION:

Type of Review: Blind Review
No. of External Reviewers: 3-5
No. of In House Reviewers: 1
Acceptance Rate: 60%
Time to Review: 2 - 3 Months
Reviewers Comments: Yes
Invited Articles: Guest Editors Welcome
Fees to Publish: 0.00 US$

MANUSCRIPT TOPICS:
Education Management/Administration; Higher Education

MANUSCRIPT GUIDELINES/COMMENTS:

Contributions on topics relating to public relations, school-community relations, audiovisuals, management and human relations are encouraged. Manuscripts should be submitted typed, double-spaced. Contributors should furnish a brief biography. Manuscripts are subject to editing for conciseness and clarity to bring the material into conformity with the Journal's style. Unsolicited manuscripts, photographs and artwork should be accompanied by a self-addressed stamped envelopes (9 x 12 and #10) for notification of receipt of manuscript and for reviewers' and editor's comments. Send SASE (#10) for guidelines.

School Public Relations Journal--A refereed journal-scholarly articles by academic/higher education authorities are refereed by an international editorial review board. The *Journal* also accepts articles by practitioners and administrators in basic (K-12) education and journalists at large.

Scope

Articles are sought on topics such as internal communication and climate, employee motivation, parent involvement, partnerships, working with the news media, community participation, audits, surveying and polls, community service programs for students, communication training, advisory committees, volunteers, writing and speaking, publications, alumni associations, foundations, mentoring, photography, and related topics.

The overall goal of the *Journal* is to support efforts to enhance/foster student achievement and staff productivity, and to provide information to build public knowledge of the value and potential benefits of a sound basic education of our youth. We advocate the concept that the school public relations function must be based on fact and reality as compared to ideals and goals of educators and the community at large.

Style

Scholarly articles can be prepared following style guidelines of the publication manual of the *Kappan Magazine* by Phi Delta Kappa. Before the start of the article, include a summary of the scope and major findings of the article in one paragraph.

We encourage authors to include photographs, drawings, and tables as appropriate.

Submissions

- Submit four copies of a manuscript with a letter from the author(s).
- Articles should be 1,000 to 3,500 words in length.
- If produced on a computer, supply a disk, clearly labeled, in ASCII format, IBM format only, with text copies.
- Include an abstract of the article and a two-three sentence credit for each author on a separate sheet.
- Advise if the article has been published or is being considered elsewhere.
- Queries for articles on specific topics are welcomed.
- SASE. Include a #10 self-addressed, stamped envelope for acknowledgement of receipt of your article. Include a 9" x 12" similar envelope for reply to submissions or queries.
- Response to an article or a query is usually conveyed to an author within 60 days.

Address Manuscripts and correspondence to Albert E. Holliday, Editor and Publisher (see address above).

Previous Journals are available in microfilm from University Microfilm Int., 300 Zeeb Rd., Ann Arbor, MI 48106.

Refer to Journal of Educational Communications (1975-83), Journal of Educational Public Relations (1984-95) and Journal of Educational Relations (19952002).

Social Policy

ADDRESS FOR SUBMISSION:

Editor
Social Policy
365 5th Avenue, Suite 3300
New York, NY 10016
USA
Phone: 212-817-1822
Fax: 212-817-2990
E-Mail: socpol@igc.apc.org
Web:
Address May Change:

PUBLICATION GUIDELINES:

Manuscript Length: 1500-3000 words
Copies Required: Two
Computer Submission: Yes
Format: N/A
Fees to Review: 0.00 US$

Manuscript Style:
    Chicago Manual of Style

CIRCULATION DATA:

Reader: Academics
Frequency of Issue: Quarterly
Copies per Issue: 3,001 - 4,000
Sponsor/Publisher: Social Policy
    Corporation
Subscribe Price: 20.00 US$ Individual
    80.00 US$ Institution

REVIEW INFORMATION:

Type of Review: Editorial Review
No. of External Reviewers: 0
No. of In House Reviewers: 3
Acceptance Rate: 21-30%
Time to Review: 1 Month or Less
Reviewers Comments: No
Invited Articles: 50% +
Fees to Publish: 0.00 US$

MANUSCRIPT TOPICS:
Higher Education; Social Studies/Social Science; Urban Education, Cultural/Non-Traditional

MANUSCRIPT GUIDELINES/COMMENTS:

Social Work

ADDRESS FOR SUBMISSION:

Cheryl Y. Bradley, Director
Social Work
NASW Press
750 First Street NE, Suite 700
Washington, DC 20002-4241
USA
Phone: 202-408-8600
Fax: 202-336-8312
E-Mail: press@naswdc.org
Web:
Address May Change:

PUBLICATION GUIDELINES:

Manuscript Length: 16-20
Copies Required: Five
Computer Submission: No
Format: N/A
Fees to Review: 0.00 US$

Manuscript Style:
Chicago Manual of Style, American
Psychological Association

CIRCULATION DATA:

Reader: Academics, Administrators
Frequency of Issue: Quarterly
Copies per Issue: More than 25,000
Sponsor/Publisher: NASW Press, National
Association of Social Work
Subscribe Price: 71.00 US$ Individual
98.00 US$ Institution
14.00 US$ Member/Part of Annual
Dues

REVIEW INFORMATION:

Type of Review: Blind Review
No. of External Reviewers: 3
No. of In House Reviewers: 1
Acceptance Rate: 11-20%
Time to Review: 4 - 6 Months
Reviewers Comments: Yes
Invited Articles: 0-5%
Fees to Publish: 0.00 US$

MANUSCRIPT TOPICS:
Elementary/Early Childhood; Social Studies/Social Science; Social Work

MANUSCRIPT GUIDELINES/COMMENTS:

Social Work, established in 1956, is a professional journal published by the NASW Press and provided to all NASW members as a membership benefit. The journal's purpose is to improve practice and advance knowledge in social work and social welfare. The editorial board welcomes manuscripts that expand and evaluate knowledge of social problems, social work practice, and the social work profession. The editor-in-chief generally selects manuscripts on specific topics from the pool of accepted articles to form theme issues. On rare occasions, the editorial board puts forth calls for papers on issues of major importance to the field.

Topics of Interest. The editorial board particularly seeks articles on the following topics:
• Research on social problems
• Evaluation of social work practice
• Advancement of developmental and practice theory
• culture and ethnicity
• social policy, advocacy, and administration.

Articles. Manuscripts for full-length articles should not exceed 20 pages, including all references and tables. The entire review process is anonymous. At least three reviewers critique each manuscript; then the editor-in-chief makes a decision, taking those reviews into account.

Note: All submissions must be typed double-spaced, including references and tables, with one inch margins on all sides.

COLUMNS

Practice Updates features perspectives, innovations, reports, and updates related to social work practice. The purpose is to inform practitioners of methods to expand upon existing practice. Case vignettes are welcomed; however, the major emphases should be placed on analysis of practice and the evidence of effectiveness. Manuscripts may be more descriptive than analytical and do not require the depth of documentation necessary for full-length articles. Manuscripts are reviewed anonymously in the same process used for articles. Although the maximum length for these manuscripts is seven pages, the journal invites shorter accounts.

Commentary offers writers an opportunity to present their critical observation on current professional issues, social problems, or policy matters. Submissions are expected to build on existing literature in the topic area. The maximum length of manuscripts for this column is six pages. The editor-in-chief reviews Commentary Submissions anonymously. (Note: This new column replaced Op-Ed and Comments on Currents,)

Points & Viewpoints provides readers an opportunity to respond substantively to an article previously published in the journal and to challenge the premises, results, or intellectual positions in that article. It was created to stimulate dialogue that helps the profession evolve. The editor-in-chief reviews all manuscripts anonymously. If a manuscript is accepted, the author of the original article will be asked to respond to it. Manuscripts may be shortened and included as a Letter to the Editor if the original author declines to respond. The maximum length for this column is seven pages.

Reviews features critical reviews of professional books, videos, software, and other media. Thoughtful critiques are essential in guiding the practitioner, educator, and student to important resources in the field. The book review editor selects books and other materials for review, solicits reviews, and makes recommendations to the editor-in-chief regarding the selection of reviews for publication. Although the journal attempts to publish all solicited reviews, publication is not guaranteed. Unsolicited reviews are not accepted.

The journal welcomes **Letters to the Editor**. Readers are encouraged to send brief comments on issues covered in the journal or other points of interest to the profession that will extend dialogue. Although we acknowledge and read all letters, not all can be published, nor can we notify authors of the decision. Selected letters may be shortened to fit the space available. Letters should be no longer than two pages.

This section describes how to assemble and submit a manuscript. Adhering to NASW Press format and style will improve the chances of acceptance if the substance of a manuscript has merit.

MANUSCRIPT PREPARATION
Appropriate Content
To determine which journal is most appropriate for your manuscript, please refer to chapter 3 in this booklet. You also should be aware that the following submissions will be rejected automatically without peer review:

- obituaries, biographical sketches, or testimonials
- organizational reports
- speeches that have not been recast in article format.

If the content is related to the mission of the journal and the manuscript is a scholarly article with utility for social work practice, the editorial boards generally will be interested in reviewing it. Editorial boards do not screen query letters.

Appropriate Length
Manuscripts submitted to any NASW Press journal should be no longer than 20 pages. You should be aware of the following information when you consider the length of your manuscript:

You should type the entire manuscript double-spaced with one-inch margins on all four sides.

- Every component of the manuscript (text, references, tables, figures) is included in the total page count.
- Editorial boards welcome short articles, and they do not equate length with quality.
- The NASW Press will return manuscripts in excess of 25 pages unreviewed.

Overwriting and excessive length for the subject at hand often result in rejection, even if the manuscript meets page limits. Consequently, you should review your manuscript carefully with an eye to tightening and condensing.

MANUSCRIPT COMPONENTS
Cover Sheet
The cover sheet should contain the following:

- the full title of the article
- information on all authors: name; highest degree, credentials, and title; full address; telephone and fax numbers, and e-mail address if available
- the date of submission.

If there is more than one author, names should be listed in the order you would prefer for the byline of a published article. Designate one author as the corresponding author. The cover sheet is the only component of the manuscript that should identify the authors in any way.

Title Page

The title page will be circulated for review with the manuscript. An effective title expresses the essence of a manuscript in as few words as possible. Conciseness and precision, the hallmarks of good writing, are particularly important for titles. Try to use key words, without resorting to jargon, so that a title will attract readers and provide an accurate picture of the article. Do not attempt to communicate all of the article's content in the title.

Abstract

The abstract should provide a distillation of the key concepts in the manuscript. Whenever possible, the abstract should be informative, and it should include theoretical concepts, major hypotheses, and conclusions. Abstracts for research papers should include the purpose of the research, the study sample size and characteristics, the measurement instruments used, and the conclusions. You should present the value of the contribution without exaggerating the results.

A comprehensive yet concise abstract is important because readers and researchers often decide to read an article on the basis of the abstract. Write the abstract as a single paragraph of about 150 words. Do not include any tables or references.

If your manuscript is accepted, the abstract will be published at the beginning of the article. Following publication of the full article, the abstract will be entered into the *Social Work Abstracts* database and will appear in the print version, as well as in SWAB+, available on CD-ROM and on Internet.

Key Words

List up to five key words that describe the content of the manuscript on the abstract page.

Example: Key words: administration, health, Hispanic, people of color, women

The NASW Press uses authors' designations of key words to develop data on manuscript submissions. In addition, if the article is accepted, the key words will appear in the journal with the abstract and in the *Social Work Abstracts* database. Key words are not necessarily used for indexing.

Text

Reviewers are looking for new work that extends the knowledge base and builds on the contribution of others. There is, however, no one formula for a successful article. You may want to keep the following in mind.

State your purpose. You should state your purpose clearly within the first few paragraphs of the article. If the reader cannot recognize what you hoped to accomplish in writing the article easily, the manuscript is likely to be rejected.

Organize. Establish a clear framework for the article and organize the manuscript so that it flows coherently. Use subheadings judiciously to help the reader track the flow of the article. If the article is organized properly, it will proceed logically and directly from the opening statements to your conclusions.

Relate your work to existing knowledge. You must relate your work to existing knowledge on the subject. However, you should not be tempted to run voluminous electronic searches and incorporate every related reference you find. Instead, use those references that demonstrate best how the new information will fill gaps in the knowledge base.

Review and rewrite. Reviewing and rewriting are basic steps in developing a manuscript for publication. As you review your work, eliminate redundancies and superfluous language. The use of pretentious jargon interferes with communication and can conceal the importance of your work. Write precisely in the active voice, use jargon only when absolutely necessary to convey specialized knowledge, and eliminate any language that might convey the perception of bias or any kind of stereotyping of people and behavior (see chapter 7). Finally, review your manuscript for spelling, punctuation, and grammatical errors. Use electronic tools, such as spell-check and a thesaurus, to assure that you have used words correctly.

References

Authors are responsible for the completeness and accuracy of the references in their manuscripts. Generally, take reference data for published material from the title page of a book or pamphlet, first page of an article, or contents page of a periodical. Take dates from the copyright page.

In general, a citation in the reference list comprises the following components in the order listed: author surname(s); author initial(s); publication date; title of article or book; for periodicals, journal name, volume number, and inclusive page numbers for the article; for books, location of publisher (city and state) and publisher name. See the subsection Reference List for examples.

- General Style Points

Arrange entries in the reference list alphabetically (by surname of the first author), then chronologically (by earliest publication date first).

In a reference that appears in parenthetical text, use commas (not brackets) to set off the date.
Example: (see Table 2 of Philips & Ross, 1983, for complete data)

Within a paragraph, do not include the year in subsequent references to a study as long as the study cannot be confused with other studies cited in the article.
Example: In a recent study, Jones (1987) compared. . . . Jones also found. . . .

Use the past tense for in-text reference citations.
Example: Hartman (1981) discussed. . .

- In-Text Author-Date Citations

Reference citations in text primarily acknowledge original specific contributions or opinions of other writers. Indicate the source of quotations in text and, for any quotes more than three words long, provide page numbers. Arrange author-date citations alphabetically in text (by surname of the first author), then chronologically (by earliest publication date first). Use a semicolon to separate reference citations in text.

Examples: (Abramovitz, 1988a; Miller, 1989; Ozawa, 1982, 1986, 1990) (Duncan & Morgan, 1979; Lindquist, Telch, & Taylor, 1983; J. Smith, 1992; P. Smith, 1992)

• Citations of Same Surname
If two authors with the same surname and year of publication are cited in text and their first initials are different, include both authors' initials in all text citations to avoid confusion.
Example: (M. Henderson, 1990; P. Henderson, 1990)

• Personal Communications
Personal communications consist of letters, telephone conversations, interviews, and the like. Because they do not provide recoverable information, personal communications are not included in the reference list. Cite personal communications in text only. Use the following style: (personal communication with [first initials and last name], [title], [affiliation], [month, day, year of communication]).
Example: (personal communication with Jane Doe, professor of social work, University of California, Los Angeles, August 5, 1995)

If the reference citation is not parenthetical, then incorporate the name, title, and affiliation outside the parentheses and put the words "personal communication" and the date inside the parentheses.
Example: J. T. Jones, professor of sociology at the University of Maryland (personal communication, June 11, 1995), suggested. . . .

Reference List
• Citation Forms
Following are examples of citations found in reference lists.

Article in an edited book
Griss, B. (1988Ò1989). Strategies for adapting the private and public health insurance systems to the health-related needs of persons with disabilities or chronic illness. In B. Griss (Ed.), Access to health care (Vol. 1, pp. 1Ò38). Washington, DC: World Institute on Disability.
Jackson, A. (1995). Diversity and oppression. In C. Meyer & M. Mattaini (Eds.), The foundations of social work practice: A graduate text (pp. 42Ò58). Washington, DC: NASW Press.

Article in a journal
Chapin, R. K. (1995). Social policy development: The strengths perspective. Social Work, 40, 506Ò514.

Book
Feldman, D. A., & Johnson, T. M. (Eds.). (1986). The social dimensions of AIDS: Method and theory. New York: Praeger.
James, F. J. (in press). Factors which shape the risks of homelessness: Preliminary observation from Colorado. Denver: University of Colorado Graduate School of Public Affairs.
Martin, E. P., & Martin, J. M. (1995). Social work and the black experience. Washington, DC: NASW Press.

McReynolds, P., & Chelune, G. J. (Eds.). (1990). Advances in psychological assessment (Vol. 6). San Francisco: Jossey-Bass.

Legal references
Follow A Uniform System of Citation (14th ed., pp. 55Ò56 and inside front cover) for citation forms of legal references.

Cite the name and year of an act in the text. If possible, cite statutes to the current official code or supplement; otherwise, cite the official session laws (see A Uniform System of Citation, p. 55, for examples).

For citations of the Federal Register, attempt to cite the original source. If the Federal Register is the original or only source the author can provide, then use the following format:
Education for All Handicapped Children Act (P.L. 94-142). (1977). Federal Register, 42(163), 42474-42518. [Note: This act does have an original source and is used as an example only.]

Newspaper
Raymond, C. (1990, September 12). Global migration will have widespread impact on society, scholars say. New York Times, pp. A1, A6.

Nonprint media
When citing a review of nonprint media, include (if available) length (number of minutes) and format (such as videocassette, audiocassette).
Breaking silence. Produced and directed by Theresa Tollini. Berkeley, CA: Future Educational Film, 1986. 132 minutes. VHS videocassette.

Paper presented at a conference
DiCecco, J. (1990, November). Using interpreters: Issues and guidelines for the practitioner in a multilingual environment. Paper presented at NASW's Annual Conference, Boston.
Romero, J. (1990, May). Culturally appropriate interventions with Hispanics. Paper presented at the Cross Cultural Competence Conference, San Diego Mental Health Services, San Diego.

Report
Schafft, G., Erlanger, W., Rudolph, L., Yin, R. K., & Scott, A. C. (1987). *Joint study of services and funding for handicapped infants and toddlers, ages 0 through 2 years* (Final Report for Contract No. 300-85-0143). Washington, DC: U.S. Department of Education, Division of Innovation and Development, Office of Special Education Programs.

U.S. Bureau of the Census. (1984). Projections of the population of the United States, by age, sex, and race: 1983 to 2080. In R. J. Koski (Ed.), *Current population reports* (Series P-25, No. 952, Tables C and F, pp. 6, 8). Washington, DC: U.S. Government Printing Office.

708

Sections of journals (other than articles)
Use brackets around departments such as Letters, Editorial, and Book Reviews in the reference list:
Spickard, P. R., Fong, R., & Ewalt, P. L. (1995). Undermining the very basis of racism-Its categories [Editorial]. Social Work, 40, 581Ô584.

Unpublished manuscript
Farber, B. A. (1979). *The effects of psychotherapeutic practice upon psychotherapists: A phenomenological investigation.* Unpublished doctoral dissertation, Yale University, New Haven, CT.

• Use of Cities and States in Reference Citations
In reference citations and in text, NASW follows Associated Press style for the omission of states and countries, except for Washington, DC. Use DC with Washington in text and in references.

Notes
Footnotes often distract readers; consequently, you should use them sparingly and incorporate them into the text whenever possible. When footnotes are essential, number them consecutively to correspond with the numbers in the text and submit them on a separate sheet. If the article is published, footnotes will appear at the bottom of the columns in which they are cited.

Tables
If you cannot present data easily and clearly in text, use a table. Tables should be self-explanatory and should supplement, not duplicate, the text. The table title should describe the contents completely so that the table can remain independent of the text. Only the highlights of the table should be discussed in the text. When you are presenting a series of tables, be consistent in terminology and format, and number them in arabic numerals in the order in which they should appear in the article. You may use standard abbreviations for nontechnical terms such as "no." for number and "%" for percent. Use footnotes to the table to explain any nonstandard abbreviations, such as "NS" for not significant and "NA" for not applicable.

Artwork
You must supply camera-ready artwork for figures and graphs that accompany articles. Artwork should not exceed 81/2 x 11 inches. You may be able to produce your artwork on your computer if you have access to a laser printer with a resolution of at least 300 dpi. Use a word-processing font, such as Times, instead of typewriter typefaces, such as Courier. If you cannot produce publication-quality art on your computer, lettering should be typeset or produced by a professional artist. All elements of each figure should be large enough to be legible even if the figures are reduced, as they generally are, for publication. Because reproduction reduces the legibility of any figure, you should start with a very clean, crisp figure. If you do not supply artwork, the NASW Press can prepare professional art and bill you for the cost. Staff can produce a cost estimate based on rough copy after an article is accepted.

GUIDELINES FOR PREPARING MANUSCRIPTS

In 1989 the Health & Social Work Editorial Board developed guidelines to assist both experienced and aspiring authors. The following is an adaptation of their work.

Content

- State your purpose early in the article.
- Develop an organizing theme and consistently relate the article to the theme.
- Start with an outline and refer to it regularly to help maintain a coherent flow.
- Prepare a short abstract to provide a general overview of the manuscript. Use an introduction to define the topic areas more specifically.
- Document all statistical statements and clearly identify opinions.
- Use case material to illustrate major theoretical concepts rather than to serve as the substance of the manuscript.
- Relate your review of the literature to your conclusion.
- Relate subject matter to the journals' editorial focus.
- Recognize that no one is as familiar with your topic as you are. Define terms and do not make too many assumptions about the reader's knowledge.
- Focus – do not try to write the definitive work on a subject in one manuscript.
- Define key concepts and relate your data to those concepts.

Writing Style

- Use the active voice whenever possible. Overuse of the passive voice takes the life out of an article. The use of the first person is appropriate for scholarly work so long as the focus is on the information in the article instead of on the author. Excessive use of "we feel," "I think," "I did," and so on emphasizes the author, whereas language such as "we studied" or "in the study we found" imparts information.
- Avoid jargon and multi-syllable words.
- Be concise. Omit unnecessary words.
- Aim for precision and accuracy. Eliminate qualifiers such as "very few" or "nearly all" that weaken the manuscript. Instead, provide comparisons that demonstrate what you mean.
- Eliminate language that might imply gender, ethnic, or other forms of discrimination, stereotyping, or bias.
- Use style manuals, a dictionary, and other resources to avoid poor grammar, misspellings, and incorrect punctuation. (Most word processors feature useful spell-check and thesaurus programs.)

Format

- Do not submit speeches unless they have been rewritten in article format.
- Use tables when they are the most efficient way to communicate information. Although tables appear impressive, sometimes the same information can be communicated more clearly and easily in a few sentences. Conversely, a well-designed table may enable you to eliminate many paragraphs.
- Make your manuscript flow logically from an interesting beginning to a justifiable conclusion.
- Use subheads to define carefully considered divisions of the topic.

- Review the journal you have selected to learn the range of topics, manuscript length, writing style, and style for footnotes and references.

Final Draft

- Ask a trusted colleague who has a publication record to review and comment before you submit.
- Incorporate comments from others as you rewrite and polish your manuscript.
- Be certain that your references and any footnotes are complete and accurate.
- Double space all sections of the manuscript, including tables, footnotes, and references.
- Proofread carefully.
- Take care with the appearance of the manuscript. It should be legible (no poor photocopies or unreadable typefaces) and clean, with no handwritten additions.
- Be certain the text contains no "About the Author" blurbs, bylines, or other references that identify you as author.
- Assemble the manuscript with cover sheet, title page, abstract, introduction, text, references, and tables and figures if used.
- Submit five copies of the manuscript.
- Notify the NASW Press immediately if you change your address or phone number.

Resubmissions

- Consider reviewers' comments objectively.
- Review the manuscript as objectively as possible.
- Use the revision to sharpen the focus of the manuscript.
- Incorporate as many of the reviewers' recommendations as possible.
- Attach a cover sheet that describes precisely how you have addressed reviewers' concerns. If you disagreed with a review and did not change some element of the manuscript, describe your rationale succinctly.

Ethics

- Obtain all necessary clearances and permissions for tables or illustrations borrowed from other sources before you submit your manuscript.
- Submit the same manuscript to only one journal at a time.
- If the manuscript is part of a series, reference all previous publications.
- Avoid overlapping submissions. Do not submit manuscripts that contain substantial portions of material contained in manuscripts already accepted or under review elsewhere.
- Submit only original material that has not been published or widely distributed elsewhere.

FORMAT FOR RESEARCH ARTICLES
2. Abstract--summarizes the entire article
- Provide five or six sentences.
- Limit to approximately 150 words.

2. **Introduction--engages the reader**
    *   State the specific purpose or goal of your study; include a statement of hypotheses.
    *   Review the literature of previous related research studies and indicate how your study is related to them. (This develops a rationale for your study.)

5. **Method--explains how you conducted your study**
    *   Describe subjects: who participated, how many, and how they were selected.
    *   Specify design by name or type: the arrangements for collecting data and how groups are collected for statistical analysis.
    *   Describe materials: measuring devices and special equipment, reliability and validity data.
    *   Detail procedures: how the study was conducted, what subjects did; also include a specific description of the intervention or independent variable sufficient for replication by others.

6. **Results--presents findings in the text and in tables and graphs**
    *   Use American Psychological Association (APA) format.
    *   Present results of all statistical tests (significant and nonsignificant) including means, standard deviations, degrees of freedom, calculated values (for example, F ratios), significance levels, and effect sizes.

5. **Discussion--gives a less technical interpretation of results, including why they turned out the way they did**
    *   Link results to literature reviewed earlier.
    *   Describe weaknesses in design and offer alternative explanations.
    *   Discuss the potential for generalizability and implications for research and practice.

6. **References--lists books and articles discussed in the text**

7. **Appendix--only if necessary for new or special materials such as a copy of a new scale or computer program**

Resources

Abbott, A. (1992). The quantitative research report. In L. Beebe (Ed.), *Professional writing for the human services* (pp. 63-85). Washington, DC: NASW Press.

American Psychological Association. (1994). *Publication manual of the American Psychological Association* (4th ed.). Washington, DC: Author.

Editor's note: Thanks are extended to Joel Fischer, University of Hawaii, Honolulu, for developing these guidelines. We offer them to readers for assistance in writing research articles and as a guide to our criteria for reviewing these articles.

MANUSCRIPT SUBMISSION

Authors should designate a journal when submitting a manuscript. Although we request computer disks when manuscripts are accepted, it is not necessary to submit a disk initially. Mail manuscripts for all NASW Press journals to

[Journal title]
NASW Press
750 First Street, NE, Suite 700
Washington, DC 20002-4241

Authors should submit five copies of their manuscript.

NASW Press journals practice strict anonymous reviews in which neither the reviewers nor the editor-in-chief learn the author's identity. Consequently, all manuscripts and correspondence regarding any article should be addressed to the NASW Press office. Editors are not able to engage in correspondence directly with authors, because doing so would abrogate the process. Manuscripts sent to an editor-in-chief at an address other than the NASW Press will be considerably delayed in review.

The NASW Press is not responsible for the loss of a manuscript in the mail. Authors should retain at least one copy of any manuscript. Manuscripts will not be returned. All manuscripts are acknowledged on receipt. The review process generally takes about three to four months.

GUIDELINES FOR PRACTICE HIGHLIGHTS AND OTHER PRACTICE DESCRIPTIONS

In 1994 the *Social Work in Education* Editorial Board developed the following guidelines for describing practice.

Purpose
- Am I doing something others should know about?
- What is the core of what I want to say?
- What should go away?

Getting Started
- Write a short paragraph and check it out with someone else. Do they understand it? Is it too broad? too narrow?
- Write an outline, laying out the various steps.
- Use outlines as a checklist.

Grab the Readers Attention
- State up front what you are attempting to do.
- Take the reader with you as you move along.
- Use existing practice as a springboard.
- Describe the problem or issue you will focus on in two paragraphs or so.

Tell What Happened

- Tell the reader what you did.
- Describe the case intervention or program in as much detail as readers need to replicate-- who was involved? what was the time span? what occurred?
- Include dialogue as appropriate.
- Use a flowchart if it makes the intervention clearer.

Help People Replicate the Practice

- What was the significance?
- Why is this practice intervention different? Is it unique?
- What impact does it have on others? On the practitioner?
- Answer the "So what?" question. What difference did it make?

Conclude the Article

- Don't just let it drop.
- Sum it up.
- Tell where you plan to go in the future--or suggest future efforts by others.

NASW PRESS GUIDELINES FOR DESCRIBING PEOPLE

To provide implementation strategies for its policy on unbiased communication (see page 19), the NASW Press has developed the following guidelines. The purposes of the guidelines are to help authors

- portray people as accurately and vividly as possible
- eliminate bias from their writing
- incorporate the richness of cultural diversity
- use language that is accessible and inviting to the reader.

All languages evolve over time, and it is likely that English will evolve to incorporate new terms for and better ways of describing people. In the meantime, the NASW Press expects authors and staff to follow the guidelines outlined in this document.

General Guidelines

Seek and use the preference of the people you write about.
Ask people you are working with how they prefer to be described and use the terms they give you. If, as often happens, people within a group disagree on preference, report the different terms and try to use the one most often used within the group. The NASW Press does not object to using alternate terms, such as black and African American, within one article or chapter as long as the content is clearly written so that readers are not confused. Be sensitive to real preferences and do not adopt descriptions that may have been imposed on people. For example, older people may say, "Oh, we're just senior citizens."

Be as specific as possible.
If you have studied work experiences among Cuban Americans, Mexican Americans, and Puerto Ricans, report on those three groups; do not lump them together as *Hispanics*.

Whenever possible, use specific racial or ethnic identities instead of collecting different groups under a general heading. If you have researched drug use among a group of people whose ages range from 65 to 75, cite their ages rather than reporting on "drug use among older people."

Describe people in the positive.
Describe people in terms of what they are, instead of what they are not. For example, do not use the terms *nonwhite* or *nonparticipant*. Remember that you are writing about people.

Help the reader see that you are writing about people, not subjects or objects. Use the terms sample or subject for statistics and describe participants as *respondents, participants, workers,* and so forth. Keep in mind that a group of 100 people who share certain characteristics also have many traits unique to them, even though those individual traits are not included in your report. Pretend that you are a member of the group about whom you are writing and see how you would react to the terms you have used to describe them.

Avoid using terms that label people.
When adjectives that describe a person's condition or status are used as nouns, they become labels that often connote a derogatory intent. For example, people who do not earn enough money to provide for their needs are often referred to collectively as the poor; use poor people if you are referring to them in the aggregate. People who have lived a long time become *the elderly* or *the aged*; if you cannot use specific ages or age ranges, use terms such as elders or older people. Do not refer to people with disabilities as *the disabled* or *the handicapped*. Note that the use of "the" in front of a noun is a good warning sign that you may be using a label.

Guidelines for Specific Populations
Age
Use *boy* and *girl* only for children and adolescents, although even for high school students, *young man* and *young woman* may be preferable. Do not use terms such as *senior citizen* or *oldster* for people who are older than 65. Use specific age ranges whenever possible. Use *aging* and *elderly* as adjectives, not as nouns.

Class
Classism often creeps into our language. Instead of assigning class to people, you should describe their situations. This does not mean that you should pretend all people have the same socioeconomic advantages, but that you should describe the advantages or lack of advantages, rather than assigning attributes to the people.

Poor Usage	Better Usage
lower class	people who are poor
underclass	with low incomes
upper class	with high incomes
the disadvantaged	with socioeconomic disadvantages

Classism often is combined with bias toward people in terms of race or ethnicity; consequently, it is doubly important to take care with language that might perpetuate discrimination.

Disability

Remember that people *have* disabilities, they are not the disabilities; in addition, the disabilities may be barriers, such as stairs or curbs, that handicap people. The following are some commonly misused terms:

Poor Usage	Better Usage
the handicapped	people with disabilities
schizophrenics	people diagnosed with schizophrenia
challenged	person who has ___
wheelchair-bound	uses a wheelchair
the blind	people who are blind
hearing impaired	hard of hearing or deaf

HIV/AIDS

Say *people with AIDS*, not *AIDS victims* or *innocent victims of AIDS*. Avoid language that may imply a moral judgment on behavior or lifestyles. Instead of *high-risk groups*, which suggests that demographic traits may be responsible for AIDS exposure, use *high-risk behavior*.

Race and Ethnicity

• Issues and Dilemmas

Traditionally, authors in the social sciences have used *minority* as a shorthand term to describe people of various races and ethnicities collectively. In these cases the term has been used in the sense of a smaller number or a population that has been oppressed or subjected to differential treatment. Authors also have used *white* and *nonwhite*, particularly in research papers, to differentiate between population groups. *Nonwhite* appears to have been used to describe collectively a diverse group of people who differ in some ways from the greater number of a population.

Another complicating factor is that not all people within specific populations agree on nomenclature, and many people use different definitions for the same words. For example, some people prefer *African American*; others within the same population say, "I am not African American; I am *black*." Some scholars use the term race to describe broad classifications of people who are presumed to have common descent and share certain physical characteristics (generally American Indian, Asian, black, and white) and reserve *ethnicity* for people who share common culture, religion, or language (often people from specific nations or countries). Others use the terms interchangeably. Some eliminate the term race entirely because they believe it is racist in itself.

• Guidelines

Styles and preferences for nouns that refer to race and ethnicity change over time. The general guidelines for discussing all people are particularly helpful when you are describing race and ethnicity. Try to ascertain what the population group prefers and use that term; recognize and acknowledge that there may be disagreement about preference within the group. Whenever possible, be as specific as possible and describe individual population groups rather than collecting many different groups under an umbrella term. If the people in your study included

Asian Americans, Hispanics, black Americans, and white Americans, do not compare the first three groups as a set with the last group. Describe them each as individual groups. If you researched experiences of a group of Asian Americans who included Chinese, Japanese, and Koreans, you should describe each national origin group individually.

You should avoid both *minority* and *nonwhite*. Many people who are described this way view the terms as pejorative and discriminatory. In addition, assuming that white people are the predominant population group is an inaccurate portrayal of most countries in the world and indeed of many areas in the United States. Some people prefer the use of people of color; however, you should be aware that this term also is imprecise and that not all people who might be included in the group under such a heading would describe themselves in this way.

Black and *white* are adjectives that should be used (in lowercase only unless they begin a sentence) to modify nouns, such as "black Americans" or "black men" or "white women." *African Americans, American Indians, Asian Americans,* and *Hispanics* are all proper nouns that should be capitalized; hyphens should never be inserted in multiword names even when the names are modifiers. Some individuals prefer to use Latino, instead of Hispanic, as the descriptive term for people of Latin American ancestry, and some use the two together. There has been considerable discussion about the use of *American Indian* versus *Native American*; many people prefer the former because it is a more precise term for the population in North America. Although the U.S. government combines *Asian* and *Pacific Islander*, most Pacific Islanders prefer that they be separated.

Poor Usage	Better Usage
minorities	specific population or "racial and ethnic groups"
tribes	people or nations
blacks	black people
nonwhites	specific populations

In addition to taking care with names of racial and ethnic groups, you should be careful with modifiers. For example, the passage "we compared the reactions of African American and Hispanic men with middle-class white men" suggests that the first two groups are in a different socioeconomic status, and given historical stereotyping, the perception is likely to be that they are in a lower status. Specify the status for all participants in your study. Describing someone as "the accomplished African American student" may suggest that this student is an exception. Describe people in terms of race or ethnicity only when the description is pertinent to the discussion.

Sex

Sexist language has no place in the professional literature. The most obvious manifestation of sexist language is the use of masculine pronouns, and there are numerous ways to avoid their use. One option is to use plural forms whenever possible. If you are writing a text or a how-to article, using the second person to address the reader directly will help you avoid having to select a masculine or feminine form and is likely to make the article more appealing to the reader. You can often substitute *we* for he and *our* or *their* for *his*. Another solution is to eliminate pronouns entirely. Inserting *him* or *her* or *he* or *she* throughout an article becomes cumbersome, although sparing use can sound natural. Do not use contrived forms such as *s/he* or *he/she*. In general, avoid alternating masculine and feminine pronouns within an article. Rather than demonstrating equality, the practice can suggest that they are interchangeable, and it is confusing to the reader.

Poor Usage	Better Usage
the social worker	social workers
will find that he	will find that they
he calls his children "kids"	we call our children "kids"
the teacher should encourage his students to write	encourage your students to write

Avoid words that suggest an overtone of judgment, that describe women in patronizing terms ("the little lady") or suggest second-class status ("authoress") or demean a woman's ability ("lady lawyer") or are rarely used to describe men ("coed"). Take care not to suggest that women are possessions of men or that they cannot carry out a role or perform a job that men do.

Poor Usage	Better Usage
policemen	police officers
man a project	staff a project
chairman	chair
housewife	homemaker
mankind	humans, human beings

It is not necessary or desirable to construct feminine versions of words that carry a masculine connotation. *Chair* or *representative* substitute much better for *chairman* or *spokesman* than *chairwoman* or *spokeswoman*. Do not specify sex unless it is a variable or it is essential to the discussion. Be sure to use parallel construction: *men* and *women*, not *men* and *females* or *girls* and *men*. *Men* and *women* are nouns, whereas *female* and *male* are best used as adjectives.

Sexual Orientation

Orientation is a state of being, and *preference* is a choice; consequently, you should not use the latter to refer to heterosexuality or homosexuality. The NASW Press uses the term *homosexual* only as an adjective. You should use *lesbians, gay men,* or *bisexual men* or *women* to refer to people whose orientation is not exclusively heterosexual.

It is important to distinguish between sexual orientation and sexual behavior. Consequently, you would not write "the client reported homosexual fantasies," but would substitute "the client reported same-gender sexual fantasies." The appropriate terms to use in describing sexual activity include *female-female, male-male,* and *same-gender,* in addition to *male-female*.

Accurate Historical Reporting

In their zeal to use appropriate language, authors sometimes try to change history. If you are quoting any document, you must quote it exactly as the words were written or said; and if you are describing a historical situation, you will likely want to use the words that were used in that context. You should, however, make the context clear. If you find the language too egregious, you may want to add a footnote saying this is not your language, but the language of the time in which it was written.

718

Clear, Accessible Writing

You are writing to communicate facts and ideas. Because you are writing for journals in the social sciences, you probably want to communicate those facts and ideas with the intent of improving human lives. To do so, you must write in such a way that you will engage readers so that they will absorb your content enough to use it.

There is no question that eliminating the old shorthand for describing people will add some length to a paper. Substituting *members of racial and ethnic groups* for *minorities* or *people with disabilities* for the *disabled* adds words, but it is more accurate and it eliminates bias. You can easily compensate for the additional length by practicing the principles of good writing. Use strong active verbs and eliminate all convoluted passive constructions. Strike out qualifiers and other redundancies:

Redundant	Simplified
successfully avoided	avoided
has the capability of	can
particularly unique	unique
most often is the case that	often is

Do not resort to euphemisms, which will weaken your message. Taking care to portray people with accuracy and sensitivity should enhance your critical analysis, not muddy it. The more clearly and simply you write, the easier you will make it for your readers to grasp complex ideas. Bring life to your writing by concentrating on the message. If you portray the people you are discussing vividly and truthfully, you will probably communicate the problems and solutions clearly.

Social Work Research

ADDRESS FOR SUBMISSION:

Cheryl Y. Bradley, Editor
Social Work Research
NASW Press
750 First Street, NE
Washington, DC 20002-4241
USA
Phone: 202-408-8600
Fax: 202-336-8312
E-Mail: press@naswdc.org
Web:
Address May Change:

PUBLICATION GUIDELINES:

Manuscript Length: 16-20
Copies Required: Five
Computer Submission: No
Format: N/A
Fees to Review: 0.00 US$

Manuscript Style:
　　Chicago Manual of Style, American
　　Psychological Assocation

CIRCULATION DATA:

Reader: Academics, Administrators
Frequency of Issue: Quarterly
Copies per Issue: No Reply
Sponsor/Publisher: NASW Press, National
　　Association of Social Work
Subscribe Price: 69.95 US$ Individual
　　99.95 US$ Institution
　　40.00 US$ NASW Members

REVIEW INFORMATION:

Type of Review: Blind Review
No. of External Reviewers: 3
No. of In House Reviewers: 1
Acceptance Rate: 21-30%
Time to Review: 2 - 3 Months
Reviewers Comments: Yes
Invited Articles: 6-10%
Fees to Publish: 0.00 US$

MANUSCRIPT TOPICS:
Social Work; Tests, Measurement & Evaluation

MANUSCRIPT GUIDELINES/COMMENTS:

Social Work Research is a professional journal committed to advancing the development of knowledge and informing social work practice. The journal is one of the chief outlets for primary research articles in social work and social welfare. As a repository for an evolving body of knowledge, it makes an important contribution to the quality of educational materials and social work practice.

The editorial board seeks manuscripts that include analytic reviews of research, theoretical articles pertaining to social work research, practice-based research, evaluation studies, and diverse research studies that contribute to knowledge about social work issues and problems. Criteria for acceptance include readability, sound methodology, and utility for practice.

History. *Social Work Research* was initiated as a section of Social Work Research & Abstracts, which was published as a dual journal from 1977 to 1993. In recognition of the growing Deed for social work research, NASW separated the two sections, primary and secondary, in 1994 and now publishes them as independent journals.

Articles. It is suggested that manuscripts for full-length articles not exceed 20 pages, including all references and tables. The entire review process is anonymous. At least three reviewers critique each manuscript; then the editor-in -chief makes a decision, taking those reviews into account.

COLUMNS

Notes on Research Methodology presents brief reports on methodological issues and should include information on the research questions and the general methodology. Submissions are selected through the standard review process. It is suggested that manuscripts be no longer than 15 pages.

Instrument Development is a forum for articles that describe the creation and testing of assessment instruments for use by social workers. The article should report process of defining questions, instrument validity, and any test results. Manuscripts should be no longer than 20 pages (including tables).

Letters from readers are strongly encouraged. Readers may react to articles published in the journal or comment on contemporary issues in social work research that have not been covered in the journal. Although space constraints preclude publishing every letter received, all will be considered. Letters should not exceed three pages.

This section describes how to assemble and submit a manuscript. Adhering to NASW Press format and style will improve the chances of acceptance if the substance of a manuscript has merit.

MANUSCRIPT PREPARATION

Appropriate Content

To determine which journal is most appropriate for your manuscript, please refer to chapter 3 in this booklet. You also should be aware that the following submissions will be rejected automatically without peer review:

- obituaries, biographical sketches, or testimonials
- organizational reports
- speeches that have not been recast in article format.

If the content is related to the mission of the journal and the manuscript is a scholarly article with utility for social work practice, the editorial boards generally will be interested in reviewing it. Editorial boards do not screen query letters.

Appropriate Length

Manuscripts submitted to any NASW Press journal should be no longer than 20 pages. You should be aware of the following information when you consider the length of your manuscript:

You should type the entire manuscript double-spaced with one-inch margins on all four sides.
- Every component of the manuscript (text, references, tables, figures) is included in the total page count.
- Editorial boards welcome short articles, and they do not equate length with quality.
- The NASW Press will return manuscripts in excess of 25 pages unreviewed.

Overwriting and excessive length for the subject at hand often result in rejection, even if the manuscript meets page limits. Consequently, you should review your manuscript carefully with an eye to tightening and condensing.

MANUSCRIPT COMPONENTS
Cover Sheet
The cover sheet should contain the following:
- the full title of the article
- information on all authors: name; highest degree, credentials, and title; full address; telephone and fax numbers, and e-mail address if available
- the date of submission.

If there is more than one author, names should be listed in the order you would prefer for the byline of a published article. Designate one author as the corresponding author. The cover sheet is the only component of the manuscript that should identify the authors in any way.

Title Page
The title page will be circulated for review with the manuscript. An effective title expresses the essence of a manuscript in as few words as possible. Conciseness and precision, the hallmarks of good writing, are particularly important for titles. Try to use key words, without resorting to jargon, so that a title will attract readers and provide an accurate picture of the article. Do not attempt to communicate all of the article's content in the title.

Abstract
The abstract should provide a distillation of the key concepts in the manuscript. Whenever possible, the abstract should be informative, and it should include theoretical concepts, major hypotheses, and conclusions. Abstracts for research papers should include the purpose of the research, the study sample size and characteristics, the measurement instruments used, and the conclusions. You should present the value of the contribution without exaggerating the results.

A comprehensive yet concise abstract is important because readers and researchers often decide to read an article on the basis of the abstract. Write the abstract as a single paragraph of about 150 words. Do not include any tables or references.

If your manuscript is accepted, the abstract will be published at the beginning of the article. Following publication of the full article, the abstract will be entered into the *Social Work Abstracts* database and will appear in the print version, as well as in SWAB+, available on CD-ROM and on Internet.

Key Words

List up to five key words that describe the content of the manuscript on the abstract page.

Example: Key words: administration, health, Hispanic, people of color, women

The NASW Press uses authors' designations of key words to develop data on manuscript submissions. In addition, if the article is accepted, the key words will appear in the journal with the abstract and in the *Social Work Abstracts* database. Key words are not necessarily used for indexing.

Text

Reviewers are looking for new work that extends the knowledge base and builds on the contribution of others. There is, however, no one formula for a successful article. You may want to keep the following in mind.

State your purpose. You should state your purpose clearly within the first few paragraphs of the article. If the reader cannot recognize what you hoped to accomplish in writing the article easily, the manuscript is likely to be rejected.

Organize. Establish a clear framework for the article and organize the manuscript so that it flows coherently. Use subheadings judiciously to help the reader track the flow of the article. If the article is organized properly, it will proceed logically and directly from the opening statements to your conclusions.

Relate your work to existing knowledge. You must relate your work to existing knowledge on the subject. However, you should not be tempted to run voluminous electronic searches and incorporate every related reference you find. Instead, use those references that demonstrate best how the new information will fill gaps in the knowledge base.

Review and rewrite. Reviewing and rewriting are basic steps in developing a manuscript for publication. As you review your work, eliminate redundancies and superfluous language. The use of pretentious jargon interferes with communication and can conceal the importance of your work. Write precisely in the active voice, use jargon only when absolutely necessary to convey specialized knowledge, and eliminate any language that might convey the perception of bias or any kind of stereotyping of people and behavior (see chapter 7). Finally, review your manuscript for spelling, punctuation, and grammatical errors. Use electronic tools, such as spell-check and a thesaurus, to assure that you have used words correctly.

References

Authors are responsible for the completeness and accuracy of the references in their manuscripts. Generally, take reference data for published material from the title page of a book or pamphlet, first page of an article, or contents page of a periodical. Take dates from the copyright page.

In general, a citation in the reference list comprises the following components in the order listed: author surname(s); author initial(s); publication date; title of article or book; for periodicals, journal name, volume number, and inclusive page numbers for the article; for books, location of publisher (city and state) and publisher name. See the subsection Reference List for examples.

- General Style Points

Arrange entries in the reference list alphabetically (by surname of the first author), then chronologically (by earliest publication date first).

In a reference that appears in parenthetical text, use commas (not brackets) to set off the date.
Example: (see Table 2 of Philips & Ross, 1983, for complete data)

Within a paragraph, do not include the year in subsequent references to a study as long as the study cannot be confused with other studies cited in the article.
Example: In a recent study, Jones (1987) compared. . . . Jones also found. . . .

Use the past tense for in-text reference citations.
Example: Hartman (1981) discussed. . .

- In-Text Author-Date Citations

Reference citations in text primarily acknowledge original specific contributions or opinions of other writers. Indicate the source of quotations in text and, for any quotes more than three words long, provide page numbers. Arrange author-date citations alphabetically in text (by surname of the first author), then chronologically (by earliest publication date first). Use a semicolon to separate reference citations in text.
Examples: (Abramovitz, 1988a; Miller, 1989; Ozawa, 1982, 1986, 1990) (Duncan & Morgan, 1979; Lindquist, Telch, & Taylor, 1983; J. Smith, 1992; P. Smith, 1992)

- Citations of Same Surname

If two authors with the same surname and year of publication are cited in text and their first initials are different, include both authors' initials in all text citations to avoid confusion.
Example: (M. Henderson, 1990; P. Henderson, 1990)

- Personal Communications

Personal communications consist of letters, telephone conversations, interviews, and the like. Because they do not provide recoverable information, personal communications are not included in the reference list. Cite personal communications in text only. Use the following style: (personal communication with [first initials and last name], [title], [affiliation], [month, day, year of communication]).
Example: (personal communication with Jane Doe, professor of social work, University of California, Los Angeles, August 5, 1995)

If the reference citation is not parenthetical, then incorporate the name, title, and affiliation outside the parentheses and put the words "personal communication" and the date inside the parentheses.
Example: J. T. Jones, professor of sociology at the University of Maryland (personal communication, June 11, 1995), suggested. . . .

Reference List

- Citation Forms

Following are examples of citations found in reference lists.

Article in an edited book

Griss, B. (1988Ò1989). Strategies for adapting the private and public health insurance systems to the health-related needs of persons with disabilities or chronic illness. In B. Griss (Ed.), Access to health care (Vol. 1, pp. 1Ò38). Washington, DC: World Institute on Disability.

Jackson, A. (1995). Diversity and oppression. In C. Meyer & M. Mattaini (Eds.), The foundations of social work practice: A graduate text (pp. 42Ò58). Washington, DC: NASW Press.

Article in a journal

Chapin, R. K. (1995). Social policy development: The strengths perspective. Social Work, 40, 506Ò514.

Book

Feldman, D. A., & Johnson, T. M. (Eds.). (1986). The social dimensions of AIDS: Method and theory. New York: Praeger.

James, F. J. (in press). Factors which shape the risks of homelessness: Preliminary observation from Colorado. Denver: University of Colorado Graduate School of Public Affairs.

Martin, E. P., & Martin, J. M. (1995). Social work and the black experience. Washington, DC: NASW Press.

McReynolds, P., & Chelune, G. J. (Eds.). (1990). Advances in psychological assessment (Vol. 6). San Francisco: Jossey-Bass.

Legal references

Follow A Uniform System of Citation (14th ed., pp. 55Ò56 and inside front cover) for citation forms of legal references.

Cite the name and year of an act in the text. If possible, cite statutes to the current official code or supplement; otherwise, cite the official session laws (see A Uniform System of Citation, p. 55, for examples).

For citations of the Federal Register, attempt to cite the original source. If the Federal Register is the original or only source the author can provide, then use the following format:

Education for All Handicapped Children Act (P.L. 94-142). (1977). Federal Register, 42(163), 42474-42518. [Note: This act does have an original source and is used as an example only.]

Newspaper

Raymond, C. (1990, September 12). Global migration will have widespread impact on society, scholars say. New York Times, pp. A1, A6.

Nonprint media

When citing a review of nonprint media, include (if available) length (number of minutes) and format (such as videocassette, audiocassette).

Breaking silence. Produced and directed by Theresa Tollini. Berkeley, CA: Future Educational Film, 1986. 132 minutes. VHS videocassette.

Paper presented at a conference
DiCecco, J. (1990, November). Using interpreters: Issues and guidelines for the practitioner in a multilingual environment. Paper presented at NASW's Annual Conference, Boston.
Romero, J. (1990, May). Culturally appropriate interventions with Hispanics. Paper presented at the Cross Cultural Competence Conference, San Diego Mental Health Services, San Diego.

Report
Schafft, G., Erlanger, W., Rudolph, L., Yin, R. K., & Scott, A. C. (1987). *Joint study of services and funding for handicapped infants and toddlers, ages 0 through 2 years* (Final Report for Contract No. 300-85-0143). Washington, DC: U.S. Department of Education, Division of Innovation and Development, Office of Special Education Programs.

U.S. Bureau of the Census. (1984). Projections of the population of the United States, by age, sex, and race: 1983 to 2080. In R. J. Koski (Ed.), *Current population reports* (Series P-25, No. 952, Tables C and F, pp. 6, 8). Washington, DC: U.S. Government Printing Office.

Sections of journals (other than articles)
Use brackets around departments such as Letters, Editorial, and Book Reviews in the reference list:
Spickard, P. R., Fong, R., & Ewalt, P. L. (1995). Undermining the very basis of racism-Its categories [Editorial]. Social Work, 40, 581Ò584.

Unpublished manuscript
Farber, B. A. (1979). *The effects of psychotherapeutic practice upon psychotherapists: A phenomenological investigation.* Unpublished doctoral dissertation, Yale University, New Haven, CT.

• Use of Cities and States in Reference Citations
In reference citations and in text, NASW follows Associated Press style for the omission of states and countries, except for Washington, DC. Use DC with Washington in text and in references.

Notes
Footnotes often distract readers; consequently, you should use them sparingly and incorporate them into the text whenever possible. When footnotes are essential, number them consecutively to correspond with the numbers in the text and submit them on a separate sheet. If the article is published, footnotes will appear at the bottom of the columns in which they are cited.

Tables
If you cannot present data easily and clearly in text, use a table. Tables should be self-explanatory and should supplement, not duplicate, the text. The table title should describe the contents completely so that the table can remain independent of the text. Only the highlights

of the table should be discussed in the text. When you are presenting a series of tables, be consistent in terminology and format, and number them in arabic numerals in the order in which they should appear in the article. You may use standard abbreviations for nontechnical terms such as "no." for number and "%" for percent. Use footnotes to the table to explain any nonstandard abbreviations, such as "NS" for not significant and "NA" for not applicable.

Artwork

You must supply camera-ready artwork for figures and graphs that accompany articles. Artwork should not exceed 81/2 x 11 inches. You may be able to produce your artwork on your computer if you have access to a laser printer with a resolution of at least 300 dpi. Use a word-processing font, such as Times, instead of typewriter typefaces, such as Courier. If you cannot produce publication-quality art on your computer, lettering should be typeset or produced by a professional artist. All elements of each figure should be large enough to be legible even if the figures are reduced, as they generally are, for publication. Because reproduction reduces the legibility of any figure, you should start with a very clean, crisp figure. If you do not supply artwork, the NASW Press can prepare professional art and bill you for the cost. Staff can produce a cost estimate based on rough copy after an article is accepted.

GUIDELINES FOR PREPARING MANUSCRIPTS

In 1989 the Health & Social Work Editorial Board developed guidelines to assist both experienced and aspiring authors. The following is an adaptation of their work.

Content

- State your purpose early in the article.
- Develop an organizing theme and consistently relate the article to the theme.
- Start with an outline and refer to it regularly to help maintain a coherent flow.
- Prepare a short abstract to provide a general overview of the manuscript. Use an introduction to define the topic areas more specifically.
- Document all statistical statements and clearly identify opinions.
- Use case material to illustrate major theoretical concepts rather than to serve as the substance of the manuscript.
- Relate your review of the literature to your conclusion.
- Relate subject matter to the journals' editorial focus.
- Recognize that no one is as familiar with your topic as you are. Define terms and do not make too many assumptions about the reader's knowledge.
- Focus – do not try to write the definitive work on a subject in one manuscript.
- Define key concepts and relate your data to those concepts.

Writing Style

- Use the active voice whenever possible. Overuse of the passive voice takes the life out of an article. The use of the first person is appropriate for scholarly work so long as the focus is on the information in the article instead of on the author. Excessive use of "we feel," "I think," "I did," and so on emphasizes the author, whereas language such as "we studied" or "in the study we found" imparts information.
- Avoid jargon and multi-syllable words.

- Be concise. Omit unnecessary words.
- Aim for precision and accuracy. Eliminate qualifiers such as "very few" or "nearly all" that weaken the manuscript. Instead, provide comparisons that demonstrate what you mean.
- Eliminate language that might imply gender, ethnic, or other forms of discrimination, stereotyping, or bias.
- Use style manuals, a dictionary, and other resources to avoid poor grammar, misspellings, and incorrect punctuation. (Most word processors feature useful spell-check and thesaurus programs.)

Format

- Do not submit speeches unless they have been rewritten in article format.
- Use tables when they are the most efficient way to communicate information. Although tables appear impressive, sometimes the same information can be communicated more clearly and easily in a few sentences. Conversely, a well-designed table may enable you to eliminate many paragraphs.
- Make your manuscript flow logically from an interesting beginning to a justifiable conclusion.
- Use subheads to define carefully considered divisions of the topic.
- Review the journal you have selected to learn the range of topics, manuscript length, writing style, and style for footnotes and references.

Final Draft

- Ask a trusted colleague who has a publication record to review and comment before you submit.
- Incorporate comments from others as you rewrite and polish your manuscript.
- Be certain that your references and any footnotes are complete and accurate.
- Double space all sections of the manuscript, including tables, footnotes, and references.
- Proofread carefully.
- Take care with the appearance of the manuscript. It should be legible (no poor photocopies or unreadable typefaces) and clean, with no handwritten additions.
- Be certain the text contains no "About the Author" blurbs, bylines, or other references that identify you as author.
- Assemble the manuscript with cover sheet, title page, abstract, introduction, text, references, and tables and figures if used.
- Submit five copies of the manuscript.
- Notify the NASW Press immediately if you change your address or phone number.

Resubmissions

- Consider reviewers' comments objectively.
- Review the manuscript as objectively as possible.
- Use the revision to sharpen the focus of the manuscript.
- Incorporate as many of the reviewers' recommendations as possible.

- Attach a cover sheet that describes precisely how you have addressed reviewers' concerns. If you disagreed with a review and did not change some element of the manuscript, describe your rationale succinctly.

Ethics

- Obtain all necessary clearances and permissions for tables or illustrations borrowed from other sources before you submit your manuscript.
- Submit the same manuscript to only one journal at a time.
- If the manuscript is part of a series, reference all previous publications.
- Avoid overlapping submissions. Do not submit manuscripts that contain substantial portions of material contained in manuscripts already accepted or under review elsewhere.
- Submit only original material that has not been published or widely distributed elsewhere.

FORMAT FOR RESEARCH ARTICLES

3. **Abstract--summarizes the entire article**
   - Provide five or six sentences.
   - Limit to approximately 150 words.

2. **Introduction--engages the reader**
   - State the specific purpose or goal of your study; include a statement of hypotheses.
   - Review the literature of previous related research studies and indicate how your study is related to them. (This develops a rationale for your study.)

7. **Method--explains how you conducted your study**
   - Describe subjects: who participated, how many, and how they were selected.
   - Specify design by name or type: the arrangements for collecting data and how groups are collected for statistical analysis.
   - Describe materials: measuring devices and special equipment, reliability and validity data.
   - Detail procedures: how the study was conducted, what subjects did; also include a specific description of the intervention or independent variable sufficient for replication by others.

8. **Results--presents findings in the text and in tables and graphs**
   - Use American Psychological Association (APA) format.
   - Present results of all statistical tests (significant and nonsignificant) including means, standard deviations, degrees of freedom, calculated values (for example, F ratios), significance levels, and effect sizes.

5. **Discussion--gives a less technical interpretation of results, including why they turned out the way they did**
   - Link results to literature reviewed earlier.
   - Describe weaknesses in design and offer alternative explanations.

- Discuss the potential for generalizability and implications for research and practice.

6. References--lists books and articles discussed in the text

7. Appendix--only if necessary for new or special materials such as a copy of a new scale or computer program

Resources

Abbott, A. (1992). The quantitative research report. In L. Beebe (Ed.), *Professional writing for the human services* (pp. 63-85). Washington, DC: NASW Press.

American Psychological Association. (1994). *Publication manual of the American Psychological Association* (4th ed.). Washington, DC: Author.

Editor's note: Thanks are extended to Joel Fischer, University of Hawaii, Honolulu, for developing these guidelines. We offer them to readers for assistance in writing research articles and as a guide to our criteria for reviewing these articles.

MANUSCRIPT SUBMISSION

Authors should designate a journal when submitting a manuscript. Although we request computer disks when manuscripts are accepted, it is not necessary to submit a disk initially. Mail manuscripts for all NASW Press journals to

[Journal title]
NASW Press
750 First Street, NE, Suite 700
Washington, DC 20002-4241

Authors should submit five copies of their manuscript.

NASW Press journals practice strict anonymous reviews in which neither the reviewers nor the editor-in-chief learn the author's identity. Consequently, all manuscripts and correspondence regarding any article should be addressed to the NASW Press office. Editors are not able to engage in correspondence directly with authors, because doing so would abrogate the process. Manuscripts sent to an editor-in-chief at an address other than the NASW Press will be considerably delayed in review.

The NASW Press is not responsible for the loss of a manuscript in the mail. Authors should retain at least one copy of any manuscript. Manuscripts will not be returned. All manuscripts are acknowledged on receipt. The review process generally takes about three to four months.

GUIDELINES FOR PRACTICE HIGHLIGHTS AND OTHER PRACTICE DESCRIPTIONS

In 1994 the *Social Work in Education* Editorial Board developed the following guidelines for describing practice.

Purpose
- Am I doing something others should know about?
- What is the core of what I want to say?
- What should go away?

Getting Started
- Write a short paragraph and check it out with someone else. Do they understand it? Is it too broad? too narrow?
- Write an outline, laying out the various steps.
- Use outlines as a checklist.

Grab the Readers Attention
- State up front what you are attempting to do.
- Take the reader with you as you move along.
- Use existing practice as a springboard.
- Describe the problem or issue you will focus on in two paragraphs or so.

Tell What Happened
- Tell the reader what you did.
- Describe the case intervention or program in as much detail as readers need to replicate-- who was involved? what was the time span? what occurred?
- Include dialogue as appropriate.
- Use a flowchart if it makes the intervention clearer.

Help People Replicate the Practice
- What was the significance?
- Why is this practice intervention different? Is it unique?
- What impact does it have on others? On the practitioner?
- Answer the "So what?" question. What difference did it make?

Conclude the Article
- Don't just let it drop.
- Sum it up.
- Tell where you plan to go in the future--or suggest future efforts by others.

NASW PRESS GUIDELINES FOR DESCRIBING PEOPLE

To provide implementation strategies for its policy on unbiased communication (see page 19), the NASW Press has developed the following guidelines. The purposes of the guidelines are to help authors

- portray people as accurately and vividly as possible
- eliminate bias from their writing
- incorporate the richness of cultural diversity
- use language that is accessible and inviting to the reader.

All languages evolve over time, and it is likely that English will evolve to incorporate new terms for and better ways of describing people. In the meantime, the NASW Press expects authors and staff to follow the guidelines outlined in this document.

General Guidelines

Seek and use the preference of the people you write about.
Ask people you are working with how they prefer to be described and use the terms they give you. If, as often happens, people within a group disagree on preference, report the different terms and try to use the one most often used within the group. The NASW Press does not object to using alternate terms, such as black and African American, within one article or chapter as long as the content is clearly written so that readers are not confused. Be sensitive to real preferences and do not adopt descriptions that may have been imposed on people. For example, older people may say, "Oh, we're just senior citizens."

Be as specific as possible.
If you have studied work experiences among Cuban Americans, Mexican Americans, and Puerto Ricans, report on those three groups; do not lump them together as *Hispanics*. Whenever possible, use specific racial or ethnic identities instead of collecting different groups under a general heading. If you have researched drug use among a group of people whose ages range from 65 to 75, cite their ages rather than reporting on "drug use among older people."

Describe people in the positive.
Describe people in terms of what they are, instead of what they are not. For example, do not use the terms *nonwhite* or *nonparticipant*. Remember that you are writing about people.

Help the reader see that you are writing about people, not subjects or objects. Use the terms sample or subject for statistics and describe participants as *respondents, participants, workers,* and so forth. Keep in mind that a group of 100 people who share certain characteristics also have many traits unique to them, even though those individual traits are not included in your report. Pretend that you are a member of the group about whom you are writing and see how you would react to the terms you have used to describe them.

Avoid using terms that label people.
When adjectives that describe a person's condition or status are used as nouns, they become labels that often connote a derogatory intent. For example, people who do not earn enough money to provide for their needs are often referred to collectively as the poor; use poor people if you are referring to them in the aggregate. People who have lived a long time become *the elderly* or *the aged*; if you cannot use specific ages or age ranges, use terms such as elders or older people. Do not refer to people with disabilities as *the disabled* or *the handicapped*. Note that the use of "the" in front of a noun is a good warning sign that you may be using a label.

Guidelines for Specific Populations
Age
Use *boy* and *girl* only for children and adolescents, although even for high school students, *young man* and *young woman* may be preferable. Do not use terms such as *senior citizen* or

oldster for people who are older than 65. Use specific age ranges whenever possible. Use *aging* and *elderly* as adjectives, not as nouns.

Class

Classism often creeps into our language. Instead of assigning class to people, you should describe their situations. This does not mean that you should pretend all people have the same socioeconomic advantages, but that you should describe the advantages or lack of advantages, rather than assigning attributes to the people.

Poor Usage	Better Usage
lower class	people who are poor
underclass	with low incomes
upper class	with high incomes
the disadvantaged	with socioeconomic disadvantages

Classism often is combined with bias toward people in terms of race or ethnicity; consequently, it is doubly important to take care with language that might perpetuate discrimination.

Disability

Remember that people *have* disabilities, they are not the disabilities; in addition, the disabilities may be barriers, such as stairs or curbs, that handicap people. The following are some commonly misused terms:

Poor Usage	Better Usage
the handicapped	people with disabilities
schizophrenics	people diagnosed with schizophrenia
challenged	person who has ___
wheelchair-bound	uses a wheelchair
the blind	people who are blind
hearing impaired	hard of hearing or deaf

HIV/AIDS

Say *people with AIDS*, not *AIDS victims* or *innocent victims of AIDS*. Avoid language that may imply a moral judgment on behavior or lifestyles. Instead of *high-risk groups*, which suggests that demographic traits may be responsible for AIDS exposure, use *high-risk behavior*.

Race and Ethnicity

- Issues and Dilemmas

Traditionally, authors in the social sciences have used *minority* as a shorthand term to describe people of various races and ethnicities collectively. In these cases the term has been used in the sense of a smaller number or a population that has been oppressed or subjected to differential treatment. Authors also have used *white* and *nonwhite*, particularly in research papers, to differentiate between population groups. *Nonwhite* appears to have been used to describe collectively a diverse group of people who differ in some ways from the greater number of a population.

Another complicating factor is that not all people within specific populations agree on nomenclature, and many people use different definitions for the same words. For example, some people prefer *African American*; others within the same population say, "I am not African American; I am *black.*" Some scholars use the term race to describe broad classifications of people who are presumed to have common descent and share certain physical characteristics (generally American Indian, Asian, black, and white) and reserve *ethnicity* for people who share common culture, religion, or language (often people from specific nations or countries). Others use the terms interchangeably. Some eliminate the term race entirely because they believe it is racist in itself.

- Guidelines

Styles and preferences for nouns that refer to race and ethnicity change over time. The general guidelines for discussing all people are particularly helpful when you are describing race and ethnicity. Try to ascertain what the population group prefers and use that term; recognize and acknowledge that there may be disagreement about preference within the group. Whenever possible, be as specific as possible and describe individual population groups rather than collecting many different groups under an umbrella term. If the people in your study included Asian Americans, Hispanics, black Americans, and white Americans, do not compare the first three groups as a set with the last group. Describe them each as individual groups. If you researched experiences of a group of Asian Americans who included Chinese, Japanese, and Koreans, you should describe each national origin group individually.

You should avoid both *minority* and *nonwhite*. Many people who are described this way view the terms as pejorative and discriminatory. In addition, assuming that white people are the predominant population group is an inaccurate portrayal of most countries in the world and indeed of many areas in the United States. Some people prefer the use of people of color; however, you should be aware that this term also is imprecise and that not all people who might be included in the group under such a heading would describe themselves in this way.

Black and *white* are adjectives that should be used (in lowercase only unless they begin a sentence) to modify nouns, such as "black Americans" or "black men" or "white women." *African Americans, American Indians, Asian Americans,* and *Hispanics* are all proper nouns that should be capitalized; hyphens should never be inserted in multiword names even when the names are modifiers. Some individuals prefer to use Latino, instead of Hispanic, as the descriptive term for people of Latin American ancestry, and some use the two together. There has been considerable discussion about the use of *American Indian* versus *Native American*; many people prefer the former because it is a more precise term for the population in North America. Although the U.S. government combines *Asian* and *Pacific Islander*, most Pacific Islanders prefer that they be separated.

Poor Usage	Better Usage
minorities	specific population or "racial and ethnic groups"
tribes	people or nations
blacks	black people
nonwhites	specific populations

In addition to taking care with names of racial and ethnic groups, you should be careful with modifiers. For example, the passage "we compared the reactions of African American and Hispanic men with middle-class white men" suggests that the first two groups are in a different socioeconomic status, and given historical stereotyping, the perception is likely to be that they are in a lower status. Specify the status for all participants in your study. Describing someone as "the accomplished African American student" may suggest that this student is an exception. Describe people in terms of race or ethnicity only when the description is pertinent to the discussion.

Sex

Sexist language has no place in the professional literature. The most obvious manifestation of sexist language is the use of masculine pronouns, and there are numerous ways to avoid their use. One option is to use plural forms whenever possible. If you are writing a text or a how-to article, using the second person to address the reader directly will help you avoid having to select a masculine or feminine form and is likely to make the article more appealing to the reader. You can often substitute *we* for he and *our* or *their* for *his*. Another solution is to eliminate pronouns entirely. Inserting *him* or *her* or *he* or *she* throughout an article becomes cumbersome, although sparing use can sound natural. Do not use contrived forms such as *s/he* or *he/she*. In general, avoid alternating masculine and feminine pronouns within an article. Rather than demonstrating equality, the practice can suggest that they are interchangeable, and it is confusing to the reader.

Poor Usage	Better Usage
the social worker	social workers
will find that he	will find that they
he calls his children "kids"	we call our children "kids"
the teacher should encourage his students to write	encourage your students to write

Avoid words that suggest an overtone of judgment, that describe women in patronizing terms ("the little lady") or suggest second-class status ("authoress") or demean a woman's ability ("lady lawyer") or are rarely used to describe men ("coed"). Take care not to suggest that women are possessions of men or that they cannot carry out a role or perform a job that men do.

Poor Usage	Better Usage
policemen	police officers
man a project	staff a project
chairman	chair
housewife	homemaker
mankind	humans, human beings

It is not necessary or desirable to construct feminine versions of words that carry a masculine connotation. *Chair* or *representative* substitute much better for *chairman* or *spokesman* than *chairwoman* or *spokeswoman*. Do not specify sex unless it is a variable or it is essential to the discussion. Be sure to use parallel construction: *men* and *women*, not *men* and *females* or *girls* and *men*. *Men* and *women* are nouns, whereas *female* and *male* are best used as adjectives.

Sexual Orientation
Orientation is a state of being, and *preference* is a choice; consequently, you should not use the latter to refer to heterosexuality or homosexuality. The NASW Press uses the term *homosexual* only as an adjective. You should use *lesbians, gay men,* or *bisexual men* or *women* to refer to people whose orientation is not exclusively heterosexual.

It is important to distinguish between sexual orientation and sexual behavior. Consequently, you would not write "the client reported homosexual fantasies," but would substitute "the client reported same-gender sexual fantasies." The appropriate terms to use in describing sexual activity include *female-female, male-male,* and *same-gender,* in addition to *male-female.*

Accurate Historical Reporting
In their zeal to use appropriate language, authors sometimes try to change history. If you are quoting any document, you must quote it exactly as the words were written or said; and if you are describing a historical situation, you will likely want to use the words that were used in that context. You should, however, make the context clear. If you find the language too egregious, you may want to add a footnote saying this is not your language, but the language of the time in which it was written.

Clear, Accessible Writing
You are writing to communicate facts and ideas. Because you are writing for journals in the social sciences, you probably want to communicate those facts and ideas with the intent of improving human lives. To do so, you must write in such a way that you will engage readers so that they will absorb your content enough to use it.

There is no question that eliminating the old shorthand for describing people will add some length to a paper. Substituting *members of racial and ethnic groups* for *minorities* or *people with disabilities* for the *disabled* adds words, but it is more accurate and it eliminates bias. You can easily compensate for the additional length by practicing the principles of good writing. Use strong active verbs and eliminate all convoluted passive constructions. Strike out qualifiers and other redundancies:

Redundant	Simplified
successfully avoided	avoided
has the capability of	can
particularly unique	unique
most often is the case that	often is

Do not resort to euphemisms, which will weaken your message. Taking care to portray people with accuracy and sensitivity should enhance your critical analysis, not muddy it. The more clearly and simply you write, the easier you will make it for your readers to grasp complex ideas. Bring life to your writing by concentrating on the message. If you portray the people you are discussing vividly and truthfully, you will probably communicate the problems and solutions clearly.

Student Affairs Journal Online

ADDRESS FOR SUBMISSION:

Steve Eubanks, Editor
Student Affairs Journal Online
SAJO Submissions
326 N. Pennsylvania
Glendora, CA 91741
USA
Phone: 626-812-3056
Fax: 626-815-3883
E-Mail: seubanks@sajo.org
Web: sajo.org
Address May Change:

PUBLICATION GUIDELINES:

Manuscript Length: 11-15
Copies Required: No Paper Copy Required
Computer Submission: Yes Disk, Email
Format: MSWord
Fees to Review: 0.00 US$

Manuscript Style:
    American Psychological Association

CIRCULATION DATA:

Reader: Administrators
Frequency of Issue: Online
Copies per Issue: Online
Sponsor/Publisher:
Subscribe Price: 0.00 US$

REVIEW INFORMATION:

Type of Review: Blind Review
No. of External Reviewers: 3
No. of In House Reviewers: 0
Acceptance Rate: 90%
Time to Review: 1 - 2 Months
Reviewers Comments: Yes
Invited Articles: 0-5%
Fees to Publish: 0.00 US$

MANUSCRIPT TOPICS:
Higher Education

MANUSCRIPT GUIDELINES/COMMENTS:

To be considered for inclusion in the SAJO journal, your submission must follow these guidelines.

Subject Matter
Submissions should contribute to a better understanding of college students, and how student affairs practitioners and professionals can better serve them. The focus of this journal is broad, and all submissions that are deemed to have importance to any facet of Student Affairs will be considered for publication.

Articles. Works published under this heading will represent what one typically considers a "journal article". Articles pertaining to primary research, new and innovative programs, technology issues, and such will be included in this section. Article submissions should generally not exceed 4,000 words in length.

Reviews. This section of the journal will contain informative reviews of books, software, internet resources, and the like. Unsolicited reviews are accepted for consideration, but are subject to a great deal of scrutiny to ensure that they are not being abused. If you know of a resource which you would like to see reviewed, please contact SAJO at info@sajo.org, and we will attempt to have it reviewed. Additionally, if you would like to write a review article, contact us about having a review topic assigned to you. Reviews should generally not exceed 1500 words in length.

Shorts. Shorts is a unique attempt to tap the creative abilities of many in the field of Student Affairs to express ideas and perspectives that are not done justice by the more formal article format. Short fiction, non-fiction, biography and poetry are prime candidates for inclusion in this section. Shorts should generally not exceed 2000 words in length.

Style
1. Submissions should be well written, and proofread. Those containing grammatical errors, spelling errors and typographical errors will be returned to the author for revision. The information and data presented in the submission should be accurate and correct.

2. Manuscripts should be submitted as either MS Word or WordPerfect files in either Windows or Macintosh format. Submissions may be sent to SAJO via e-mail or on a 3.5" diskette. Tables and figures should be in separate files in .GIF or .JPG format, and should be referred to in the body of the text in such a way that a hypertext link to the figure can be created.

E-mail submissions should be sent to submit@sajo.org
1. The words "Submission to SAJO" should appear in the subject line of your message.
2. The following information should appear in the body of the e-mail message.
   a. Your Name
   b. The e-mail address where you would like to receive responses to your article
   c. The journal section for which you are submitting (Articles, Reviews or Shorts)
3. The submission itself, as well as any graphic files should be included as attachments to your e-mail.

Regular mail submissions should be sent to SAJO Submission, 326 N. Pennsylvania, Glendora, CA 91741.
1. Affix a label to your 3.5" diskette on which your name, and the format of the disk appear (Windows or Mac).
2. Include an 8.5" x 11" sheet of paper on which you have typed the following information:
   a. Your Name
   b. The e-mail address where you would like to receive responses to your article
   c. The journal section for which you are submitting (Articles, Reviews or Shorts)

3. Each submission should include a descriptive title which should appear at the top of the document. You should also indicate the section to which you are submitting (Articles, Reviews or Shorts)

4. Citations referred to in the manuscript should be referenced in APA style. Additional references may be included in the document, before the "References" section. Quotations of 300 or more words from a single source require copyright permission from the original author. See our Copyright Information page for more information.

5. Submissions should not contain any references to the author's name or institutional affiliation in the body of the text, since they will be reviewed by a blind review process. If this type of information is necessary to the finished work, it will be added after the work is accepted for publication.

6. Do not submit work that is under consideration by any other publication. If your submission has been previously published in part or in whole, you must disclose that fact at the time it is submitted to SAJO. SAJO generally only publishes material that has not been previously published, but will consider each case individually.

Editorial Review Process
You are probably wondering what happens to your submission once you have sent it to us. These are the steps that your submission will go through.
1. The submission is received by SAJO.

2. The submission is distributed to three members of the Editorial Board. The only identifying mark on your submission at this time is the tracking number assigned to your article at the time it is received by SAJO.

3. The reviewing members of the Editorial Board will read your submission, and record their comments. This is the stage that takes the greatest amount of time.

4. The reviewers return your submission along with their comments and their recommendation regarding acceptance to the SAJO office.

5. Your submission is returned to you along with the comments of the reviewers. At this time, you will also learn whether or not your article has been accepted for publication.

It is a rare case for any submission to be accepted for publication immediately. Almost all manuscripts are returned be the reviewers with comments for the author to use in rewriting.

Information on Acceptance
Acceptance for publication in the SAJO Journal is complex. First, your submission must be recommended by at least two of the three reviewers. SAJO reserves the right to modify articles that we publish to fit the style and space needs of the journals. While we will not alter the substance of your submission, it is rare that any article will appear in the journal exactly as it appeared when you submitted it.

Studies in Continuing Education

ADDRESS FOR SUBMISSION:

David Boud, Editor
Studies in Continuing Education
University of Technology Sydney
Faculty of Education
PO Box 123
Broadway NSW, 2007
Australia
Phone: +61 2 9514 3945
Fax: +61 2 9514 3933
E-Mail: David.Boud@uts.edu.au
Web: www.carfax.co.uk/sce-ad.htm
Address May Change:

PUBLICATION GUIDELINES:

Manuscript Length: 26-30
Copies Required: Three
Computer Submission: Yes
Format: MSWord
Fees to Review: 0.00 US$

Manuscript Style:
American Psychological Association

CIRCULATION DATA:

Reader: Academics
Frequency of Issue: 2 Times/Year
Copies per Issue: Less than 1,000
Sponsor/Publisher: Studies in Continuing
Education, Inc.; Carfax Publishing
(Taylor & Francis Group)
Subscribe Price: 52.00 US$ Individual
172.00 US$ Institution

REVIEW INFORMATION:

Type of Review: Editorial Review
No. of External Reviewers: 3
No. of In House Reviewers: 0
Acceptance Rate: 21-30%
Time to Review: 2 - 3 Months
Reviewers Comments: Yes
Invited Articles: 0-5%
Fees to Publish: 0.00 US$

MANUSCRIPT TOPICS:
Adult Career & Vocational

MANUSCRIPT GUIDELINES/COMMENTS:

Aims and Scope
Studies in Continuing Education is a scholarly journal concerned with all aspects of continuing, professional and lifelong learning. It aims to be of special interest to those involved in:

• Continuing professional education
• In-service training
• Staff development
• Training and development
• Human resource development

Studies in Continuing Education publishes material which will contribute to improving practice in the field of continuing education and of bringing theory and practice into closer association. Contributions are sought on all aspects of the field. These include: accounts of new initiatives, discussions of key issues, review articles, reports of research and development, and reflections on theory and practice. Papers drawing upon any one or more perspectives on the field are welcome. Of particular interest are contributions from practitioners in any area who may wish to engage in critical reflection on their own practices. Book reviews and reviews of other published material are also included.

World Wide Web

Full details of Studies in Continuing Education, including contents pages, can be found on the Carfax Home Page at: http://www.carfax.co.uk/sce-ad.htm and on the website of Professor David Boud at: http://www.education.uts.edu.au/ostaff/staff/david_boud.html

Note to Authors please make sure your contact address information is clearly visible on the outside of all packages you are sending to Editors. Send Manuscripts to Professor Boud.

Form of Submission

Articles should be written in a style that is accessible to those not familiar with the specialisation of the author. They should normally be in the range of 5,000 to 8,000 words. All articles will be refereed, normally by specialists in the area of the contribution and by others to assess their broader interest. Manuscripts are accepted for consideration on the understanding that they are original material and are not being considered for publication elsewhere.

In preparing articles for publication, authors should follow the style conventions of the American Psychological Association (Publication Manual, 3rd edition). Contributors without ready access to this will normally find all they need to know by inspection of any issue of Studies in Continuing Education. Please note that non-sexist language should be used throughout and the convention for citing references should be carefully followed.

A copy on disk or by e-mail attachment should be submitted in addition to the paper-based submission. The following electronic formats are acceptable: text and tables in Microsoft Word or Wordperfect (Macintosh or PC), diagrams and figures in PICT, JPEG, GIF or TIFF formats.

Offprints

Fifty offprints of each paper are supplied free. Additional copies may be purchased and should be ordered when the proofs are returned. Offprints, together with a complete copy of the relevant journal issue, are sent by accelerated surface post about three weeks after publication.

Copyright

It is a condition of publication that authors vest copyright in their articles, including abstracts, in Taylor & Francis Ltd. This enables us to ensure full copyright protection and to disseminate the article, and the journal, to the widest possible readership in print and electronic formats as appropriate. Authors may, of course, use the article elsewhere after publication without prior permission from Carfax, provided that acknowledgement is given to the Journal as the original source of publication, and that Carfax is notified so that our records show that its use is properly authorized.

Studies in Educational Evaluation

ADDRESS FOR SUBMISSION:

David Nevo, Editor
Studies in Educational Evaluation
Tel Aviv University
School of Education
Tel Aviv, 69978
Israel
Phone: +972 3 6408479
Fax: +972 3 6407125
E-Mail: dnevo@post.tau.ac.il
Web: www.elsevier.nl
Address May Change:

PUBLICATION GUIDELINES:

Manuscript Length: 21-25
Copies Required: Three
Computer Submission: Yes
Format: MSWord
Fees to Review: 0.00 US$

Manuscript Style:
    American Psychological Association

CIRCULATION DATA:

Reader: Practicing Teachers, Academics,
    Administrators, Counselors, Evaluators
Frequency of Issue: Quarterly
Copies per Issue: No Reply
Sponsor/Publisher: Tel Aviv Univ. Sch. of
    Edu., UCLA Grad. Sch. of Edu., IPN
    Univ. of Kiel/ Elsevier Science
Subscribe Price: 63500.00 JPY Japan
    536.00 US$ Countries not Japan/Europe
    478.00 Euro European Countries

REVIEW INFORMATION:

Type of Review: Blind Review
No. of External Reviewers: 3
No. of In House Reviewers: 1
Acceptance Rate: 50%
Time to Review: 4 - 6 Months
Reviewers Comments: Yes
Invited Articles: 0-5%
Fees to Publish: 0.00 US$

MANUSCRIPT TOPICS:

Curriculum Studies; Education Management/Administration; Program, School, and Personnel Evaluation; Student Assessment; Tests, Measurement & Evaluation

MANUSCRIPT GUIDELINES/COMMENTS:

Description

Studies in Educational Evaluation publishes original reports of evaluation studies. Four types of articles are published by the journal:

a) empirical evaluation studies representing evaluation practice in educational systems around the world;
b) theoretical reflections and empirical studies related to issues involved in the evaluation of educational programs, educational institutions, educational personnel and student assessment;
c) articles summarizing the state-of-the-art concerning specific topics in evaluation in general or in a particular country or group of countries;
d) book reviews and brief abstracts of evaluation studies.

742

Information For Contributors

Manuscripts can be submitted in triplicate to the editors at one of the three centers in Tel Aviv, Kalamazoo, and Kiel.

On all matters of style (bibliography, figure and table preparation, etc.) authors are referred to the *Publication Manual of the American Psychological Association*, 3rd edition (copyright 1983, American Psychological Association, 1200 17th St., N.W., Washington, DC 20036, U.S.A.).

Authors' names and affiliations should be submitted on a separate page with their full correspondence address including fax and telephone numbers and e-mail addresses.

A short abstract (100-120 words) should also be on a separate page.

Authors whose manuscripts have been accepted for publication will be asked to submit material on a 3 1/2 inch diskette using Macintosh or IBM compatible word processor in Microsoft Word format.

Authors should include up to six keywords with their article. The controlled list of keywords is based on the *ERIC* list of index descriptors and includes: program evaluation; teacher evaluation; personnel evaluation; student evaluation; school-based evaluation; school supervision; evaluation utilization; evaluators; evaluation methods. In addition, authors may include one or two "free" keywords if they wish to do so. All tables and charts should be prepared in photo-ready form.

All authors must sign the "Transfer of Copyright" agreement before the article can be published. This transfer agreement enables Elsevier Science Ltd to protect the copyrighted material for the authors, but does not relinquish the author's proprietary rights. The copyright transfer covers the exclusive rights to reproduce and distribute the article, including reprints, photographic reproductions, micro form or any other reproductions of similar nature and translations, and includes the right to adapt the article for use in conjunction with computer systems and programs, including reproduction or publication in machine-readable form and incorporation in retrieval systems. Authors are responsible for obtaining from the copyright holder permission to reproduce any figures for which copyright exists.

Author Enquiries

For enquiries relating to the submission of articles (including electronic submission), the status of accepted articles through our Online Article Status Information System (OASIS), author Frequently Asked Questions and any other enquiries relating to Elsevier Science, please consult http://www.elsevier.com/locate/ authors/

For specific enquiries on the preparation of electronic artwork, consult
http://www.elsevier.com/locate/authorartwork/

Contact details for questions arising after acceptance of an article, especially those relating to proofs, are provided when an article is accepted for publication.

Teaching & Learning

ADDRESS FOR SUBMISSION:

Jeanette Bopry, Editor
Teaching & Learning
University of North Dakota
College of Education & Human
   Development
Box 7189
Grand Forks, ND 58202
USA
Phone: 701-777-3574
Fax: 701-777-4365
E-Mail: jeanette_bopry@und.nodak.edu
Web: See Guidelines
Address May Change:

PUBLICATION GUIDELINES:

Manuscript Length: 16-25
Copies Required: Three
Computer Submission: Yes Disk, Email
Format: MSWord
Fees to Review: 0.00 US$

Manuscript Style:
   American Psychological Association

CIRCULATION DATA:

Reader: Academics
Frequency of Issue: 3 Times/Year
Copies per Issue: Less than 1,000
Sponsor/Publisher: College of Education
   and Human Development, University of
   North Dakota
Subscribe Price: 12.00 US$ Annual US
   22.00 US$ Annual International
   22.00 US$ Two Years US

REVIEW INFORMATION:

Type of Review: Blind Review
No. of External Reviewers: 2
No. of In House Reviewers: 1
Acceptance Rate: 40%
Time to Review: 4 - 6 Months
Reviewers Comments: Yes
Invited Articles: 0-5%
Fees to Publish: 0.00 US$

MANUSCRIPT TOPICS:
Perspectives on Teaching/Learning; Teacher Education

MANUSCRIPT GUIDELINES/COMMENTS:

Teaching and Learning is a refereed journal devoted to the values of thoughtful observation as an educational method, of description as a technique for understanding, and of lived experience as a source of knowledge construction. The journal is being converted to the online environment. Three electronic issues will be published during the year; the hardcopy will equal the complete volume, published once per year.

We encourage the submission of articles, essays and critical commentary grounded in observed experience in natural settings, of parts of reflective journals, of situated descriptions of teaching/learning practice, of action-oriented research, of ethnographic studies, of semiotic analyses, and of evaluation studies. We will also consider creative works focused on issues related to teaching and learning.

744

We define teaching and learning broadly and invite contributors to stretch or dissolve traditional categories of education. We invite contributions from educators, critical theorists, researchers, social scientists, human-service professionals, historians, philosophers, administrators, students, parents, and artists.

Due to the interdisciplinary character of this journal, articles should be written in a manner that facilitates communication across domains; a style of intelligent informality is preferred. Please provide three printed manuscripts in American Psychological Association (APA) style, double-spaced, with wide margins. Manuscripts will not be returned except for editorial purposes. Manuscripts may also be submitted as e-mail attachments in Word format. All manuscripts should be accompanied by a brief biography of the author or authors. Submissions should be directed to:

Teaching & Learning: The Journal of Natural Inquiry and Reflective Practice
College of Education and Human Development
University of North Dakota
PO Box 7189
Grand Forks, ND 58202-7189
Email Contact: Jeanette Bopry, Editor (bopry@und.nodak.edu)

Website: www.und.nodak.edu/dept/end/journal.htm

Teaching & Learning is published with three electronic issues per year; the hardcopy equals complete volume, published once per year.

Teaching English in the Two-Year College

ADDRESS FOR SUBMISSION:

Howard Tinberg, Editor
Teaching English in the Two-Year College
777 Elsbree Street
Fall River, MA 02720
USA
Phone: 508-678-2811 ext 2567
Fax: 508-675-2294
E-Mail: htinberg@bristol.mass.edu
Web: www.ncte.org/tetyc
Address May Change:

CIRCULATION DATA:

Reader: Academics
Frequency of Issue: Quarterly
Copies per Issue: 3,001 - 4,000
Sponsor/Publisher: NCTE
Subscribe Price: 15.00 US$

PUBLICATION GUIDELINES:

Manuscript Length: 11-15
Copies Required: Three
Computer Submission: No
Format: N/A
Fees to Review: 0.00 US$

Manuscript Style:
, Modern Language Association

REVIEW INFORMATION:

Type of Review: Blind Review
No. of External Reviewers: 2
No. of In House Reviewers: 2
Acceptance Rate: 21-30%
Time to Review: 2 - 3 Months
Reviewers Comments: Yes
Invited Articles: 0-5%
Fees to Publish: 0.00 US$

MANUSCRIPT TOPICS:
Bilingual/E.S.L.; Curriculum Studies; English Literature; Higher Education; Languages & Linguistics; Reading; Teacher Education

MANUSCRIPT GUIDELINES/COMMENTS:

TETYC tries to serve the pedagogical and theoretical needs of two-year college English instructors. Its authors attempt to aid their colleagues in coping with the two-year college instructor's increasingly complex and pressured career by providing articles of practical and theoretical import. What are our editorial attitudes and goals? The editors feel these are well and properly mated at *TETYC*. Indeed, their combination forms an essential part of our editorial philosophy. We care about our authors' manuscripts and the quality of their lives and professional careers, about providing our readership with a professional forum of which they can be justly proud. These concerns are our goals.

Operating practices? Authors often want to know what types of material we like to publish, what kinds of articles we seek currently. First, we demand quality writing: quality of thought, research, and execution in areas of interest to our readership. Defining areas of interest has given us some difficulty.

Two-year college instructors are omnivorous; their tastes are discerning, but also wide ranging: composition theory and practice, developmental studies, technical writing, literature instruction, creative expression, the nature of language and learning theory, and the profession and its status. One almost feels guilty ending any list of their interests.

After appropriate subject matter, we also look for originality. Since we keep well abreast of what has been written and what is being written, we occasionally reject well-written articles reiterating an "oft repeated" idea or technique. Some seventy-five percent of rejected submissions exhibit either poor writing or repeated themes.

An article must, however, be more than timely and well written; it must also meet *TETYC's* needs. In each edition, we seek a balance between the purely pedagogical and the theoretical.

In addition, *TETYC* concerns itself deeply in professional issues and the creative spirit of our readership and does not shy away from controversial points of view. Therefore, articles cogently addressing the lives and times of our profession receive serious consideration by the editors. And we seek to print brief creative expressions from our readership, recognizing that our creative natures often express most appropriately key aspects of our professional natures.

"But don't you give preference to articles from two-year college personnel?" True, a hefty number of our best submissions come from two-year college persons. But our editorial taste is whetted by quality writing appropriate for the needs of *TETYC's* readership; the author's employer whether a two-year school or four-year school or private business or government agency) concerns us little.

The Submission Process
What actually happens to a manuscript once submitted? *TETYC* policies derive from the "Guidelines" of the Authors and Editors of *Learned Journals: "Procedures and Protocol"* by Caroline O. Eckhardt printed in Editors' News (Spring 1978): 23-31. These "Guidelines" have been endorsed by the MLA Conference of Editors of Learned Journals (CELJ), of which *TETYC* is a member.

When your manuscript arrives, the editors promptly send you a receipt letter stating that your manuscript will be reviewed and that you will receive an editorial decision about its publication within three months. From experience, we have learned it takes us three months to circulate your manuscript among our staff and forward our decision to you.

After the review, you receive notice of acceptance or rejection. An accepted manuscript is added to the current file and published as soon as scheduling permits.

Occasionally, we send a letter of provisional acceptance asking you to revise your manuscript and resubmit it for review. The "Guidelines" advise authors that in "most cases a letter or provisional acceptance should be regarded as merely evidence of the editor's willingness to consider the article again in revised form. Courtesy requires that the author reply, indicating whether revision is indeed planned, and if so, by approximately what date the article will be resubmitted."

When all goes well in journal publishing, it goes very well, but when it goes poorly, it is painful. Multiple submissions, evaluation delays, disputed evaluations, and publication delays all create pain, and the "Guidelines" have established "conventions and courtesies" to give fast-acting relief to authors and editors.

Sequential vs. Multiple Submissions

Sequentials are painless but multiples hurt. In a sequential submission you offer exclusive evaluation rights of your manuscript to one journal, and if your submission does not work out, you simply try another journal and another until you receive satisfaction. With a multiple submission, however, you offer your manuscript to several journals simultaneously. The "Guidelines" state: "An author should submit to one journal at a time; an editor should give a decision by a known date; after that date, it is to be understood that the author is free to submit the manuscript elsewhere."

Evaluation Delays

Summer vacations, beginnings and endings of terms, pressing institutional chores-- all can create delays. However, the "Guidelines" do have something to say on the subject: "In general three months is adequate time for evaluation"; unless the editor has written to request an extension of exclusive rights (and to explain the delay)…"

Notice of Rejection

Like most authors, you probably want to know why if your manuscript is rejected. The CELJ agrees that authors should receive a full explanation, but CELJ also recognizes that most editors and staff lack the time for so monumental a task. The "Guidelines" comment that "editors and reviewers cannot afford to serve as unpaid writers and subject matter consultants, which is what they would be doing if they were to comment at length on how to rehabilitate each unacceptable manuscript." "Therefore, the "Guidelines" suggest that "a form letter (e.g., a notice saying merely 'Your article is not suitable to our needs' or 'We are unable to publish your contribution') is quite permissible when the submission is so far off base that the author could have seen why simply by reading several issues of the journal."

Naturally, the "Guidelines" also advise authors to consider a letter of rejection as final and not to dispute the decision.

In other cases, it is the editor's responsibility to offer some explanation to the author. "Ideally, this explanation will be a summary of the reviewers' evaluations."

Publication Delays

"Authors should regard a publication delay of a year or two as normal. When the delay will exceed two years, or when the estimated publication date specified in the letter of acceptance will be missed by more than two issues, the author should be notified and be given the option of withdrawing the article for submission elsewhere."

Closing Note

Publication of *TETYC* requires discipline and months of precious time; still, the editors do enjoy their task like true gourmets enjoy an elegant smorgasbord--not every dish proves delicious, but so many are that we rise after every issue for another serving.

Manuscript Information For Contributors
Typing: double or triple spaced
Preferred Length: articles, 11-15 typed pages; notes, 2-3 typed pages; book reviews, 2-3 typed pages
Documentation: according to *MLA Style Manual 1989*; notes after text; hold notes to a minimum
Copies: two (original and duplicate)
Envelope: a stamped, addressed return envelope must accompany manuscripts
Editorial Report: time varies; usually within three months
Payments: two complimentary copies
Copyright: National Council of Teachers of English

Teaching of Psychology

ADDRESS FOR SUBMISSION:

Randolph A. Smith, Editor
Teaching of Psychology
(See GUIDELINES for Departmental
  Editors and Submission Addresses)
Ouachita Baptist University
Department of Psychology
Arkadelphia, AR 71998-0001
USA
Phone: 870-245-5108
Fax: 870-245-5086
E-Mail: smithr@obu.edu
Web: www.ithaca.edu/beins/top/top.htm
Address May Change:

PUBLICATION GUIDELINES:

Manuscript Length: 6-30/See Guidelines
Copies Required: Five
Computer Submission: No
Format: N/A
Fees to Review: 0.00 US$

Manuscript Style:
  American Psychological Association

CIRCULATION DATA:

Reader: Academics
Frequency of Issue: Quarterly
Copies per Issue: 3,001 - 4,000
Sponsor/Publisher: Lawrence Erlbaum
  Associates
Subscribe Price: 29.00 US$ Individual
  140.00 US$ Institution
  170.00 US$ Foreign

REVIEW INFORMATION:

Type of Review: Editorial Review
No. of External Reviewers: 3
No. of In House Reviewers: 0
Acceptance Rate: 21-30%
Time to Review: 1 - 2 Months
Reviewers Comments: Yes
Invited Articles: 0-5%
Fees to Publish: 0.00 US$

MANUSCRIPT TOPICS:
Adult Career & Vocational; Curriculum Studies; Educational Psychology; Teaching
Psychology at All Levels

MANUSCRIPT GUIDELINES/COMMENTS:

Content
Teaching of Psychology is devoted to improvement of the teaching/learning process at all
educational levels from the secondary school through college and graduate school to
continuing education. The journal includes empirical research on teaching and learning:
studies of teacher or student characteristics; subject matter or content reviews for class use;
investigations of student, course, or teacher assessment; professional problems of teachers;
essays on teaching; innovative course descriptions and evaluations; curriculum designs;
bibliographic material; demonstrations and laboratory projects; book and media reviews; news
items; and readers' commentary.

Topical Articles include a range of content troth broader to more specialized applicability. Articles may vary in length from 2,500 to 7,000 words. The editor may solicit manuscripts deemed to he of significance to the readership.

Methods And Techniques papers are those describing demonstrations, laboratory projects, other learning/teaching devices, or instrumentation (1,000-2,000 words). Articles for this section must include some type of empirical assessment* of the pedagogical effectiveness or value of the technique.

Faculty Forum items may cover the full range of the journal's content policy, including commentary, criticism, or opinion. Brief contributions of innovative procedures, courses, or other materials are especially appropriate (1,200 words or less). Some Forum articles may not require evaluations.

Computers In Teaching articles examine the integration of computer technology and the teaching of psychology. Articles may review commercial or public domain software, describe innovative uses of existing or new computer technology, or assess the effectiveness of computer technology for the teaching of psychology. Articles describing computer assisted teaching methods must include empirical verification* of the utility of the technique. Articles for this section may take the form of Topical Articles, Methods and Techniques, or Faculty Forum.

*Articles for all sections should include empirical assessment of the contribution whenever possible. Ideally, the empirical assessment should directly measure the impact of the technique on student learning (e.g., a pretest/posttest analysis of learning) rather than student self-report of learning.

Manuscript
Submit five copies of all manuscripts. Manuscripts will not be routinely returned to authors. Manuscripts should be prepared according to the *Publication Manual of the American Psychological Association* (4th ed.). Manuscripts should include an abstract that does not exceed 120 words. The cover letter should include a word count for the manuscript (not including title page, abstract, or references), a complete mailing address for each author, and the telephone number of the author to whom editorial correspondence is to be addressed. Figures should be in camera-ready condition.

Masked (blind) reviews are an option at the request of the author(s). Authors submitting manuscripts for masked review should specifically state this request in their cover letter. Each copy of the manuscript should have a separate title page with all author information and notes. This information should not appear elsewhere in the manuscript. Authors should take care to ensure that the manuscript contains no clues as to identity.

Submit manuscripts for Methods and Techniques to Peter J. Giordano, Department of Psychology, Belmont University, Nashville, TN 37212.

Send manuscripts for Computers in Teaching to David J. Pittenger, Department of Psychology, University of Tennessee at Chatanooga, 615 McCallie Avenue, Chatanooga, TN 37403.

Send ideas for The Generalist's Corner to Jane Halonen, Department of Psychology, James Madison University, Harrisonburg, VA 22807.

Submit all other manuscripts to Randolph A. Smith, Department of Psychology, Ouachita Baptist University, Arkadelphia, AR 71998--0001.

Address correspondence about news items to David E. Johnson, Department of Psychology, John Brown University, Siloam Springs, AR 72761; e-mail: djohnson@jbu.edu.

Address other inquiries to Bernard C. Beins, Department of Psychology, Ithaca College, Ithaca, NY 14850-7290.

Contributors are responsible for all statements made in their work, and for obtaining permission from copyright owners if they use an illustration or lengthy quote (over 100 words) published elsewhere. Contributors should write to both publisher and author of such material, requesting nonexclusive world rights in all languages for use in the article and all future editions of it.

Manuscripts will be evaluated on the basis of style as well as content. Some minor copyediting may be done. but authors must take responsibility for clarity, conciseness, and felicity of expression.

Teaching Statistics

ADDRESS FOR SUBMISSION:

Gerald Goodall,Editor
Teaching Statistics
The Royal Statistical Society
12 Errol Street
London, EC1Y 8LX
UK
Phone: +44 (0) 2076 388998
Fax: +44 (0) 2072 567598
E-Mail: g.goodall@rss.erg.uk
Web: science.ntu.ac.uk/rsscse/ts
Address May Change:

PUBLICATION GUIDELINES:

Manuscript Length: 6-10
Copies Required: Two
Computer Submission: Yes Disk, Email
Format: MSWord, PC Format
Fees to Review: 0.00 US$

Manuscript Style:
    Chicago Manual of Style

CIRCULATION DATA:

Reader: Practicing Teachers, Academics
Frequency of Issue: 3 Times/Year
Copies per Issue: 1,001 - 2,000
Sponsor/Publisher: Applied Probability
    Trust; International Statistical Institute;
    Royal Statistical Society
Subscribe Price: 35.00 US$ Individual
    49.00 US$ Institution

REVIEW INFORMATION:

Type of Review: Editorial Review
No. of External Reviewers: 2
No. of In House Reviewers: 1
Acceptance Rate: 75%
Time to Review: 1 - 2 Months
Reviewers Comments: No
Invited Articles: 0-5%
Fees to Publish: 0.00 US$

MANUSCRIPT TOPICS:
Curriculum Studies; Mainly for Teachers, Not Researchers; Science Math & Environment;
Teacher Education

MANUSCRIPT GUIDELINES/COMMENTS:

Scope
Teaching Statistics is aimed at teachers and students aged up to19 who use statistics in their
work. The emphasis is on *teaching* the subject and addressing problems which arise in the
classroom. The journal seeks to support not only specialist statistics teachers but also those in
other disciplines, such as economics, biology and geography, who make widespread use of
statistics in their teaching. *Teaching Statistics* seeks to inform, enlighten, stimulate, correct,
entertain and encourage. Contributions should be light and readable. Formal mathematics
should be kept to a minimum.

Contributions
Contributions are welcomed in the form of articles, notes, letters, problems, news, and smaller
items such as poems, quotations or cartoons. Articles may be of a general nature or aimed
specifically at one of our specialist sections

Classroom Notes	- shorter items containing good ideas worth sharing
Computing Corner	- new developments and ideas in statistical software
Curriculum Matters	- addressing curriculum issues nationally and internationally
Data Bank	- interesting data sets and what to do with them
Historical Perspective	- the lives of statisticians and history of statistics
Project Parade	- reporting on a successful project or suggesting ideas
Practical Activities	- ideas for 'hands-on' classroom practicals in statistics
Research Report	- accessible reports on research in statistical education
Standard Errors	- exposing and correcting common 'howlers'
Statistics at Work	- accounts of what statisticians do in the real world

Articles should be as concise as possible and will not normally be accepted if they exceed 3000 words in length, or would occupy more than four pages of the journal. Diagrams, photographs and illustrations are particularly welcomed. Authors should examine carefully a recent issue of *Teaching Statistics* and conform to the journal's style with respect to headings, summary, keywords, references, spellings, and so on. However, it is not necessary for authors to prepare articles in the two-column format used in the journal.

Initial submissions should be made as TWO paper copies or, *by prior arrangement* with the editor, electronically (Microsoft Word document, PC format). Diagrams, photographs and illustrations should be submitted either as camera-ready copy or electronically (TIF files strongly preferred).

Copyright
Copyright of all published articles will be held by the Teaching Statistics Trust. Once an article has been accepted for publication authors will be required to transfer copyright to the Trust and declare in writing that the article has neither previously been published, nor will be submitted for publication elsewhere.

Editorial Address
Mr Gerald Goodall, Editor *Teaching Statistics*, Royal Statistical Society, 12 Errol St., London EC1Y 8LX, UK. **Tel:** 020 7638 8998, **Fax:** 020 7256 7598, **Email:** g.goodall@rss.org.uk

Tech Trends

ADDRESS FOR SUBMISSION:

Don E. Descy, Editor-in-Chief
Tech Trends
Minnesota State University
125 Memorial Library
Mankato, MN 56002
USA
Phone: 507-389-5244
Fax:
E-Mail: descy@mankato.msus.edu
Web: www.aect.org
Address May Change:

PUBLICATION GUIDELINES:

Manuscript Length: 3-6
Copies Required: Three
Computer Submission: Yes
Format: MSWord
Fees to Review: 0.00 US$

Manuscript Style:
American Psychological Association

CIRCULATION DATA:

Reader: Practicing Teachers, Academics,
   Administrators
Frequency of Issue: 6 Times/Year
Copies per Issue: 4,001 - 5,000
Sponsor/Publisher: Association for
   Educational Communications and
   Technology (AECT)
Subscribe Price: 55.00 US$ Individual
   100.00 US$ Institution
   85.00 US$ Journal w/Membership

REVIEW INFORMATION:

Type of Review: Blind Review
No. of External Reviewers: 2
No. of In House Reviewers: 1
Acceptance Rate: 29%
Time to Review: 2 - 3 Months
Reviewers Comments: Yes
Invited Articles: No Reply
Fees to Publish: 0.00 US$

MANUSCRIPT TOPICS:
Adult Career & Vocational; Curriculum Studies; Education Management/Administration;
Educational Technology Systems; Library Science/Information Resources; Teacher
Education; Tests, Measurement & Evaluation

MANUSCRIPT GUIDELINES/COMMENTS:

Tech Trends, published by the Association for Educational Communications and Technology
(AECT), seeks authoritative articles that focus on the practical applications of technology in
education and training.

Guidelines
Tech Trends is a periodical for professionals. Write in a clear, conversational style. You
should not be afraid to write in the first person (if you are involved in an exciting project) or
the second person (if you want to tell someone how to do something). *Tech Trends* is a
peer-reviewed publication. All manuscripts are read by a panel of consulting editors and other
professionals with expertise in the topic presented by the author. Text and references should

conform to the style set forth in the *Publication Manual of the American Psychological Association* (4th ed.).

Manuscript submission
Your manuscript should be approximately 1000-4000 words in length (or 3-6 pages double-spaced). Please submit three copies of the manuscript. Because articles are reviewed without bias, two of the copies should be without author identification. The manuscript should be accompanied by a brief biological paragraph for each author and an abstract, not to exceed 150 words, that summarizes the article.

Please include a diskette containing the manuscript in a Rich Text Format (.rtf) file or as a Microsoft Word file. We strongly encourage you to include figures, tables, photographs, or other graphics to illustrate your article. We also encourage you to include a photograph of yourself for possible use with your article. Please send photographs as prints - black and white is preferred, but color is also acceptable. As an alternative, you may send photos electronically in separate files, in .eps, .tif, or .jpg format, with a resolution of 300 dpi or higher. Please send other illustrations electronically, or as separate files on diskette; line art and graphics should be sent as .eps, .tif, or. jpg files, with resolution of at least 300 dpi. Captions, well labeled, should be included in a separate file or listed and labeled at the end of your manuscript. *Tech Trends* assumes no responsibility for unsolicited manuscripts and materials.

Complimentary copies
We will send you two complimentary copies of the issue in which your article appears.

Copyright
If your manuscript is accepted for publication in *Tech Trends,* you will be asked to sign a standard publication form that permits us to editor article to conform to our style and format. This form also assigns to *Tech Trends* the copyright to your article. You will also confirm that the manuscript is original and has not been submitted, accepted, or published elsewhere.

Submissions and queries
Send manuscripts or query letters to:
Don E. Descy, Ph.D.
Editor-in-Chief, *Tech Trends*
125 Memorial Library
Minnesota State University
Mankato, MN 56002.

Technical Communication Quarterly

ADDRESS FOR SUBMISSION:

Mary M. Lay, Editor
Technical Communication Quarterly
University of Minnesota
Department of Rhetoric
64 Classroom Office Bldg.
1994 Buford Avenue
St. Paul, MN 55108
USA
Phone: 612-624-2262
Fax: 612-624-3617
E-Mail: mmlay@umn.edu
Web: www.attw.org
Address May Change:

PUBLICATION GUIDELINES:

Manuscript Length: Up to 8,000 words
Copies Required: Four
Computer Submission: Yes On Acceptance
Format: ASCII, WP, Word
Fees to Review: 0.00 US$

Manuscript Style:
, MLA

CIRCULATION DATA:

Reader: Academics
Frequency of Issue: Quarterly
Copies per Issue: 1,001 - 2,000
Sponsor/Publisher: Association of Teachers
   of Technical Writing
Subscribe Price: 20.00 US$ Student
   40.00 US$ Individual
   75.00 US$ Institution

REVIEW INFORMATION:

Type of Review: Blind Review
No. of External Reviewers: 3
No. of In House Reviewers: 1
Acceptance Rate: 21-30%
Time to Review: 2 - 3 Months
Reviewers Comments: Yes
Invited Articles: 6-10%
Fees to Publish: 0.00 US$

MANUSCRIPT TOPICS:
Educational Technology Systems; Higher Education; Languages & Linguistics; Technical Communication

MANUSCRIPT GUIDELINES/COMMENTS:

Technical Communication Quarterly, (Journal of the Association of Teachers of Technical Writing) is an academic, peer-reviewed journal published in English. The subject classification is Scientific/Technical. The publication schedule is February, May, August, November.

Send submissions directly to
Mary M. Lay, *TCQ,* Department of Rhetoric, University of Minnesota, 64 Classroom Office Building, 1994 Buford Avenue, St. Paul, MN 55108. mmlay@umn.edu

All submissions are assumed to be original, verified, unpublished, and not under present consideration by any other publisher.

Follow these guidelines when preparing manuscripts for submission:

- Send an original and three copies of manuscript. Prepare a floppy disk for submission when article is accepted. Place entire manuscript in one document using ASCII, Word, WordPerfect, or Macintosh text files.
- Prepare cover sheet with title of the manuscript, author's name, place of affiliation, mailing address, phone number, and a 35-word biographical sketch.
- Do not make references to the author in the text or on any page besides the cover sheet.
- Center title on top of first page of text.
- Do not exceed 8,000 words in the text.
- Provide a 50-75 word informative abstract.
- Tables and figures should appear on separate pages at the end of the text.
- Provide camera-ready quality copies of all figures.
- Include no footnotes.
- Indicate italics by underscoring or italicizing.
- Indicate a first-level, or primary, header by boldface or all capital letters.
- Indicate a second-level, or secondary, header by indenting and boldface or all capital letters.
- Use the parenthetical method for citing a reference in the text, according to The MIA Style Manual (1999).
- Provide a list of works cited at the end in a section called "Works Cited."
- Follow The MLA Style Manual in the "Works Cited" section.
- Include first names of all authors in "Works Cited" and first mention in text.

Techniques: Connecting Education and Careers

ADDRESS FOR SUBMISSION:

Susan Reese, Editor
Techniques: Connecting Education and
   Careers
Association for Career and
   Technical Education
1410 King Street
Alexandria, VA 22314
USA
Phone: 703-683-3111
Fax: 703-683-7424
E-Mail: susan@printmanagementinc.com
Web:
Address May Change:

PUBLICATION GUIDELINES:

Manuscript Length: 6-10
Copies Required: One
Computer Submission: Yes
Format: MSWord
Fees to Review: 0.00 US$

Manuscript Style:
   See Manuscript Guidelines

CIRCULATION DATA:

Reader: Practicing Teachers
Frequency of Issue: 8 Times/Year
Copies per Issue: More than 25,000
Sponsor/Publisher:
Subscribe Price: 39.00 US$
   78.00 US$ Overseas

REVIEW INFORMATION:

Type of Review: Editorial Review
No. of External Reviewers: 0
No. of In House Reviewers: 2
Acceptance Rate: 0-5%
Time to Review: 4 - 6 Months
Reviewers Comments: No
Invited Articles: 21-30%
Fees to Publish: 0.00 US$

MANUSCRIPT TOPICS:
Adult Career & Vocational; Counseling & Personnel Services; Education
Management/Administration; Educational Technology Systems; Gifted Children; Higher
Education; Rural Education & Small Schools; Secondary/Adolescent Studies; Special
Education; Teacher Education; Tests, Measurement & Evaluation

MANUSCRIPT GUIDELINES/COMMENTS:

How to Write It. *Techniques* is a popular magazine, which means its style is journalistic, not
academic. The approach is direct and conversational. Always keep your audience in mind
when you write: Is the article appropriate for the readers? Use active words and phrases to
evoke precise images. State the main idea right away, and then develop it thoroughly in the
article. Steer clear of jargon and support all generalizations with specifics, including analysis,
examples, quotations and statistics. No footnotes, please. Whenever possible, "personalize"
articles by adding the human element--put actual people in your stories.

How It's Edited. *Techniques* editors sometimes make substantial edits and revisions to manuscripts that are accepted for publication. They often call authors for more information which is then added into the article. Authors do have an opportunity to discuss changes with the editors before articles are printed. A research paper or thesis that may be entirely appropriate in academic circles is NOT what we're looking for.

How Much to Write. Feature articles generally should be between 1,500 and 2,500 words--that's about eight to ten typed, double-spaced manuscript pages. "Forum" (opinion) articles are about 850 words. "It Works" pieces should be about 1,000 words.

When the Article Iis Due. Manuscript deadlines usually are three months before the cover date of the magazine issue. For example, copy for the October issue is due July 1. In some cases, you and the editor may agree on a different due date. Either way, please be sure to contact us if you're finding it difficult to meet an assigned deadline. Note: Unsolicited manuscripts can take six months to process. You may save time by calling the editors to discuss your proposed article before submitting a manuscript.

Pictures and Graphics. If you have or can obtain professional-quality photographs (preferably color slides or prints) and material for graphics (such as statistics for charts and graphs) to illustrate your article, please send them in with your manuscript. The author is responsible for obtaining permission to publish the photos submitted.

Other Things We Need. For the author biography at the end of the article, submit two or three sentences describing your experience and qualifications, including your job title and employer. We'll send you an edited copy of your article for your review along with a copyright assignment form.

How to Send Your Article. We prefer to receive your article on an IBM-compatible computer disk, with an indication of the word processing system you used and file name for your article. We also need a double-spaced hard copy. Be sure to include your name, address, phone number, fax number and e-mail address. Send your article to: Associate Editor, Techniques, 1410 King St., Alexandria, VA 22314.

Getting Published. About 90 percent of the editorial in *Techniques* is written by staff and freelancers. Occasionally the editors will accept or solicit articles from educators or other experts who are not professional writers when they are seeking a particular perspective. On average, less than 5 percent of the unsolicited feature articles received each year are accepted. However, the rate of acceptance is much higher for "Forum" and "It Works" articles (see descriptions below). Starting with the September 1998 issue, *Techniques* will pay $50 for each "Forum" and $25 for each "It Works" or book review it publishes. (Contributions to other departments are not compensated.)

- **Forum**--Bylined opinion pieces on current trends in the connecting worlds of education and work.

- **It Works**--Bylined, concise articles about successful programs and practices in the field.

- **Books**--Consider reviewing a book of interest to our readers or Let us know of a noteworthy new book.

- **Calendar**--Lists dates and events of interest to educators and other school-to-careers professionals.

- **State Update**--News of vocational education legislation, programs and people in each state.

- **Letters To The Editor**--Write in to respond to something you read in Techniques. We try to print all that we receive.

Send All Articles And Queries To: Associate Editor, Techniques
1410 King Street
Alexandria, VA 22314

Check out our editorial calendar at www.acteonline.org

Trusteeship

ADDRESS FOR SUBMISSION:

Daniel J. Levin, Editor
Trusteeship
Association of Governing Boards of
    Universities and Colleges
One Dupont Circle, Suite 400
Washington, DC 20036
USA
Phone: 202-296-8400
Fax: 202-223-7053
E-Mail: danl@agb.org
Web:
Address May Change:

PUBLICATION GUIDELINES:

Manuscript Length: 7-12
Copies Required: One
Computer Submission: Yes
Format: IBM, ASCII
Fees to Review: 0.00 US$

Manuscript Style:
    Associated Press Stylebook

CIRCULATION DATA:

Reader: , CEOs, Trustees, Administrators of
    Higher Education
Frequency of Issue: Bi-Monthly
Copies per Issue: More than 32,000
Sponsor/Publisher:
Subscribe Price:
    Avail. to Assn. Members

REVIEW INFORMATION:

Type of Review: Editorial Review
No. of External Reviewers: 0
No. of In House Reviewers: 3
Acceptance Rate: 50%
Time to Review: 1 Month or Less
Reviewers Comments: No
Invited Articles: 31-50%
Fees to Publish: 0.00 US$

MANUSCRIPT TOPICS:
Education Management/Administration; Governance, Public Policy, Tuition, Tenure; Higher Education; Issues Affecting College & University Boards

MANUSCRIPT GUIDELINES/COMMENTS:

Checking a recent issue of *Trusteeship* (Previously *AGB Reports*) will give you a good idea of our usual article length, plus the range of topics we address. Our guidelines follow:

1. Articles should be approximately 7-12 pages long, typed double-spaced, and written in clear, lively, jargon-free prose. Articles may also be submitted on an IBM-compatible disk in MS Word or ASCII or via e-mail to danl@agb.org

2. Our readers are lay trustees and academic executives and administrators; their concerns are higher education governance and policy, especially how trustees can do their jobs more effectively. Our articles are generally of four types: (1) practical advice, information, and how-to examples; (2) discussions of emerging trends in or related to higher education; (3)

reports of research related to higher education governance and policy; and (4) ideas and issues that governing boards will find interesting and provocative.

We like articles that contain a strong lead sentence, lots of specifics, examples, and case studies. We don't use footnotes or references, and we discourage the use of charts, graphs, and illustrations--unless that is the best way to present the material. Camera-ready copy for graphics must be supplied by the author.

3. Authors are notified when we receive their article. Our editorial staff reviews each manuscript, and occasionally a manuscript will be more broadly distributed for review. This process usually takes about one month.

4. When an article is accepted, authors are asked to sign a copyright release form that also grants us permission to edit the article to conform to our style and format and to submit a brief biographical sketch. After editing, we send galleys to the author for approval.

5. Like most professional journals, we do not guarantee publication, even if we have solicited the article. We make every effort, however, to assist authors in making their work suitable for our audience. We also do not promise to publish accepted articles in any specific issue of *Trusteeship*.

6. We welcome inquiries in advance of submissions. Please contact the Publications Department if you have an idea or article you think may be appropriate. Often we can help authors shape an article while it is in preparation, shortening the editorial process for everyone involved.

Understanding Statistics

ADDRESS FOR SUBMISSION:

Brian Everitt, Editor
Understanding Statistics
Institute of Psychiatry
Biostatistics and Computing
Decrespigny Park
London, SE5 8AF
UK
Phone: +44 (0) 2078 480309
Fax: +44 (0) 2078 480281
E-Mail: B.Everitt@iop.kcl.ac.uk
Web: iop.kcl.ac.uk
Address May Change:

PUBLICATION GUIDELINES:

Manuscript Length: 16-20
Copies Required: Five
Computer Submission: No
Format: N/A
Fees to Review: 0.00 US$

Manuscript Style:
American Psychological Association

CIRCULATION DATA:

Reader: Practicing Teachers, Academics
Frequency of Issue: Quarterly
Copies per Issue: No Reply
Sponsor/Publisher: Lawrence Erlbaum
Associates
Subscribe Price: 40.00 US$ Individual
150.00 US$ Institution
36.00 US$ Electronic Only

REVIEW INFORMATION:

Type of Review: Editorial Review
No. of External Reviewers: 2
No. of In House Reviewers: 1
Acceptance Rate: 21-30%
Time to Review: 2 - 3 Months
Reviewers Comments: Yes
Invited Articles: 0-5%
Fees to Publish: 0.00 US$

MANUSCRIPT TOPICS:
Educational Psychology; Statistics in Psychology

MANUSCRIPT GUIDELINES/COMMENTS:

Editorial Scope
Understanding Statistics aims to make psychologists and other behavioral scientists aware of relevant recent developments in statistics, point out current poor practice in their use of statistics, illustrate innovative uses of software, highlight software inadequacies, and generally make non-statisticians in a variety of disciplines more aware of what modern statistics has to offer them. This journal welcomes well written articles presenting non-technical accounts of the use of recently developed statistical methods in the social and behavioral sciences as well as, articles illustrating the advantages of newer statistical methodologies over those traditionally used in these disciplines. In addition, this journal publishes articles that point out examples of current bad practice in the application of statistics by researchers in the area and describes innovative uses of software.

764

Audience
Researchers, teachers, and students in psychology, education, and related disciplines, and statisticians giving statistical courses in these areas.

Instructions to Contributors
Manuscripts must be in typewritten form with 1.5" margins on all sides. Type all components double spaced, including title page, abstract, text, acknowledgements, references, appendices, tables, figure captions and footnotes. Indicate in the manuscript approximately where each figure or table is to be positioned. Page 1 should contain the article title, author(s) affiliation(s), a short form of the title (less than 48 characters and spaces), and the name and complete mailing address of the author to whom correspondence should be sent. Page 2 should contain a 150-200 word abstract. All pages should be numbered (except camera-ready artwork pages). Prepare manuscripts according to the *Publication Manual of the American Psychological Association* (4th ed.), paying particular attention to references and citations and following "Guidelines to Reduce Bias in Language."

In a cover letter, include the contact author's address and telephone and fax numbers and state that the manuscript includes only original material that has not been previously published and that is not submitted for publication elsewhere. Authors are responsible for all statements made in their work and for obtaining permission to reprint or to adapt a copyrighted table or figure or to quote at length from a copyrighted work. Authors should write to the original author(s) and original publisher to see if permission is required and to request nonexclusive world rights in all languages to use the material in the current article and in future editions. Include copies of all permissions and credit lines with the manuscript.

Authors should send four copies and one original manuscript to:
Professor Brian Everitt
Department of Biostatistics and Computing
Institute of Psychiatry
Denmark Hill, London, SE5 8AF
England

Urban Anthropology

ADDRESS FOR SUBMISSION:

Jack R. Rollwagen, Editor
Urban Anthropology
The Institute, Inc.
56 Centennial Avenue
Brockport, NY 14420
USA
Phone: 716-637-2684
Fax: 716-395-2684
E-Mail:
Web:
Address May Change:

PUBLICATION GUIDELINES:

Manuscript Length: 15-60
Copies Required: Three
Computer Submission: Yes
Format: for Accepted Manuscript Only
Fees to Review: 0.00 US$

Manuscript Style:
See Manuscript Guidelines

CIRCULATION DATA:

Reader: Academics
Frequency of Issue: Quarterly
Copies per Issue: Less than 1,000
Sponsor/Publisher:
Subscribe Price: 15.00 US$ Individual
80.00 US$ Institution

REVIEW INFORMATION:

Type of Review: Blind Review
No. of External Reviewers: 2
No. of In House Reviewers: 1
Acceptance Rate: 21-30%
Time to Review: 2 - 3 Months
Reviewers Comments: Yes
Invited Articles: 50% +
Fees to Publish: 0.00 US$

MANUSCRIPT TOPICS:
Social Studies/Social Science

MANUSCRIPT GUIDELINES/COMMENTS:

Manuscripts submitted for publication in *Urban Anthropology* and *Studies Of Cultural Systems and World Economic Development* (hereafter *UAS*) must conform to the following requirements.

1. All manuscripts submitted must be on 8 1/2 X 11 inch, paper and must be supplied in triplicate.

2. Manuscripts must be typed in black ink, using one side of the sheet of paper only. All typed material must be double spaced including all text, notes, and quotations. Liberal margins must be provided.

3. Notes should be kept to a minimum and should be numbered consecutively through the manuscript. All notes should appear at the end of the text of the manuscript, beginning on a separate sheet of paper labeled "Notes."

4. Sources cited in the body of the text will appear at the end of the manuscript in a section entitled "References Cited" and will begin on a separate sheet of paper. Sources in the references cited section will contain all information normally required and will conform to styles current in *UAS* (a variant of the style found in the *American Anthropologist*). References to those sources that appear in the text of the manuscript will appear in parenthetical form, e.g. (Malinowski 1918:121). When the name of the author has been mentioned in the text, only the date and page need be included, e.g. (1918:121).

5. Illustrations (photographs, drawings, diagrams, and charts) are to be numbered in one consecutive series of Arabic numerals. Photographs should be large, glossy prints, showing high contrast. Drawings should be prepared with India ink. Either the original drawings or high-quality photographic prints are acceptable. Identify figures on the back with author's name and number of the illustrations. Each figure should have an accompanying caption. The list of captions for illustrations should be typed on a separate sheet of paper.

6. Tables should be numbered and referred to by number in the text. Each table should be typed on a separate sheet of paper and should have a descriptive title.

7. An abstract of up to 200 words must accompany the manuscript submitted for publication. This abstract will appear at the beginning of the article in *UAS*. Abstracts of all articles published in *UAS* will also appear in *Abstracts In Anthropology, Current Contents, Marriage And Family Review, MLA International Bibliography, Sage Urban Studies Abstracts, Social Sciences Citation Index, And Sociological Abstracts*. Abstracts submitted must not have appeared in any form prior to publication in *UAS*.

8. Submission is a representation that the manuscript has not been published previously and is not currently under consideration for publication elsewhere. A statement transferring copyright from the authors (or their employers, if they hold the copyright) to the Institute for the Study of Man, Inc. will be required before the manuscript can be accepted for publication. The Editor will supply the necessary forms for this transfer. Such a written transfer of copyright, which previously was assumed to be implicit in the act of submitting a manuscript, is necessary under the new U.S. Copyright Law in order for the publisher to carry through the dissemination of research results and reviews as widely and effectively as possible.

9. Authors whose manuscripts are accepted for publication in *UAS* are urged to submit the final, corrected and revised copy on computer diskette, accompanied by a paper copy printed from that diskette. The most appropriate format is Apple Macintosh diskette copies of the manuscript using Microsoft Word software or Macwrite. However, 3.5" IBM or IBM compatible diskettes using Word Perfect, or some other standard word processing software are also acceptable. If this is contemplated, please contact the editor prior to submission for instructions.

Manuscripts should be sent in triplicate to the Editor: Jack R. Rollwagen, Editor, Department of Anthropology, SUNY College at Brockport, Brockport, New York 14420, USA.

WebNet Journal

ADDRESS FOR SUBMISSION:

Gary Marks, Editor
WebNet Journal
c/o Joe McDonald
ONLINE SUBMISSION ONLY
AACE
P.O. Box 3728
Norfolk, VA 23514-3728
USA
Phone: 757-623-7588 ext. 232
Fax: 757-997-8760
E-Mail: pubs@aace.org
Web: www.aace.org/pubs/submit.asp
Address May Change:

PUBLICATION GUIDELINES:

Manuscript Length: Max/30
Copies Required: No Paper Copy Required
Computer Submission: Yes Online
Format: MSWord, html, rtf
Fees to Review: 0.00 US$

Manuscript Style:
American Psychological Association

CIRCULATION DATA:

Reader: Practicing Teachers, Academics,
 Administrators
Frequency of Issue: Quarterly
Copies per Issue: Online
Sponsor/Publisher: AACE
Subscribe Price: 85.00 US$ Individual
 120.00 US$ Institution

REVIEW INFORMATION:

Type of Review: Blind Review
No. of External Reviewers: 2-4
No. of In House Reviewers: 2
Acceptance Rate: 11-20%
Time to Review: 1 - 2 Months
Reviewers Comments: Yes
Invited Articles: 11-20%
Fees to Publish: 0.00 US$

MANUSCRIPT TOPICS:
Business Oriented Topics; Education Management/Administration; Educational Technology Systems; Higher Education; Science Math & Environment

MANUSCRIPT GUIDELINES/COMMENTS:

The *WebNet Journal--Internet Technologies, Applications & Issues* is a quarterly print magazine written for an international readership of researchers, developers, and Internet users in educational, business, and professional environments. As we strive to define a new age— networked, decentralized and anti-hierarchical—through our research, application development, and exploration of the issues at hand, the *WebNet Journal* serves as a unique and innovative forum.

This forum enables top academic and corporate laboratory researchers, developers, business people, and users to collaborate and exchange ideas on a broad range of current topics that impact their respective activities.

All feature articles are carefully peer-reviewed and selected by a respected international editorial review board based on merit and perceived value of the content for readers. Columnists offer how-to articles and expert commentary on the latest developments.

Guidelines

Publishing policy and selection of articles are governed by the editorial objectives of AACE, by each Journal's content, and by the general guidelines that follow.

Please only send all submissions electronically via the **Journal Submissions Form** found on the journal website.

Editorial Objectives

AACE publications have the overall objective to advance the knowledge, theory, and quality of teaching and learning at all levels with computing technologies. The international readership of each Journal is multidisciplinary and includes professors, researchers, classroom teachers, developers, teacher educators, and administrators.

Editorial objectives are to:
- Serve as a forum to report the interdisciplinary research, development, integration, and applications of computing in education.
- Contribute toward the professional development of all who seek in-depth yet practical knowledge about the important research results, latest developments and applications of teaching and learning with computers.
- Present articles of interest on educational computing problems.
- Provide creative ideas, practical strategies, and experiences on instruction with computers.
- Offer information on various aspects of computer literacy for educators.
- Provide information on new computer materials, methods of use, and evaluative criteria.

General Guidelines

Material must be original, scientifically accurate, and in good form editorially. The manuscript should be informative, summarizing the basic facts and conclusions, and maintaining a coherence and unity of thought.

Tutorial or how-to-do-it articles should preferably include a section on evaluation. Controversial topics should be treated in a factually sound and reasonably unbiased manner.

The format of headings, tables, figures, citations, references, and other details should follow the *(APA)* style as described in the *Publication Manual of the American Psychological Association* available from *APA*, 750 1st St., NE, Washington, DC 20002 USA.

Preview

Manuscripts sent to the Editor for review are accepted on a voluntary basis from authors. Before submitting an article, please review the following suggestions. Manuscripts received in correct form serve to expedite the processing and prompt reviewing for early publication.

Spelling, punctuation, sentence structure, and the mechanical elements of arrangements, spacing, length, and consistency of usage in form and descriptions should be studied before submission. Due to the academic focus of AACE publications, the use of personal pronoun (I, we, etc.) and present tense is strongly discouraged.

Pre-publication
No manuscript will be considered which has already been published or is being considered by another journal. Authors should include a statement with their letter that the manuscript has not been published and is not under consideration elsewhere.

Copyright
These journals are copyrighted by the Association for the Advancement of Computing in Education. Material published and so copyrighted may not be published elsewhere without the written permission of the AACE.

Author Note(s)
Financial support for work reported or a grant under which a study was made should be noted just prior to the Acknowledgments. Acknowledgments or appreciation to individuals for assistance with the manuscript or with the material reported should be included as a note to appear at the end of the article prior to the References.

Handling of Manuscripts
All manuscripts are acknowledged upon receipt. Review is carried out as promptly as possible. The manuscript will be reviewed by at least two members of the Editorial Review Board, which takes usually no more than two months. When a decision for publication or rejection is made, the senior author or author designated to receive correspondence is notified. At the time of notification, the author may be asked to make certain revisions in the manuscript, or the Editor may submit suggested revisions to the author for approval.

Presentation
Accepted Submission File Formats - All submissions must be sent in electronic form using the Article Submission Form. **No hard copy submission papers will be accepted.** A format which best preserves the "document look" is preferred. Do NOT submit compressed files. Do not use any word processing options/tools, such as--strike through, hidden text, comments, merges, and so forth.

Submit your manuscript in either of the following formats:
- **WORD** - Microsoft Word (preferred)
- **RTF** - Rich Text Format
- **HTML**

Manuscripts should be double-spaced and a font size of 12 is preferred. All graphics should be embedded in the file in the correct location of the paper. Do not send separate graphic files or compressed files.

Length - In general, articles should not exceed 30 double-spaced pages. Long articles, or articles containing complex material should be broken up by short, meaningful subheads.

Title sheet - Do NOT include a title sheet. Manuscripts are blind reviewed so there should be no indication of the author(s) name on the pages.

Abstract - An informative, comprehensive abstract of 75 to 200 words must accompany the manuscript. This abstract should succinctly summarize the major points of the paper, and the author's summary and/or conclusions.

Citations
Citations should strictly follow *American Psychological Association (APA)* style guide. Examples of references cited within the texts of articles are as follows: (Williams, Allen, & Jones, 1978) or (Moore, 1990; Smith, 1991) or Terrell (1977). In citations, et al., can only be used after all authors have been cited or referenced. As per *APA* all citations must match the reference list and vice versa. Over use of references is discouraged.

Quotations
Quoted material of more than two lines should be set in a narrower width than the remainder of the text but continue to double space. At the close of the quotation, give the complete source including page numbers. Copy all quoted material exactly as it appears in the original, indicating any omissions by three spaced periods.

A block quote must be a minimum of 40 words or four lines, single spaced (not 20 and double spaced as is presently noted).

Tables and Figures
All tables and figure graphics must be embedded within the file and of such quality that when printed be in camera-ready form (publication quality). Within the submitted file, number and type captions centered at the top of each table. Figures are labeled at the bottom of the figure, left justified, and numbered in sequence.

Terminology and Abbreviations
Define any words or phrases that cannot be found in Webster's Unabridged Dictionary. Define or explain new or highly technical terminology. Write out the first use of a term that you expect to use subsequently in abbreviated form. Abbreviations (i.e., e.g., etc.) are only acceptable in parenthesis, otherwise they must be spelled out, that is, for example, and so forth, respectively. Please avoid other foreign phrases and words such as via.

Mathematics
Math or other formulas'/codes/programs/text tables, should be submitted as graphics (jpeg, gif, tiff, png), graphics should be embedded in the file where they are to appear. (Do not send separate files.) Graphics, tables, figures, photos, and so forth, must be sized to fit a 6 x 9 publication with margins of: top, 1," inside 1," outside, .75," and bottom, 1," an overall measurement of 4 ½ X 6 ¾ is the absolute limit in size. A table or figure sized on a full size 8 ½ by 11 piece of paper does not always reduce and remain legible. Please adhere to the size stipulation or your manuscript will be returned for graphics/figure's or tables to be re-done.

Program Listings

Program listings will appear with the published article if space permits. Listings should be publication quality. The brand of computer required should be included. Lengthy program listings (more than four 6 x 9 pages) can not be published, but may be made available from the author; a note to that effect should be included in the article.

References

A **maximum** of 40 references is recommended. References should strictly follow the *APA* style guide. References must be checked with great care. All references should be in alphabetical order by author (unnumbered), as shown below. In the references there are no spaces between the author's initials. Use the following style when referencing a book or an article in a periodical:

O'Shea, T., & Self, J. A. (1983). *Learning and teaching with computers.* Englewood Cliffs, NJ: Prentice-Hall Inc.

Porter, R., & Lehman, J. (1984). Projects for teaching physics concepts using a microcomputer. *Journal of Computers in Mathematics and Science Teaching, 3*(4), 14-15.

Post-publication

Upon publication, each author will receive a complimentary copy of the journal issue in which the article appears and an article reprint order form.

Please carefully read and adhere to these guidelines. Manuscripts not submitted according to the guidelines must be returned.

Please only send all submissions electronically via the **Journal Submissions Form**.

All correspondence concerning your submission should be directed to the Publications Coordinator at: pubs@aace.org.

Women in Higher Education

ADDRESS FOR SUBMISSION:

Mary Dee Wenniger, Editor
Women in Higher Education
1934 Monroe Street
Madison, WI 53711-2027
USA
Phone: 608-251-3232
Fax: 608-284-0601
E-Mail: women@wihe.com
Web: www.wihe.com
Address May Change:

PUBLICATION GUIDELINES:

Manuscript Length: 6-10
Copies Required: One
Computer Submission: Yes Disk, Email
Format: MSWord
Fees to Review: 0.00 US$

Manuscript Style:
    Associated Press Stylebook

CIRCULATION DATA:

Reader: Administrators, Women
    Academics, Staff, Students
Frequency of Issue: Monthly
Copies per Issue: 2,001 - 3,000
Sponsor/Publisher:
Subscribe Price: 99.00 US$
    66.00 US$ Introductory Rate
    40.00 US$ Students

REVIEW INFORMATION:

Type of Review: Editorial Review
No. of External Reviewers: 0
No. of In House Reviewers: 1
Acceptance Rate: 50%
Time to Review: 1 Month or Less
Reviewers Comments: Yes
Invited Articles: 50% +
Fees to Publish: 0.00 US$

MANUSCRIPT TOPICS:
Education Management/Administration; Higher Education; School Law; Women, Gender
Equity

MANUSCRIPT GUIDELINES/COMMENTS:

We are delighted to welcome submissions from subscribers, administrators and faculty in
higher education, and organization leaders with information on topics relevant to our readers.
Your interests are ours! We strive to take scholarly ideas and make them comprehensible
without academic gobbledegook, using small words and short sentences. It's journalism, not
scholarship.

Newsletter Mission
To provide women on campus with practical ideas and insights to be more a effective in their
careers arid their lives, gaining the power they need to win respect influence others, sell ideas
and take their rightful place in leading society. Mission: *To enlighten, encourage, empower
and enrage women ors campus, building a network of women in higher education who can be
successful using cooperation and teamwork to make a difference in using alternative styles
and strategies to improve higher education for employees and students.*

Subscribers Profile
A New Subscriber Interest Inventory, sent with subscriber's first issue, slows they are:

- School type: Almost evenly divided (40-60) between two-year and four-year schools.
- School size: Even more evenly divided (55-45) between fewer than and more than 5,000 students.
- Jobs: More than 70% are administrator; and 15'% faculty, the rest a mixture.
- Sex: More than 98%, are women.
- Age: Likely to be in their 40s (52%), with some younger (24% in their 30s), and some older (24% in 50s).
- Especially interested in; leadership skills (84%), advice from successful women on campus (70%), gender equity issues (56%), communication techniques (52%), new research on gender differences (44%) as well as career strategies, new programs, legal updates, ending sexual harassment, mentors & role models.

Style
For the best notion of what works, read the, issues closely Use small words, be clear, use active instead of passive voice, aim for "a good read," be upbeat and positive, think "What can we learn from this? and gave practical ideas and recommendations, concrete examples Put yourself in the head of the reader and think "What would I want to know?" about your topic. Do I really care? Might my idea work on other campuses?

Departments
(word counts are estimates BEFORE EDITING HERE and are extremely flexible)
In Her Own Words - 1200 words - opinions, controversial or subjective insights on relevant topics
What Should She Do? - 300 words - answers to dilemmas posed by typical readers
Moveable Type-1100 words - synopsis of a useful book on women in higher education /work
Profile - 1,4M words - a woman leader in higher education
News/ Research Briefs - 300 words - short reports of interest, mostly from scholarly journals
News Features - 9111) wards -new programs on your campus, speeches, major research of interest

Compensation
Knowledge that you are sharing your knowledge with a network of other women in higher education to help make a difference on campuses across the USA and Canada; additions to your vita; building your national reputation, plus establishing ties to national conferences in higher education through exposure here.

The Next Step
Call Editor Mary Dee Wenniger (608) 25'1-3232 to discuss what you have in mind, and whether it would fit with the news journal's editorial perspective. Writers can send their copy on a disk or via e-mail to women@wihe.com (Best to send both within an e-mail message AND as an attachment-one will work!) Editors then work their magic on it, and fax back a revised draft to the writer, who then can edit for her changes We look forward to relevant articles of interest to our more than 12,000 discerning readers!

12 Tips for Writers Submitting Articles to Women in Higher Education
Thank you for submitting your work to WIRE. Since most writers contribute to a variety of publications, it occurred to me that if I provide a few stylistic guidelines for what I do to make: your article into a finished piece appropriate for WIHE, perhaps my job of editing articles would take less time each month. And then I can spend more time. playing in my red convertible.

1. Our job is to translate scholarly BS into easily readable words and usable ideas, however complex. Sometimes it's very hard work to ditch the jargon and lingo, but it's very important.

2. Use *AP* style, not *APA*. We are journalists, not scholars. That means spell out all numbers smaller than nine, and write out 10 or above. Capitalize: sparingly.

3. Our unique style is to keep it short and sweet. So we spell words like dialog and catalog without the extra "uc" on the end. Use the % symbol instead of writing it out.

4. In a listing of three things, there is no comma before the "and" that precedes the third item.

5. Never use the words "implement" or "approximately." Use "institution" only in referring to "institutional culture." Otherwise, it's a "school," which is not always 100% accurate but avoids the longer word- Try to use short, simple words rather than long, ostentageous ones.

6. Vary sentence construction by using clauses and phrases, but always seek parallel construction- The best writers work very hard to avoid starting a paragraph with the worthless words "A" or "?The." Stand on your head to avoid using the boring, passive tense.

7_ List contacts at the end of all articles. If you speak with or e-mail a person, ask how she would prefer to be contacted (phone., e-mail, snail mail, fax) and be sure it's acccurate.

8. Spell out all months and days of the week.

9. Use direct quotations only if they're especially clever, pithy, unique, appropriate or in some way special. Otherwise, paraphrase them to keep the text shorter and sweeter. Try not to break up a quotation within a sentence as it slows down the reader. But do use some quotations.

10. Length is always an issue. If I ask for one page, about 1,000 words will fit. If you are a good, tight writer, do not give me 1,300 words for an article, more like 1,050. If you are a loose writer, try to tighten up your own stuff so I don't have to edit your 1,300 words down to 1,000. Pull quotes and photos take up extra space, so I may still have to edit down your article to fit.

11. It's perfectly OK to include heds and suhheds in your article, but I may change them.

12. Your own ideas for articles are always welcome!

Young Exceptional Children

ADDRESS FOR SUBMISSION:

Eva Horn, Editor
Young Exceptional Children
University of Kansas
521 JR Pearson
1122 West Campus Road
Lawrence, KS 66045-3101
USA
Phone: 785-864-0615
Fax: 785-864-4149
E-Mail: evahorn@ukans.edu
Web: www.dec-sped.org/yec
Address May Change:

PUBLICATION GUIDELINES:

Manuscript Length: 11-15
Copies Required: Five
Computer Submission: No
Format: N/A
Fees to Review: 0.00 US$

Manuscript Style:
American Psychological Association

CIRCULATION DATA:

Reader: Practicing Teachers
Frequency of Issue: Quarterly
Copies per Issue: 5,001 - 10,000
Sponsor/Publisher: Division for Early
Childhood, Council for Exceptional
Children
Subscribe Price: 20.00 US$ Individual
35.00 US$ Institution
40.00 US$ International

REVIEW INFORMATION:

Type of Review: Blind Review
No. of External Reviewers: 3
No. of In House Reviewers: 0
Acceptance Rate: 37%
Time to Review: 4 - 6 Months
Reviewers Comments: Yes
Invited Articles: 0-5%
Fees to Publish: 0.00 US$

MANUSCRIPT TOPICS:
Elementary/Early Childhood

MANUSCRIPT GUIDELINES/COMMENTS:

Young Exceptional Children is a peer-reviewed publication produced by the Division for Early Childhood (DEC) of the Council for Exceptional Children (CEC), designed for teachers, early care and education personnel, administrators, therapists, family members, and others who work with or on behalf of children from birth through eight years of age who have identified disabilities, developmental delays, are gifted/talented, or are at risk of future developmental problems. *Young Exceptional Children* is published four times per year and serves as a practitioner's magazine and as a complement to the DEC's Journal of Early Intervention, as well as the major source of printed communication between DEC and its membership.

Young Exceptional Children is designed to assist practitioners and family members in their daily activities with young children. Articles are sought which have a sound base in theory or research, yet are written for practitioners and families. Articles should be reader-friendly, and written for a broad audience which includes professionals from a variety of disciplines, family members, and paraprofessionals. Technical terms which might not be familiar to all of these groups should be explained.

Information should be clearly presented using descriptions, vignettes, or examples so translation into practice will be facilitated. We accept 8-12 page manuscripts as well as 1-2 page position or opinion papers.

Photo Submissions
Contact Eva Horn for consent forms then mail photos/consent forms to her. Please include name, address, and telephone number of photographer. Photos will not be returned.

Agreements
To be considered for review, an article must meet the following criteria:
1. It must be no more than 12 pages, double-spaced, including references.
2. It must be considered functional and useful for practitioners and families.
3. It must not have been previously published in or under review for another publication.
4. DEC must be given an exclusive option on possible publication for a period of five months following receipt of the article.
5. The author assumes responsibility for publication clearance in the event the article was presented at a professional meeting of another organization or was developed for a funding agency.

Format Guidelines
In preparing an article for publication, authors must use the following guidelines:
- Double space text, including quotations.
- Use 12-point Times New Roman font with margins set to one inch.
- Keep article length under 12 pages, double-spaced, including tables, figures, and references.
- Follow the format rules of the American Psychological Association (APA). Authors are advised to consult the Publication Manual of the American Psychological Association (5th ed.).
- Prepare a cover sheet with all authors' full names, professional degrees, addresses with zip code, and phone numbers and/or e-mail addresses. The author names should not appear at any other place in the article.
- We strongly encourage the use of printed photos to highlight the manuscript. These should be included at the time of submission. *Note:* Photos cannot be returned.

Submit five hardcopies of the article to:
Eva Horn, Dept. of Special Education, 521 JR Pearson, 1122 West Campus Road, University of Kansas, Lawrence, KS 66045-3101; Phone (785) 864-0615; Fax (785) 864-4149, E-mail evahorn@ukans.edu

Journal Name	Type Review	No. Ext. Rev.	Accept. Rate	Page
Perspectives: The New York Journal of Adult Learning	Blind	2	New J	648
Public Personnel Management	Blind	3	50%	667
Rehabilitation Counseling Bulletin	Blind	3	40%	672
Research in Post-Compulsory Education	Blind	2	21-30%	676
Rhetoric Review	Blind	2	11-20%	679
Studies in Continuing Education	Editorial	3	21-30%	739
Teaching of Psychology	Editorial	3	21-30%	749
Tech Trends	Blind	2	29%	754
Techniques: Connecting Education and Careers	Editorial	0	0-5%	758

Art/Music

Journal Name	Type Review	No. Ext. Rev.	Accept. Rate	Page
American Indian Culture and Research	Blind	3+	21-30%	14
American Scholar	Editorial		0-5%	35
Creativity Research Journal	Blind	3+	11-20%	207
Education Research and Perspectives	Blind	1		230
Education Review	Blind	0	95%	232
Educational Forum	Blind	3+	6-10%	246
Educational Gerontology	Blind	3	21-30%	251
Essays in Education	Blind	2	50%	279
Harvard Educational Review	Blind	3+	11-20%	304
Journal for Specialists in Group Work	Blind	2	21-30%	347
Journal of Creative Behavior	Blind	2	11-20%	451

Audiology/Speech Pathology

Journal Name	Type Review	No. Ext. Rev.	Accept. Rate	Page
Education Research and Perspectives	Blind	1		230
Education Review	Blind	0	95%	232
Educational Forum	Blind	3+	6-10%	246
Educational Gerontology	Blind	3	21-30%	251
Exceptional Children	Blind	2	11-20%	286
Exceptional Parent	Editorial	0	6-10%	290
Journal of Gerontology: Psychological Sciences	Peer	2	15%	506

Bilingual/E.S.L.

Journal Name	Type Review	No. Ext. Rev.	Accept. Rate	Page
Applied Psycholinguistics	Editorial	2	21-30%	55
Assessing Writing	Blind	2	21-30%	59
Bilingual Family Newsletter (The)		0	70%	79
Chemical Engineering Education	Editorial	3	48%	108
Children & Schools	Blind	3	21-30%	110
Community College Review	Blind	2	21-30%	180
Contemporary Educational Psychology	Blind	3	11-20%	183
Education Research and Perspectives	Blind	1		230
Education Review	Blind	0	95%	232
Educational Forum	Blind	3+	6-10%	246
Essays in Education	Blind	2	50%	279
Exceptional Children	Blind	2	11-20%	286

Curriculum Studies

Journal Name	Type Review	No. Ext. Rev.	Accept. Rate	Page
Bilingual Family Newsletter (The)		0	70%	79
British Educational Research Journal	Blind	2-3	11-20%	86
Catalyst for Change	Editorial	3+	50%	103
Cognitive Psychology	Editorial	3	11-20%	130
Cognitive Science	Editorial	3	11-20%	140
Community & Junior College Libraries	Editorial	1	80%	169
Contemporary Educational Psychology	Blind	3	11-20%	183
Education Research and Perspectives	Blind	1		230
Education Review	Blind	0	95%	232
Educational & Psychological Measurement	Editorial	2	11-20%	235
Educational Forum	Blind	3+	6-10%	246
Educational Gerontology	Blind	3	21-30%	251
Educational Leadership	Editorial	0	6-10%	254
Educational Perspectives	Editorial			263
Essays in Education	Blind	2	50%	279
Exceptional Children	Blind	2	11-20%	286
Journal of Chinese Language Teachers Association	Editorial	1	21-30%	388
Journal of Educational Psychology	Blind	2	11-20%	491
Reading Professor (The)	Blind	3	60%	670
Teaching English in the Two-Year College	Blind	2	21-30%	745

Religious Education

Journal Name	Type Review	No. Ext. Rev.	Accept. Rate	Page
British Educational Research Journal	Blind	2-3	11-20%	86
Christian Higher Education: An Int'l Journal of Applied Research & Practice	Blind	3	21-30%	128
Counseling and Values	Blind	2	21-30%	201
Education Research and Perspectives	Blind	1		230
Education Review	Blind	0	95%	232
Educational Forum	Blind	3+	6-10%	246
Educational Gerontology	Blind	3	21-30%	251
Journal of Thought	Blind	2	21-30%	587

Rural Education & Small Schools

Journal Name	Type Review	No. Ext. Rev.	Accept. Rate	Page
British Educational Research Journal	Blind	2-3	11-20%	86
Catalyst for Change	Editorial	3+	50%	103
Education Research and Perspectives	Blind	1		230
Education Review	Blind	0	95%	232
Educational Forum	Blind	3+	6-10%	246
Educational Leadership	Editorial	0	6-10%	254
Essays in Education	Blind	2	50%	279
Futurist	Editorial	0	21-30%	295
International Journal of Leadership in Education	Blind	3+	40%	327
Journal of Community Development Society	Blind	3+	45%	435
Journal of Educational Administration	Blind	3	21-30%	473
Journal of School Violence	Blind	2	New J	564
Planning and Changing	Blind	Varies	45%	652

Journal Name	Type Review	No. Ext. Rev.	Accept. Rate	Page
School Administrator (The)	Editorial	0	21-30%	681
Techniques: Connecting Education and Careers	Editorial	0	0-5%	758

School Law

Journal Name	Type Review	No. Ext. Rev.	Accept. Rate	Page
American Educational Research Journal (AERJ)	Blind	3+	7-13%	9
Brigham Young University Education and Law Journal	N/A	1	Varies	83
Christian Higher Education: An Int'l Journal of Applied Research & Practice	Blind	3	21-30%	128
Community College Journal of Research and Practice	Blind	3	21-30%	178
Education and the Law	N/A	1		221
Education Research and Perspectives	Blind	1		230
Education Review	Blind	0	95%	232
Educational Administration Quarterly	Blind	3	6-10%	237
Educational Forum	Blind	3+	6-10%	246
Educational Perspectives	Editorial			263
Essays in Education	Blind	2	50%	279
Harvard Civil Rights-Liberties Law Review	Editorial	3+	6-10%	302
Journal of Clinical Psychology	Blind	2	21-30%	398
Journal of College and University Law	Editorial	1	40%	411
Journal of Education Finance	Blind	3	21-30%	458
Journal of Educational Administration	Blind	3	21-30%	473
Journal of School Leadership	Blind	3	6-10%	561
Journal of School Violence	Blind	2	New J	564
Journal of Student Financial Aid	Blind	3+	21-30%	579
Migration World	Blind	3	21-30%	618
NACADA Journal	Blind	0	40%	628
National Forum of Educational Admin. and Supervision Journal (NFEAS Journal)	Blind	3+	21-30%	639
School Business Affairs	N/A	3+		686
Women in Higher Education	Editorial	0	50%	772

Science Math & Environment

Journal Name	Type Review	No. Ext. Rev.	Accept. Rate	Page
American Scholar	Editorial		0-5%	35
British Educational Research Journal	Blind	2-3	11-20%	86
Catalyst for Change	Editorial	3+	50%	103
Cognitive Science	Editorial	3	11-20%	140
Contemporary Educational Psychology	Blind	3	11-20%	183
Education Research and Perspectives	Blind	1		230
Education Review	Blind	0	95%	232
Educational Forum	Blind	3+	6-10%	246
Educational Leadership	Editorial	0	6-10%	254
Essays in Education	Blind	2	50%	279
Journal of College Science Teaching	Blind	2	40%	416
Journal of Creative Behavior	Blind	2	11-20%	451

Journal Name	Type Review	No. Ext. Rev.	Accept. Rate	Page
Multicultural Perspectives	Blind	3	21-30%	621
Psychology in the Schools	Blind	2	21-30%	664
School Administrator (The)	Editorial	0	21-30%	681
School Foodservice & Nutrition	Editorial	0		689
School Psychology International	Blind	3	21-30%	695
Techniques: Connecting Education and Careers	Editorial	0	0-5%	758

Teacher Education

Journal Name	Type Review	No. Ext. Rev.	Accept. Rate	Page
British Educational Research Journal	Blind	2-3	11-20%	86
Catalyst for Change	Editorial	3+	50%	103
Christian Higher Education: An Int'l Journal of Applied Research & Practice	Blind	3	21-30%	128
College & University Media Review	Blind	3	80%	159
College Teaching	Editorial	2	40%	167
Education and Urban Society	Blind	3		223
Education Research and Perspectives	Blind	1		230
Education Review	Blind	0	95%	232
Educational Evaluation & Policy Analysis	Blind	3	11-20%	242
Educational Forum	Blind	3+	6-10%	246
Educational Perspectives	Editorial			263
Educational Policy	Blind	2	21-30%	265
Essays in Education	Blind	2	50%	279
Exceptional Children	Blind	2	11-20%	286
Harvard Educational Review	Blind	3+	11-20%	304
Intercultural Education	Editorial		60%	320
International Journal of Leadership in Education	Blind	3+	40%	327
Journal of Agricultural Education	Blind	2	21-30%	353
Journal of Chinese Language Teachers Association	Editorial	1	21-30%	388
Journal of College and University Law	Editorial	1	40%	411
Journal of College Science Teaching	Blind	2	40%	416
Journal of Computing in Higher Education	Blind	2	21-30%	440
Journal of Creative Behavior	Blind	2	11-20%	451
Journal of Instructional Psychology	Editorial	1	50%	519
Journal of Professional Studies	Blind	3	11-20%	549
Journal of School Leadership	Blind	3	6-10%	561
Journal of Statistics Education	Blind	3	21-30%	574
Journal of Thought	Blind	2	21-30%	587
Language, Culture and Curriculum	Blind	2	50%	592
Leadership Magazine	Editorial	0	31%	596
Lifelong Learning in Europe (LLINE)	Blind	2		609
Multicultural Perspectives	Blind	3	21-30%	621
National Forum of Educational Admin. and Supervision Journal (NFEAS Journal)	Blind	3+	21-30%	639
Nurse Educator	Blind	2	11-20%	645
Research in Post-Compulsory Education	Blind	2	21-30%	676
Teaching & Learning	Blind	2	40%	743

Journal Name	Type Review	No. Ext. Rev.	Accept. Rate	Page
Education Review	Blind	0	95%	232
Educational Forum	Blind	3+	6-10%	246
Educational Leadership	Editorial	0	6-10%	254
Educational Policy	Blind	2	21-30%	265
Educational Studies: A Journal in Foundations of Education	Editorial	2-4	50%+	267
Essays in Education	Blind	2	50%	279
Exceptional Children	Blind	2	11-20%	286
Futurist	Editorial	0	21-30%	295
Harvard Educational Review	Blind	3+	11-20%	304
International Electronic Journal for Leadership in Learning	Blind	3	21-30%	323
International Journal of Leadership in Education	Blind	3+	40%	327
Journal for Specialists in Group Work	Blind	2	21-30%	347
Journal of Adult Development	Blind	3	40%	350
Journal of Communications & Minority Issues	Blind	2	40%	434
Journal of Community Development Society	Blind	3+	45%	435
Journal of Community Psychology	Blind	2	11-20%	438
Journal of Instructional Psychology	Editorial	1	50%	519
Journal of Latinos and Education	Blind	2	New J	526
Journal of Multicultural Counseling and Development	Blind	2	11-20%	540
Journal of School Leadership	Blind	3	6-10%	561
Journal of School Violence	Blind	2	New J	564
Journal of Thought	Blind	2	21-30%	587
Leadership Magazine	Editorial	0	31%	596
Multicultural Perspectives	Blind	3	21-30%	621
National Forum of Educational Admin. and Supervision Journal (NFEAS Journal)	Blind	3+	21-30%	639
Planning and Changing	Blind	Varies	45%	652
Research in Post-Compulsory Education	Blind	2	21-30%	676
Rhetoric Review	Blind	2	11-20%	679
School Foodservice & Nutrition	Editorial	0		689
Social Policy	Editorial	0	21-30%	700

Notes

Notes

Notes